The Vietnam War

The Vietnam War

Vietnamese and American Perspectives

MARK BRADLEY
JEFFREY CLARKE
WILLIAM DUIKER
DAVID W. P. ELLIOTT
JAMES P. HARRISON
GEORGE C. HERRING
DAVID HUNT
PAUL JOSEPH
BEN KIERNAN
NGO VINH LONG
KRISTIN PELZER
RONALD H. SPECTOR
KEITH W. TAYLOR
TRAN VAN TRA
GEORGE R. VICKERS
MARILYN B. YOUNG

Edited by Jayne S. Werner
and Luu Doan Huynh

M. E. Sharpe
Armonk, New York
London, England

Library of Congress Cataloging-in-Publication Data

The Vietnam War: Vietnamese and American perspectives/
edited by Jayne S. Werner and Luu Doan Huynh.
p.   cm.
Includes index.
ISBN 1-56324-057-2
1. Vietnamese Conflict, 1961–1975.
I. Werner, Jayne Susan.
II. Huynh, Luu Doan.
DS557.7.V5662   1992
959.704′3—dc20
92-30989
CIP

Printed in the United States of America

The paper used in this publication meets the minimum requirements of
American National Standard for Information Sciences—
Permanence of Paper for Printed Library Materials,
ANSI Z39.48–1984.

BM (c)   10   9   8   7   6   5   4   3   2   1

The Southern Emperor Rules the Southern Land

The Southern emperor rules the Southern land.
Our destiny is writ in Heaven's Book.
How dare you bandits trespass on our soil?
You shall meet your undoing at our hands.

—Ly Thuong Kiet, 1076

[The South refers to the land ruled by the Vietnamese, as distinguished from the North, ruled by the Chinese.]

The United States and all other countries respect the independence, sovereignty, unity, and territorial integrity of Vietnam as recognized by the 1954 Geneva Agreements on Vietnam.

—Article 1, Paris Peace Agreement, January 27, 1973

Contents

Part Two: The War from the American Side

Part Three: The War in the South and Cambodia

Part Four: Retrospective and Postwar Issues

The Contributors

Mark Bradley is a doctoral candidate in the Department of History at Harvard University and an associate of the Center for International Affairs at Harvard. His dissertation, "Making Cold War: Vietnam and the United States, 1941–1954," explores Vietnamese and American mutual perceptions and their impact on policy in an analysis of the origins of the Cold War in Vietnam.

Jeffrey J. Clarke is Chief Historian at the U.S. Army Center of Military History in Washington, D.C. and associate professor at the University of Maryland–Baltimore County. He has traveled to both north and south Vietnam, and has authored several works on military history including *Advice and Support: The Final Years, 1965–63*.

William J. Duiker is professor of East Asian history at The Pennsylvania State University. A former foreign service officer, he is the author of numerous articles and books on modern China and Vietnam, including *The Communist Road to Power in Vietnam* (1981) and *Vietnam Since the Fall of Saigon* (1989).

David W.P. Elliott is H. Russell Smith professor of government and international relations at Pomona College. He is a graduate of Yale University and received a Ph.D. from Cornell University. During the period 1963 to 1973, Elliott spent six years in Vietnam with the United States Army, the Rand Corporation, and as a graduate student. He is the editor of *The Third Indochina Conflict* (1980) and is currently at work on a study of the war in the Mekong Delta, 1954–1975.

James P. Harrison is professor of history at Hunter College, CUNY. A former air force pilot, he is a specialist on the history of communism in Vietnam and China and author of *The Endless War: Vietnam's Struggle for Independence* and *The Long March to Power: A History of the Chinese Communist Party*.

George C. Herring is alumni professor of history at the University of Kentucky. His recent work has focused on U.S. involvement in Vietnam and includes *America's Longest War: The United States and Vietnam, 1950-1975* (revised edition 1985) and *The "Negotiating Volumes" of the Pentagon Papers* (1983).

David Hunt is associate professor of history and co-director of the William Joiner Center at the University of Massachusetts/Boston. He is the author of *Parents and Children in History* and of various articles on peasants and revolutions in France and Vietnam.

Luu Doan Huynh served in the anti-French resistance movement (1945–54) as a soldier and government official. From 1984 to 1987 he was counselor of the Vietnamese Embassy in Australia. He is currently senior research fellow in the Institute of International Relations in Hanoi. He is co-author of *President Ho Chi Minh and Vietnam's Diplomacy*, 1990.

Paul Joseph is the chair and associate professor of sociology at Tufts University. His most recent book is *Peace Politics: The United States Between the Old and New World Orders.*

Ben Kiernan was born in Melbourne, Australia, in 1953. He is associate professor of history at Yale University, author of *How Pol Pot Came to Power* (1985), and co-author of four other books on modern Cambodia, including *Pol Pot Plans the Future*, a collection of internal documents of the Khmer Rouge regime. He is now working on a history of that regime.

Ngo Vinh Long is associate professor of Asian history at the University of Maine. He is author of *Before the Revolution: The Vietnamese Peasants under the French* (1991) and co-editor of *Coming to Terms: The United States, Indochina, and the War* (1991).

Kristin Pelzer is professor of Southeast Asian Studies at the University of Hawaii. Her publications include *Postwar Vietnam: Dilemmas in Socialist Development*, "Vietnam War, Socialism and the Politics of Gender Relations," in S. Kruks, R. Rapp, and M. Young, eds., *Promissory Notes: Women in the Transition to Socialism*, and "Socio-Cultural Dimensions of Renovation in Vietnam: Doi Moi as Dialogue and Transformations in Gender Relations," in William S. Turley and Mark Selden, eds., *Reinventing Vietnamese Socialism: Doi Moi in Comparative Perspective.*

Ronald Spector is professor of history and international affairs at George Washington University. He is the author of two books on the Vietnam War—*Advice and Support: The Early Years of the U.S. Army in Vietnam* and *After Tet: The Bloodiest Year.*

Keith W. Taylor is associate professor of Vietnamese cultural studies at Cornell University and author of *The Birth of Vietnam* (1983).

Tran Van Tra was commander of the People's Liberation Armed Forces of South Vietnam from 1963 to 1975 and deputy commander of the Ho Chi Minh Campaign that liberated the South. His memoirs of that campaign are in *Vietnam: History of the Bulwark B–2 Theatre*, vol. 5: *Concluding the 30 Years' War*, published in 1983.

George R. Vickers is professor of sociology at Brooklyn College and the Graduate Center of the City University of New York. He is the author of *The Formation of the New Left*, and has written extensively about the antiwar movement in the United States during the Vietnam War. His current work focuses on U.S. military strategy and the dynamics of revolutionary movements in Central America.

Jayne Werner is associate professor of political science at Long Island University and associate research scholar at Columbia University. She is co-author (with David Hunt) of a forthcoming book entitled *The American War*.

Marilyn B. Young is professor of history at New York University. She has written on the Chinese revolution, U.S.–East Asian relations, and issues of gender and socialism. Her most recent book is *The Vietnam Wars: 1945–1990*.

Acknowledgments

The editors would like to acknowledge the assistance and support of various individuals and institutions in making this book possible. We are grateful to Ambassador Trinh Xuan Lang, permanent representative of Vietnam to the United Nations, for his active support during the visit of General Tran Van Tra and Luu Doan Huynh to the United States. Several members of the Vietnamese Mission gave generously of their time and translation skills, in particular Tran Minh Dung. We are also grateful to the School of International and Public Affairs at Columbia University, former dean Alfred Stepan, and the Southern Asian Institute. Long Island University generously provided Jayne Werner with released time from teaching duties to work on the book.

But it is with particular gratitude that we wish to thank Cora Weiss and the Samuel Rubin Foundation for their support for what seemed to be a most impractical project—bringing former Vietnamese military and diplomatic personages to the United States for a conference at a time of virtually no official contact between the United States and Vietnam. Surprisingly, the State Department granted visas, save for Nguyen Thi Dinh, the former deputy commander of the PLAF and president of the Women's Union in Hanoi. We are saddened that Nguyen Thi Dinh passed away on August 26, 1992, as this book was being readied for the printer. In many respects, the Vietnam War is still not over. Without the stimulation and interaction between the Vietnamese visitors and the American scholars, many of whom came to New York on short notice and at personal expense, this book would not have materialized.

General Tran Van Tra graciously granted us permission to translate and publish his article on the Tet Offensive, which is virtually unknown in the West, even in secondary sources on the history of the Vietnam War.

Many others assisted in this project. We would like to acknowledge the help of Tran Phuong Hoa and Mimi Dinh and the support of officials in the Foreign Ministry in Vietnam. A special note of thanks goes to Marilyn Flaig for the index. Finally, but most definitely not least, Michael Weber, our editor at M.E. Sharpe, signed on to the project at an early stage and provided unfailing assistance each step along the way.

Introduction

The Vietnam War: Vietnamese and American Perspectives

Jayne Werner and Luu Doan Huynh

This book is the result of an extraordinary conference held in the fall of 1990 at Columbia University to investigate the Vietnam War from both U.S. and Vietnamese perspectives. The conference included presentations from twenty-two scholars, including two from Vietnam. Although all the papers were prepared in advance for the meeting and were meant as a basis for the exchange of viewpoints and approaches to the war, the presence of General Tran Van Tra as part of the Vietnamese delegation became a focal point around which discussion revolved, animating the entire proceedings. Tran Van Tra is widely regarded as the key "southern" revolutionary figure from the war period. Aside from his military and diplomatic positions, he is also known to Americans through his memoirs, *History of the Bulwark B2 Theatre*, published in Vietnamese in 1982 and translated into English and published by the Foreign Broadcast Information Service (an arm of the CIA) in 1983.[1] In Vietnam, this book was abruptly withdrawn from circulation after its publication due to disapproval by some top officials.

The Columbia conference was the second in a series of meetings between Americans and Vietnamese on the war. The first meeting, held in Hanoi in 1988 in the form of a seminar, occurred under the auspices of the Institute of Military History (Vien Lich Su Quan Su).[2] Both meetings were cosponsored on the U.S. side by the Southern Asian Institute at Columbia University, and funding was provided by the Samuel Rubin Foundation. The experience of these meetings, from both the Vietnamese and the American sides, was universally judged to be positive and creative. Although much has been written about the war, its historiography is still incomplete and there is a great deal to be gained from collaborative efforts.

The Columbia conference, from which this volume is derived, was unique in that it brought together for the first time three streams of scholarship on the war that had been largely self-contained. The first stream comprises work by U.S. diplomatic historians, who treat the war primarily as a function of U.S. foreign policy, using sources such as archival records, interview material, and secondary sources. The second comprises U.S. Vietnam scholars, whose scholarly agenda is much broader than the war and whose sources include fieldwork in Vietnam and documents in the Vietnamese language. The third are the Vietnamese themselves, who are either scholars of the war or who were actively involved in it as military commanders, political figures, or diplomatic officials.

U.S. diplomatic historians approach the war through U.S. eyes and view U.S. policy judgments about Vietnamese behavior or actions in this context. There is a sense of unipolarity in some of these accounts, however illuminating they are as far as U.S. policy is concerned. Vietnam scholars have tended to judge the war as merely an episode in Vietnam's long struggle against foreign invasion. In this instance, the "American" war is as episodic as the "French" war or "Japanese" wars, or indeed the millenial Chinese occupation before these. Vietnam scholars also often reflect a viewpoint held in Vietnam that aside from the American war being one of many wars, it is also time to put the war behind us and move on to more pressing and urgent problems of economic survivability. Vietnamese official viewpoints on the war have tended, of course, to follow a "party line," and at any rate can be expected to try to justify a certain point of view. Nonetheless, aside from the archival record on both sides, the most important primary sources for researching the war remain the few figures on both sides who held authoritative positions during the war and who are still alive.

At the conference, and as this volume shows, contact and cross-fertilization among these three streams of scholarship enriches them all, and is indeed necessary for a more balanced view of the war.

All the chapters in this book were revised for publication following the conference. Parts One and Two focus on the interpretation and the evolution of Vietnamese strategy and analyze the essential nature of the war, mostly on the battlefield, but also how it was "read" from Washington. The crucial "stages" or turning points of the war are examined, as is the U.S.–Vietnamese relationship, in a historical light that takes account of the relevance of China. An analysis of the impact of the antiwar movement on U.S. policymaking is offered. In Part Three, the progression of the war in southern Vietnam, including the role of the Saigon regime, is explored and its impact on Cambodia is assessed. The chapters in the concluding part deal with the ways Americans and Vietnamese remember the war and differentiate between key events in the war.

Taken as a whole, the book clarifies the combination of the political and military dimensions of revolutionary activity that was characteristic of Vietnamese strategy. This is still not well understood in the United States. The political struggle remained paramount in the thinking, initiatives, and even goals of the Communist Party until late in the war when military factors finally took over. The essential strength of the revolution, however, always resided in its political character, even up to 1975. The United States and its allies in Saigon invariably turned toward and relied on military means to win the war, since they had overwhelming military means at their disposal and confidence in the effectiveness of these means. The U.S. side and the Saigon government never succeeded in capturing the political mantle from the revolutionary forces, represented in the South[3] by the National Liberation Front (NLF). The revolutionary forces, for their part, realized this, and adjusted their strategic thinking accordingly. As Tran Van Tra noted during the conference,

> When the U.S. introduced ground forces in 1965, our assessment was we didn't have the strength to cope with both the U.S. Army and the Saigon Army. We understood the U.S. was a superpower. We were just a small country, not strong enough to cope with such a rich and powerful country. Thus, we did not advocate a policy of destroying the U.S. militarily.

Tran Van Tra noted that even the Tet Offensive was not considered to be an "offensive" or an all-out effort to attain a military victory because the Vietnamese knew they could not defeat the U.S. militarily.

The war was neither a purely "conventional" war nor a solely unconventional, or guerrilla, war. The Vietnam War was a unique combination of both. It can be analyzed as a "revolutionary war," as discussed by George Vickers in "U.S. Military Strategy and the Vietnam War" (chapter 6). In this sense, U.S. military strategists erred in their assumption that the war was primarily conventional in nature. As explained by Tran Van Tra in his discussion of the Tet Offensive (chapter 3), guerrilla, regular forces and other types of units operated side by side, and mass actions were organized inside the zones of the Saigon regime. There were careful political preparations in advance of Tet 1968 and the Final Offensive in 1975 by revolutionary cadres who were living in the cities. The Vietnam War was different from the civil war in China, where main-force units of the People's Army attacked one city after another. The mixture of units, combined with mass action, made Vietnam a war "without a front and without a rear." As explained by Tran Van Tra, Vietnamese military strategy always reflected local realities in Vietnam and essentially differed from Maoist strategy. The goal was not for the countryside to surround the cities. Vietnamese strategy consisted primarily in trying to "weaken the aggressive will of the enemy." This was a political goal as much as a military one. To some extent, it was also a psychological goal. However, it dealt not only with perception but with a conscious decision on the part of the United States to cease hostilities. As Tran Van Tra notes, the revolutionaries could not force the United States to disengage from the war. Their aim was simply to thwart or to block the U.S. effort and its desire to continue the war. David Elliott points out in chapter 4, "Hanoi's Strategy in the Second Indochina War," that the Vietnamese revolutionaries used a kind of "strategic judo" in their approach to the war.

This is where the question of stalemate comes in. Was the Vietnam War a "stalemate"? Was the aim of U.S. policymakers to stalemate the war, and did U.S. warmakers perceive "winning the war" in terms of achieving a stalemate? Did the Vietnamese also perceive winning in terms of achieving a stalemate?

The chapters in this book point to an inescapable irony—both the United States and the Vietnamese saw stalemate as a way to "win" the war. As Leslie Gelb and Richard Betts argue in their book *The Irony of Vietnam: The System Worked,*[4] two successive U.S. presidents sought not to lose the Vietnam War only until the next election. Actually winning (militarily) was less important than not being blamed for "losing" another country to communism or being soft on communism. But "stalemate" seems to have worked more to the advantage of the Vietnamese revolutionary side. By denying victory to the United States; by preventing the revolving-door governments in Saigon from gaining political legitimacy; by being able to mount impressive, damaging, and unanticipated military operations against the United States and the Saigon army at unpredictable times; by foreclosing the strategic options available to the other side; by in effect "forcing" the United States to react, to try to ascertain what to do next; by continuously keeping the ball in the U.S. court, the Vietnamese side played a kind of cat and mouse game in which the United States fought the war on the defensive, spread out, with inconclusive results. Stalemate in this sense meant wearing out the other side. As Henry Kissinger noted in a 1968 article, the guerrillas in southern Vietnam would win by not losing.

The significance of the Tet Offensive, then, comes into clearer focus. If the aim of the revolutionaries was not to win the war militarily but to demonstrate both the inconclusiveness of waging the war at its existing level and that a major and highly controversial decision by U.S. policymakers would have to be made to escalate the war in order to win it, then Tet 1968 accomplished its objective. Stalemate, seen in this light, strengthened the ability of the revolutionary side to enter a "new stage" in the war and eventually prevail. Tran Van Tra argues in his Tet chapter that although the offensive did not allow the revolutionaries to overthrow the Saigon regime, it was a *strategic* turning point and victory, and hence a military success since it forced the U.S. hand and led directly to peace talks. This is regardless of whether the U.S. or Saigon forces were defeated in situ (an unrealistic goal, Tra argues). The goal of the Tet Offensive was not to destroy the U.S. Army and force a retreat. But Tet was a qualified military success. The anticipated general insurrection in the cities to seize power from the Saigon regime did not materialize. Without the Tet Offensive, however, Tra maintains that the Ho Chi Minh campaign toppling the Saigon regime in 1975 would not have been possible.

Tran Van Tra's chapter on the Tet Offensive casts doubt on current theories of revolution which focus exclusively on structural, contextual and sociological/historical variables of revolution. According to Theda Skocpol, "Revolutions are not made; they come."[5] Tran Van Tra's chapter demonstrates that revolution is a purposive act, guided by strategic thought and planning. As he shows, the Tet Offensive was an integral part of "people's war" and constituted a *strategy* designed to win the war. It can also be noted that as such, it was hardly a last-gasp effort by a desperate and beleaguered guerrilla army.

Robert McNamara, as Lyndon Johnson's secretary of defense, realized the war was stalemated as early as 1965 and thought that escalation would be seen as the only way out. In chapter 8, "The Strange 'Dissent' of Robert S. McNamara," George Herring shows that McNamara also realized this carried enormous risks and would not necessarily enable the United States to win the war. He put forward the option of a political settlement, which was rejected. McNamara's dissent led to his departure from the administration in February 1968. The tragedy is that he never revealed his misgivings publicly.

Stalemate and the inconclusiveness of the war also operated on a different level. Ronald Spector speculates in his chapter "'How Do You Know If You're Winning?': Perception and Reality in America's Military Performance, 1965–1970" that the Vietnam War was more like World War I than any other major twentieth-century war. In both cases, the soldiers who fought became disillusioned, confused, and dispirited. There was an absence of a "meaningful measurement of military success and clear view of what would constitute victory." Many GIs in Vietnam did not believe in the war. Tet 1968 accelerated their disillusionment, sense of loss, and perception that the war lacked purpose.

The enormous loss of life and sheer destruction caused by the war is discussed by James Harrison in chapter 7, "History's Heaviest Bombing." Harrison wonders how the Vietnamese revolutionaries were capable of sustaining some of the most intensive bombing in history. In chapter 3, "Tet: The 1968 General Offensive and Uprising," Tran Van Tra offers a partial answer—the revolutionaries' belief that theirs was a "just war," their implacable determination and spirit of self-sacrifice, and their confidence in being able to maintain the upper hand strategically on the battlefield.

On the U.S. side, the elusive military victory and inflated policy pronouncements from Washington were elements in the rise of an influential antiwar movement. Paul Joseph argues in chapter 10 that this movement had a greater impact on U.S. policymakers than is generally recognized. While it did not succeed in transforming either the goals of U.S. policy in Vietnam or the purposes of U.S. intervention, the antiwar movement did manage to "block and/or reduce the scale of military strategies that were necessary to achieve those objectives." U.S. policymakers, then, were constrained in escalating the war both by domestic political pressures and by moves on the battlefield coming from the revolutionary forces. It is interesting to note Tran Van Tra's estimation of the impact of the

U.S. antiwar movement. He discounts its decisive impact on Washington, arguing that U.S. policymakers were primarily influenced by what was happening on the battlefield. However, in his comments at the Columbia conference he said that the antiwar movement heartened the revolutionary forces on moral grounds and was a source of great encouragement.

Was the Vietnamese revolution in the South "northern" or "southern"? This question continues to vex many who study the war. Tran Van Tra argued at the conference that the military leadership in charge of prosecuting the war in the South remained southern, up to the end. As military units of the North Vietnamese army—the People's Army of Vietnam (PAVN)—increasingly came South after 1965, they were integrated into existing People's Liberation Armed Forces (PLAF) forces. It often took up to a year for PAVN units to become fully operational, and they relied on the southern guerrillas for logistical and intelligence support. Northerners retained control of the overall direction and strategic planning of the war by virtue of their key posts in the Political Bureau in Hanoi. But southern commanders were given a great deal of latitude in their regions despite often acrimonious disagreements over strategic and tactical issues (which "northern" personnages in the Political Bureau did not always win).

The decision to accelerate the revolutionary struggle in the South in 1959 revolved around a debate as to whether to emphasize political or military struggle. The Fifteenth Plenum of the Central Committee, which met in January 1959, announced that both political and military struggle would be used. This amounted to an intensification of the revolutionary struggle in the South and is widely seen as the beginning of "armed struggle" there. Yet as William Duiker concludes in chapter 2, "Waging Revolutionary War: The Evolution of Hanoi's Strategy in the South, 1959–1965," it is misleading to portray this debate in terms of a North–South confrontation. Le Duan, General Secretary of the Party (in the North), argued then and later that the primary reliance should still be placed on political struggle. Military means should not be the primary tool in confronting the United States and the Ngo Dinh Diem regime.

Tran Van Tra noted that it is correct to interpret the Party Plenum's Resolution 15 as a result of pressure from revolutionaries from the South. "People in the South wanted to arm themselves in self-defense. The central government in Hanoi wanted to have a peaceful political struggle." But Resolution 15 "advocated political struggle as the main role and armed struggle as a supplement to the political struggle." Tra went on to say, "Since 1945, even though there was North and South, we always believed that Vietnam was one country, and that the strategic leadership would be in Hanoi." Even after 1968, when many revolutionary cadres in the South were killed, the "North" still did not impose its will over the South, according to Tra. In two years time the southern revolution was able to recover from its losses, rebuild its bases, and play an important role in the events leading up to 1975.

Kristin Pelzer's chapter, "Love, War, and Revolution: Reflections on the

Memoirs of Nguyen Thi Dinh," explores the sources of revolutionary motivation for southerners through the reminiscences of a Viet Cong general, who happened to be a woman. The bonds of family love and devotion were key elements in the revolutionary consciousness of Ba Dinh, as she was known. Personal vignettes of the war by "the other side" undermine accepted images of the Viet Cong's inhumanity and violence usually held in the United States and are a necessary corrective in balancing Western perceptions of the "enemy." Racial stereotypes associated with U.S. military intervention in Vietnam in fact go back to the very first U.S. contacts with the young revolutionary government of Ho Chi Minh. In chapter 1, "An Improbable Opportunity: America and the Democratic Republic of Vietnam's 1947 Initiative," Mark Bradley shows how American diplomats implicitly questioned the Vietnamese capability for an independent government and misinterpreted the Democratic Republic of Vietnam's motives for desiring to establish diplomatic relations with the United States. The United States in 1947 rejected a positive initiative by the Vietnamese government to establish diplomatic contact. Furthermore, although by 1947 China was engulfed in civil war and could play no role in Vietnam, China was an important factor in U.S. policymaking with regard to Vietnam. The United States during this period tended to rely on outsiders' judgments about Vietnam, especially those of European diplomats and American officials stationed in China.

Part Three of this book deals with the war in southern Vietnam primarily during the years of the Nixon administration. Jeffrey Clarke's chapter 11, "Civil-Military Relations in South Vietnam and the American Advisory Effort," argues that the U.S. political advisory program was transferred to the military chain of command, with mixed results. Internal politics, rather than military considerations, continued to dictate the priorities of the Saigon regime. The result was that the Saigon regime remained just as ineffective militarily as it was undemocratic politically.

Despite the intensification of the war under Nixon, the revolutionary side continued to search for a diplomatic formula that would bring the war to an end. The Provisional Revolutionary Government (PRG) put forward an offer in July 1971 to negotiate an end to the war on the basis of the complete withdrawal of U.S. troops and the return of U.S. prisoners of war. It insisted the United States end its support of the Thieu regime and allow a more neutral regime which would be willing to enter into talks with the PRG with an aim to forming a coalition government. These points were rejected by Nixon and Kissinger, but some political advantage did accrue to the Communist side as a result. The initiative accelerated a desire for an end to the war among political circles in Saigon. In the end, the population under the control of the Thieu regime became increasingly critical of its prowar policies. Ngo Vinh Long argues in chapter 13, "Post–Paris Agreement Struggles and the Fall of Saigon," that the internal political and economic weakness of the Thieu regime spelled disaster for Thieu and would have caused the collapse of his regime whether or not U.S. aid was cut off. The final military denouement, unanticipated as much by the revolutionary side as by the pro-Saigon forces, was in effect a coup de grace.

In Cambodia, as Ben Kiernan shows in "The Impact on Cambodia of the U.S. Intervention in Vietnam," chapter 14, U.S. intervention was the decisive factor in the rise of Pol Pot. Although U.S. complicity in the coup against Sihanouk in 1970, which permitted the United States to engage in full-scale military activity in Cambodia, cannot be definitively proved, Kiernan offers evidence that the U.S. Special Forces, rather than the CIA, may have prompted the coup. These processes were set in motion well before Nixon invaded Cambodia in May 1970.

The chapters in Part Four look at the war from the historical vantage point of several years following the U.S. withdrawal. Tran Van Tra suggests in chapter 15, "The War That Should Not Have Been," that an important missed opportunity were the Geneva Agreements of 1954, which, if followed, could have prevented an outbreak of hostilities between the United States and the Communists. There were other opportunities for a political settlement even after U.S. military intervention, which would have obviated the need for a military solution. To Tran Van Tra, the United States fundamentally misconceived the nature of the Vietnamese revolution and paid heavily for it.

Luu Doan Huynh explains in chapter 16, "The American War in Vietnamese Memory," the devastating consequences the war had for the Vietnamese people, who continue to pay a heavy price for a war fought on their own territory. Yet, incredibly, today they display little rancor toward Americans and do not consider the United States to be their enemy. And, he notes, while there have been bad losers on the American side, there have been bad winners on the Vietnamese side.

Marilyn Young's "The Vietnam War in American Memory," chapter 17, explores the ways Americans have tried to alleviate the pain of Vietnam and how the collective memory of Vietnam is still influenced by military interventions elsewhere, notably the war in the Persian Gulf. The quick victory in the Gulf War appeared to ease some of the pain, but the stigma of Vietnam remains. In chapter 18, David Hunt examines the war from the vantage point of a former antiwar activist who goes back to Vietnam many years after the war.

Finally, in chapter 19, "China and Vietnam: Looking for a New Version of an Old Relationship," Keith Taylor shows how the historical development of the Vietnamese revolution in the twentieth century distanced Vietnam from the Chinese cultural and political orbit, which, ironically, U.S. intervention in Vietnam had the effect of counteracting. He argues that the U.S. relationship with Vietnam has always served to support Chinese interests in the region, despite the avowedly anti-Chinese aims of U.S. containment policy. It can be added that grim anti-communism in the wake of the Korean War, among other things, perceived China as a vassal of the Soviets and the Vietnamese fight for independence as part of China's scheme for expansion in Southeast Asia. This may have been the key factor that led to the outbreak of hostilities between the United States and Vietnam. The need to uncouple U.S.-Vietnamese relations from U.S.-

Chinese relations is both a lesson of the past and a test for the future.

Notes

1. Tran Van Tra, *Vietnam: History of the Bulwark B2 Theatre*, vol. 5: *Concluding the 30 Years War* (Washington, D.C.: Foreign Broadcast Information Service, Southeast Asia Report, No. 1247, Joint Publication Research Service (JPRS) 82783, February 2, 1983).

2. The papers from this meeting are published in Jayne Werner and David Hunt, *The American War* (Ithaca, NY: Cornell University Southeast Asia Publication Series, forthcoming).

3. "North" and "South" refer to regions of Vietnam and are commonly capitalized in Vietnamese historiography of the war. This capitalization in this volume, however, does not imply they were separate nations.

4. Leslie Gelb and Richard K. Betts, *The Irony of Vietnam: The System Worked* (Washington, D.C.: Brookings Institution, 1977).

5. Theda Skocpol, *States and Social Revolution*. New York: Cambridge University Press, 1979, p. 17. Quote attributed to Wendell Philipps. See also Jack Goldstone et al. *Revolutions of the Late Twentieth Century*. Boulder: Westview Press, 1991.

Part One

The Vietnamese Revolution and Political/Military Strategy

1

An Improbable Opportunity: America and the Democratic Republic of Vietnam's 1947 Initiative

Mark Bradley

Shortly after the outbreak of the First Indochina War, Ho Chi Minh's Democratic Republic of Vietnam (DRV) launched a four-month diplomatic initiative in the spring and summer of 1947 designed to secure the support of the Truman administration. Centered in Thailand, the Vietnamese effort was led by Pham Ngoc Thach, deputy minister in the Office of the President and one of three men who directly advised Ho Chi Minh. From April to June, Thach presented a series of substantive proposals to representatives of the American government and business community in Bangkok aimed at winning American confidence and assistance: calls for recognition of the DRV and mediation of the war with the French; requests for economic rehabilitation loans and promises of economic concessions to American businesses; and appeals for technical assistance and cultural exchange.

The Vietnamese initiative inspired the Truman administration's only sustained internal reexamination of its relationship with the DRV between 1946 and 1949. The initiative prompted efforts to reestablish direct diplomatic contact with the DRV as well as a comprehensive evaluation of Ho Chi Minh's government and its willingness to accept American advice and guidance. Nonetheless, the DRV's initiative ended in failure. As with Ho Chi Minh's better known efforts to seek American support in 1946 and 1949,[1] the administration met the Vietnamese proposals with public silence. By the fall of 1947, the Truman

3

administration hesitantly began to embrace French efforts to organize a non-communist, nationalist alternative to the DRV, a policy that culminated in American recognition of the Associated States of Vietnam under the former emperor, Bao Dai, in February 1950.

Despite its failure, the DRV initiative and the reactions of the Truman administration to it provide new evidence about the character of Vietnamese and American policy toward each other in the late 1940s, a period contemporary critics of American policy termed a "lost opportunity"[2] for closer relations between the United States and the DRV. First, this episode permits a reexamination of the nature and aims of the DRV's diplomacy. The character of Pham Ngoc Thach's proposals to the Truman administration and the domestic context from which they emerged suggest that, rather than viewing world politics solely through a Leninist prism, Ho Chi Minh and the DRV took a pragmatic approach to foreign relations in this period. Second, this episode illustrates the factors that influenced the Truman administration's policy toward the DRV. In part, it sustains the conclusions of scholars like Gary R. Hess who argue that anti-communism and French pressure framed administration policy in Vietnam.[3] But it also demonstrates the institutional processes by which French concerns made their way into American policy deliberations. More importantly, the administration's reaction to the DRV initiative reveals the roles that ambivalent attitudes toward the Nanjing[4] government in China and culturally based judgments of the DRV's incapacity for independent government played in shaping the administration's unfavorable perceptions of Vietnamese communism.

Spring of 1947 was a time of internal crisis for the DRV. After nine months of often acrimonious diplomatic negotiations over the terms of Vietnamese independence, war broke out between the French and the DRV in December 1946.[5] The first three months of the Indochina War brought sustained military defeat and escalating administrative chaos, putting the continued survival of Ho Chi Minh's government in jeopardy. Moreover, with Soviet diplomacy focused on Europe and the Chinese Communists preoccupied by civil war, the DRV faced almost complete isolation from the Communist world. In large measure, pragmatism rather than ideology shaped the DRV's efforts to address this crisis. With the possibility of external assistance from the Communist world foreclosed, the DRV's diplomacy focused on the United States and the Nanjing government in China. At the same time, the Vietnamese government launched a series of internal reforms aimed not so much at socialist revolution as at boosting its popular legitimacy and developing military and economic self-sufficiency.

The Vietnamese government's national authority quickly eroded as the DRV's army faltered under the strong French military challenge at the outbreak of the Indochina War. French armed forces took most of the provincial capitals of Bac Bo and Trung Bo[6] in January 1947. By early February, the imperial capital of Hue had fallen to the French after a six-week siege. In mid-February, after two months of sporadic fighting, Vietnamese forces withdrew from Hanoi which once again fell under French control. The adverse military situation prompted Ho Chi Minh to move his government from Hanoi to the jungles of Thai Nguyen in northern Bac Bo to escape French capture. Although the government in Thai Nguyen retained loose control of most of rural Bac Bo, the central state apparatus built by the DRV in 1945 and 1946 ceased to function by March 1947. As one contemporary critic noted in the DRV newspaper, *Su That* (Truth), "plans were slow in coming out" and "orders and instructions were not complete." Each rural community, this critic continued,

> simply followed its own developments concerning tactics and organization. At the same time the way our cadres worked was also poor so that each time an order to set something in motion needed coordination it seemed to be too difficult.[7]

The crisis precipitated by military defeat and the collapse of the government's administrative structure were compounded by the DRV's isolation from its potential allies in the communist world. No evidence of sustained contact or of financial and technical assistance from the Chinese Communist Party (CCP), the Soviet Union, or the French Communist Party in the spring and summer of 1947 is available.[8] Support from the CCP, increasingly important to the DRV after 1949, was insignificant in this period. The CCP, preoccupied with fighting the Nanjing government in Manchuria and northern China in early 1947, served as a model for Vietnamese military strategy, but offered no financial or technical assistance. Nor did the Soviet Union extend substantial guidance or assistance to the Vietnamese. Concerned with events in Europe, including the communist struggle for power in France, the Soviets expressed sympathy for the Vietnamese cause but remained noncommittal about the specific levels of assistance the Vietnamese might receive.[9] The French Communist Party remained aloof from the DRV until its ejection from the French ruling coalition in the spring of 1947; even then, however, members were able to offer little more than internal party resolutions to secure the withdrawal of French troops.

Against this backdrop of internal crisis and international isolation, the DRV sent Pham Ngoc Thach to Bangkok in the spring and summer of 1947 to seek the Truman administration's support.[10] Two elements comprised the DRV initiative: efforts to convince the administration of the moderate and independent character of the Vietnamese government and calls for American political, economic, and cultural assistance. Thach's contacts with the American embassy in Bangkok between April and May were directed at the former. In frequent conversations with the assistant military attache to the Bangkok embassy, Lt. Col. William Law, and with American businessmen, Thach sought to inform the American government of developments in Indochina from the DRV's perspective, demonstrate the moderate character of the Vietnamese regime, and convey the DRV's capability and seriousness of purpose.

During this initial phase of the DRV initiative, Thach submitted two Vietnamese documents to the American government that illustrate the nature of his efforts. The first was a series of answers Thach gave on April 9 to questions formulated by Law and Edwin F. Stanton, the American ambassador to Thailand. Thach's responses stressed the broad composition of the Vietnamese government and the nationalist orientation of communism in Vietnam. "The actual government," Thach said, "is . . . of broad national makeup, comprised of men from all three regions of the country." The cabinet ministers "are not associated with a particular party," he continued, rather, the "choice of ministers has been made in consideration of their worth and popularity." Emphasizing its nationalist program rather than a commitment to socialist revolution, Thach argued that communism in Vietnam since 1932 had embodied "the spirit of national resistance against French colonialism" and "is nothing more than a means of arriving at independence." Thach also sought to reassure the administration about the DRV's economic program, claiming that "the government" and "the communist ministers . . . favor the development of capitalist autonomy and call on foreign capital for the reconstruction of the country."[11]

In a second Vietnamese document, Thach sought to translate these broader appeals into concrete proposals aimed at increasing American confidence in the DRV's capabilities. This document, a memorandum to representatives of the American International Engineering Group in Bangkok, is one of several Thach prepared and distributed to American firms in Thailand. It offered a quid pro quo: guarantees of monopolistic economic concessions to American business in return for agricultural and industrial equipment as well as $10 million to $20 million in American rehabilitation loans. Of particular interest are what Thach termed the "economic privileges" the DRV was willing to grant to American firms. The strangest, perhaps, was tourism; at a time of political and socioeconomic turmoil, Thach called Vietnam "an ideal country for tourists." More serious were promises of tax-free monopolies for American imports and for the rice export trade, potentially the largest in Asia, as well as calls for establishment of small American manufacturing plants in Vietnam. Significantly, in view of Thach's efforts to demonstrate conciliation toward the French, an American rubber concession was specifically excluded from the proposal. "The majority of rubber fields' owners are French," Thach said, "so we cannot guarantee the monopoly of export because it is necessary to give some economic interests to the French."[12]

The moderate image Thach sought to convey to the Truman administration in the initial phase of the DRV's initiative was reinforced by his own appointment and a subsequent reshuffling of the DRV cabinet. By selecting Thach to represent the DRV to the Truman administration, Ho Chi Minh sought to communicate a conciliatory message to the Americans. Thach had been a member of the Viet Minh executive committee, which oversaw efforts to establish a provisional government in Nam Bo in August and September of 1945. Thach's formal position was commissioner for foreign affairs; in that role he had served as the

Vietnamese liaison for the U.S. Office of Strategic Services (OSS) in the fall 1945 "Embankment" mission to Saigon led by Peter Dewey. The leadership of the DRV, particularly Ho Chi Minh, saw Dewey's mission, along with another OSS mission led by Archimedes Patti to Hanoi, as the high point of Vietnamese-American cooperation. The selection of Thach to meet American officials in 1947 may be seen as an effort to capitalize on this favorable association.[13] Ho Chi Minh also hoped to influence favorably American perceptions of his government's composition through his appointment of Hoang Minh Giam, the leader of the Vietnamese Socialist Party, as foreign minister in March and a shift in the composition of his cabinet in July. Three Communist ministers were dismissed in the July cabinet reshuffle, including Defense Minister Vo Nguyen Giap (who continued to run the army), and were replaced by non-Communists who supported Ho's policies.[14]

Thach's calls for direct American assistance to the Vietnamese government in late May and early June opened the final phase of the DRV initiative. This was preceded on May 8 by Foreign Minister Giam's appeal to the Truman administration for American diplomatic recognition, a policy Giam claimed "would increase United States prestige and influence . . . and establish peace in Southeast Asia."[15] The substance of Thach's message was more pragmatic: "we recognize the world-politics of the U.S. at this time does not permit taking a position against the French." Instead, Thach appealed for political, economic, and cultural assistance from the Truman administration. He sought American mediation of the Indochina War to guarantee a settlement with France either through tripartite discussion or the presentation of the Vietnamese case before the United Nations by the Philippines. Thach explicitly disavowed any interest in American weapons, repeating the request he made of American businessmen for a substantial loan to provide capital and technicians for economic reconstruction and development. He also expressed concern that the Vietnamese had "seen U.S. culture only through the French 'prison' [sic]" and proposed the establishment of joint scientific organizations, funding for a chair in American literature at the University of Hanoi, and scholarships for Vietnamese students at American universities to foster enhanced mutual understanding.[16]

The absence of documentation on the processes of Vietnamese decision making in undertaking the initiative to the Truman administration makes it difficult to authoritatively address DRV motivations and aims.[17] In one view of Vietnamese diplomacy, most recently put forward by Ton That Thien,[18] the DRV's ideological solidarity with the Soviet Union prevented it from undertaking any sustained relationship with the non-Communist world. Party doctrine, Thien argues, viewed diplomacy as part of the political and military struggle to achieve a proletarian revolution in Vietnam. In this view, any effort to gain external support from the non-Communist world was little more than a tactical maneuver to be quickly abandoned when the government's revolutionary aims had been achieved.

Despite the adherence of much of the DRV's leadership to Marxism-Leninism, the DRV initiative to the Truman administration and the context from which it emerged suggest that a pragmatic concern to build an independent nationalist state was more important to the DRV than Soviet ideological influence. The urgent sense of domestic crisis, limited diplomatic options, the careful selection of Thach to meet with American diplomats in Bangkok, and the character of the messages he delivered convey a seriousness of purpose on the part of the DRV to develop a closer relationship with the Truman administration. In particular, Thach's appreciation for the constraints acting on American policy and his interest in economic and cultural, as well as political, assistance are indicative of the DRV's interest in developing a realistic and long-term alliance with the United States.

The pragmatic spirit that animated Thach's mission is also reflected in the nature of the DRV's other efforts to address the crisis it faced in 1947. Along with the initiative to the United States, Ho Chi Minh sought to enlist the confidence and support of the Nanjing government in China throughout most of 1947. At the outbreak of the Indochina War, the DRV, despite traditional Vietnamese distrust of China and the predatory actions of the Chinese occupation forces in Hanoi in the fall and winter of 1945, made strenuous efforts to protect Chinese refugees caught in the crossfire of initial skirmishes between French and Vietnamese troops in Hanoi and Haiphong. In February of 1947, the DRV planned to send a four-man delegation to Nanjing, a mission its leader Nguyen Duy Thanh, chief of the Chinese section of the DRV's Foreign Ministry, termed an effort "to get rid of the French, with the help of the Chinese."[19]

While a February French offensive in Bac Bo forced the abandonment of the mission, the DRV renewed its efforts in the spring of 1947. At the Asian Relations Conference held in New Delhi in March and April, the head of the Vietnamese delegation, Tran Van Giau, met with delegates from the Nanjing government.[20] No substantive agreements were reached, but the selection of a senior official like Giau, who had led the Viet Minh's 1945 provisional government in Nam Bo, to lead the delegation indicates the continued importance attached to the Chinese relationship.[21]

Ho Chi Minh's efforts to foster Chinese support continued into the summer at a time when many observers believed Chiang Kai-shek's armies would shortly defeat the CCP's main force. In a July interview, Ho sought to draw an ideological link between the DRV and the Nanjing government, claiming: "We are realizing the People's Three Principles of Asia's great revolution, as stated by Dr. Sun Yat-sen, though the French reactionary colonialists mistook them for the 'class principles' of Karl Marx."[22] The DRV's last efforts at diplomacy with Nanjing ended in failure. In October 1947, a seven-man delegation led by Thanh entered China only to be arrested by local Nanjing authorities in Jingshi and held there until the following February. Despite Nanjing's efforts to disavow the actions of its local representatives, Thanh returned to Vietnam upon his release rather than continue on to Nanjing.

Far-reaching internal reforms accompanied the DRV's diplomatic initiatives, suggesting that the DRV's leadership was prepared to develop domestic autonomy if its efforts to win American and Chinese assistance failed and reinforcing the DRV's pragmatic outlook. In April 1947, a central party cadre conference issued a directive calling for an immediate shift to guerrilla tactics in order to regain the initiative against the French. As part of this shift, all villages under the DRV's control were instructed to establish self-defense militia units, and training in guerrilla warfare began in newly liberated areas. Domestic weapons manufacturing also increased, with the construction of major factories at Phu-Tho in Bac Bo and at Thap Muoi in Trung Bo and the establishment of local arms workshops producing bazookas, grenades, pistols, rifles, and machine guns.[23]

The DRV also renewed efforts to launch moderate forms of socioeconomic reform, including calls for increased food and industrial production, revived efforts to reduce land rents by 25 percent, and intensified literacy drives. The DRV's policy toward the reduction of land rents illustrates the character of these efforts. Rather than undertaking full-scale land reform to achieve a socialist transformation of the countryside, the DRV sought to alleviate rural distress by reducing rents while maintaining existing land ownership patterns to keep local notables and rich peasants in the nationalist coalition against the French.[24]

The DRV's overtures to the Truman administration in the spring and summer of 1947 came at a time of increasing resolve in American policy toward Europe and of continued indecision and growing frustration in East Asia. With the announcement of the Truman Doctrine in March and the Marshall Plan in June, American efforts to contain Soviet expansionism in Western Europe began to find full expression. Among policy planners in Washington, the political and economic stability of France was a particularly high priority.[25] But policy toward East Asia, particularly China, remained fluid. Throughout 1947, the administration debated the efficacy of continued support to Chiang Kai-shek in the civil war between the Nanjing government and the Chinese Communists.[26] The Chinese issue was particularly acute for George Marshall, who returned from a failed effort to mediate the civil war shortly before becoming secretary of state in February 1947. Both resolve in Europe and indecision in East Asia, along with unfavorable notions of the Vietnamese capacity for self-government, shaped the administration's response to the DRV initiative.

The Truman administration's response to the DRV's efforts in March and April of 1947 to demonstrate its moderate character was initially quite favorable, prompting Secretary Marshall's approval of plans by American diplomats in Southeast Asia to reestablish direct diplomatic contact with Ho Chi Minh's government. In response to Hoang Minh Giam's appointment as foreign minister in March, James O'Sullivan, the American vice-consul at Hanoi, cabled Washington: "Giam is a 'moderate' with whom the French might deal."[27] The American ambassador to Thailand, Edwin F. Stanton, favorably characterized Thach as "a man of intelligence and very considerable energy." Moreover, Stanton commented that the "disillusionment felt by members of the Vietnamese government with the French communists" in large measure explained Thach's "desire to contact the American authorities" and "enlist our support."[28]

On April 24, O'Sullivan cabled Secretary Marshall and proposed that he meet directly with Pham Ngoc Thach in Bangkok. O'Sullivan had met Thach in Hanoi before the outbreak of the Indochina War had forced Ho's government into the jungles of Thai Nguyen. While O'Sullivan did not share Stanton's favorable impression of Thach, calling him "a very shifty character," O'Sullivan was convinced that Thach was "close to Ho Chi Minh" and that "conversations with him would probably result in his revealing more information than he realized." Concerned about allaying what he termed "French suspicions," O'Sullivan suggested that official connections with this initial visit could be avoided by authorizing him leave to travel to Bangkok at his own expense.[29] Within a week, Marshall cabled his approval, both for the meeting itself and for the arrangements O'Sullivan had proposed. Of particular interest to Marshall were the answers Thach might give to questions about the "extent of communist control" in the DRV and "the degree of subservience to Moscow to be expected of communist leaders."[30]

O'Sullivan's proposed meeting, however, was soon abandoned. Ambassador Stanton cabled Marshall on May 7, informing him that Thach had left Bangkok. At the same time, he mentioned that Tran Van Giau remained in Bangkok and could serve as a "useful contact." Stanton recognized Giau as the former head of the Viet Minh's provisional government in Nam Bo in late summer and early fall of 1945 and more recently as head of the Vietnamese delegation to the New Delhi Asian Relations Conference. But Stanton expressed doubts about O'Sullivan meeting any Vietnamese representative, suggesting that such an encounter "would certainly come to the attention of the French legation officials who might attach undue significance" to it.[31] Two days later, Marshall cabled O'Sullivan to withdraw his approval for the meeting with Thach; without reference to the possibility of initiating contact with Giau, Marshall cited Thach's absence and concerns over French reaction as reasons for the change.[32]

In part, O'Sullivan's failure to meet Thach in Bangkok reveals the importance that the Truman administration attached to its commitment to the French in Vietnam. O'Sullivan's caution, Stanton's doubts, and Marshall's reversal reflect American sensitivity to French opinion. Stanton's efforts to keep Thach's contacts with the American embassy in Bangkok outside regular diplomatic channels reinforce this conclusion. Appreciating what he called the "delicacy of the situation in Indochina," Stanton argued that "utmost discretion is essential in dealings with Vietnamese officials." Stanton used his assistant military attache, Lt. Col. Law, as an intermediary in all of the Bangkok embassy's dealings with Thach. Law, who had served a tour of duty in Kunming near the Sino-Vietnamese border during World War II, had established contact with local representatives of the DRV shortly after his appointment in May 1946.[33] At no time did Stanton acknowledge in writing any communication from Thach, arguing "it is better for Law to make informal contact . . . even though these contacts are well known to the French."[34]

The Truman administration's hesitancy to reestablish direct contact with the DRV was also influenced by the administration's shifting perceptions of Chiang Kai-shek's government in China. In April of 1947, while Thach sought to win American confidence in Bangkok, the DRV renewed its efforts to foster Chinese support in meetings between Tran Van Giau and representatives of the Nanjing government at the Asian Relations Conference in New Delhi. At the same time, the Truman administration was expressing repeated concern over the Nanjing government's policy toward the DRV. As Secretary Marshall told Charles S. Reed, the American consul at Saigon, shortly after he approved O'Sullivan's meeting with Thach: "the Chinese cannot be expected to follow a clear and simple policy, but the Department assumes any Vietnamese government acceptable to the Chinese . . . may be considered free of predominant connections to the Communist International." Marshall added, however, that the evidence of Chinese attitudes and policy toward the DRV was "so far conflicting."[35]

At issue were two contradictory views of Chinese intentions in Indochina, a debate that reflected sharp divisions within the American embassy in China on the nature of the Nanjing regime.[36] John L. Stuart, a former missionary and president of Yenching University who became the American ambassador to China in 1946, was a vocal champion of Chiang Kai-shek and took a sympathetic view of Chiang's policy toward Vietnam. As he confidently told Secretary Marshall in a May 1947 cable, even the French ambassador to China agreed that the Chinese had abandoned their designs on Indochina in 1946 and now supported French policy in the region.[37] Against Stuart's favorable assessment, W. Walton Butterworth, a career foreign service officer and counselor to the American embassy in China, represented the view of most professional diplomats in the embassy. Butterworth insisted that Chiang was corrupt and untrustworthy and intended to place Indochina under Chinese influence or direct control. As early as March of 1947, Butterworth told Marshall that the Chinese believed "no consideration is due France." Warning that Nanjing's calls for the protection of ethnic Chinese in Vietnam could serve as a pretext for military intervention, Butterworth raised "the likelihood that the Sudeten pattern would be followed" by the Chinese in Indochina, an ominous reminder of Hitler's policy toward Czechoslovakia in 1938.[38]

Between Marshall's approval of O'Sullivan's meeting with Thach in Bangkok on May 2 and the reversal of his decision seven days later, the debate over Chinese intentions reemerged in reports from Reed in Saigon and O'Sullivan in Hanoi on the attitudes of the Chinese consul generals in Vietnam toward the DRV. Echoing Stuart's view of Chinese policy, Reed reported that the Chinese consul general to Saigon, Ing Fong Tsao, supported French policies. Ing believed, Reed's report argued, that the DRV was "completely controlled by Communist elements whose idea of a nationalist state is but a prelude to an eventual communist state." Ing's willingness to work with Bao Dai and other Vietnamese non-Communist nationalists, Reed suggested, demonstrated Chinese willingness to mediate the Franco-Vietnamese conflict.[39] O'Sullivan's report on the attitude of Yuen Tse Kien, the Chinese consul general in Hanoi, reinforced Butterworth's less favorable assessment of Chinese intentions. Commenting that Yuen's support for the DRV against the French "ha[d] never wavered" since his appointment in the fall of 1945, O'Sullivan reported that Yuen "reasons that if Vietnam were independent and began to play the Moscow game too strongly the Chinese would be able to handle the situation."[40]

Had the Truman administration accepted one or the other view of Chinese intentions in Indochina, the significance of the DRV's appeals to the Nanjing government might have been clearer. If the Chinese had been seen as intent upon wresting control of Vietnam from the French, Ho Chi Minh's efforts to seek the assistance of the Nanjing government might have provided the administration with evidence that the DRV was too closely tied to a government hostile to American commitments in the region. Or, had the Chinese been viewed as sympathetic to the French, perhaps even willing to mediate Franco-Vietnamese differences, the DRV's appeals to Nanjing might have appeared to American policymakers as confirmation of conciliation and moderation on the part of the Vietnamese. In the event, the Truman administration was left with the sense that the Nanjing government was "playing Vietnam so that China will have two strings to her bow."[41] Just as sensitivity to French opinion prompted caution in the administration's response to the DRV, continuing uncertainty over Chinese intentions shaped its ambiguous perceptions of the DRV's Chinese initiatives and contributed to Marshall's hesitancy to reestablish diplomatic contact with the Vietnamese.

With the possibility of direct contact between the Truman administration and the DRV foreclosed, the administration's attention to the DRV initiative waned until Thach's June appeal for American support and assistance was conveyed to Washington. In mid-July, Marshall asked American diplomats in Saigon and Hanoi for an appraisal of the DRV should events force the French to recognize the DRV as the legitimate government in Vietnam. Marshall's request, the only intensive effort by the Truman administration between 1946 and 1949 to examine the nature of Ho Chi Minh's government, raised five broad questions: Did Communist influence in the DRV put Vietnam in the Soviet camp? What was Ho Chi Minh's connection to Moscow? Did most Vietnamese understand the meaning of communism? Would the DRV, without French pressure, permit "free expression" or become a "police state under one-party rule"? And, finally, what was the attitude of the Vietnamese people toward the United States?[42]

In the view of Charles S. Reed, the American consul in Saigon, Ho Chi Minh's direct ties to Moscow were extremely limited. Nonetheless, Reed suggested that Ho's forceful leadership, along with the inability of the majority of the Vietnamese population to understand Western notions of self-government, might prompt the emergence of a Communist state in Vietnam antithetical to American interests. "Soviet policy toward Vietnam," Reed told Marshall, "appears to be one of remote control rather than of open support." Reed argued that "there is no proof that he [Ho] has renounced his communist training. . . . [A] wily opportunist, Ho will take any aid coming his way to gain his ends without disclosing his ultimate intentions." Reed asserted that Ho's leadership represented an "aggressive minority" who "could bring about the evolution of a communist state even if the majority of the Vietnamese are not particularly interested in the communist message."

Unfavorable perceptions of the Vietnamese capacity for self-government underlay Reed's analysis. Reed viewed the capabilities of the Vietnamese through a prism of racial stereotypes. "Few of the Annamites are particularly industrious," Reed reported, nor were they noted for their "honesty, loyalty or veracity." And while he added that the Vietnamese national character may be "a direct and pernicious result of decades of French maltreatment," Reed insisted that "the great bulk of the population was not prepared for self-government." Despite France's previous record, Reed concluded that the removal of "French pressure and the absence of Western democratic control" would make it impossible to prevent a "police state" with "Communist leanings."[43]

Writing from Hanoi, Vice-Consul James O'Sullivan voiced a more moderate view of Ho Chi Minh's Communist connections and the aims of the DRV. Echoing some of the themes that arose in Pham Ngoc Thach's portrayal of Ho's regime, O'Sullivan argued that:

> [the] influence of the Communists in the present government would not be sufficient to put Viet Nam squarely in the Soviet camp although there would be pull in that direction. . . . Ho's very great reluctance to admit that he is Nguyen Ai Quoc or to show any connection whatsoever with Russia is indicative of his realization that he must deal with the West. Ho wrote twenty-five years ago that national revolution must precede Communist revolution in Indochina and it is obvious his first concern is to get rid of the French here. He is trying to obtain aid wherever he can and will tend to be oriented toward the source from whence the assistance came.

Patriotism and nationalism, O'Sullivan suggested, formed the basis of the DRV's appeal. "Most Vietnamese," O'Sullivan asserted, "do not really understand" the meaning of communism "as an international form" nor would "they care if it was thoroughly explained to them." Like Reed, although without his racial rhetoric, O'Sullivan argued that the Vietnamese had "no democratic tradition" and speculated on the possible "danger of a police state under one-party rule."[44]

Although Marshall had limited his request to reports from Reed and

O'Sullivan, Jefferson Caffery, the American ambassador to France, also cabled his views of the DRV to Marshall. Far more alarmed than American diplomats in Vietnam about Ho Chi Minh's relationship to the Soviet Union, Caffery claimed that

> [the] absence of any widespread belief in or sympathy for Communism among the masses of Ho Chi-Minh's admirers and their apparent apathy towards Communist teachings cannot seriously be regarded in these times as potent factors against the establishment of a government which would follow Moscow's directions. Recent experiences have shown only too well how a relatively small, but well-trained and determined, minority can take over power in an area where democratic traditions are weak. Nor can remoteness of Moscow be regarded as an adequate safeguard. From Ho Chi-Minh's past career there can be little doubt but that he maintains close connections in Communist circles.[45]

Caffery's perceptions were also shared by William C. Bullitt, the American ambassador to the Soviet Union in the mid-1930s and, later, to France before the outbreak of World War II. In a series of conversations with the State Department's Division of Philippine and Southeast Asian Affairs in the spring of 1947, Bullitt claimed that if Vietnam were "liberated under the present government," the DRV "would immediately be run in accordance with dictates from Moscow." Bullitt's suspicions about Vietnamese communism were compounded by the same unfavorable notion of Vietnamese capabilities that Reed reported from Saigon: "The Annamese are attractive and even lovable," Bullitt claimed, but "essentially childish."[46]

Only Marshall's query about Vietnamese perceptions of the United States yielded a uniform response, suggesting that all of these observers viewed the Vietnamese through the prism of superior notions of American political culture. O'Sullivan's sentiment that "Vietnamese people here still regard the United States as a promised land and earthly paradise" resonates throughout these reports. Reed did interject a cautionary note, suggesting that "if American advice and action run counter to what [the Vietnamese] think is the full sum of their desiderata, the U.S. might not be so popular." But the others shared O'Sullivan's view that the Vietnamese were "exceedingly sensitive to United States opinion and unquestionably would accept American advice."[47]

Although the reports Marshall received did not result in any change in American policy toward the DRV, they illustrate the factors that shaped the administration's perceptions of Vietnamese communism and its rejection of the DRV initiative. The reports of Caffery and Bullitt reveal how French views forcefully made their way into American policy discussions. Both of their reports, far more strident than those of American diplomats in Vietnam on the extent of Soviet influence over the DRV, paralleled French efforts to shift international perceptions of the Indochina War from a colonial struggle to an anti-

Communist crusade. American diplomats in Vietnam often dismissed French claims. As O'Sullivan told Marshall in a July 1947 cable, "it is curious that the French discovered no Communist menace in the Ho Chi Minh government until . . . it became apparent that the Vietnamese . . . would not bow to French wishes."[48] But with Caffery and Bullitt, both influential senior diplomats, presenting similar arguments, the French position gained enhanced legitimacy in American policymaking circles. Caffery, sixty-one in 1947, had served in the foreign service since 1913 with high level postings in Japan, Latin America, and Western Europe. Bullitt, fifty-six in 1947, was also an experienced diplomat. O'Sullivan's junior status may have encouraged the administration to diminish his more moderate portrait of the DRV. O'Sullivan, thirty-one in 1947, had joined the foreign service just five year earlier; his appointment as vice-consul to Hanoi was his first significant post.[49]

These reports also reflect how little information American diplomats had on which to base their evaluations of the DRV. No new information is presented in these cables, nor are their characterizations of the DRV backed by any systematized sets of evidence. Particularly significant is the absence of any discussion of the internal crisis facing the Vietnamese government, the ways in which Soviet influence might be brought to bear on the Vietnamese, or the character of the DRV's efforts at internal reform. The differences among these reports, more of tone than substance, are better accounted for by individual temperament or the geographic setting of the authors' posts. Reed, who doubted the existence of strong ties between the DRV and Moscow but remained skeptical of Vietnamese ability to maintain an independent Communist state, spent most of his professional life in colonial enclaves, first as a representative of an American rubber company in Sumatra during the 1920s, later as a young foreign service officer in Shanghai and Beijing in the 1930s, and finally as American consul in Saigon just before and immediately after World War II. Reed's post in Saigon, the center of non-Communist nationalism, would have provided him with access to both anti-French and anti-Communist viewpoints. O'Sullivan's post in Hanoi and his access to high-ranking members of the DRV's cabinet before the outbreak of the Indochina War would have increased his exposure to DRV viewpoints and helps to account for his more nuanced view of Vietnamese communism.

Caffery and Bullitt's sympathy to French perceptions of the DRV reflects their willingness to rely on French judgments of Vietnamese politics as well as their individual backgrounds. Caffery, a Louisiana Catholic of French ancestry, was popular with the French government, holding an honorary degree from the University of Lyon along with other French honorific awards. Bullitt's personal ties to France were also very strong. After leaving his post as ambassador to France, he enlisted in the French army in 1944, serving as an infantry major, and was later made a commander in the French Legion of Honor. Moreover, Bullitt was an outspoken anti-Communist; his experiences as American ambassador to the Soviet Union at the high point of Stalin's purges had convinced him of "Soviet fanaticism bent on world domination."[50]

A unanimous distrust of the Vietnamese capacity for self-government and a sense of the superiority of Western political culture emerges from these reports as well, suggesting that an American cultural chauvinism also shaped the administration's perceptions of Vietnamese communism and its rejection of the DRV initiative.[51] Whether expressed in racial terms, like Bullitt's characterization of the Vietnamese as "children," or in the confident assumption of Vietnamese deference to American advice and models, all of these reports view the majority of the Vietnamese population as passive, uninformed, and vulnerable to outside control. For policymakers like Marshall, concerned with the extent of Soviet influence over the DRV, these images of the Vietnamese must have been particularly disturbing. If the Vietnamese were unfit for political independence and self-government, as all of these reports appeared to confirm, the potential for an independent and moderate communist government under DRV auspices surely appeared remote.

Contemporary critics of the Truman administration's policy toward Vietnam, such as veteran Asian correspondent Robert Shaplen,[52] have called the period from 1946 to 1949 a "lost opportunity" for Vietnamese-American relations. In the view of Shaplen and others, the administration made a "serious mistake" in not dealing more realistically with the DRV. Had Ho Chi Minh been "Titofied" and Vietnam considered a Southeast Asian Yugoslavia, the "whole course of events . . . might have been altered."[53] The DRV's initiative toward the Truman administration in the spring and summer of 1947 does confirm some aspects of the lost opportunity thesis. The DRV's response to the crisis it faced in 1947 illustrates the pragmatic approach that shaped Vietnamese policy in this period. Whether seeking American and Chinese mediation of the war with the French, fostering American economic and cultural ties, building military and economic self-sufficiency, or undertaking moderate forms of socioeconomic reform, the policies of the DRV suggest that, in spite of the adherence to Marxism-Leninism by much of the regime's leadership, Soviet direction and ideological influence were far less important to the DRV than the creation of an independent nationalist state. Moreover, the Vietnamese initiative coincided with the first efforts by policymakers to implement what John Lewis Gaddis termed the "wedge strategy" of America's emerging containment doctrine.[54] Aimed at reducing Soviet influence and power by promoting fragmentation in what was perceived as a Soviet-backed international Communist movement, the wedge strategy produced American support for Tito's break with the Soviet Union in 1948 and encouraged "Asian Titoism" by leaving open the possibility of American cooperation with the People's Republic of China in 1949.

Although the Vietnamese initiative confirms some aspects of the lost opportunity thesis, American and Vietnamese misperceptions over the aims and meaning of the DRV initiative suggest that powerful obstacles blocked the development of closer relations between the United States and the DRV. If the objectives of DRV policy held an internal logic for the Vietnamese, they were not always perceived in the same way by the Americans. From the Vietnamese perspective, seeking assistance from both the Truman administration and the Nanjing government to mediate the Indochina War seemed mutually reinforcing. For the American government, however, suspicious of Nanjing's intentions in Indochina and uncertain over its East Asia policy, the DRV's appeals to China heightened administration fears of the Vietnamese susceptibility to outside control. There were also misperceptions on the Vietnamese side. Thach and the leadership of the DRV may have perceived as normal the channel of communication with the American government in Bangkok through Lt. Col. Law. As Thach's only direct American contact, Law held a position similar to those of the American OSS officers who worked with the DRV in 1945. In view of Thach's favorable experiences with the OSS mission to Saigon and Ho Chi Minh's successful interactions with the OSS and American military personnel in Bac Bo, the administration's selection of Law as an intermediary with the Vietnamese might have initially been interpreted by the DRV as an encouraging sign of American interest in its appeals. But for the Americans, the use of Law, an assistant military attache, suggests the relatively low priority initially accorded to Thach's mission and demonstrates the extent of administration efforts to keep its contacts with the Vietnamese out of normal diplomatic channels.

The Truman administration's acceptance of the DRV initiative was further impeded by the factors that shaped the administration's image of Vietnamese communism, which differed from those that framed its views of communism in China and Yugoslavia. Unlike the State Department's political reporting on Mao's China, the administration's assessments of Ho Chi Minh and the DRV came from two major sources—American diplomats in Vietnam and France. In this way, the pessimistic accounts of Soviet influence in the DRV from the American embassy in France made their way into policy discussions along with the more moderate reports of American diplomats in Vietnam. By contrast, American diplomats in China reported directly to the secretary of state without significant challenge from their colleagues in Western Europe.[55] Reporting on political developments in China and Yugoslavia, where American diplomats were better trained in area studies and language, also tended to be more sophisticated than the evaluations of Vietnamese policy produced by American diplomats in Vietnam and France. Even more important, racial stereotyping of the Vietnamese national character and a sense of the superiority of Western political culture, which often substituted for accurate political reporting from Vietnam, prompted the administration to distrust the Vietnamese capability for independent government and heightened its fears of the DRV's susceptibility to Soviet control. The contrast with reports from Belgrade and Moscow on Tito and the Yugoslav Communists in 1948 is sharp; while American diplomats were concerned about Tito's Marxist-Leninist ideology, Tito or the Yugoslavs' capacity for independent self-government was never at issue.[56]

Despite evidence that the DRV's diplomacy and domestic policies favored pragmatism over ideology, misperceptions on both sides contributed to the failure of the DRV initiative. Together with the administration's unfavorable images of Vietnamese communism, shaped by its commitments to France in Western Europe, an ambivalent policy in China, and suspicion over the capability of the Vietnamese to create an independent government, these misperceptions rendered the DRV initiative in the spring and summer of 1947 not so much a lost opportunity as an improbable one.

Notes

I gratefully acknowledge support for my research from the Fulbright-Hays Doctoral Dissertation Research Abroad Program, the Association for Asian Studies, Woodrow Wilson Center for Scholars, John Anson Kittridge Educational Fund Trust, and the Center for International Affairs and Charles Warren Center at Harvard University. I wish to thank my sponsors in Vietnam, the Institute of History and the National Center for the Social Sciences of Vietnam. I also wish to thank Pierre Brocheux, Bui Dinh Thanh, David Chandler, David Elliott, George C. Herring, Gary R. Hess, Hue-Tam Ho Tai, Akira Iriye, Luu Doan Huynh, Walter LaFeber, Ernest R. May, William Stueck, Stein Tønnesson, Tran Huy Dinh, and Marilyn B. Young for helpful comments on various drafts of this article.

1. For the substance of Ho Chi Minh's appeals to the United States in 1946, see copies of his letters to President Truman reprinted in *United States–Vietnam Relations, 1945–1976: Study Prepared by the Department of Defense* (Washington, D.C.: U.S. Government Printing Office, 1971), Book 1, Part I, C–57–102. On Ho's efforts in 1949, see *Newsweek*, April 25, 1949: 44; and *Nation*, September 10, 1949: 244. For an analysis of American responses, see Gary R. Hess, *The United States' Emergence As a Southeast Asian Power* (New York: Columbia University Press, 1987), 193–208, 325–26.

2. American journalists such as Harold R. Issacs and Robert Shaplen are most closely associated with this interpretation. See, for instance, Issacs, *No Peace for Asia* (New York: Macmillan, 1947), 170–76.

3. Hess, *The United States' Emergence,* 313, 314–17; for an expanded treatment of these themes, see also his "The First American Commitment in Indochina: The Acceptance of the 'Bao Dai Solution,' 1950," *Diplomatic History* 2, 4 (Fall 1978): 331–50; on the influence of French pressure as early as spring 1945, see George C. Herring, "The Truman Administration and the Restoration of French Sovereignty in Indochina," *Diplomatic History* 1, 2 (Spring 1977): 97–117.

4. This chapter favors Pinyin transcriptions for Chinese place names but follows the more familiar Wade-Giles romanizations for such individuals as Chiang Kai-shek.

5. On Franco-Vietnamese negotiations in 1946 and the coming of war in Vietnam, see Ellen J. Hammer, *The Struggle for Indochina* (Stanford: Stanford University Press, 1954), 148–91; and Stein Tønnesson, *1946: Déclenchement de la guerre d'Indochine: les vêpres tonkinoises du 19 décembre* (Paris: L'Harmattan, 1987).

6. This chapter favors Vietnamese, rather than the more common French, terms for regional divisions of the country in this period. Bac Bo, like the French term Tonkin,

refers to northern Vietnam; Trung Bo, like Annam, refers to central Vietnam; Nam Bo, like Cochinchina, refers to southern Vietnam. For the Vietnamese, French terms like Annam, a Chinese word meaning "Pacified South," evoke memories of both Chinese and French colonialism. Vietnamese appelations are not always more "natural." As Patricia M. Pelley argues in her "Writing Revolution: The New History in Post-Colonial Vietnam" (Ph.D. diss., Cornell University, 1991), the postcolonial state sought to undo French terms in part to naturalize or legitimate the historical novelty of the nation-state. Focusing on the development of a nationalist and culturalist conception of the Vietnamese state after 1955, Pelley suggests that a stress on the homogeneity and permanence of the Vietnamese state obscures the presence of historically conditioned internal divisions such as ethnic heterogeneity, differing historical settlement patterns in the North and South, and the tenuous links between regional economies.

7. *Cuoc Khang Chien Than Thanh cua Nhan Dan Viet Nam* [The Sacred Resistance War of the Vietnamese People] (Hanoi: Nha Xuat Ban Su That, 1958–60), vol. 2, 40–41. This source is a four-volume compilation of articles from the official press, including *Su That* [Truth], *Sinh Hoat Noi Bo* [Inner Life], and *Nhan Dan* [The People] for the period September 1945 to July 1954.

8. On Vietnamese relations with the CCP, see Hoang Tranh, *Ho Chi Minh voi Trung Quoc* [Ho Chi Minh and China] (Nha Xuat Ban Sao Moi, 1990); King C. Chen, *Vietnam and China, 1938–1954* (Princeton: Princeton University Press, 1969), 187–95; and Greg Lockhart, *Nation in Arms: The Origins of the People's Army of Vietnam* (Boston: Allen and Unwin, 1989); on Soviet influence in Vietnam, see Charles B. McLane, *Soviet Strategies in Southeast Asia* (Princeton: Princeton University Press, 1966), 261–345; on the relationship between the DRV and the French Communist Party, see Alain Ruscio, *Les communistes français et l'Indochine* (Paris: L'Harmattan, 1985); and McLane, *Soviet Strategies*, 423–43.

9. Conversations with University of Hanoi historians Pham Xanh and Do Quang Hung in 1992 yielded an alternative explanation for the lack of Soviet support for the DRV in this period. They argue that Stalin's distrust of Ho Chi Minh's revolutionary credentials significantly reduced Soviet interest in the DRV. Beginning with the rise of the ultra-leftist revolutionary line adopted at the Sixth World Congress of the Comintern in 1928, Xanh and Hung assert, Stalin criticized Ho's emphasis on national liberation rather than proletarian social revolution and remained skeptical of Ho's aims for the DRV until Mao effected a rapprochement between Stalin and Ho in 1950. Because party archives remained closed to foreign researchers in 1992, I was unable to confirm Xanh and Hung's thesis. On the origins of Stalin's distrust of Ho, see Do Quang Hung, "Chu Tich Ho Chi Minh Trong Thoi Ky 1934–1938, Roi Sang Them Cho Van De Dan Toc Hay Quoc Te? [Ho Chi Minh in the Period 1934–1938, Clearly for Nationalism or Internationalism?]," in *Ho Chi Minh: Anh Hung Giai Phong Dan Toc Danh Nhan Van Hoa* (Hanoi: Nha Xuat Ban Khoa Hoc Xa Hoi, 1990), 28–36.

10. Thach worked out of the DRV's diplomatic mission in Bangkok. Established in 1946, this five-man office engaged in intelligence gathering, dissemination of information and propaganda, clandestine arms purchases, and efforts to gain diplomatic representation in various Southeast Asian countries. For an analysis of DRV activities in Thailand during this period, see Christopher E. Goscha, "Thailand and the Vietnamese Resistance against the French" (Master's thesis, Australian National University, 1991), 121–64; and Vien Quan He Quoc Te Bo Ngoai Giao, *Chu Tich Ho Chi Minh voi Cong Tac Ngoai Giao* [Ho Chi Minh and Foreign Relations] (Hanoi: Nha Xuat Ban Su That, 1990), 129–31.

11. "Transmission of Questions Answered by Pham Ngoc Thach," Stanton to Marshall, May 14, 1947, Box 4; Confidential Records of the Saigon Consulate; Records of the

Department of State Foreign Service Posts, 1936–54; Record Group (RG) 84; National Records Center, Washington, D.C.

12. "Memo to International Engineering Company," Stanton to Marshall, April 24, 1947, Box 4, RG 84.

13. Biographical material on Pham Ngoc Thach is based upon conversations with scholars at the Institute of History, Hanoi, Vietnam, in 1989 and 1992, and "Note sur la personnalité de Monsieur Pham Ngoc Thach," December 1947, "Communisme et relations Moscou-Hanoi-Chine," 174, Indochine, Asie-Oceanie 1944–1955, Archives Diplomatiques, Ministère des Affaires Etrangères, Paris, France. On the relationship between the DRV and the OSS during World War II, see Archimedes L. Patti, *Why Vietnam? Prelude to America's Albatross* (Berkeley: University of California Press, 1980); Stein Tønnesson, *The Vietnamese Revolution of 1945: Roosevelt, Ho Chi Minh and De Gaulle in a World at War* (London: Sage Publications, 1991); Peter Dennis, *Troubled Days of Peace: Mountbatten and the South East Asia Command, 1945–46* (New York: St. Martin's Press, 1987); Peter M. Dunn, *The First Vietnam War* (New York: St. Martin's Press, 1985); and Ngoc An, "Bo Doi Viet-My [The Vietnamese-American Army]," *Tap Chi Lich Su Quan Su* [Journal of Military History] no. 10 (1986): 18–20, 31. The DRV's 1947 intention to capitalize on its favorable wartime relations with the OSS was confirmed in my interview with Hoang Minh Giam, DRV foreign minister (1946–54), Hanoi, Vietnam, July 8, 1989.

14. Hammer, *Struggle for Indochina*, 204.

15. The text of Giam's appeal is contained in O'Sullivan to Marshall, May 9, 1947; *Foreign Relations of the United States 1947, VI: The Far East* (Washington, D.C.: U.S. Government Printing Office, 1972), 95.

16. "Questionnaire Received from Dr. Thach," Stanton to Marshall, July 9, 1947, Box 4, RG 84.

17. At the time of my research in Vietnam, the archives of the party and Foreign Ministry remained closed to American researchers. A similar problem confronts scholars of foreign policy in the People's Republic of China (PRC). For two quite different approaches to the problem of sources that consider PRC diplomacy in the late 1940s and address issues similar to those raised by the Vietnamese case, see Michael H. Hunt, "Mao Tse-tung and the Issue of Accomodation with the United States, 1948–1950" and Steven M. Goldstein, "Chinese Communist Policy Toward the United States: Opportunities and Constraints, 1944–1950" in *Uncertain Years: Chinese-American Relations, 1947–1950*, Dorothy Borg and Waldo Heinrichs, eds. (New York: Columbia University Press, 1980), 185–278.

18. Ton That Thien, *The Foreign Politics of the Communist Party of Vietnam: A Study of Communist Tactics* (New York: Crane Russak, 1989), 57–65.

19. Nguyen Duy Thanh, *My Four Years with the Viet-Minh* (Bombay: Democratic Research Service, 1950), 18; Hoang Tranh, *Ho Chi Minh voi Trung Quoc* [Ho Chi Minh and China] (Nha Xuat Ban Sao Moi, 1990), 209–17.

20. Chen, *Vietnam*, 175–76.

21. The selection of Tran Van Giau to represent the DRV with China points to the presence of some ambiguity in the DRV's diplomatic strategy, suggesting, as Huynh Kim Khanh argues in his study of Vietnamese communism, that the role of class and nationalism continued to be a "thorny issue" for the DRV leadership. Unlike the more moderate Thach, Giau is often characterized by Western scholars of Vietnamese communism such as Khanh and Philippe Devillers as an uncompromising internationalist. When Ho Chi Minh dissolved the Indochinese Communist Party (ICP) in November 1945 to minimize official Communist presence in the DRV, Giau and other like-minded leaders of the ICP reorganized in the form of the Marxist Study Group, which stressed internationalist no-

tions of radical social revolution over the DRV's more moderate policy of all-class nationalism. Moreover, as chairman of the Viet Minh executive committee in Nam Bo, Giau oversaw radical efforts to consolidate control in Saigon and the south in 1945 and 1946, including the assassinations of prominent Vietnamese Trotskyists and anti-Communists. Before his appointment to lead the Vietnamese delegation to the New Delhi conference, however, Giau was forced to undergo *kiem thao* (self-criticism) and was removed from leadership positions in Nam Bo. For Khanh's analysis of Vietnamese communism, which stresses the roles of patriotism and the indigenization of proletarian internationalism in shaping its independent character, see his *Vietnamese Communism 1925–1945* (Ithaca, NY: Cornell University Press, 1982). A focus on the indigenization of external ideas by Vietnamese Communists prior to 1945 also informs Hue-Tam Ho Tai, *Radicalism and the Origins of the Vietnamese Revolution* (Cambridge, MA: Harvard University Press, 1992); and David G. Marr, *Vietnamese Tradition on Trial, 1920–1945* (Berkeley: University of California Press, 1981). On Tran Van Giau, see Khanh, *Vietnamese Communism*, 255, and Philippe Devillers, *Histoire du Viêt-Nam de 1940 à 1952* (Paris: Editions du Seuil, 1952), 144–76, 197, 247.

22. *Bulletin of the Vietnam-American Friendship Association*, New York, July 7, 1947, cited in Virginia Thompson and Richard Adloff, *The Left Wing in Southeast Asia* (New York: William Sloane Associates, 1950), 42.

23. On the April directive, see William J. Duiker, *The Communist Road to Power in Vietnam* (Boulder, CO: Westview Press, 1981), 131; on local arms workshops, see Lockhart, *Nation in Arms*, 207–8.

24. Andrew Vickerman, *The Fate of the Peasantry: Premature 'Transition to Socialism' in the Democratic Republic of Vietnam*, Yale University Southeast Asian Studies Monograph Series, No. 28 (New Haven: Yale Center for International and Asian Studies, 1986), 49–72; for an analysis of the impact of DRV military and socioeconomic reforms on one Bac Bo village, see Hy V. Luong, *Revolution in the Village: Tradition and Transformation in North Vietnam, 1925–1988* (Honolulu: University of Hawaii Press, 1992), 147–58.

25. On the origins of containment and the Marshall Plan, see John Lewis Gaddis, *Strategies of Containment: A Critical Appraisal of Postwar American National Security Policy* (New York: Oxford University Press, 1982), 25–88; and Michael J. Hogan, *The Marshall Plan: America, Britain, and the Reconstruction of Western Europe, 1947–1952* (Cambridge: Cambridge University Press, 1987); on the role of France in American policy toward Western Europe, see John W. Young, *France, the Cold War and the Western Alliance, 1944–49: French Foreign Policy and Post-War Europe* (Leicester: Leicester University Press, 1990); and Irwin M. Wall, *The United States and the Making of Postwar France, 1945–1954* (Cambridge: Cambridge University Press, 1991).

26. On confusion in the Truman administration's policy toward China, see Ernest R. May, *The Truman Administration and China, 1945–1949* (Philadelphia: J.B. Lippincott Company, 1975); Dorothy Borg and Waldo Heinrichs, eds., *Uncertain Years: Chinese-American Relations, 1947–1950* (New York: Columbia University Press, 1980); and Nancy Bernkopf Tucker, *Patterns in the Dust: Chinese-American Relations and the Recognition Controversy, 1949–50* (New York: Columbia University Press, 1983).

27. O'Sullivan to Marshall, March 28, 1947, *FRUS 1947*, VI: 83.

28. Stanton to Marshall, April 24, 1947, Box 4, RG 84.

29. O'Sullivan to Marshall, April 24, 1947, Box 4, RG 84.

30. Marshall to O'Sullivan, May 2, 1947, Box 4, RG 84.

31. Stanton to Marshall, May 7, 1947, *FRUS 1947*, VI: 92.

32. Marshall to O'Sullivan, May 9, 1947, Box 4, RG 84.

33. Note, March 30, 1946, "Activités americaines en Indochine," 11, Conseiller Politique, Haut-Commissarait de France en Indochine, Centre des Archives d'Outre Mer, Archives Nationales, Aix-en-Provence, France.

34. Stanton to Marshall, May 7, 1947, *FRUS 1947*, VI: 92.

35. Marshall to Reed, May 3, 1947, *FRUS 1947*, VI: 90.

36. On divisions in the American embassy in China, see May, *Truman Administration*, 12–14.

37. Stuart to Marshall, May 15, 1947, *FRUS 1947*, VI: 90.

38. American embassy, China, to Marshall, March 16, 1947, Box 4, RG 84.

39. Reed to Marshall, April 29, 1947, Box 4, RG 84; Reed to Marshall, May 3, 1947, *FRUS 1947*, VI: 99.

40. O'Sullivan to Marshall, May 3, 1947, *FRUS 1947*, VI: 90.

41. Reed to Marshall, May 7, 1947, *FRUS 1947*, VI: 94.

42. Marshall to Reed, July 17, 1947, *FRUS 1947*, VI: 117.

43. Reed to Marshall, July 11, 1947, and July 24, 1947, *FRUS 1947*, VI: 114–15, 124–25.

44. O'Sullivan to Marshall, July 21, 1947, *FRUS 1947*, VI: 121–22.

45. Caffery to Marshall, July 31, 1947, *FRUS 1947*, VI: 128.

46. "Memorandum of Conversation between Bullitt and Ogburn," May 29, 1947, Box 4, RG 84.

47. O'Sullivan to Marshall, July 21, 1947, *FRUS 1947*, VI: 122; Reed to Marshall, July 24, 1947, *FRUS 1947*, VI: 125.

48. O'Sullivan to Marshall, July 19, 1947, FRUS 1947, VI: 120. For one example of these French claims, see the *New York Times* despatch of July 15, 1947, in which the French government officials argue that "Ho Chi Minh worked for independence for Indochina with the sole purpose of making the country a vassal to Moscow."

49. Biographical information on Jefferson Caffery, William C. Bullitt, James O'Sullivan, and Charles S. Reed was obtained from the U.S. Department of State, *Biographic Register* (Washington, D.C.: U.S. Government Printing Office, 1940–47); material on Bullitt is supplemented by Will Brownell and Richard N. Billings, *So Close to Greatness: A Biography of William C. Bullitt* (New York: Macmillan, 1987).

50. Hugh DeSantis, *The Diplomacy of Silence: The American Foreign Service, the Soviet Union, and the Cold War, 1933–1947* (Chicago: University of Chicago Press, 1983), 33. For an extended analysis of Bullitt's anti-communism, see Beatrice Farnsworth, *William C. Bullitt and the Soviet Union* (Bloomington: Indiana University Press, 1967).

51. My thinking on the connection between an American sense of the superiority of Western political culture and the Truman administration's perceptions of and policies toward the Vietnamese communists is influenced by Michael Adas, who in his *Machines as the Measure of Men: Science, Technology, and Ideologies of Western Dominance* (Ithaca: Cornell University Press, 1989) suggests that European perceptions of the material superiority of their scientific thought and technical innovations, rather than simple racism, shaped attitudes toward and interactions with peoples they encountered overseas in the nineteenth century.

52. Robert Shaplen, *The Lost Revolution: The U.S. in Vietnam, 1946–1966* (New York: Harper and Row, 1955). Shaplen's evaluation of Truman administration policy originally appeared much earlier in the *New Yorker*.

53. Shaplen, *The Lost Revolution*, 27–28.

54. For Gaddis' discussion of the wedge strategy, see his *The Long Peace: Inquiries into the History of the Cold War* (New York: Columbia University Press, 1987), 149–64.

55. On this point I follow the suggestion of John Lewis Gaddis, based on his conver-

sations with John Cady, professor of history at Ohio University; see Gaddis, *The Long Peace*, 90, 269, note 112.

56. See, for instance, Ambassador to the Soviet Union (Smith) to Secretary Marshall, July 1–2, 1948; *Foreign Relations of the United States 1948, IV: Eastern Europe and the Soviet Union* (Washington, D.C.: U.S. Government Printing Office, 1974), 1082–84; Chargé in Yugoslavia (Reams) to Marshall, July 7 and September 15, 1948, *FRUS 1948*, IV: 1088–92, 1106–10; and Ambassador to Yugoslavia (Cannon) to Secretary Marshall, October 28 and November 24, 1948, *FRUS 1948*, IV: 1113–16.

2

Waging Revolutionary War: The Evolution of Hanoi's Strategy in the South, 1959–1965

William Duiker

Did the United States fight the wrong war in Vietnam? Did it adopt a counter-guerrilla strategy in a conflict that, from Hanoi's point of view, was essentially conventional in nature? That issue was debated actively by U.S. policymakers during the Vietnam War, notably during the Kennedy administration, when advocates of a primarily "political" or "military" approach competed briefly for control over U.S. strategy in South Vietnam. More recently, it has been the subject of lively interest among historians, journalists, and foreign policy analysts, with no signs of abatement or of any prospective consensus emerging on the subject for the forseeable future.[1]

This is not a topic of mere academic interest. In fact, it is one of the key bones of contention in the running debate over the "lessons of Vietnam," a debate that centers around the fundamental issue of how the United States can and should react to the rise of revolutionary insurgencies and other political and military disturbances in the post-Vietnam era. To some, the primary lesson of the Vietnam War was that the failure to apply the full weight of its military and technological superiority cost the United States victory in the war. Others counter that the salient lesson of Vietnam is that external power cannot overcome a revolutionary movement with a solid base of support among the mass of the population.[2]

This is not the place to undertake a lengthy evaluation of U.S. war strategy in Vietnam. But the appearance of a number of new documentary sources on Hanoi's conduct of the war in South Vietnam does offer an opportunity to enhance our understanding of Communist war strategy and to determine whether, as some have alleged, Hanoi used guerrilla tactics as a stratagem to hoodwink the United States, while intending to win by conventional military means all along.

The tradition of combined political and military struggle has a long pedigree in Communist revolutionary strategy in Vietnam. The first explicit reference to the idea came shortly after the formation of the Viet Minh Front by the Indochinese Communist Party (ICP) at the beginning of World War II, when the party's founder and leader Ho Chi Minh called for an approach that would begin with political struggle and move gradually toward an emphasis on armed conflict as the revolution reached its height. Although party sources have not elaborated in detail on the reasons for Ho's choice of approach, it is clear from the context that he realized that the ICP would need time to build up its military forces for a major effort to seize power from the Japanese occupation forces and the returning French troops at the end of the war. In the meantime, the party, through the medium of the Viet Minh Front, would build up a mass base among the local population.[3]

As it turned out, the August Revolution that brought the Viet Minh to power in North Vietnam in the late summer of 1945 was more political than military in nature, as the surrender of Japan left a military vacuum that Ho Chi Minh's small but well-trained revolutionary forces were able to fill with a minimum of violence. The August Revolution model, involving the seizure of power by means of a popular uprising supported by selected attacks on the part of armed revolutionary units, would later assume an almost sacred quality in the minds of party strategists, a Vietnamese equivalent of the model of the October Revolution of 1917 in Russia. Undoubtedly one reason for its appeal was the belief that, unlike the latter (when Lenin admitted that the Bolsheviks did not have widespread popular support), the August Revolution had triumphed precisely because the Viet Minh Front had already won wide acceptance as the legitimate representative of the great mass of the Vietnamese population.

Unfortunately for the party and its supporters, the course of events in the immediate postwar period would soon demonstrate that more than human spirit was required to triumph over the power of modern weaponry. When negotiations with the French broke down in the fall of 1946, Ho Chi Minh and his colleagues discarded the strategy applied during the August Revolution and adopted a revised version of the Chinese model of "people's war." This Maoist concept of three-stage warfare, beginning with a stage of retrenchment and culminating in a conventional assault on enemy forces in the major urban areas, does not entirely neglect the importance of political struggle, but the latter is clearly subordinated to the buildup of revolutionary armed forces for a final confrontation with the enemy on the battlefield.

During the opening years of the Franco–Viet Minh conflict, party strategists applied the three-stage concept in Indochina, with some variations to take into account local conditions and circumstances. By 1951, however, the disadvantages of the Maoist model became increasingly apparent, at least as applied in Vietnam, where the revolutionary forces could not hope to achieve absolute military superiority over their adversary. In the last years of the war, Viet Minh strategy concentrated on achieving limited military victories on the battlefield that could contribute to a satisfactory peace agreement at the conference table.[4]

The Geneva Conference of 1954 resulted in a compromise settlement of the Franco–Viet Minh conflict, dividing the country in half, with Ho Chi Minh's Democratic Republic of Vietnam (DRV) in the North and a non-Communist state in the South. Party leaders were now faced with the new problem of achieving reunification of their divided land. The Chinese model of people's war did not seem appropriate for several reasons:

1. pressure from Hanoi's allies, China and the Soviet Union, who wished to avoid a resumption of the conflict in Indochina;
2. the expectation (or the hope) that reunification could take place through national elections, as called for by the political declaration at Geneva;
3. the conviction that, even in the absence of national elections, the new government of Ngo Dinh Diem in Saigon would gradually disintegrate under the pressure of the revolutionary movement in the South, leading eventually to a takeover on the model of the August Revolution by means of a general uprising supported by low-level paramilitary forces.

Under any of the above circumstances, an extensive role for the main force units of the People's Army of Vietnam (PAVN) would probably not be necessary.[5]

It was not long, however, before some leading party cadres operating in the South began to argue that such expectations were overly optimistic. Not only had the Diem regime refused to hold consultations on national elections with representatives of the DRV, but Diem's control over the southern provinces was tightening, rather than disintegrating. In 1956, the party's leading representative in South Vietnam, Politburo member Le Duan, began to press for a more active approach to protect the southern revolutionary movement from Diem's security forces. In a report that he wrote to the central party leadership sometime in the late summer or fall, Le Duan argued that a more aggressive combination of political and military struggle would be needed to bring the Saigon regime to its knees.[6]

Le Duan's report was approved at the Eleventh Plenum of the Party Central Committee in December, which now adopted a new policy to strengthen the revolutionary movement in the South to enable it to defend itself against counterrevolutionary terror. In fact, party leaders in Hanoi had apparently already begun to question the assumption that national reunification could be achieved by peaceful means. At the Ninth Plenum in April 1956, Ho Chi Minh had argued that recent Soviet speculation over the possibility of a "peaceful road to socialism" was irrelevant in countries like Vietnam where the aggressive nature of

U.S. imperialism and its ally in Saigon might compel the people to resort to armed struggle. At the Conference of Communist Parties of Socialist Countries held in Moscow in November 1957, he lobbied successfully for a statement to this effect to be included in the final conference communique.[7]

Still, although party leaders were aware of the possibility of a return to war, most still assumed that the two zones could be reunified under Hanoi's authority without a return to the primarily military approach that they had adopted in their war against the French in 1946, and hoped that the Saigon regime would collapse as a result of a strategy relying principally on what was termed the "political force of the masses." Past U.S. behavior in China and Korea was cited as evidence that Washington would hesitate to become actively involved militarily in an area of clearly secondary importance to American national security.[8]

But in early 1959, party leaders revised their views of the situation and decided that the basic road to a revolutionary victory in the South was by means of violent struggle, through a revolutionary war to achieve the reunification of the two zones. That decision, approved by the Fifteenth Plenum of the Central Committee in January and announced in May, was not specific on what strategy should be adopted, merely announcing that both political and military struggle would be required. According to a history of the war published recently in Hanoi, the plenum resolution merely stated that the "political force of the masses" would be the primary instrument of the revolutionary movement, supported by armed forces "to a greater or lesser degree, depending on the situation."[9]

Why Hanoi decided to accelerate the revolutionary struggle in the South in early 1959 has been a matter of lively debate among scholars and other foreign policy analysts in the West. Some have maintained that party leaders in the North were belatedly and perhaps reluctantly reacting to pressure from their colleagues stationed in South Vietnam, who argued that the movement must either take up arms or be destroyed by the repressive efforts of the Diem regime.[10]

There seems to be some merit to this argument. There is no doubt that some of the leading cadres in the South had been arguing for several years that a more active effort would be needed to bring the revolution there to a successful conclusion. But it is probably misleading to portray the debate in terms of a North–South confrontation, or to assert that the former preferred a political solution and were persuaded against their best judgment to accept a military one. As we have seen, a number of party leaders in the North (including Ho Chi Minh, Vo Nguyen Giap, and of course Le Duan himself) had been aware for years that armed struggle in some form might be required to bring about national reunification.

If there was a debate at the Fifteenth Plenum, then, it was probably more about timing and the proper balance of political and military struggle to be adopted than about whether to shift to a more active approach, although some might have been reluctant to return to a strategy of revolutionary war. Le Duan, now acting general secretary of the party and generally recognized as the party's leading expert on conditions in the South, probably argued for a variation of the

August Revolution model, with partial insurrections in rural areas leading to the formation of liberated base areas and culminating in a general uprising in the cities. In this version, the main role would still be played by the political force of the masses, with assistance from armed revolutionary units to reduce the strength of Saigon's armed forces, formally known as the Army of the Republic of Vietnam (ARVN).[11]

In the end, the Fifteenth Plenum approved a decision to return to the strategy of revolutionary war to achieve the liberation of the South, using an as yet undetermined combination of political and armed struggle. According to sources in Hanoi, it was seen at the time as a crucial moment in the Vietnamese revolution, and the leadership took time to evaluate the situation in the South and to seek support from its allies before issuing the final resolution in May.

For the next two years, the party attempted to increase the strength of the revolutionary armed forces by recruiting efforts within South Vietnam, supplemented by the limited infiltration of cadres and materiel from the North. As the level of violence escalated, the debate over strategy continued. Some leading southern cadres were critical of the alleged overemphasis on political struggle and apparently argued for more stress on military activities and a qualified return to the Maoist strategy of people's war that had been applied during the war against the French, with revolutionary forces in the rural areas surrounding and eventually attacking the enemy bastions in the cities.

Le Duan attempted to counter such views. In a letter to Nguyen Van Linh, his successor as the party's senior representative in South Vietnam, Le Duan pointed out that the revolutionary movement was still weak, while the Diem regime still retained the loyalty of the majority of the armed forces. The primary advantage of the revolution, he said, lay in its political superiority over its rival, and this must be used to the greatest advantage. Such a strategy would also serve to reduce the likelihood of direct U.S. intervention in the South.[12]

The debate apparently was not fully resolved by the autumn of 1960, because the party's Third National Congress, meeting in September, did not make any significant decisions affecting the existing strategy, simply noting that the period of stability in the South was at an end and a period of disintegration under way. To take advantage of this favorable new stage of the revolution, the Third Congress decided to place military and political struggle on an equal footing in the South, while heightening the level of support from the North. It apparently did make one concrete decision, approving a plan to form a new united front to seek political support among the population in South Vietnam. This would become the famous National Liberation Front, formed in December.[13]

The following January, the Politburo met, in the words of an official history of the war, to "concretize" the results of the Third Party Congress. The resolution issued at the end of the meeting was decidedly optimistic, echoing the views of the Party Congress by noting that the period of stability of the Saigon regime was at an end, and a period of continuous crisis was about to begin. In the North, the DRV was stronger and moving toward socialism. Based on that analysis, the Politburo called for an intensification of the military effort in the South aimed at final victory through a combined General Offensive and Uprising, with intensified military attacks in rural areas (now divided into two regions, the Central Highlands and the Mekong River Delta) coordinated with a mass popular insurrection in the major cities. To provide centralized direction for the effort, in September the Regional Committee for the South (*Uy ban Nam Bo*) was transformed into a Central Office for South Vietnam (*Trung uong cuc Mien Nam*, also known as COSVN) similar to the one that had existed in the South during the previous war against the French.[14]

In letters written to Nguyen Van Linh, Le Duan—formally named general secretary at the Third Party Congress—described the recent decisions and added his own appraisal of the overall situation. The revolution in the South was progressing well, he said, but it was still in the "first stage" of development, since enemy military strength was still substantially intact and many ARVN troops were still ambivalent about the revolution. Criticizing some southern leaders for their recent tendency to feel that the general uprising could be launched without extensive prior preparation (such as the formation of liberated base areas and the adoption of a strategy of protracted war), Le Duan warned Linh not to be impetuous, noting that a greater emphasis on military struggle might provoke an enemy reaction and make the party's legal activities more difficult to carry out. Citing the examples of the Bolshevik Uprising and the August Revolution, he pointed out that revolution could not succeed unless the enemy's armed forces had been militarily defeated or undermined by internal subversion.[15]

During the remainder of 1961, the party's southern leadership carried out the joint politico-military strategy that had been devised at the Politburo meeting in January. Revolutionary forces, newly unified under the name of the People's Liberation Armed Forces (PLAF), began to increase in numbers, and the first main force units were organized in July. Liberated base areas under the control of the PLAF expanded while the political problems of the Diem regime intensified. Such harbingers of success, however, were counterbalanced by growing indications that the new Kennedy administration in Washington had decided to escalate U.S. involvement in the war. The number of American advisers began to increase well beyond the limits set by the Geneva Accords and Washington announced a new counterinsurgency strategy to cope with the increased threat from the insurgent forces. A key element in that strategy was the construction of so-called "strategic hamlets" (*ap chien luoc*) to protect the rural population from the revolution.

The decision by the Kennedy administration to escalate American involvement in the conflict complicated strategic planning in Hanoi. In February 1962 the Politburo met to evaluate the situation and concluded that the struggle in the South had now turned into a protracted war, but had not essentially changed the balance of forces between the revolution and the Saigon regime. The growing

U.S. military role necessitated an increase in the military strength of the PLAF, with a particular emphasis on the buildup of guerrilla forces at the regional level. But political struggle continued to receive close attention, and the COSVN leadership was criticized for an excessive emphasis on military struggle and an erroneous belief that a revolutionary "high tide" was just around the corner.[16]

The importance of achieving a proper balance of political and military activity came into even sharper focus as a result of the negotiated settlement of the conflict in Laos reached in July, a settlement that raised hopes in Hanoi for the possibility of a similar agreement in South Vietnam. In a letter to Nguyen Van Linh that same month, Le Duan pointed out that a flexible use of political and military tactics had enabled the revolutionary forces in Laos to win a significant victory at the conference table. Without the battlefield successes achieved by Laotian guerrilla forces, the United States would not have been forced to agree to a settlement. But if those forces had realized even greater success, it might have provoked the United States into open intervention. How far we win, and how far they lose, he said, is very important.

The experience of Laos, Le Duan continued, provided a useful lesson on how to carry on the struggle in South Vietnam, where it was highly important to keep the United States in the stage of Special War (e.g., fighting the war with South Vietnamese troops rather than introducing U.S. combat forces). In fact, he warned, the danger of direct U.S. military intervention was even greater in South Vietnam than it was in Laos since the former, unlike the latter, does not have a direct border with China. As a result, if the war in the South was pushed "beyond reasonable limits," it could result in "some bad consequences."

The goal in South Vietnam, he concluded, was to win while at the same time preserving world peace, to make the United States lose, but up to a tolerable point where it would be willing to accept a negotiated settlement of the war. The enemy must thus be foiled rather than totally defeated, while at the same time the ground for a diplomatic settlement must be prepared by tightening links with progressive and neutralist elements in the South who might serve in a future coalition government in Saigon. Party leaders in Hanoi were wary that a negotiated settlement might arouse anger among party operatives in the South, and Le Duan attempted to reassure them that this was but a temporary "transitional step" to total victory in the South.[17]

As it turned out, the Kennedy administration rejected Hanoi's overtures for a political settlement in South Vietnam, and party strategists were compelled to return to their earlier plans for a combined General Offensive and Uprising. A resolution issued by the Politburo after a meeting held in December called for intensified efforts to strengthen the revolutionary armed forces while expanding liberated areas and destroying the enemy's strategic hamlets. In a speech given the following March, Le Duan warned that because of imperialist aggression, the working class, while seeking to make revolution by peaceful means, had no alternative but to make preparations for a seizure of power by violence.[18]

During the next several months, the party's southern leadership focused on the effort to destroy the strategic hamlet program and cope with increased enemy mobility brought about by the use of helicopters. Although histories of the war written by Vietnamese historians point to the battle of Ap Bac in January 1963 as a firm indication that the PLAF had mastered the challenge, Le Duan's assertion that the results of the battle aroused profound discouragement in Washington remains debatable, since most U.S. intelligence estimates published during the spring were guardedly optimistic about the military situation. As it turned out, it was Diem's political weakness rather than the situation on the battlefield that led to growing anxiety in Washington and the overthrow of his regime by a military junta in November.

At first Hanoi appeared uncertain how to react to the November coup, not only because party leaders were initially unclear over the attitude of the new leadership in Saigon, but also because of the uncertainty over the possible reaction in Washington. In December, Hanoi convened its Ninth Plenum to assess the situation. The Central Committee concluded that the United States could react to heightened revolutionary pressure in two possible ways: by maintaining the existing strategy of Special War, or by moving to a higher level of commitment, involving the introduction of U.S. combat troops. It was the consensus view that the Johnson administration would be most likely to escalate if it became convinced that the revolutionary forces would be unable to resist a growing U.S. presence. Such a development would be unacceptable to Hanoi, since it would make it significantly more difficult to maintain the momentum of the revolution.

The Ninth Plenum therefore approved a decision to strengthen the PLAF as rapidly as possible in order to realize a basic change in the balance of forces and achieve victory in a short time. In that process, the role of armed struggle was seen as "direct and decisive," since the most urgent task was to destroy the ARVN in preparation for a General Offensive and Uprising.

There have been persistent reports of disagreement within the party leadership over how to respond to the overthrow of Ngo Dinh Diem, and some may have called for the direct intervention of the PAVN in the struggle in the South. In the end, however, the introduction of large numbers of North Vietnamese main force units was rejected, probably out of the fear that such actions could trigger an escalation of the U.S. role in the war. The plenum did call for increased aid from the North to deal with the heightened U.S. military effort, but indicated that the roles of the two zones would continue to be different, thus implying that the PAVN would play, at most, a limited combat role in the South.[19]

Party leaders were well aware that the decision to increase the level of violence in the South would strain relations with Moscow, and possibly with Beijing, and for that reason Hanoi sent out a circular letter to fraternal parties explaining the decision and promising that even if the United States should intervene directly in the South, the DRV would restrain Washington from extending the war to North Vietnam.[20]

Over the course of the next twelve months, Hanoi's gamble proved to be, on most counts, a success. Bolstered by the modest infiltration of PAVN units from the North, the PLAF imposed severe losses on the armed forces of the Saigon regime, while the political situation in South Vietnam continued to deteriorate. By the fall of 1964 U.S. intelligence estimates were predicting a Communist victory within six months in the absence of a major U.S. response. On the international scene, Hanoi's bid to win Soviet support had no immediate effect in Moscow, but the fall of Nikita Khrushchev from power in October 1964 brought to office a new Soviet leadership somewhat more willing to follow the Vietnamese lead in Southeast Asia.

At a meeting of the Politburo in early 1965, Hanoi attempted to press its advantage, approving an accelerated effort to destroy the South Vietnamese armed forces and prepare conditions for a general uprising in the major cities. In a report on the results of the meeting to Nguyen Chi Thanh, the new COSVN chief in the South, Le Duan raised the fundamental question: could the PLAF defeat the ARVN before it had a chance to revive (as had taken place in Laos) or the United States decided to intervene? If so, Washington would have no choice but to negotiate a compromise settlement and withdraw.

Le Duan answered the question in the affirmative. He admitted that the balance of forces was not as favorable to the revolution as had been the case just before the Geneva Conference of 1954, but asserted that the guerrilla movement was stronger now and the overall political situation was more favorable. If several ARVN divisions could be disabled and others lured out of the cities through guerrilla attacks in rural areas, urban uprisings in major cities like Saigon, Da Nang, and Hue would have a good chance of success. Then politics would become a key factor, as a coalition of neutralist forces, secretly guided by the party, could form a government in Saigon and ask the United States to withdraw. Le Duan admitted that there was no guarantee of success, but quoted Lenin: let's act and then see. Even if we do not succeed, he said, we can always retire and try again.[21]

But Hanoi once again miscalculated the U.S. reaction. Beginning in February, the Johnson administration announced a bombing campaign against the North and began to introduce U.S. combat troops into the South. A few days after the first troop announcement in Washington, the party Central Committee held its Eleventh Plenum in Hanoi. According to one source, some members wanted to avoid a direct confrontation with the United States and seek a negotiated settlement but, perhaps persuaded by Le Duan's confidence, the party ultimately opted to maintain the existing strategy to "win a decisive victory within a relatively short period of time" while preparing for the possibility of a large-scale introduction of U.S. combat troops.[22]

But Lyndon Johnson's decision to add additional troops during April and May forced Hanoi to recognize that a basic change had taken place in the attitude in Washington. In a letter to Nguyen Chi Thanh in May, Le Duan conceded that if

U.S. troop levels in South Vietnam reached 100,000 or even 200,000, the revolutionary forces would lack the military power to inflict "mortal blows" on the enemy. The large-scale introduction of U.S. troops would also reduce the rate of infiltration from the North and put pressure on revolutionary base areas. But Le Duan insisted that Washington was still afraid of a protracted war and hoped for a negotiated settlement, and he pressed his colleagues not to abandon the existing strategy. Even if the United States should move to a Limited War (*khang chien cuc bo*) with 250,000 to 300,000 troops, he said, we can return to a protracted war, which is their most vulnerable point, since history shows that they lack the patience to fight more than three or four years. If the Americans want a protracted war, he concluded, we will give it to them.[23]

By the end of the summer, with the projected size of the American presence in South Vietnam nearing 200,000, it was clear that Le Duan's "worst case" scenario had become a reality. It was also painfully evident that Hanoi's allies were not prepared to respond actively to the U.S. escalation of the war. The Vietnamese had hoped that the People's Republic of China would keep the United States guessing as to its own intentions. But during the summer, Beijing signaled to Washington that it would not directly enter the war unless the United States attacked China.[24]

In September, the Politburo met to consider its options. Party leaders now realized that they lacked the capacity to achieve a complete military victory in the South. But according to the report that Le Duan sent to COSVN a few weeks later, Hanoi was also convinced that the United States remained vulnerable. The Johnson administration dared not attack the North directly, for it would face the united strength of the entire socialist camp. At the same time the American people lacked the patience to fight and win a protracted war. So a "decisive victory" (here Le Duan distinguished the idea of a decisive victory, which he compared to the battle of Dien Bien Phu, from a total victory) was still possible through a coordinated General Offensive and Uprising, even if the United States should increase its presence to half a million troops. The key to success was to destroy the bulk of South Vietnamese troops while doing sufficient damage to American forces to compel the Johnson administration to withdraw.[25]

The Politburo's decision was confirmed at the Twelfth Plenum in December. Hanoi would match the U.S. escalation and maintain an offensive strategy in the South. But the goal would not be a total military victory but rather to use a combination of political, military, and diplomatic techniques to force the United States to get bogged down in a protracted war and defeat it at that level.[26]

In a letter to a colleague, Politburo member Le Duc Tho explained the decision. Tho admitted that the situation had changed since the previous plenum in March with the addition of 200,000 U.S. troops, and that the opportunity to achieve a quick victory had passed. Sometimes, he noted, the revolution in the South has developed more rapidly than we expected. Such was the case in recent months, when the Saigon regime disintegrated so quickly that revolutionary forces did not have adequate time to complete the destruction of its armed forces.

Tho also admitted that the divisions within the socialist community were a distinct disadvantage. Previously, he said, we could rely on our socialist allies; now we must do it ourselves. But he reaffirmed the conclusion of the Twelfth Plenum that a flexible combination of military and political struggle was the best strategy to pursue. Citing the examples of Laos, Algeria, and World War II, he said that history showed there were many ways to win.[27]

Conclusions

What conclusions can be drawn from the above account? Perhaps the most salient point is that although party leaders moved steadily from a primarily political to a predominantly military approach between 1959 and 1965, even in the shadow of the U.S. escalation of the mid-1960s they viewed political struggle as a crucial component of their revolutionary strategy in the South. The validity of that assumption, of course, is dependent on acceptance of Hanoi's definition of "political struggle," which, in this context, means a primarily nonviolent but vigorous and sometimes extralegal effort to bring down a hostile regime.

Secondly, it seems clear that the party embarked on the road to revolutionary war in the South with some reluctance. This is not to say, as some have done, that the central leadership in the North was forced into the decision by pressure from comrades in the South. In fact, as we have seen, some leading party figures in Hanoi were probably convinced from the outset that the military option would be necessary. But most appeared to recognize the risks involved in a return to revolutionary war, not only in terms of the cost in human lives but even more in terms of the danger of a direct U.S. role in the war. Hanoi was willing to go to considerable lengths to prevent that from taking place.

One reason that Hanoi preferred the political option, of course, is that party leaders were convinced from the start that here they possessed a clear advantage over the enemy. We need not accept their assumption that this superiority necessarily had any moral basis to recognize the validity of their conviction that in the absence of foreign intervention, the revolutionary movement would have had little trouble in besting their rivals within the political arena. When they found themselves at a military disadvantage, they made use of their political advantage as a counterweight.

Finally, it is clear that party leaders, or at least the ruling group around Ho Chi Minh and Le Duan, were quite flexible in their approach to the problem, and were willing to use whatever means were necessary—political, military, diplomatic, or a combination of all three—in order to complete reunification with the South. If necessary, as had occurred in 1946 and again in 1954, they were prepared to go through a "transitional phase" (by which was meant a neutralist coalition government) in order to give the United States a face-saving way out of its predicament. Perhaps the most telling phrase in one of the documents cited here is Le Duan's simple statement that if U.S. leaders want a protracted war, we will give it to them. We will fight, he said, whatever way the United States wants.

In that sense, it can be said that the conflict became a predominantly military struggle with the characteristics of a conventional war not, as some have said, because Hanoi planned it that way but because the United States wanted it that way. Given Hanoi's political superiority over its rivals in the South and the ineluctable reality of U.S. technological superiority, it must have seemed in Washington the easier way out. The results have proven otherwise.

Notes

The author would like to express his appreciation to the Institute for Arts and Humanities at the Pennsylvania State University for providing a grant that assisted in the preparation for this chapter.

1. For the policy debate over a political versus a military approach during the Kennedy administration, see Roger Hilsman, "Two American Counterstrategies to Guerrilla Warfare: The Case of Vietnam," in Tang Tsou, ed., *China in Crisis*, vol. 2, *China's Policies in Asia and America's Alternatives* (Chicago: University of Chicago Press, 1968). The primary exponent of the view that it was a conventional war all along is Harry Summers; see his *On Strategy: A Critical Assessment of the Vietnam War* (Novato: Presidio Press, 1982).

2. One recent exponent of the view that the primary lesson of Vietnam is that the United States must never leash the power of its armed forces is President George Bush. See his comments at the White House in reference to the war in the Persian Gulf in the *New York Times*, January 17, 1991. For an overview, see John M. Gates, "Vietnam: The Debate Goes On," in Lloyd J. Matthews and Dale Brown, eds., *Assessing the Vietnam War* (McLean, VA: Pergamon-Brassey's, 1987).

3. For a reference to the need for a joint political-military strategy, see *Histoire de la Revolution d'Aout* (Hanoi: Foreign Languages Press, 1972), 66, 68. Also see Vo Nguyen Giap's *Tien Len Con Duong Vu Trang Tranh Dau* [Advance on the Road to Armed Struggle], in *Van Kien Dang, 1930–1945* [Party Documents, 1930–1945] (Hanoi: Center for the History of the Party, 1978), vol. 3, 381.

4. The classical statement of the Vietnamese version of people's war is Truong Chinh's *The Resistance Will Win*, written in 1947. In Truong Chinh's formulation, which was undoubtedly approved by the party leadership as a whole, the Chinese model was adapted to local conditions and circumstances in Vietnam, but was still a recognizable imitation of Mao's own ideas. For an English-language version, see Truong Chinh, *Selected Writings* (Hanoi: Foreign Languages Press, 1977), 85–211. For another reference to the three-stage concept, see *Van Kien Dang, 1945–1954* (Hanoi: Center for the History of the Party, 1978), vol. 2, part 1, "Cuoc Truong Ky Khang Chien Cua Dan Toc Ta," p. 12.

5. The party's decision to seek a peaceful reunification of the country was announced by Ho Chi Minh at a plenary meeting of the Central Committee in July 1954. For an English-language version of the speech, see Ho Chi Minh, *Selected Writings* (Hanoi: Foreign Languages Press, 1977), 172–83. A version in *quoc ngu*, is located in Ho Chi Minh, *Toan Tap*, vol. 6 (1951–1954), 578–592.

6. The pamphlet is located in Race Documents, a microfilm series located at the Center for Research Libraries in Chicago, Illinois. See no. 1002.

7. See *United States–Vietnam Relations, 1945–1967* (Washington, D.C.: U.S. Government Printing Office, 1971), vol. 2, 46–48. Ho's speech at the April 1956 plenum is in *Toan Tap*, vol. 7 (1954–1957), 426–430.

8. This belief is discussed in the resolution issued at the end of the party's Ninth Plenum in December 1963. For an English version, see *Vietnam Documents and Research Notes* (VDRN), no. 96.

9. *Cuoc Khang Chien Chong My Cuu Nuoc, 1954–1975: Nhung Su Kien Quan Su* [Vietnam: The Anti–U.S. Resistance War for National Salvation, 1954–1975: Military Events] (Hanoi: Nha Xuat Ban Quan Doi Nhan Dan, 1980), 49. The book was translated into English by the Joint Publications Research Service (JPRS), and the comment is located on 29–30. For the convenience of readers I will hereafter cite page numbers from the English-language version. Hereafter CKC.

10. For example, see George McT. Kahin, *Intervention: How America Became Involved in Vietnam* (New York: Alfred A. Knopf, 1986), 8. For critical comments on Kahin's thesis, see Carlyle Thayer, "Revisionism in Communist Vietnamese Historiography: The Issue of Central Party Control over the Southern Party Organization, 1954–1961," presented to the Senior Seminar Series organized by the Department of Pacific and Southeast Asian History, Research School of Pacific Studies, Australian National University, August 8, 1989.

11. For Le Duan's view, see his *Thu Vao Nam* [Letters to the South] (Hanoi: Su That, 1986), 33.

12. Ibid. Letter to Muoi Cuc Nguyen Van Linh, April 1961, 45. A comment about Maoist people's war is located on 33.

13. For a reference to the need for a new united front in the South, see *Third National Congress of the Vietnam Workers' Party* (Hanoi: Foreign Languages Press, 1960), vol. 3, 24–26.

14. The Politburo meeting is mentioned in CKC, 46.

15. Le Duan, *Thu Vao Nam*, letters of February and April 1961.

16. The resolution issued by the Politburo at the end of the meeting is contained in *Mot So Van Kien Cua Dang Ve Chong My Cuu Nuoc* [Selected Party Documents Relating to the Anti–United States National Salvation Struggle] (Hanoi: Su That, 1985), vol. 1, 136–58. For evidence of Hanoi's criticism of COSVN actions, see Douglas Pike, microfilm series entitled Documents of the National Liberation Front, Document 257.

17. Le Duan, *Thu Vao Nam*, Letter of July 1961.

18. CKC, 50. Le Duan's speech was broadcast by NCNA, April 15, 1963.

19. VDRN, Document no. 96. The original version is in *Mot So*, vol. 1, 159–210.

20. VDRN, Document no. 98.

21. Lu Duan, *Thu Vao Nam*, Letter to Xuan [Nguyen Chi Thanh], February 1965.

22. CKC, 69. *Mot So*, vol. 1, 211–29, has the resolution.

23. *Thu Vao Nam*, Letter to Xuan, May 1965.

24. For a comment and references, see my *China and Vietnam: The Roots of Conflict* (Berkeley: Institute of East Asian Studies, 1986), 49.

25. Le Duan, *Thu Vao Nam*, Letter to Xuan, November 1965.

26. CKC, 84–85. The resolution is in *Mot So*, vol. 2, 5–34.

27. U.S. Department of State, *Working Paper on North Vietnam's Role in the War in South Vietnam* (Washington, D.C.: U.S. Government Printing Office, 1968), Item no. 32.

3

Tet: The 1968 General Offensive and General Uprising

General Tran Van Tra

The Context of the General Offensive and General Uprising of 1968

The Simultaneous Uprisings in 1960 (the partial armed uprising of the people to seize power in the countryside) turned the revolution in the South into a guerrilla war, a people's war against the U.S. aggressors' Special War (which was part of the "flexible response" strategy).[1] Subsequently, the military victories of Ap Bac (1963) and Binh Gia–Ba Gia (winter–spring 1964–65), together with the movements to destroy the "strategic hamlets" in the countryside and the political struggle in the urban areas, created a crisis leading to the collapse of the dictatorial and fascist regime of Ngo Dinh Diem and the successive puppet regimes, *driving the U.S. imperialists' Special War into a dead end.*[2]

Faced with this situation, the White House and the Pentagon came to the conclusion that the main cause for their failure lay with North Vietnam and that if they launched massive air attacks against the North they could win the war. On February 13, 1965, President Johnson ordered the beginning of Operation Rolling Thunder, a long-prepared non-stop air war against the Democratic Republic of Vietnam.

The original Vietnamese text of this chapter was published as "Tet Mau Than, Chien Cong Hien Hach" [Tet, The Year of the Monkey, a Glorious Feat of Arms], part 1, and "Thang Loi va Suy Nghi ve Thang Loi" [Victory and Reflections on Victory], part 2, in *Tap Chi Lich Su Quan Su* [Journal of Military History], February 1988, 8–23 (part 1), and April 1988, 36–45 (part 2). The translation presented here is by Ngo Vinh Hai, Do Le Chau, and Jayne Werner. The translation starts with page 2 of the April article, the first page in the original being devoted to introductory comments. All end-of-chapter notes are by the editors, except where noted.

General Westmoreland, commander of the U.S. Expeditionary Corps in South Vietnam, however, predicted that it would not be until June at the earliest that the bombing of the North would show some results. Meanwhile, the South Vietnamese army was in need of U.S. assistance to sustain its defense lines now being threatened by the growing strength of the Viet Cong and to develop its own forces in an "orderly manner." Westmoreland warned, "if there is a counter-attack by the V.C. [Viet Cong] in the summer, one cannot expect the South Vietnamese army to hold out long enough for the bombings to show effect. . . . All indications show that the government of Vietnam (the puppets) may collapse and there is a clear possibility that the Viet Cong will be able to successfully consolidate its power."[3]

So as a "quick fix," to save the puppet army from defeat and the Saigon regime from imminent collapse, which could lead to a pullout of U.S. forces from strategically important Southeast Asia, the White House hurriedly sent in troops, launching a devastating Local War[4] in South Vietnam. [Ed. note: Nearly 200,000 troops were sent in, which Westmoreland hoped would give him enough strength to seize the initiative from the Viet Cong in 1966.] Westmoreland thus hoped he could shift to the offensive and, with additional reinforcements, defeat the enemy by the end of 1967. . . .[5]

As soon as the United States started the Local War in 1965, our Party concluded that the United States was forced to introduce its own troops because it was losing the war. It had lost the political game in Vietnam. It could no longer use the mask of nationalism of its puppet regime to conceal its aim of aggression. In terms of military strategy, it had also lost the Special War, which meant using American arms and dollars and Vietnamese blood. Because of this strategically passive and losing posture, the United States and puppet forces were not strong, despite their large numbers and modern weaponry. We therefore retained our winning posture and the strategic initiative, and could afford to continue our attacks in order to find the most effective fighting methods. The enemy was still bewildered by the new battlefield, new people and circumstances, and even a new form of war. This testified to our Party's clear-sightedness and proved our leadership and the field command's judgment to be correct. We had gone through two seasons of the enemy's strategic counterattacks, defeating a force of almost half a million U.S. troops and about as many puppet and Allied troops. . .

The more we fought, the stronger our political and military forces became, both quantitatively and qualitatively. The progressive world was on our side against the unjust and cruel war. The United States was failing politically both at home and around the world.

We were winning and we held the initiative despite the difficulties and weaknesses we had in replenishing our forces, building our political strength and conducting mass movements in urban areas, and ensuring material and technical supplies. However, these were difficulties in the context of a favorable situation. As for the United States, its numerous difficulties resulted from a war that had reached its peak but still offered no way out. President Johnson had to make a definite and important decision: either yield to the military and escalate the war, expanding it to the whole of Indochina (including an invasion of North Vietnam), or listen to McNamara and several high-level civilian officials, and de-escalate the war and negotiate with Hanoi and the Viet Cong. He could not afford to stay at the crossroads any longer, "gradually escalating," preventing the collapse of the Saigon army, while gradually "squeezing" Hanoi to come to terms with the United States. To encourage Johnson to "charge ahead," the "hawks" distorted reports, drawing optimistic pictures of the situation. A March 1967 telegram from Westmoreland to the Pacific Military Command said,

> As a result of our buildup and successes, we were able to plan and initiate a general offensive. We now have gained the tactical initiative, and are conducting continuous small and occasional large-scale offensive operations, to decimate enemy forces; to destroy enemy base areas and disrupt his infrastructure; to interdict his land and water LOC's and to convince him, through the vigor of our offensive and accompanying psychological operations, he faces inevitable defeat.[6]

However, the entire United States could not help but sicken of the deadlock in South Vietnam and the fact that the heavy losses in the air war over North Vietnam were not compensated by any tangible political or military results. Differences within the United States and Saigon ranks were widening. The antiwar movement of the American people intensified. So did the world's condemnation of the war. All of this forced an extremely cautious stand on Johnson who was further frustrated by the gloomy prospects for the 1968 presidential election.

This provided us with a very important opportunity to push Johnson into making a decision which would lead to a strategic shift in our favor. In revolution and war, it is essential to size up the situation and seize the right opportunity, to decide and act in a resolved, timely, and appropriate manner to win. This work requires talent and artful skills. If the opportunity is missed, the situation will take an undesirable turn and can result in failure. At these junctures, it is more often than not that one is not fully aware of every detail in the situation of one's forces and the enemy's. Some elements emerge clearly, but others remain murky, yet need to be tackled with clear-sightedness and correct analyses.

Strategic Decision for the General Offensive–General Uprising[7]

In judging this situation, the Political Bureau of the Party Central Committee noted, "the situation allows us to shift our revolution to a new stage, that of decisive victory." It adopted a resolution on the immediate goals and tasks:

> Our great and urgent task now is to mobilize the greatest efforts of our Party, armed forces and people in both regions [the North and the South] to move our

revolutionary war to the highest level and achieve decisive victory through a
General Offensive and General Uprising, and realize the strategic objectives
set by the Party.

These objectives were:

- To break down and destroy the bulk of the puppet troops, topple the puppet
  administration at all levels, and take power into the hands of the people.
- To destroy the major part of the U.S. forces and their war materiel, and
  render them unable to fulfill their political and military duties in Vietnam.
- On this basis, to break the U.S. will of aggression, force it to accept defeat in
  the South and put an end to all acts of war against the North. With this, we
  will achieve the immediate objectives of our revolution—independence,
  democracy, peace, and neutrality for the South—and we can proceed to
  national reunification.

The Resolution continued,

In the course of our utmost efforts to achieve these objectives, we will have
multiplied our strength and accelerated the weakening of the enemy. This will
ensure us the capability to deal successfully with any situation in the war. . . .
The coming General Offensive and General Uprising will be the first stage in a
process involving a very fierce and complex strategic offensive which will
combine military and political attacks to be carried out by all the three forces
in all three strategic zones in combination with the diplomatic offensive. Military attacks by the armed forces on the main fronts and the uprising of the
people in large urban areas are the two main thrusts.

The Resolution also noted,

We will be launching this General Offensive and General Uprising in a circumstance where the enemy is not exhausted by a world war (as in the Russian
October Revolution, or our August Revolution), but at a time when it still
retains more than a million troops and a large war potential.
   Regarding the measures to be taken, we shall launch not only a General
Offensive but also, simultaneously, a General Uprising. We will strike with
strength and power at the enemy's main force army corps in the capital and
other cities to create conditions for millions of people in enemy-held urban and
rural areas to rise up and coordinate with our military forces to break up and
destroy enemy troops, overthrow the nerve center of the Southern puppet
government, frustrate and fundamentally paralyze the war machine of the
United States and its allies, turn the enemy's rear and strategic reserves into
our own, force a quick shift in the balance of forces to our advantage and to the
disadvantage of the enemy, and win a decisive victory.
   The main principles are to concentrate most intensely and appropriately our
military and political forces on opening fierce attacks in the main strategic
directions, stage continuous and decisive attacks on the most vital points of the

United States and puppet forces, win by every means victories at the decisive theaters, maintain at all costs the element of surprise, . . . constantly promote victory, shatter all enemy counterattacks, and pursue the enemy hot-on-his-heels to ensure the biggest victory.

The Resolution also foresaw these three contingencies:

Contingency I: We win overwhelming victories in all important theaters, successfully stage attacks and uprisings in crucial areas and large urban centers and smash all enemy counterattacks, making the enemy unable to recover; we crush its aggressive will, and force it to give up and enter into negotiations to end the war on our terms.

Contingency II: We win in many theaters, but the enemy can still regroup and, with reinforcements from outside, can regain important positions, large urban centers—particularly the capital—and continue to rely on their bases in order to hold out against us.

Contingency III: The United States mobilizes and sends in large reinforcements, and steps up the war in North Vietnam, Laos, and Cambodia in order to change the course of the war and remedy its losing position.

We thus have to exert extraordinary efforts, summon up all our spiritual strength and forces to fight determinedly for the biggest win as envisaged in Contingency I.

Contingency III is the least possible, but we still have to be constantly ready to cope with any situation that may emerge.

As for the combination of struggle on the diplomatic front and the General Offensive, the Resolution said,

Our diplomatic activities must be aimed at attacking the enemy when he is confused and passive militarily and politically, while at the same time, opening the way for the enemy to negotiate on the most favorable terms for us. We must prepare plans and options for negotiations with the enemy as and when he is forced to talk with us. The plans must be specific and aimed at putting an end to the war of aggression, bringing about the withdrawal of the United States and its allied forces, and ensuring the right of the South Vietnamese people to determine their own government.

The Political Bureau made an appeal to the people "to overcome all hardships and sacrifices, challenges and difficulties, to courageously and resourcefully carry out the 'General Offensive and General Uprising' to bring our struggle against the U.S. aggressors for national salvation to complete victory, so as to accomplish our cause of national liberation and reunification."

Preparations for and Implementation of the General Offensive–General Uprising

It was not until the end of October and the beginning of November 1967 that the Party Central Office for the South,[8] Regional Command (B2), and a number of key cadres at the key fronts (Eastern area and Saigon–Gia Dinh) were informed of the Political Bureau's Resolution, and began discussing its general directives and details. As "N" Day, the date chosen for the General Offensive, had been fixed—Tet Mau Than, that is, the New Year's Day of the lunar year of the Monkey (January 31, 1968)[9]—only three months were left for all the preparations at the front. These included setting the operation and battle plans; organizing military, political, and proselytizing forces; readying the battlefield; positioning the troops; organizing the material supplies; and disseminating instructions and giving ideological guidance to all regions, military zones, divisions, regiments, provinces, cities, districts, villages, and urban wards. This was too short a time for such a colossal and complex undertaking. It required the extraordinary efforts of hundreds of thousands of devoted and self-sacrificing revolutionaries. In fact, the key front of Saigon–Gia Dinh, the capital of the puppets and the nerve center of U.S. forces, was surrounded with multilayered defenses. Therefore any timely preparation would not have been possible without the previous planning and preparations made since 1964–65, in line with Resolution 9 adopted by the Party Central Committee (Third Congress) in December 1963. This Resolution characterized the war in the South as one against foreign aggression, which at the same time was a civil war against the reactionaries and counterrevolutionaries. It was drawn from the experiences of the nine years of war against the French and, especially, the almost ten years of fierce and diversified struggle of the southern people against the United States and its puppet regime. It put forth the line of combining political struggle with military attacks. It affirmed that this line was for long-term application to the whole war. It said, "general offensives and general uprisings will be the natural outcome of the line of combining political with military struggle."

On the basis of this Resolution, the Regional Command (B2),[10] which was responsible for both tactical and strategic operations at the key front of Saigon–Gia Dinh, was obliged to figure out ways for its implementation and to ready itself in the spirit of constantly holding the initiative. A General Offensive–General Uprising was a major strategic move in itself, since it was to take place in the biggest city in the country and was designed to topple the central puppet government and paralyze the U.S. forces' nerve center. It was extremely difficult and complicated and required thorough and time-consuming preparation. It was all the more so for us since we were in the middle of a big war in which the enemy was many times larger in numbers and better equipped, and was holding most of the strategic positions. Without our previous preparations, when the opportunity arose we would certainly be relegated to the sidelines. For this offensive, we could not wait until the water reached our feet to jump, so to speak. Our responsibility was so great that, in the strategic sense, we had to prepare in advance. Therefore, after Resolution 9 was adopted, the Regional Command spent months on end designing a plan for a General Offensive–General Uprising in Saigon. Under this plan, preparations were made step by step, focusing on the creation, organization, and disposition of political, military, and proselytization forces. Completed by the end of 1964, the plan envisaged specific tasks for the front, specified the enemy targets to be destroyed, and categorized them into three groups. The first, and main, group consisted of:

• The Saigon Office of the General Staff (military command)
• The Office of the Special Forces of the Capital (defense of the inner city)
• The Office of the National Police (which would repress the people's uprisings)
• Tan Son Nhat airport (to neutralize the enemy's control of the air)
• The Presidential Palace of the Saigon Government (where the highest power resided)

These five targets were to be destroyed simultaneously and seized at all costs for the General Offensive–General Uprising to be carried out in the heart of the enemy's capital city.

The second group of targets, which was also very important, included Radio Saigon, post offices, the U.S. embassy, the Saigon Navy Command, the residence of the chief of Gia Dinh province, Chi Hoa Prison, the command centers of the armored and artillery forces, the Quang Trung military training center, the Bien Hoa air base, and the headquarters of the Third Corps of the Saigon army. The third group included warehouses, ports, economic and logistical installations, power stations, and government offices.

The basic guiding method was to combine attacks by military units with mass urban uprisings, attacks from within the cities with those from outside, and military activities in rural areas with those in urban centers. The offensive was to be continuous, going from one victory to another, all the way to complete victory.

To fight in such a way, different military forces had to be formed to suit different targets so that a force smaller in number could fight a force larger in strength. The quantity of troops was crucial, although their quality and whether or not they were seasoned fighters and had the ability to maintain absolute secrecy were paramount. Therefore, it was of utmost importance that, at a very early stage, we build special mobile attack units and on-the-spot sapper units[11] and pre-assign them to each and every target. The units were to be supported by local masses, and provided with caches and camouflage for their personnel and ammunition. They were to monitor their targets closely, conduct thorough reconnaissance, and constantly improve and adjust their battle plans and tactics according to the latest developments and activities at their targets. Shock battalions of the regular army and local battalions, which were thoroughly familiar with the local terrain and situation—and had their guerrilla bases in the vicinity of their targets—were assigned to approach each main target and provide timely support for the special attack and sapper forces, regular and local. Next in line were the regional and main force regiments and divisions which would stand ready to move in to destroy the enemy resistance and repulse any counterattacks.

Field dispositions and commands were arranged according to the five main targets, which were all to be simultaneously attacked and seized. The character, disposition and terrain, and location of these targets had to be determined in relation to their immediate suburban areas. Our military forces were to start from their forward bases closest to the targets and, in strict coordination and command, were to quickly close in on their pre-assigned targets to discharge their duties. The whole theater therefore had to be reorganized into five wings, each assigned a section of the inner city where its main target was located and a suburban stretch connecting the target with its base, which would serve as its springboard. In other words, when preparations for the General Offensive–General Uprising were to begin, the provincial military organizations in the Eastern area, Zone Seven, and the Saigon–Gia Dinh Zone had to be dissolved and reorganized into five new zones. A sixth zone was also needed to coordinate activities in the center of Saigon. Each zone was to have its own command responsible for both political and military activities, and all were to be placed under the General Command responsible for the whole city, or rather, for the whole Eastern area of South Vietnam. The plan was approved by the Central Office for the South which gave top-secret access to only a few regional staff officers.

Proceeding from this plan of 1965, five shock battalions meant for the five wings were set up. They were carefully trained in combat tactics in rural and urban terrains. By the end of 1965, these battalions began to move in the vicinity of their respective wings to acquaint themselves with the terrain and to train in actual combat situations. At the same time, selections were made to find soldiers and cadres for sapper units to be assigned to the chosen targets, first, targets in category one, then, categories two and three. Efforts were also made to build local underground mass bases for each special attack and sapper unit, establish its munitions caches and design ways to bring in the munitions. Along with organizing the military force in each area where a target was located, mass organizations with Party cells forming their leadership were set up in each district, ward, and street area. Intelligence services and proselytization branches deployed their agents for tasks which had been assigned to them by their upper levels according to the plan. Pending the order for action, all these pre-organized units would remain in their localities and carry on their periodically assigned duties while building up their forces, sharpening their skills, digging in and preparing themselves for long-term objectives. In this manner, the mass political forces and the Party leadership would be tempered every day in the practice of political struggle, and weak links could be properly strengthened and adjusted according to the plan for the uprising.

Regrettably, during 1966–67, updates of the plan were not made as required by the vital needs arising in the field, because the higher command considered it more important to concentrate on fighting the U.S. forces. Therefore, when the

Party Political Bureau adopted the Resolution on launching the General Offensive–General Uprising, the field command was caught somewhat by surprise and had to hurriedly review the old plan and set out to complete it. The time allowed for completing the remaining monumental work was three months. In fact, without the preparations made in 1964–65, our main forces would hardly have been able to accomplish this challenging task, since each level was required to immediately design and submit both an overall plan and specific plans for each target, which were to be detailed down to the methods of attack and unit forces to be used, so that their respective higher commands would have time to approve and coordinate planning with other units. The plan for the B2 theater (Southern Central Vietnam and South Vietnam), and especially the plan for the Saigon–Gia Dinh front, had to be approved by the Party Central Committee.

Since the Party and mass organizations in the inner cities were still weak, the Central Office for the South was hard pressed to quickly bring in more cadres from the delta provinces to beef up those in crucial areas. However, according to plan, prior to "N" Day, we launched strong attacks on Khe Sanh (January 20, 1968) in order to draw a large number of U.S. and Saigon puppet troops from the inner cities to this remote but important area, to divert the enemy's attention and thus help our urban forces in the secret deployment of their units. A "technical" problem developed in our strategic coordination: in Tri Thien and the Fifth Zone (including the Central Highlands), the attacks took place twenty-four hours ahead of those in the B2 theater. This happened because the B2 command based its timing on the old lunar calendar, which heretofore had been in use, while the Fifth Zone and Tri Thien fronts, which were under the direct command of the Party Central Committee, used the new lunar calendar, which had just been revised and was in effect in Hanoi. Unfortunately, this revision threw off the timing for the opening attacks, since there was a twenty-four-hour difference between the two calendars. This gave the enemy enough time to alert its troops, cancel the Tet truce, cancel all leaves, recall its troops, and strengthen its defenses. The surprise factor, which should have been the top priority for the B2 theater, which included Saigon, the number-one target, was no more. Tactically, this made it more difficult for the attackers. However, in terms of strategy, a few days difference in the baptism of fire at different fronts in the whole region did not diminish the overall excellence of our coordination. We brought the war to every corner of the enemy's rear and to the nerve center of the U.S. and Saigon forces. In Westmoreland's own words, we brought it into the "enemy's base areas." On the first day of attack, our army and people hit six cities, forty-four provincial centers, and hundreds of district towns.

At the Tri Thien–Hue, Fifth Zone, and Central Highlands fronts, where our troops and people were the first to open fire, the enemy was taken completely by surprise. The assaults continued unabated. Most outstanding was our success in taking full control of Hue, holding up and repelling the enemy's counterattacks for twenty-five successive days and nights. This provided a tremendous encouragement for the whole country, especially the key front—Saigon–Gia Dinh. In the Mekong Delta, we seized control of the provincial towns of Ca Mau, Tra Vinh, My Tho, Ben Tre, and An Giang and a number of targets in other provincial towns, and took over many district towns and military posts.

At the key front of Saigon–Gia Dinh, from the night of January 30 and early morning of January 31, most of the designated targets were attacked. In a deft and courageous assault, special attack units attacked and occupied the radio station for many hours, the U.S. embassy, a part of the Presidential Palace, and Gates 4 and 5 of the Office of the General Staff of the Saigon army. Shock battalions and their local counterparts seized control of the Phu Dong Armored Vehicle Barracks and the Co Loa Artillery Camp, and destroyed many pieces of artillery, armored vehicles, arsenals, the Quang Trung Training Center, and parts of the western end of Tan Son Nhat airport, along with a number of airplanes. For many days, our troops controlled an area of Binh Hoa district, Cay Thi intersection, the Phu Tho racetrack, and the Saigon Women's Military Cadets School. Also seized were the Nguyen Tri Phuong, Trieu Da, Nguyen Kim, and Nguyen Lam areas. At the Lu Gia, Le Dai Hanh, and Nguyen Van Thoai residential areas, and the Thiet Market, the battles between our troops and the enemy were extremely fierce.

In the south and southwest quadrants of the key front, we seized the area of the Hoi Dong factory, the Third Bridge, and the Binh Dong rice granary; we held them for four days running. A unit attacked Nhi Thien Duong Bridge and penetrated enemy defenses in the Phu Dinh area, the Ceramics Kiln, and the Binh Tay Wine Company between the Hau Giang and Thap Muoi avenues. This group then moved across Duong Cong Trung Avenue to the Thiet Market, converging with incoming forces from the west. The Hoa Van[12] force mobilized local people to seize control of districts 5, 6, 10, and 11. To the east and northwest of the main front, our troops secretly closed in on and overran the district police headquarters at Hang Xanh, held the area, and wiped out a counterattacking commando battalion.

People in many places took to the streets, such as in districts 7 and 8, the Hang Xanh Binh Hoa intersections, the Tran Quoc Toan Market, the Phu Tho racetrack, Go Vap, the Bamboo Bridge, and Phu Lam areas. A dispatch of the French Press Agency (AFP) on February 3 reported, "U.S. intelligence services now acknowledge that the majority of the population knew about the Viet Cong's preparations for the Offensive, but no one said a word,"[13] and "it is said that in a number of Saigon districts and in areas in the Delta, there are separate demonstrations in support of the Viet Cong, and occasionally government soldiers refusing to open fire."[14] In other places, where our troops had not yet arrived, or where fierce battles were still being fought, with incessant bombing and factory buildings collapsing, unarmed people could not rise up to seize control of their areas. Indeed, any military attack should always be one step ahead of any political activity if it is to provide effective leverage for a successful political uprising. This is also a principle of uprisings during wartime, which is different from uprisings under conditions of political struggle only.

In close coordination with the special attack and sapper units and shock battalions, regiments and divisions of the regular army simultaneously sprang assaults on Bien Hoa airport and the Second Field Command Headquarters of the U.S. forces; took control of the Tam Hiep intersection (Bien Hoa); attacked the Fifth Division in Ben Cat; destroyed a U.S. battalion in Phu Giao; destroyed and pinned down the U.S. First Infantry Division at Cu Chi; held back the U.S. Twenty-fifth Division; and crossed the Tra Canal (Hoc Mon) to join local forces in attacks on the northern end of Tan Son Nhat airport, and also backed up the shock battalions in repelling enemy counterassaults.

Further back from the main front, local military forces and the people staged an uprising and destroyed the Phu Khuong military section (Tay Ninh), occupied Long Khanh province, the Tuc Trung section and Long Dat district town (Ba Ria), and attacked the Phuoc Binh provincial town (Phuoc Long).

These events took place from January 31 to February 25. In this period, we attacked many targets as planned, and destroyed a large number of enemy troops and their materiel. However, except for Hue, which we held for twenty-five days, we were not able to hold any of our objectives for very long, and had to fend off ferocious counterattacks. Toward the end of the period, we had to retreat to our strategic positions in the outlying areas to maintain them as staging areas for later attacks. In the meantime, we consolidated our forces, fought back enemy counterattacks, and prepared ourselves for the second phase of the offensive.

On the enemy's part, having witnessed the frustration and incompetence of the puppet army in defending the cities, U.S. troops hastily abandoned their "search and destroy" activities in the "priority areas" of "the enemy's base areas" and returned to the cities in order to join in counterattacks and clear and hold the cities. U.S. troops were most heavily concentrated in Khe Sanh and Saigon— from its downtown area to the outskirts. They launched large counterassaults, such as "Operation Victory" in March in the Saigon–Gia Dinh and in the eastern theaters, engaging the First, Ninth and Twenty-fifth U.S. Divisions, and brigade-size units of paratroopers, marines, commandos, and police. The total number of troops involved was 50,000.

Results of these activities were reported to be "not very good." However, they did help consolidate the enemy's defense posture in the capital city. The puppets immediately suspended the demobilization of all servicemen, recalled discharged soldiers and officers, drafted students and teachers, set up self-defense forces, erected bunkers, and put up barbed wire around important military and government offices in the inner parts of cities. Close to "N" Day for Phase II and alarmed by news from Viet Cong defector Tam Ha, the enemy put its troops on top alert, suspending all leaves of absence and stepping up defense activities.

As for the first phase of the offensive, the Party Central Committee and the

Central Office for the South both concluded that we had won a substantial victory because we hit the enemy right at its nerve center, delivering a direct political and economic blow and causing the enemy its biggest losses so far. The enemy's control over the rural areas shrank as a result.

Our shortcomings and weaknesses were that we were not able to destroy a significant number of enemy forces and their top leaders. The operations were not effective enough to lend leverage to the people's uprising. Mass organizations and proselytization forces were not adequate to encourage the people to rise up en masse. However, our attacks sent shudders through the enemy's vital points, and destabilized its military, political, and economic foundations throughout South Vietnam. The enemy reacted strongly, though it betrayed many weaknesses and was still unable to regroup properly. This provided an opportunity for us to continue strong assaults and compensate for our earlier shortcomings in order to win even bigger victories.

On the night of May 4 and the early morning of May 5, Phase II of our offensive began. Our forces in all the cities and provinces in the B2 theater opened the push with artillery fire of all types on the targets before our ground forces closed in. At key points, some of our special attack units had suffered such losses in Phase I that they could only mount independent attacks to seize a few targets, such as the television center and the Phan Thanh Gian Bridge. The rest of the special units joined ranks with regular ground forces converging onto their targets from various directions. Our artillery fire hit a good number of important targets in and around Saigon such as the Presidential Palace, the residence of the U.S. ambassador, the U.S. embassy compound, the National Police Office, the Navy Command, the Capital City Command, Tan Son Nhat airport, and the new Port of Saigon. The shock and local battalions, together with the regular army forces, thrust deeper into the city center and occupied the larger areas for a longer period of time than during Phase I.

The puppet army acknowledged,

> This time the enemy made use of lapses in our defense line and sneaked in before we knew it. Before opening fire, the enemy had placed its troops at all the key vantage points in large buildings, factories and places of worship. Also, in open and raised areas, it dug fox holes and trenches. When we managed to bombard the areas it had seized, its forces were reinforced at night. It was very difficult for us to liberate those areas. We were thus forced to use the air force and armored vehicles to check the enemy's advance and destroy its entrenched forces.[15]

The areas that we attacked and managed to hold included many important points in both Saigon–Gia Dinh and Cholon. They were Go Vap, Gia Dinh, Cay Thi and Cay Queo areas, the Bang Ky Bridge, the Binh Loi Bridge, the Son Bridge, Binh Hoa, the Le Van Duyet Cemetery, and the Chuong Cho intersection. To the south, areas held included the fourth district, Khanh Hoi, the Tan

Thuan Bridge, the seventh and eighth districts, the "Y-shaped" bridge, and Pham The Hien and Au Duong Lan wards. Places seized in the west were the Bamboo Bridge, Binh Thoi, Phu Tho Hoa, the Phu Tho racetrack, Ba Hat, the Bay Hien intersection, the Lai garden, areas in Minh Phung, and the sixth district. Other places captured in the western front included Hau Giang, Tran Quoc Toan, and Monk Van Hanh avenues, the Administrative Building of the fifth district, the Phu Lam, Nguyen Trai, Phung Hung, Dong Khanh, Khong Tu, Tong Doc Phuong, and Nguyen Van Thoai avenues, the An Dong Market, the Binh Tien area, and the Binh Tay Wine Company.

In Phase II, although the enemy was not caught by surprise and, in fact, had strengthened its defenses after Phase I, the puppet troops still could not cope with our attacks. Its defense lines were broken through and its forces were overrun in many places, putting the U.S. forces on the defensive and forcing them to mount their own counterattacks. The U.S. Ninth Division had to enter the inner city while the First and Twenty-fifth Divisions moved to the north and the west. U.S. armed helicopters, jet fighters, and propeller bombers wantonly fired and dropped 350 kg bombs on residential areas, burning and ruining houses in larger residential areas that were under our control. Moreover, in areas where we had put up barricades and in big buildings where we maintained our vantage points, armored vehicles and tanks of the U.S. Ninth Division shelled streets to destruction before U.S. and puppet ground troops slowly opened their counterattacks. At Cay Thi and in Cholon and many other areas, the enemy sprayed or shelled our troops with toxic chemicals to force them out so the masked enemy could move in and retake these places. The fight in the inner city was extremely ferocious. The enemy had absolute superiority over us in air power, armor firepower, and troop strength. They opened fire recklessly at civilians as well.

Phase II, from May 5 to June 18, 1968, testified clearly to the courage and resourcefulness of our armed forces and the revolutionary masses. It was during this phase that the American and puppet troops suffered fairly heavy losses. The U.S. forces massed in defense in the city's outlying areas and lost one battalion after another and hundreds of tanks and armored vehicles at Vinh Loc and Duc Hoa in engagements with our main force units. Puppet troops suffered their fair share of losses in the inner city. General Nguyen Ngoc Loan, general director of the National Police, was wounded in both legs near Phan Thanh Gian Bridge. (He was the killer who shot a bound Viet Cong prisoner in the head in a Saigon street in Phase I.) Col. Luu Kim Cuong, commander of the Thirty-third Air Force Division and the Tan Son Nhat military complex, was killed at the airport. At Minh Phung Avenue, near Cholon, Col. Dam Van Qui was killed in his jeep by a B–40 rocket. But the puppet army's heaviest loss was sustained at Khong Tu Avenue where almost the whole military command suffered casualties. Six officers were killed: Lt. Col. Nguyen Van Luan, Saigon Police director; Lt. Col. Le Ngoc Tru, commander of the Fifth District Police Battalion; Lt. Col. Doan Ba Phuoc, commander of the Fifth Commando Police Battalion; Lt. Col. Pho Quoc

Chu, director of the Port of Saigon; Maj. Nguyen Ngoc Sinh, assistant director of the Saigon Police; and Maj. Nguyen Bai Thuy, director of the Saigon Security Office. Many others were critically wounded, including Col. Nguyen Van Cua, mayor of Saigon; Col. Nguyen Van Giap, commander of the Capital City Zone; and Lt. Col. Tran Van Phan, assistant general director of the National Police.

In Phase II, although the enemy was no longer taken by surprise, it was still taken aback by the intensity and broad range of the attacks, the depth of our thrusts into the inner city, and the magnitude of its losses. The five successive months of the General Offensive–General Uprising, from January 31 to June 16, 1968, were a period of utterly vicious battles that were fought mainly in the cities and their outlying areas, especially in Saigon, the largest city in the South, where the terrain was complicated with numerous tall buildings and houses, and where the U.S. and puppet armies had concentrated their forces and could employ all their weaponry, including heavy artillery, tanks, aircraft, and even toxic chemicals.

In face of this situation, with the approval of the Central Office for the South, the Regional Command Center decided to launch Phase III of the General Offensive in the Tay Ninh–Binh Long Theater in order to:

- wipe out a part of the U.S.-puppet mobile units, the main force defending Saigon.
- attract the enemy's ground and artillery forces to the defense lines and loosen its defense system in inner Saigon and vicinity (and in provincial towns) in order to prepare for the fourth phase of the General Offensive.
- punish the enemy ringleaders, expand our control in rural areas, and further build up our political and military forces.

Phase III of our offensive took place from August 17 to September 23, 1968. With the main attacks now directed at rural areas, the results were considerable. In the eastern part of the battle zone, the bulk of the U.S. forces and a part of the puppet army were rushed from Saigon to Tay Ninh and Binh Long to engage our troops. And while in the Fifth Zone we were wreaking havoc on the "Americal" Division and regular forces of the Saigon army in eastern Tam Ky and Quang Ngai, southwestern Dac Lac, northern Kon Tum, and pressing hard on the enemy at Route 9 in Tri Thien, our regional regular forces in Tay Ninh and Binh Long launched fierce attacks on the newly arrived units of the First and Twenty-fifth U.S. Infantry Divisions. With the special technique of "*danh nhoi, danh boi,*"[16] we destroyed twelve U.S. motorized infantry battalions, one battalion and several companies of the puppet army thus scoring greater results than expected. Many rural areas in the Mekong Delta were liberated. In the West alone, we seized control of eighty-eight villages and about 2,000 hamlets with a population of 1.5 million.

Despite our big victory, the general situation in the entire southern theater, especially in the cities, was no longer in our favor. Enemy troops were constantly reinforced. Fresh troops from the United States arrived in waves in the South. The puppet army also increased forces through the draft. They staged fierce counterattacks to strengthen the defense of the cities, and at the same time executed an emergency pacification program in rural areas. Meanwhile our forces were not replenished, in troop strength or munitions. The Central Office for the South and the Regional Command therefore called off the General Offensive–General Uprising instead of launching its fourth phase.

In summary, the General Offensive–General Uprising went on for almost the whole of 1968, mostly the first half of the year. It was conducted in close combination with our struggle on the diplomatic front, whose outcome, in turn, was proportional to our successes on the battlefield. After our first phase, which involved two months of fierce fighting in the southern cities, President Johnson discharged General Westmoreland and replaced him with his assistant, General Creighton Abrams. The "search and destroy" strategy was replaced by "clear and hold," in line with the policy of "Vietnamization" and de-escalating the war. On March 31, 1968, Johnson ordered a partial bombing halt over North Vietnam, and declared: " . . . I shall not seek, and I will not accept, the nomination of my Party for another term as your President,"[17] and offered peace talks. On April 3, we accepted, and both sides started negotiations on venues and the composition of the negotiating parties.

A day in the war was never too short, and was often measured by the death of hundreds and thousands of people. But it was not until the end of the second— and even the third—phase of the General Offensive–General Uprising on November 1, 1968, that the United States declared an end to the air war against North Vietnam. On November 13, 1968, the State Department made this sly announcement: "The U.S. agrees to bilateral talks with the U.S. and the Republic of Vietnam on the one side and North Vietnam and whomever it may be on the other." Indeed! Even as it was forced to swallow a bitter pill and open its eyes to the true strength of its adversary, the United States was still trying to disallow its shame. Was it not a fact that the "whomever" was the one who had truly given it a blow to remember? On December 10, 1968, the delegation of the National Liberation Front (NLF) of South Vietnam arrived in Paris for the four-party peace talks.

Reflections on Victory

In southern Vietnam, 1967 marked the fiercest year in the Local War. Our army and people heroically and successfully repulsed two successive seasons of U.S. strategic counterattacks, with a resounding victory over the U.S. search and destroy operation "Junction City." We were able to strike and win and maintain our initiative on the battlefield. This was not because our armed forces were bigger and stronger than those of the enemy but rather because our strategic line for the war was correct, and our decisions as to the choice of tactics and operations to carry them out were flexible and appropriate. We combined the strengths of military action with political agitation and proselytization of enemy troops and personnel,[18] and waged the struggle both at home and abroad. This was the combined force of a highly developed people's war—a just war. Up to that point in the conflict, the balance of forces between the two sides was still very unequal: the enemy was many times stronger in terms of troop strength, weaponry, and technical know-how. The United States still possessed great potential for operations involving rapid reinforcement and resupply. In the meantime, having engaged them in Operation Junction City, we had yet to make up for our losses in troop strength and ammunition. Many of our units were yet to be regrouped. Our army and people had fought with boundless courage, displayed tremendous talent, exerted great physical and mental effort, overcame untold hardships, and made enormous sacrifices.

Considering this situation, the Political Bureau of the Party Central Committee made a complete analysis of both sides and proceeded to identify the turning point of the war. The party concluded that confusion prevailed in the enemy ranks, which were divided between the "hawks" and the "doves" and that the U.S. president was at a crossroads. It recognized this precious opportunity to make a great strategic move on the battlefield in order to "shift our revolution to a new stage, that of decisive victory." This decision reflected the wisdom and acumen of the party's military leadership. Recognizing the turning point in war is an enormously difficult task. It will be a brief interlude because both sides will try to reverse the unfavorable situation and create a strategic opening to victory. It requires not only talent and experience but patience and courage. However, once one recognizes the turning point, it is even more difficult to determine what action to take, and the method and scope necessary to achieve the strategic goal. These types of decisions require both sides to make logical deductions on the basis of a thorough knowledge of the situation at hand, and to undertake meticulous studies and intricate calculations. This was particularly the case for us in 1967, given the balance of forces between us and the enemy. The Party Political Bureau observed that "the enemy has not yet been exhausted," and "still has over a million troops and enormous war resources," and that the United States was still capable of "mobilizing great reinforcements for their forces." This was also "the process in which the enemy will stage a fierce counterattack to regain lost positions of strategic importance," the Political Bureau further noted.

That conclusion notwithstanding, our goal was still to "destroy and break up the bulk of the puppet armed forces, overthrow the puppet administration at all levels, take power into the hands of the people," and "destroy the major part of the U.S. forces and war materiel." This goal, in fact, surpassed our actual capabilites by many times. First, we were still incapable of destroying an important part of the U.S. forces and war materiel and equipment. Our ground force was only one-fifth that of the U.S. and puppet infantries, and they had absolute superiority in the air and in naval and motorized power. The United States had been involved in the war for many years, spending hundreds of billions of dollars with the determined view to containing communist expansion in Asia. They would not give up easily, even if we achieved our goal on the battlefield. They still had enormous war resources and modern equipment. They could reinforce quickly and mount savage counterattacks. Second, since we could not destroy an important part of the U.S. force or defeat the U.S. troops, we were naturally unable to "destroy and break up the bulk of the puppet armed forces and overthrow the puppet administration at all levels." So, it was completely unrealistic for us to set the goal of the General Offensive–General Uprising in terms of "taking complete power into the hands of the people," which our cadres and combatants would interpret as dealing the enemy a "knock-out" blow. Since the General Offensive could not destroy the bulk of enemy forces—meaning that our attacks could not be decisive—simultaneous uprisings by the masses would be less than successful. The enemy could then ruthlessly suppress them with the kinds of weapons at its disposal. Therefore, although the Political Bureau correctly identified the turning point of the war and clearly discerned the precious opportunity it offered for timely and strategic action to "shift our revolution to a new stage, that of decisive victory," thus reflecting the acumen of our leadership, the approach we employed and the concrete strategic goals we set for the General Offensive–General Uprising were in effect unrealistic and beyond our reach. They also underestimated the U.S. reaction and its capabilities.

Huge as the implementation of this goal was, however, the Political Bureau gave each strategic level on the battlefield only three months to prepare. This was too short a time, since each level, military and political, had to make all-round preparations while still carrying out routine combat duties. It was everybody's understanding that we had many limitations: our troop strength was still not sufficiently replenished and our ammunition was low. (In fact, we had been fighting and seizing enemy weapons to stay in combat.) Our food supplies were short, communications poor—especially given the divided battlefield. Our chosen method of combat in such a large city as Saigon was not to attack in waves but with small units. We were unfamiliar with the maze of roads in Saigon and had to thread our way through the enemy's outer defenses, skirting its strong positions to approach important targets in the inner city. Aside from this, our units had to break through the defenses and meet the counterattacks of an enemy that was superior in terms of troop strength and fire power and also familiar with the terrain. This was a monumental task requiring time-consuming reconnaissance and study of the topography, the appropriate disposition of units and tactical training, and so forth. Even if we had had adequate modern equipment, it would not have been easy to organize the proper communications-and-command setup in each wing and each individual unit, and coordinate the operations during the attack for every unit and wing—all in a very short time.

When "N" Day arrived, however, our combatants at all positions opened fire at their predetermined targets in perfect strategic coordination. What made this success possible? It was none other than faith in victory, the determination to win, and the boundless courage and self-sacrifice of our combatants, from the highest ranking commanders to the foot soldier who had just enlisted on the eve of the Lunar New Year. There were, of course, a small number of cowards who chose to live in shame rather than die a glorious death. While the strategic coordination in the whole South was excellent, operational coordination-and-command was very confused. This resulted from our inadequate preparations and, in particular, lack of equipment. Even the field commander of the main theater of Saigon, who was assigned from the Central Office for the South and the Southern Command, was not completely aware of the situation at the front, nor was he provided with reports from all wings and units as the General Offensive began. This was despite the fact that representatives from the southern Command had been assigned to all units of the southern wing. And although the commanders of the offensive, as well as those of every zone (and even units), did go out to the field, they were only able to get a partial picture of the situation.

Both wings and units were unable to maintain close contact with their own lower levels and with one another. Because of this, it was impossible to relay orders and coordinate reinforcements. Units had to act on their own, based on their preassigned tasks and targets. This limited their success, and also posed no small risk to themselves. In fact, the fighting efficiency of our combatants and cadres, and of our special attack groups and small infantry units, was very high. However, the outcome could have been much better had the command-and-coordination of each attack, as well as the entire campaign, been more efficient, and had we had more forces to solidify our victories and push ahead. In much the same way, if we had had reinforcements to broaden our attacks from Hue, instead of just defending the citadel city, we could have achieved a bigger victory. It was the same with Saigon. If we had had reinforcements to expand our bridgeheads in areas we had seized and to maintain our control on all five directions of attack, as well as better communications among our forces, this would have led to greater results. Unfortunately, our overall strength, our organizational work, and our preparations had only reached a level that was insufficient for achieving greater success. Success was thus limited to the level of the highest possible effort. Any higher goal, such as to destroy the bulk of enemy forces to give rise to a general uprising and put total power into the hands of the people, was only an illusion.

A great success of Tet Mau Than,[19] which many viewed as a miracle, was that the secrecy of our goal and actions was maintained until the very baptism by fire; this greatly surprised the enemy. A book on military history published by the General Staff of the puppet army with the endorsement of its chief, Gen. Cao Van Vien, conceded, "an obvious fact was that the plan for the General Offensive/General Uprising had been kept secret until the attack broke out throughout the country." So we and the enemy agreed on that score. The fact of the matter is tnat in war, secrecy and surprise are guarantees for victories, strategic, tactical, and operational alike. However, it is important to understand these factors properly. Many will see secrecy as merely a requirement for the timing of an attack. That is not incorrect. However, this was only one of the secrets of Tet Mau Than. In fact, if the timing of an attack is the only secret in a military campaign, its usefulness will soon be exhausted.

The most important secret was our method of attack, strategically, tactically, and operationally. This factor made Tet Mau Than famous around the world and caught the enemy completely off guard, making the Pentagon and White House alike unable to anticipate our next moves. All of a sudden, within twenty-four hours, all the most secure areas in the enemy's rear—including cities, provincial capitals, and towns, which prior to the Lunar New Year's Eve still appeared a world away from the war—came under simultaneous attack. The most important points—from the office of the General Staff of the puppet army to the headquarters of the Capital City Military Zone, from the puppet regime's Presidential Palace to the U.S. embassy compound—all fell under fierce assaults. An AFP dispatch on February 3 reported, "this was probably the largest battlefield of the war. The whole of Vietnam is under fire, from Khe Sanh to Ca Mau."[20]

The war positions of both sides were reversed: in no time, the rear was turned into the front, and the latter into the former. Crack units, which had been sent to the "enemy's base areas" to "search and destroy," were all recalled on the double to "their own strongholds" to rescue the nerve center, to try to check and counterattack the enemy, and then to "clear and hold" till the very day they were forced to pull out of the war. The AFP dispatch remarked, "U.S. power has lost its prestige. The mightiest army in the world has been driven onto the defensive over the whole territory. At times, it has been overwhelmed."[21]

This obviously was the result of our unique fighting method in the revolutionary war. It combined armed uprisings, that is, attacks from within, with military assaults from without and simultaneous uprisings in all places. It also combined attacks of all forms, by units of all types and sizes, either by individuals or by small or large army units which were knitted together with different means of organization and provided with different levels of equipment. It was also the result of diverse efforts to integrate the actions of the revolutionary masses—in both the urban and rural areas—with the activities of the armed forces in combined offensives and uprisings. Some observers assert that there was only a general offensive and not an uprising in our 1968 campaign. This is a denial of the truth and is wrong. In fact, we had planned and made every effort to carry out a General Offensive–General Uprising. But our General Offensive was not up to the level that would enable a general uprising to take place. And without this indispensable condition during wartime, an uprising could not materialize. However, this does not mean that there were no uprisings in various places and at various times. It was impossible to stage the types of attacks we did during the

1968 campaign without mass uprisings. Our method of attack was truly unique for any war, past and present. Our strength was born of a combined military and political effort, both at home and abroad.

Aside from the timing and method of attack, the large scale, high intensity, and strength of our attacks constituted another surprise factor. They took place throughout the South. Extremely savage battles were fought over the course of more than half a year. This was beyond the enemy's expectations. It had never anticipated such strong determination, persistence, resourcefulness, and strength from an enemy it tended to dismiss. In his review of the combat year of 1967, which was made public on January 27, 1968, U.S. Field Commander General Westmoreland said, "Interdiction of the enemy's logistics train in Laos and North Vietnam by our indispensible air efforts has imposed significant difficulties on him. In many areas the enemy has been driven away from the population centers; in others, he has been compelled to disperse and evade contact, thus nullifying much of his potential. . . . Enemy bases, with sparse exception, are no longer safe havens. . . ."[22] The General Staff of the puppet army also commented, "strategists and tacticians say that the Viet Cong can only stage large attacks from starting-bases in border areas. But such attacks will meet with failure. Regarding the hinterland, military experts estimate that the enemy can only launch attacks with the engagement of battalion-sized units to attract attention. But even so, the attacks will not last long if the enemy does not want to be destroyed."[23]

As Tet Mau Than was unfolding, however, the attacks "took the U.S. Command and the U.S. public by surprise, and their strength, length, and intensity prolonged this shock." And "for the President, the shock and disappointment were especially serious."[24] In its book, *Vietnam—The Decisive Hour*, AFP commented, "The American General John Chaisson of the U.S. Command [under Westmoreland] said that the Viet Cong offensive on Tuesday was a 'big surprise' for the U.S. command. 'Our intelligence services did not inform us that the offensive would be as widespread and as massive as it was. . . . The most serious mistake of our intelligence services, without doubt, was that they did not believe that the Viet Cong could mobilize such a large number of personnel and unleash such fierce attacks in such close coordination and high intensity.'"[25] For the two years prior to Tet Mau Than, the United States always said that "the enemy's morale had been shaken."[26] Such confidence was belied by the secrecy and surprise of Tet Mau Than. This was impossible for the enemy to understand. And even when events had completely unfolded, their surprise still continued.

Tet Mau Than was a period of extremely intense fighting in both the cities and their outlying areas. The repeated and sustained attacks and counterattacks caused more losses to both sides than in any previous period of the war. According to enemy statistics, which were presumably lower than the actual figures, in February and March alone, U.S. forces suffered 24,013 casualties [sic] and lost

552 aircraft and a large number of warehouses and war material. As for the puppet army, a report by Westmoreland recognized that it had been weakened by casualties and desertions during the attacks. As for our side, we also sustained the biggest losses in military and political forces, especially the high-ranking and local cadres who, as demonstrated throughout our war and revolution, were always those who marched ahead of the masses at the most critical times and in the most dangerous places. These losses, both in troop strength and materiel, caused us untold difficulties in coping with the enemy's frenzied counterattacks and rapid pacification activities in the 1969–70 period when the Vietnamization policy was put in place. In fact, we had great trouble resupplying our forces in time, while the U.S. and Saigon reinforcements were huge and swift. The enemy took advantage of this period to mount continuous attacks, pushing us away from the cities and driving our regular army to the border areas. We also lost control of many rural areas, where our bases in the villages were severely disrupted. With this momentum, the enemy thought that it could push on and destroy us completely by widening the war to Laos to cut off the Truong Son trail[27] at Route 9 in southern Laos, overthrowing Sihanouk to expand the war to Cambodia to seal off our transit route from the Sihanoukville Port, and at the same time dragging the peace talks in Paris to a dead end. It was thus an extremely difficult situation in which we seemed to be on the decline. Not a few people, who judged things by their appearances, jumped to the conclusion that Tet Mau Than was a failure. Even a number of cadres of various ranks, who were faced with the enemy's intense counterattacks and its pacification operations and Phoenix program on the battlefield after Tet Mau Than, were not aware of the extent of our victory and doubted the explanations from the higher command. Only in times like these could we see clearly the firmness and consistency of our leadership at all levels and how they helped change the course of each battle and the whole war. However, even when the revolutionary forces had regained their strength and moved forward in 1971–72, to the signing of the Paris Agreement, and even after our total victory in 1975, some people still harbored naive thoughts that:

• we failed militarily but won politically during the 1968 General Offensive–General Uprising.
• the U.S.-puppet forces won militarily but were defeated psychologically, and that led to their political defeat.

Some people even believed the American hawks' smug arguments that we had won in Washington and not on the battlefield. This meant that Washington was forced to withdraw due to its internal conflicts and psychological panic, and not because of an impossible Vietnamese victory over an overwhelmingly rich and strong United States. What an example of blind xenophilia. How could one accept the argument that we were crushed on the battlefield, beaten to rags and tatters, and then all of a sudden handed a psychological and political victory by an enemy—the chieftain of all imperialist forces—who was paralyzed by its own frustration and internal splits and who graciously bestowed this glorious victory on us? In fact, there is never an easy "political" victory won by the grace of Heaven or through an enemy's mercy without first having to shed blood and scatter bones on the battlefield, especially in a big war such as ours.

Let us take a closer look at the enemy in order to understand ourselves better. On February 12, General Westmoreland, a man of constant optimism who always fed the U.S. president rosy reports about the war, hastily reported to the Joint Chiefs of Staff and the secretary of defense that "as of February 11, 1968 Military Assistance Command, Vietnam (MACV) reports that attacks have taken place on 34 provincial capitals, 64 district towns and all of the autonomous cities."[28] General Westmoreland also said that the enemy was able to accomplish that while "committing only 20 to 25 percent of his North Vietnamese forces . . . as gap fillers where VC strength was apparently not adequate to carry out his initial thrust on the cities and towns."[29] The United States shifted its strategy from "search and destroy" to "clear and hold," from escalating the war to de-escalating it, from halting the air war over the North to sitting down at the peace talks. This was not the result of psychological or political pressure, or due to moments of frustration on the part of experienced and seasoned U.S. leaders. By the end of February, back from Saigon where he was sent on an inspection tour of the battlefield and discussions with Westmoreland, General Wheeler, Chairman of the Joint Chiefs of Staff, reported his findings to the president and proposed that the war be widened with an additional 206,756 troops, to be sent during the last six months of 1968. This would bring the strength of the U.S. force in Vietnam to its peak of 731,756 troops. The president asked Clark Clifford, his new secretary of defense, to form a group of senior advisers to study U.S. policy. This group became embroiled in intense debates with the military. The Pentagon study showed that the debates were intense and lasted for three weeks. The memorandum prepared by the Clifford group proposed to do " 'a little bit more of the same' to stabilize the military situation, plus a level of mobilization in order to be prepared to meet any further deterioration in the ground situation."[30] However, President Johnson was forced to seek a new strategy and a new road to peace.

In their writings on the events in February and March of 1968, Pentagon analysts concluded that the Tet General Offensive had finally forced President Johnson to accept the advice of his civilian advisers and the intelligence community that he had persisted too long in "seeking a military victory." The analysts wrote,

> In March of 1968, the choice had become clear-cut. The price for military victory had increased vastly and there was no assurance that it will not grow again in the future. There were also strong indications that large and growing

elements of the American public had begun to believe that the costs had already reached unacceptable levels and would strongly protest a large increase in that cost.[31]

The political reality that faced President Johnson was that "more of the same" in South Vietnam, with an increased commitment of American lives and money and its consequent impact on the country, accompanied by no guarantee of military victory in the near future, had become unacceptable to these elements of the American public. The optimistic military reports of the progress in the war no longer rang true after the shock of the Tet Offensive. Thus the president's decision to seek a new strategy and a new road to peace. . . .[32]"

In his *Anatomy of a War*, the well-known American historian Gabriel Kolko wrote,

> The 1968 Tet Offensive was the most important and most complicated development of the Vietnam War. . . . [I]t nonetheless came as a shock. . . . It was this new American readiness to limit its commitments and later partially to disengage . . . that was the major outcome of the Tet offensive. . . . Tet revealed that it was time to focus on the limits of the system. To have pursued the scale of escalation to an even higher level would have wreaked an untold amount of damage on America's economic position at home and abroad, on its military power elsewhere, and on its political life—a price scarcely any serious person proposed to pay. The offensive brought these processes to a head, and from this viewpoint the Revolution had attained a decisive advantage in its overall struggle.[33]

Thus, the top U.S. leaders as well as objective American historians shared a clear-cut evaluation of Tet Mau Than.

The change in U.S. strategy in South Vietnam, the halt in its air war against the North, and its agreement to sit down for peace talks were in fact decided in March 1968, that is, after the first phase of Tet Mau Than. But only after a period of fierce combat on the battlefield, after the second phase of our assaults on Saigon, and the third phase of our attacks in the countryside, and not until November, did the United States declare a complete halt to the air war and accept the National Liberation Front as a party to the peace talks in Paris. This is quite under-standable. In any war—especially one as big as the one in Vietnam—the outcome of the fighting on the battlefield is the decisive factor for all developments on the political and diplomatic fronts. Military success will determine the extent of political success. One never suffers a military defeat yet wins political victory, nor are diplomatic skills at peace talks independent from the fighting on the battlefield. The end of 1968 and the beginning of 1969 saw the start of the peace talks in Paris, but in the years 1969 through 1970 the enemy thought that they would win on the battlefield, and therefore dragged on the talks, ultimately bringing them to a dead end. But in 1971, the situation on the battlefield again turned to our favor, and in 1972 the U.S.-puppet forces suffered heavy defeats in the South. Then the United States lost the battle of "Dien Bien Phu in the Air"[34] over Hanoi–Hai Phong. Only then were they forced to sign the Paris Agreement. The agreement provided for a cease-fire and the setting up of a tripartite coalition government. However, since the enemy still harbored the stubborn illusion that its "Vietnamization of the war" could succeed, they continued the war in an attempt to scrap the agreement so that Nguyen Van Thieu could rule the South under U.S. control. Therefore, we were compelled to mount the Ho Chi Minh Campaign—the spring 1975 General Offensive–General Uprising—to achieve total victory.

To evaluate any period of history or an enormous event like Tet Mau Than, it is very important that our assessment be based on its concrete and clear-cut results. We cannot be superficial or let ourselves be misled by prejudices.

The General Offensive and Uprising of Tet Mau Than—as it was then called, although the General Uprising was not a success—matched the conditions at the time. Despite the fact that the General Uprising did not take place and power was not turned over to the people, Tet Mau Than was still a great victory, creating the most important strategic turning point of the war, eventually leading us to total victory.

Tet Mau Than in fact shook the enemy's aggresive will to its foundation and put an end to the U.S. dream of achieving "victory" by escalating the war; it awakened the United States to the fact that might, resources, and money have their limits; and it highlighted the conclusion that the United States was not strong enough to force another nation—even a smaller and weaker one—to kneel down and surrender if that nation's desire for independence and freedom was strong.

It also forced the United States to take other actions: shift its strategy from an offensive "search and destroy" to a defensive "clear and hold"; de-escalate the war gradually; adopt the "Vietnamization of the war"; cut back its commitment and gradually bring its troops home to consolidate the U.S. military might that had declined to a dangerously low level; prop up its severely weakened economy; and heal the seriously polarized American body politic.

The United States was forced to drop its conquering club and sit down for peace talks, not only with the socialist North, now a feared and respected opponent, but also with the NLF as one of the four sides in the negotiations, since the latter had proved itself a force of real power on behalf of the people of southern Vietnam and a negotiator of real value. The United States also had to halt completely and unconditionally the air war over the North for the talks to begin.

Tet Mau Than "shifted our revolutionary war onto a new stage, that of decisive victory." Earlier, Uncle Ho and the Political Bureau of the Party Central Committee had decided that since we were not able to defeat both the United States and the puppet forces at the same time, we had to first drive the United

States out, then do away with the puppets to complete our victory. "Knowing both oneself and others" is a trait of the wise and the brave. Tet Mau Than forced the United States to de-escalate and gradually extract itself from the war through the "Vietnamization" process. This created favorable conditions for our successes in the spring of 1975 that eventually led us to total victory in the historic Ho Chi Minh Campaign. Therefore, it is no exaggeration to say that had it not been for Tet Mau Than, "April 30" would not have occurred. In fact, Tet Mau Than opened a new strategic stage, which concluded on April 30, 1975.

The intention to stage the General Offensive–General Uprising to transfer all power into the hands of the people in 1968, at a time when the United States maintained a half-million troops and even had plans to further escalate the war to seek victory, clearly was not in line with Uncle Ho's correct and astute strategic guidance, which was: "First, drive the U.S. out, then topple the puppets." We were not able to simultaneously carry out both segments of the General Offensive–General Uprising. Our inability was determined by the reality of the balance of forces at the time. However, we did stage a campaign with victories that forced the United States to pull out, beginning in 1969, and paved the way for the puppet regime's fall in 1975. In other words, despite the fact that we had set too lofty and unrealistic a goal, our armed forces and people, in response to the Party Political Bureau's appeal, exerted extraordinary efforts, endured all kinds of hardship and sacrifice, courageously overcoming all trials and difficulties, and, as a result, won a decisive victory that created a strategic turning point and paved the way for the next stage of the war—total victory. In that way, our people and armed forces were following the guiding line of Uncle Ho and our Party. It was they, the masses, who made history.

With the above analysis of Tet Mau Than, we now can conclude that the offensive was a tremendous victory, that it ushered us into a decisive phase of our road to victory in the extremely fierce thirty-year war of our heroic people. However, we paid a high price. Tens of thousands of our best cadres and combatants laid down their lives, as did tens of thousands of our fellow countrymen and compatriots in towns and villages. However, without such sacrifices, would such a glorious victory have been possible? The blood shed by our fallen heroes, both combatants and civilians, during Tet Mau Than was of absolute value and worthy of the magnitude of the victory, and will forever be held in gratitude by their children for generations to come. Their sacrifice was valuable not only for Tet Mau Than itself, but also for the entire final stage of the war. It played a decisive role in our total victory on April 30. Whereas in 1968 we fought to drive out the United States, that is, the main enemy, in 1975 we pushed on with the Ho Chi Minh Campaign and toppled the now-abandoned puppet regime, the other enemy. Tet Mau Than therefore provided us with the key to total victory in the war. The Simultaneous Uprisings in Spring 1960, the "Drive America Out" Campaign in Spring 1968, and the "Total Victory" Campaign in Spring 1975 were the three strategic milestones of the war and the three most beautiful springs in the twenty-one years of the Vietnamese people's heroic, fierce, and gloriously triumphant struggle against the United States. They were beacons for national salvation under the leadership of the Vanguard Party of the working class.

There is another major question about Tet Mau Than which I wish to raise only as a topic of discussion in this chapter, and which calls for further in-depth research before it can be fully understood. The question is, Why did victory not accrue to those who had the overwhelming force in battle, and what was the secret of our success and victory?

At that time, our infantry in all of the South was less than 300,000 strong, while the U.S., puppet, and allied forces had more than 1.2 million troops. The ratio was nearly one to five. On top of that, our infantry was supported by just a few lightly armed units, such as engineering, artillery, signal, and transport. Meanwhile, the enemy was backed by a wide variety of armament, had absolute superiority in firepower and mobility, in tanks and other armored vehicles, and wielded total control of the air, sea, inland waterways, land routes, and dense population centers. That is not to mention U.S. forces in the Seventh Fleet and at bases in Japan, as well as contingents from the Philippines and Thailand, which also participated in the war. However, we still held the initiative on the battlefield, both strategically and tactically. We also held the initiative in opening attacks while the U.S.-puppet forces only counterattacked on the defensive. The attackers were lesser in strength, but their will overwhelmed the morale of the numerically superior defenders. The fact that we won and the enemy lost was due to the genius of our military leadership, the superiority of our revolutionary military art, and the combined result of all our splendidly victorious engagements throughout the battle zone, including encounters in which whole units laid down their lives. Certain people must have seen those battles as defeats, and could only see the dark side of death. But in our eyes, these fallen heroes had won. They gave their lives so that life could go on, and it was precisely for that reason that they plunged forward at the enemy with all their hearts and minds. There were units that went into battle from which not a single soldier returned. They can be compared to those patriotic soldiers who used their own bodies to seal up the enemy's firing holes so that their comrades could move forward, who charged into the enemy lines, setting off grenades in their hands, who carried bombs and charged at enemy tanks. They were just like those Soviet pilots who flew their planes into the enemy's during their great war of national defense in World War II. The only difference, if there was any, was between individual heroism on the one hand and collective heroism on the other. If we look at things from the perspective of a typical conventional war where the balance of forces between the two sides decides victory or defeat, we will be left without an answer to the above question. Or else we would think it was all a miracle. The General Offensive–General Uprising of Tet Mau Than was an outstanding example of a revolutionary war combined with armed insurrection. It was in line with the rule of offensive-cum-uprising and uprising-cum-offensive. It was brought about by the combination of military and political struggle, a merging of proselytization, armed force, and the forces of the revolutionary masses, as well as the progressive people around the world—including those in the enemy countries. The military units in this type of revolutionary war were in fact a strong organization of the revolutionary masses and were only one of the forces of the revolutionary masses. The Party-led revolutionary masses also had other forces at their disposal, such as the village militia, the political struggle units (including the long-haired army and the popular forces for multifaceted struggle in urban areas[35]), the proselytization of enemy troops, and those engaged in espionage and sabotage activities within the enemy's ranks. So, it is incorrect to assess the balance of forces according to the alignment of military forces only. Ours was a just war against foreign aggression and a traitorous puppet regime, against brutality and injustice, for national independence and freedom, and for human dignity. The war was thus in tune with the conscience of our time. Our aggregate forces were therefore stronger than those of the enemy, and the difference was hardly determinable by arithmetic calculation. Those who would refute the importance of mass uprisings and insurrections would find themselves thinking according to stereotypes, which is alien to our revolution and to warfare. Lenin, the brilliant leader of the world revolutionary movement, once said,

> There are no miracles in nature or history, but every abrupt turn in history, and this applies to every revolution, presents such a wealth of content, unfolds such unexpected and specific forms of struggle and alignment of forces of the contestants, that to the lay mind there is much that must appear miraculous.[36]

Tet Mau Than was exactly like that.

Notes

1. "Special War" was defined by the Vietnamese revolutionaries as U.S.-sponsored war by local client forces but not direct U.S. intervention. "Tong dong khoi" is translated as "Simultaneous Uprisings."

2. Political Bureau Resolution, December 1967.

3. *The Pentagon Papers*. [In original.]

4. "Local War" refers to the period of the massive introduction of U.S. troops into South Vietnam.

5. The author spends several pages reviewing the failure of the new "search and destroy" strategy of Westmoreland: the Viet Cong withstood successfully the large-scale operations launched by Westmoreland during the two dry seasons of 1965–66 and 1966–67 and continued to mount guerrilla and sometimes regiment and division-size attacks; the air war reached its peak at the end of 1967, both in the South and the North, but came to a stalemate like the ground war. U.S. forces could not seize the initiative, and needed more reinforcements to continue the war. Casualties of the U.S. and Saigon forces were high and victory was not in sight.

6. Senator Mike Gravel, ed., *The Pentagon Papers*, vol. 4 (Boston: Beacon Press, 1971), 428.

7. *"Tong cong kich-tong khoi nghia."*

8. *"Trung Uong cuc"*: Central Office for South Vietnam—the southern branch of the Vietnam Workers' Party Central Committee, which represented the Party and conducted all military and political activities in South Vietnam. Sometimes translated as COSVN.

9. "Tet Mau Than" is thus the term generally used for the "Tet Offensive" (not used by the author). It can also be translated as "Spring 1968" or "Tet 1968," but refers specifically to the first day of the new lunar year. In broader terms, however, Tet Mau Than refers to the entire campaign of the General Offensive and General Uprising that occurred throughout 1968.

10. The B2 theater comprised Southern Central Vietnam and South Vietnam. See Tran Van Tra, "Vietnam: History of the Bulwark B2 Theatre, vol. 5: Concluding the 30-years War," translated by the Foreign Broadcast Information Service (Washington, D.C.: JPRS, Southeast Asia Report, No. 1247, No. 82783, February 2, 1983).

11. *"Don vi biet dong, dac cong,"* or *"cac luc luong biet dong, dac cong."* The latter were special attack units belonging to both the regular and guerrilla forces. They were specially equipped and trained, and were used for attacks on important targets in the enemy's rear, particularly in the nerve centers. *Biet dong* units were usually assigned to densely populated urban areas controlled by the Saigon regime. These terms are sometimes translated as "sappers" or "commandos." Both types of units were highly trained, were used for the most difficult targets, and relied on secrecy and surprise. They attacked bases and other installations. *Biet dong* troops, however, operated mainly in the urban areas. The term "special attack unit" can refer to both types of units.

12. *Hoa Van*: agitation activities among people of Chinese origin.

13. Agence France Presse, *Vietnam: L'Heure decisive. L'Offensive du Tet (fevrier 1968)* (Paris: Robert L'affont, 1968), 94.

14. Ibid., 95.

15. Documents of the Office of the General Staff of the puppet army. [In original.]

16. *Danh boi*: a tactic using the element of surprise to attack enemy forces already engaged in a combat operation, with a view to inflicting as many casualties as possible. As a *danh boi* attack is being concluded (the remaining enemy troops are in deep confusion and suffer hearby losses while newly arrived reinforcements are not yet in a position to deploy effectively and stabilize the situation), new, strong, and repeated attacks (*danh nhoi*) are launched in order to wipe out the remaining enemy forces and the newly arrived reinforcements.

17. *The Pentagon Papers*, vol. 4, 602.

18. "*Binh van*" troops were proselytization of enemy troops. They operated in Saigon-controlled zones.

19. See note 10.

20. Agence France Presse, *Vietnam: L'Heure decisive*, 91.

21. Ibid.

22. *The Pentagon Papers*, vol. 4, 538.

23. *L'offensive generale des Viet Cong au Tet Mau Than 1968*. [In original.]

24. *The Pentagon Papers*, vol. 4, 539.

25. Agence France Presse, *Vietnam: L'Heure decisive*, 87, 91–92.

26. Ibid., 92.

27. The Ho Chi Minh trail.

28. *The Pentagon Papers*, vol. 4, 539.

29. Ibid., 585.

30. Ibid., 603.

31. Ibid., 603.

32. Ibid., 603.

33. Gabriel Kolko, *Anatomy of a War* (New York: Pantheon Books, 1985), 303, 306, 322, 335.

34. The Christmas bombings of 1972.

35. The "long-haired army": female cadres and supporters of the National Liberation Front who lived in the Saigon-controlled zones and organized demonstrations and other propaganda work against the Saigon regime and U.S. army. *"Cac luc luong dau tranh nhieu mat"*: patriotic masses mobilized to wage struggles against the enemy through multiple forms (legal, semilegal, illegal) and in many fields of activity (political, military, economic, and cultural). The "long-haired army" was part of the *luc luong dau tranh nhieu mat* in the cities and countryside.

36. V.I. Lenin, "Letters from Afar, First Letter, The First Stage of the First Revolution," in *Collected Works*, vol. 23. M.S. Levine, Joe Fineberg, et al., trans. (Moscow: Progress Publishers, 1981), 297.

4

Hanoi's Strategy in the Second Indochina War

David W.P. Elliott

As the United States moved toward the momentous 1965 decision to send ground combat troops to Vietnam, the decision makers whose views carried the day felt that while the results were not guaranteed, they could at least control the terms under which the war was fought. This assumption was proved wrong, though it took some time for the realization to sink in. Failure to understand the opponent's strategy was the main cause of this misperception.

Key U.S. decision makers thought that the Vietnamese were carrying out a Chinese-inspired "war of national liberation" and were therefore using Chinese strategic precepts to do so. A desire to exploit an imputed connection with China for propaganda purposes seems to have diminished the U.S. impulse to take a closer look at what the Vietnamese actually said about their strategic intentions, often in widely publicized open writings. Another American conviction was that in a confrontation between a superpower and a third world state, the superpower would naturally dictate the terms under which the war was fought and shape its situational logic. Finally, for much of the war it was felt that communist strategy was based on the aim of winning a clear-cut military victory. The logic of this position was that denial of victory to Hanoi would mean victory for the United States. All of these assumptions proved erroneous.

At the center of the 1965 debate in Washington over Hanoi's intentions was the assertion of then Secretary of Defense Robert MacNamara and General Westmoreland that Hanoi was moving into the "Third Stage" of Maoist guerrilla warfare, massing regular troops for set piece battles to terminate the conflict. Most of President Johnson's civilian advisers rejected this claim, though in the end they acknowledged that the military situation could not be salvaged without direct U.S. military intervention. The civilian dissenters did not reject the view that Hanoi was following a Maoist blueprint, but disagreed on the degree to which the strategic plan had been implemented. Both sides were mistaken.

Although in the First Indochina War against the French the Viet Minh had employed a version of the Maoist model of guerrilla war, they abandoned it and by 1961 had moved to a very different strategy which aimed at countering the new U.S. "flexible response" doctrine of President Kennedy. Just as "flexible response" required a capability of meeting the enemy at various levels of force, the Vietnamese response centered on devising a strategy to cope with each scale of escalation that the United States could employ in Vietnam. "Coping" did not require the direct military defeat of U.S. forces but simply preventing them from achieving a decisive outcome at each level of escalation. In so doing, Hanoi could deny the United States its objective and raise the costs of conflict by creating a strategic stalemate that would ultimately exhaust the resources, patience, and political capital of its adversary.

At times U.S. strategy mirrored that of Vietnam, but was unable to achieve the same results with that strategy. During the pre-1965 "advisory" phase of the war General Westmoreland's predecessor nurtured the hope of being able to bring the war to a decisive termination by a "spasm" of violence in which every military unit of the Saigon government would attack simultaneously throughout the country, a curious preview of the 1968 Tet Offensive but with the roles reversed. Given the thinking that this approach represented, it was only natural that many Americans concluded that the Tet Offensive was a once- and-for-all final effort by Hanoi to bring the war to a close which, by its military failure, signaled the beginning of the end for the revolutionary side. As the subsequent discussion of Hanoi's strategy suggests, the ultimate purposes of the Tet Offensive were somewhat different.

Another example of parallel thinking between the United States and Hanoi was the declared U.S. objective in intervening in 1965. Success or "victory" was defined as avoiding defeat. As the *Pentagon Papers* commented, "the definition of 'win,' i.e. 'succeed in demonstrating to the VC that they cannot win,' indicates the assumption upon which the conduct of the war was to rest—that the VC would be convinced in some meaningful sense that they were not going to win and that they would then rationally choose less violent methods of seeking their goals."[1] Four years later in a celebrated essay on Vietnam in *Foreign Affairs*, Henry Kissinger ruefully concluded that "the guerrilla wins if he does not lose," reversing the 1965 logic of American strategy. This insight succinctly, if belatedly, encapsulated the concept underlying Vietnamese revolutionary strategy in the Second Indochina War.

One of the crucial tasks of scholarship on the Vietnam War is to unite what have up to now been separate tracks in the study of this conflict. The works on Hanoi's strategy have usually been written by and for specialists on Vietnam, and have only infrequently reached out to diplomatic historians who study U.S. decision making in the Vietnam conflict. Vietnam's own writings on the history of the conflict have generally been accessible only to specialists on Vietnam. As the conference at Columbia convincingly demonstrated, these three perspectives, while valuable on their own terms, are even more significant when they are brought together and analyzed in relation to each other.

An Overview of the Development of Vietnamese Strategic Thinking

During the war against the French (1946–54), Vietnamese strategy was initially guided by a three-phase scheme borrowed from the Chinese and further refined, notably in the writings of Truong Chinh. This model envisaged three phases of revolutionary war starting from the strategic defensive, building bases in the countryside, achieving a state of strategic parity or equilibrium and, finally, surrounding the cities and advancing to a "general counteroffensive." Despite the fact that many Western writers on revolutionary war asserted that this scheme carried over into what shall be referred to here as the Vietnam War (1954–75), a major change of concept had in fact taken place. When and why this happened is a key issue of the historiography of the war.[2]

In part, the abandonment of the Maoist three-phase scheme was the result of an inherent flaw recognized during the war against the French when the Vietnamese forces prematurely moved to phase three, had to de-escalate, and were faced with the problem of explaining how a dialectical and inevitable progress through stages could be reversed. If the general counteroffensive failed it would be demoralizing to go back to the second phase of strategic equilibrium, which would seem to be the only logical option in this approach. More fundamental, perhaps, was the fact that the nature of the task in the Vietnam War had changed from the military defeat of an already entrenched colonial ruler to the prevention of the United States from following in their footsteps. The best strategy was obviously one that would forestall deeper American involvement, if at all possible.

Thus the guiding concept changed from one that was predominantly offensive and military to a primarily defensive and psychological strategy. Rather than culminating in an apocalyptic counteroffensive shattering the enemy's military forces, the purpose of military action in the anti-American strategy would be to deter and dissuade the United States from deeper involvement and to exhaust the strategic options open to Washington—a kind of strategic judo. This strategy would not rely on the direct military defeat of the United States, but rather would erode the very foundations of American policy and render U.S. military action inconclusive.

It is ironic that the Vietnam War ended with precisely the apocalypse that had been envisaged by the Maoist general counteroffensive scheme, with tanks crashing through the gates of the Presidential Palace in Saigon and the stunning collapse of the Saigon armed forces. This was an outcome that was compatible with some elements of Vietnamese strategy, notably the General Offensive, but had not really been envisaged by the revolutionary leaders, who were still in a process of redefining their strategy after the departure of the American ground troops. This period from 1973 to 1975 is one of the most interesting but least understood phases of the war with respect to strategic objectives and planning, and would greatly benefit from any insight that Hanoi strategists and historians could provide.

The evolution of Vietnamese strategy in the post-1954 period was a gradual process of accretion of new thinking and new strategic precepts, making it difficult to date the point at which a fully formulated version of an "anti-American strategy" was in place. Its origins roughly coincided with the new Kennedy administration's more aggressive approach toward Vietnam. Certainly, by the end of the Ngo Dinh Diem era the main outlines of such a strategy were discernible.

Replacing the three phases of the Maoist concept, three types of warfare or three strategic options open to the United States were envisaged. By relying on a proxy or client Vietnamese government, the United States could obtain its objectives at relatively low cost. This was the Special War (*chien tranh dac biet*) option. If it failed, the United States would face the choice of either acknowledging defeat or introducing its own troops. This escalation of the conflict was termed Limited War (*chien tranh cuc bo*), a Korean-type intervention by U.S. troops which would be limited to the territory of South Vietnam. If this too failed, Washington would again be confronted with a choice between escalation and defeat. Expanding the war beyond the confines of South Vietnam would raise the prospect of Chinese or even Soviet intervention and, of course, expanded infiltration of North Vietnamese troops, further complicating American calculations and raising the costs of attaining their objectives.

In essence, this strategy was designed to force a choice between disengagement and escalation on the United States, and was based on the assumption that these were the only strategic options open to the United States. If these options were all eliminated, the strategy would succeed. Of course, the strategy would be most successful if the United States could be convinced or compelled to choose disengagement at a low level of involvement. As it turned out, the war passed through the Special War and Limited War phases, escalating to a level of unprecedented devastation before President Johnson finally acknowledged that the costs of further escalation were unacceptable.

The Strategic Model

Any model of conflict strategy must start with a definition of the main problem. This generally means a clear definition of the primary enemy who will be the main target of the strategy. Almost all other aspects of strategy flow logically from this determination: the mix of military and political approaches, the correct united front strategy to build the most effective coalition against the enemy, the military methods to be employed, and the role of diplomacy. This seems both obvious and simple. But while the United States was the clear main enemy for most of the period under consideration, it was not always clear what the position of the Saigon government and army was.

For much of the Second Indochina War, the Saigon regime was treated as an appendage of the United States, though there were frequent shifts in policy on how much attention should be diverted from the Americans to deal with Saigon. As will be discussed below, the strategic model based on the assumption that the United States was the main enemy dictated an approach that was as much political and psychological as military, and not based on the necessity of conclusively defeating the opponent on the battlefield. This concentration on the United States also appears to have created problems for Hanoi's planners following the departure of U.S. troops.

The fundamental objective of the strategic model used by Hanoi in the Second Indochina War was to understand the options open to the United States for maintaining its interests in South Vietnam and formulate ways of eliminating these options. The emphasis was not on a military defeat of the United States but, rather, on exhausting the strategic possibilities open to it. The key was to defeat the "aggressive will" (*y chi xam luoc*) of the United States—a psychological objective more than a military one.

An important requirement for devising a response to the American intervention was to formulate a strategic model that would not rely on or emphasize a favorable balance of force—at least in straight numerical terms. Such a favorable balance of force had been implicit in the "three-phase model" and was a logical prerequisite for breaking out of the strategic equilibrium stage and moving on to the general counteroffensive. Even though superiority in numbers was not a stated criterion of the three-phase view and even though balance of forces could be calculated by factoring in political elements of strength to balance the quantitative gap in numbers and qualitative gap in weapons, it would clearly be preferable to have a concept that would not highlight the ways in which the United States and its allies were superior to the revolutionary forces. Far better, instead, to focus on their weaknesses and vulnerabilities.

In the "three types of war" or "three-option" view, there were only three ways the United States could attain its goals in Vietnam. First was Special War, by working through the Saigon government and its armed forces. This would clearly be the preferable option in terms of cost and avoidance of direct involvement. If this did not work, two options remained. In the event the Saigon regime proved ineffective or was in danger of collapse the United States might have to intervene directly with its own troops, but restricting its involvement within the territory of South Vietnam in a Limited War. If Limited War did not succeed, a final option existed: widening the war beyond the territory of South Vietnam in a General War, with the risk of expanded North Vietnamese, Chinese, or even Soviet involvement.

A primary goal of political and military action was to force the United States to recognize the unviability of each of these options, and force a choice between de-escalation leading to eventual withdrawal, on the one hand, and escalation, which was a more costly and risky option, on the other. Unlike the Maoist "three-phase" strategy, which was specifically designed to move from defense to offense and which assumed that the ability to control the outcome of the conflict would come from imposing one's will on the other side, this "three types of war" or "three-options" concept relied primarily on frustrating the offensive capabilities of the other side and inducing a state of psychological exhaustion, clearly a more reactive strategy even at the most intense levels of conflict.

The highest level of this model, then, is the reactive orientation just described. The means to achieve this are a combination of military and political pressures. Diplomacy must go hand in hand with the efforts to deny success in South Vietnam itself. Within South Vietnam, a proper balance must be struck between political and military activity within each geostrategic region. The mountain-forest regions (*rung nui*) were suitable for large military units and a predominantly military approach. Military and political action were to be pursued simultaneously in the populated delta countryside, while the cities were suitable for political action. Each strategic region supported the others. The threat of the big units in the mountains relieved pressure from the guerrillas in the delta, who in turn recruited and sent supplies to the big units. Both regions supported a base structure and zone of control which isolated the cities and allowed political activities to be more effective there. The "three points of attack" (*ba mui giap cong*) of military action, political action, and military proselytizing to weaken the morale of the Saigon army reflect this attempt to coordinate different aspects of revolutionary struggle. A key element of revolutionary strategy, the united front, may be considered a subcategory of the political element of the "three points of attack."

There should also be an overall balance between the "three types of forces"—main force, local force, and guerrilla units. The big units would cast an umbrella of security over the bases of the smaller units which, in turn, could operate in areas too constricted or exposed for the big concentrated units. Both types of force protected the activities of the political cadres. With the significant exception of a period in 1964 and early 1965, when the main forces were expanded at the expense of the other two, strenuous efforts were devoted toward maintaining this balance, until the Tet Offensive when the southern guerrilla forces were decimated. The Spring Offensive of 1972 was, in part, designed to restore this balance, and the strategy prior to the realization in late 1974 that the war might be won by a big-unit offensive also seems to have been predicated on restoring the guerrilla movement in the southern deltas to play their part along with the big northern units.

With a predilection for triangular symmetry, the strategic model might be summarized as follows:

Three types of war
Three strategic zones
Three "points of attack"
Three types of forces

Methods of calculating balance of forces and their implications are an essential feature of any strategic model. During the Second Indochina War there was much discussion about the balance of forces within the context of the "three-option model." Much of this discussion emphasized ways in which the political disparity in strength favoring the revolutionary side, or the general flow of strategic momentum, compensated for any disparity in numbers and weapons. But the logic of the "three-options" theory led to an emphasis on creating a stalemate, not a military victory through achieving superior force. Calculations of the military balance became a guiding element in strategy at only two points of the revolution. The first was following the overthrow of Ngo Dinh Diem in 1963, and the second was the final phase of the conflict in late 1974 and early 1975.

A final point about the model of revolutionary strategy is that it should contain guidelines for determining when the favorable strategic moment (*thoi co chien luoc*) has arrived. In the "three-phase model" this was presumably when the balance of forces (especially military force) tilted in favor of the revolutionary side. In the "three-options" model the guidelines for determining the propitious strategic moment do not seem to be built into the schema. Perhaps this accounts for the fact that many of the questions about Hanoi's strategy revolve around how and why these strategic opportunities were identified. It also is related to the problem of determining when a long-term strategy of protracted struggle is preferable and when it is advantageous to switch to maximum military effort, another much debated element of Vietnamese strategy during the war.

The General Offensive and Uprising

One crucial element of Vietnamese strategic thinking remained constant during the shift from "three phases" to "three types of war," the General Offensive and Uprising. But the actual role this concept played during the post-1960 period varied greatly, and its relationship to the various "triangles" of the model are unclear. It was first put in the background during 1961–62 when the stress in strategic thinking was on an interim coalition-neutralization solution, then pushed aside again in the rush to win a decisive military victory over Saigon's army in 1964–65, and further deferred while the immediate problem of responding to direct U.S. intervention was solved.

The Tet Offensive was thought by General Westmoreland and others to be a last-gasp effort, because it billed itself as a General Offensive and Uprising, logically the final stage of revolutionary war. The offensive was beaten back and the uprising did not take place in the cities, as General Tra comments, because of the fierce battles taking place in the streets. (It should be noted that something approximating an uprising did take place in some rural areas of the Mekong Delta during the first month of the Tet Offensive when Saigon forces were forced to evacuate large portions of the countryside).

Although this was a logical inference, given the previous stress on the General Offensive and Uprising and the use of the term during Tet 1968, the presence of U.S. troops fundamentally altered the situation. Under this circumstance, a General Offensive and Uprising could not aim at terminating the conflict, but only altering the context in which the war was fought. The complexities of applying a concept designed to deal with the internal opposition to an intervention by an external superpower probably accounts for some of the ambiguity in the way the General Offensive and Uprising was defined and interpreted during the long and shifting course of the war.

Because the term "General Offensive and Uprising" often conjures up the image of an apocalyptic grand finale to the Maoist "Third Stage," it is important to note that the Vietnamese thought that the concept of the General Offensive and Uprising was quite different from the Chinese model. The introduction to Le Duan's writings on revolutionary strategy quotes him as saying:

> The revolution in the South will not follow the path of protracted armed struggle, surrounding the cities by the countryside and advancing to the liberation of the entire country by using military forces as China did, but will follow a Vietnamese path. That means there will be partial uprisings and establishment of base areas, and there will be a guerrilla war leading to a general uprising which will primarily use political force in coordination with armed forces to grasp political power in the hands of the people.[3]

As the editors of Le Duan's writings note, this early stress on the general uprising should not be interpreted as a solely political mass movement like the 1945 August Revolution, but had to be based on military strength as well. "The general uprising absolutely must be coordinated with the general offensive. . . .The general uprising cannot possibly succeed if the enemy hasn't been militarily defeated and can still use instruments of violence to oppose the revolution."[4] This is possibly an allusion to the experience of the Tet Offensive.

The General Offensive and Uprising resurfaced in Le Duan's writings of 1967 in anticipation of the Tet Offensive, but the broad range of possible situations and definitions of the concept that he offered rendered it a less than precise guide for strategic planning. Following the Tet Offensive the General Offensive and Uprising appears to have receded in prominence. During the Spring 1972 Offensive the stress was on the military situation in the countryside. After 1973 the focus was on coping with the immediate problems of the cease-fire. Perhaps the General Offensive and Uprising was revived in the planning of 1974, but the uprising element of this concept was obviated by the swift and conclusive military victory of 1975. All this leaves unclear the role that this venerable concept actually played in Vietnamese strategic thinking during the Second Indochina War.

What is evident, however, is that the General Offensive and Uprising could only be conclusive if it involved just the two Vietnamese parties to the conflict. As the analyses of the Tet Offensive made clear, it was not intended to directly sweep away the U.S. forces, but rather shake the foundation on which U.S. intervention rested, the Saigon government.

Evolution of the Strategic Model

The origins of the "three-option" model may be traced to the Kennedy strategy of "flexible response."[5] At the beginning of the insurgency, Hanoi and the revolutionaries in the South had several problems. First was the "peaceful coexistence line" of the Soviet Union, which posed a constraint on the extent to which Vietnam could mount an armed challenge to American interests in the region. Although Hanoi reluctantly acceded to southern pressure to allow limited armed activity, this remained an issue in the initial phase of the conflict, and was linked to a second problem: striking a proper balance between political and military pressure on the Saigon government. There was also a question of how to overcome a very unfavorable balance of forces. Finally there was the question of the extent to which revolutionary strategy should be aimed primarily at the local enemy, the Saigon government, and how much at the international aspect of the problem, the United States.

These problems were not all resolved simultaneously. Although it lies beyond the scope of this essay to trace the exact evolution of the strategic model within which the Tet Offensive was formulated, some stages of development may be suggested. The first was the resolution of the balance between political and military action. This was a complex process, and was the subject of much debate within the party. Following the decision in 1959 to authorize armed struggle in self-defense, the debate intensified as the movement grew. As William Duiker's careful study of revolutionary strategy has shown, there was a tendency among southern revolutionaries in 1961–62 to place their focus on political struggle, because in their view this was the most vulnerable dimension of the Diem regime. Even after the Kennedy administration stepped up its military assistance to South Vietnam, the party cautioned against a predominantly military response. As Duiker notes, the party concluded that a "mature revolutionary situation did not yet exist in South Vietnam."[6]

As a result of the unfavorable military balance of force that existed at the time, the party focused on how it could neutralize its opponent's strengths while building up its own forces. The Chinese model of protracted struggle was an obvious candidate, and had been used against the French. It was, however, rejected. In a letter to Nguyen Van Linh in February 1961, Le Duan noted that after the initial success of the insurgency, "thanks to armed activities, there arose the view that the revolution in the South should progress according to the laws of armed struggle, surrounding the cities in the countryside as in China." Rejecting this approach, Le Duan said, "I have reminded you that you comrades must be patient and take the direction of relying primarily on political forces and political struggle to advance to the general uprising, while at the same time *expanding the bases and going all out to build up military forces to push the revolution ahead*."[7] His analysis made it clear that the unfavorable military balance would take some time to overcome.

Despite the political weakness of the Diem administration, Saigon was still a formidable military opponent, supported by the resources of the United States. Although revolutionary propaganda treated Saigon and the United States as a single entity, "My-Diem" (the "U.S.-Diem clique") they were faced with the problem of minimizing the extent of U.S. involvement while maximizing the pressures on Saigon. Duiker writes that the

> key to success would be the ability of the party's forces in the South to bring Saigon to the point of collapse without at the same time provoking Washington to increase the level of U.S. involvement in South Vietnam, or even take the war to the North. For this reason a combination of political struggle with low-level guerrilla warfare was considered most appropriate. The objective would be not to inflict a total defeat on the enemy, but to create a "no-win" situation and lead Washington to accept a political settlement and the formation of a coalition government including the NLF in Saigon.[8]

The role that diplomacy and coalition government played in early revolutionary strategy has generated debate over the sincerity of Hanoi in offering a compromise solution, and the role of the National Liberation Front (NLF) in the revolutionary struggle.[9] Whatever Hanoi's estimate of the durability of a coalition solution, it was an early indication of a mode of strategic thinking that was mainly focused on how to exploit the vulnerabilities of a stronger opponent, rather than relying mainly on building up sufficient military strength to dictate the outcome.

A characteristic of Hanoi's strategic thinking is a reliance on analyzing the logic of a strategic position, and refining it into scenarios of action. The key assumption is that the situational logic constrains the opponent and limits his possibilities, and that strategy should be directed toward exploiting the contradictions of the opponent's position. Revolutionary strategy will be tailored to this goal and is, in this sense, reactive—dependent on the actual or potential actions of the opponent. "Resolution 9," the new strategic guidance from Hanoi following the overthrow of Ngo Dinh Diem in 1963, is perhaps the most comprehensive example of the categories of revolutionary strategy discussed in this essay, and a very good example of the use of scenarios in strategic planning. Even in the post-1975 era, the interviews with Foreign Minister Thach on diplomatic problems often contain lengthy analyses of possible scenarios or situational conditions, with the implication that Vietnam will adapt its response to whatever scenario its diplomatic antagonists select.

Hanoi's "three-option" strategy was a response to the Kennedy administration's flexible response strategy, though it was not fully formulated until the post-1963 crisis and the escalation of U.S. involvement brought on by the weakness of a succession of caretaker Saigon governments. In another letter to Nguyen Van Linh in South Vietnam dated July 1962, Le Duan noted the new U.S. approach. "At present, in order to cope with the forces of revolution, they have posited three types of war: all out war (*chien tranh tong luc*), Limited War (*chien tranh cuc bo*), and counter-guerrilla warfare to repress the national liberation movements, which they call Special War (*chien tranh dac biet*).[10]

Le Duan commented on internal differences among American leaders on the willingness to resort to war and added that the scale and intensity of the war in South Vietnam would not depend only on the intentions of the United States but also on the development of revolutionary war throughout the world. He further mentioned that the interests of the entire socialist world in preserving the peace would have to be taken into account even while Vietnam struggled to achieve its own goals.[11] As time went on, the broader international factors, while still significant, played a less prominent role in Vietnam's strategic calculation, as it became more and more focused on the specific and immediate actions of the United States.

Hanoi's concern during the Kennedy years was how to counter the U.S. strategy of Special War. The obvious remedy was to undermine the instrument of this policy, the Saigon government. In this regard, the battle of Ap Bac was perceived as a major strategic turning point, offering the prospect that the southern revolutionaries could militarily defeat the Saigon government if the United States did not intervene.

Strategic Turning Points in the Conflict

Since Hanoi's strategy was designed to progressively shut off all avenues of victory to its opponent, it necessarily concentrated on doing everything possible to demonstrate the futility of each policy option. This in turn helps explain why Hanoi gave so much prominence to particular battles that they regarded as symbolic turning points in the war. They hoped to convince their opponents that the current policy was leading nowhere, and force a reevaluation.

Because of the importance of impressing the lessons of these turning points on their opponents, Hanoi regarded the military battles that were the signposts of these critical strategic junctures more in terms of their political and educational significance than in terms of their direct or lasting impact on the military balance of forces. This does not, of course, mean that the military efforts were regarded as secondary. They were indispensable. Without them the political point could not be made. But in the end the ultimate strategic significance of these pivotal battles went far beyond their immediate military results.

The Ap Bac battle in early 1963 showed that the revolutionaries could cope with heliborne troop assaults and were capable of standing up to Saigon's main forces, and was viewed by Hanoi as the beginning of the end for Special War, since it showed they could not be militarily defeated by the Saigon army. At the Binh Gia battle at the end of 1964, several regiments of the ARVN (Army of the Republic of South Vietnam) were badly mauled, demonstrating that it was only a matter of time before Saigon's forces were militarily defeated, a conclusion that was soon shared by Washington as well.

In 1968 the Tet Offensive marked the failure of Limited War, the option of winning by direct U.S. military victory within South Vietnam, and forced the choice of withdrawal or further escalation of the war beyond the boundaries of South Vietnam, with the attendant risks and costs that President Johnson had sought to avoid. The 1972 Spring Offensive was regarded by Hanoi as demonstrating the failure of "Vietnamization."

Closer examination of some of these turning points can serve both to illustrate how Vietnam's strategic model worked and to raise some unanswered historiographical questions has well. Three episodes in particular merit further discussion. One is the reaction of Hanoi to the collapse of the Diem government in 1963 and the subsequent U.S. decision to send ground forces to Vietnam. A second is the Tet Offensive. Third, Hanoi's response to the post-1973 period following the U.S. withdrawal of troops also raises some intriguing questions.

Following the battle of Ap Bac in January 1963 the military dimension of Hanoi's strategy became more prominent. One reason was that the United States had not responded to offers to settle the war politically through a coalition-neutralization formula. It thus became imperative to demonstrate that the alternative of Special War would not work. The political instability of the Diem government in the urban areas offered military opportunities as well, as demoralization of Saigon's forces reached the countryside. William Turley's authoritative account of the Second Indochina War notes that it was at this juncture that:

> To equip COSVN for the coming armed struggle, the Central Committee assigned another member, Lieutenant General Tran Van Tra in 1963. A native of Quang Ngai province and a party member since 1938, Tra had been appointed commander and political officer of the Saigon Gia-Dinh special zone as well as southern regional commander in 1950. He had regrouped to the north in 1954, became a deputy chief of the PAVN general staff in 1955, and was said by defectors to have gone abroad for training. Taking over as the head of COSVN's Central Military Committee in 1963 Tra began to organize a command staff for the lower half of the south (or B2) that fell under COSVN's jurisdiction.[12]

Turley's account also remarks on the arrival in the South in 1964 of two higher ranking generals, Nguyen Chi Thanh and Tran Do, with the mission of implementing a new strategy which would take into account a new situation.[13]

After the overthrow of President Diem in November 1963, a great opportunity opened up to the revolutionary side, but one that also entailed great risks. They could push ahead and escalate the military struggle, but the risks were (1) that the United States would be forced to intervene by the rapid deterioration of the situation, and (2) that the taxation and conscription necessary to intensify the military struggle would have adverse political effects over the long term. Resolution 9 of the Lao Dong Party Central Committee meeting in December 1963 specifically addressed both the dangers and the opportunities. "We have sufficient conditions to quickly change the balance of forces in our favor," it said. Saigon's weaknesses "are obvious and have increased after the battle of Ap Bac, especially after the overthrow of Diem's regime. A strong development of the Revolution will cause many more troubles for the enemy and bring about a quicker disorganization of this armed forces and government. *The Revolution in SVN will inevitably evolve into a General Offensive and Uprising to achieve the complete victory*" (italics in original).

In the event the United States intervened directly, this scenario would not apply. The document said that in this case the revolution in Vietnam will meet more difficulties and the struggle will be harder. In this case the revolution might have to go through a period featuring "complex forms and methods" of struggle before victory is attained—in Duiker's view "an obvious allusion to the possibility of a negotiated settlement."[14] The General Offensive and Uprising and final victory would be reached through an incremental "step-by-step" process. Complete victory would have to be preceded by a "transitional period" of uncertain duration.

Even though this discouraging possibility was discussed, Resolution 9 concluded that even if the United States intervened, they would be entering the conflict on the unstable foundation of the Saigon government and army and must "still use the henchman's army as the main force." The resolution maintained that history has shown that the South Vietnamese "have the determination, strength and patience to crush any of the U.S. imperialists schemes and plans, and finally force them to withdraw from Vietnam as the French did."[15]

"To many observers," writes Duiker, "Hanoi's decision to escalate was somewhat of a puzzle. Given the risks of U.S. intervention and the progressive disintegration of the GVN, why did the party feel compelled to take the gamble?"[16] His answer is twofold. First there were the lessons of Vietnamese revolutionary history on the importance of armed struggle. But beyond this, Duiker argues, was a feeling by Hanoi that if Washington was faced with a sudden and irreversible deterioration of the situation in South Vietnam, it might decide (as it had done in the case of China) that intervention could not succeed. "Consequently, a determined effort to overturn or at least seriously weaken the Saigon regime in a relatively short time was vital."[17]

As in the Tet Offensive of 1968, Hanoi wanted to push the situation forward to the point that their opponent would be compelled to make a decision. The calculated risk was that it would produce a decision not to intervene. This proved to be wrong. In fact, Hanoi's decision to escalate produced the opposite and unwanted result of U.S. intervention. Once again, however, it was not a question of moving to a Maoist "Third Stage" that underlay this decision. It was, rather, an attempt to shape the situational context and influence the course of action of an adversary—that is, the military escalation of 1964–65 was aimed as much at Washington as at Saigon.

In the same way, the subsequent Tet Offensive of 1968 was aimed more at Washington than Saigon, in the sense that it hoped to compel a decision by the United States to withdraw and negotiate. But as will be argued below, the Tet Offensive was not calculated by Hanoi simply to create a propaganda splash aimed at panicking the U.S. public, any more than the military offensive of 1964–65 was a mere exercise in psychological warfare. Still, there were some real costs attached to this 1964–65 escalation. It unbalanced the relationship between main force and guerrilla units and between the Mekong Delta and other strategic zones of South Vietnam and had the political costs noted above.[18] For example, Le Duan wrote, "I am not clear whether the level of contribution of the people in Nam Bo is high or low, but in Region V it appears as though the troop support tax is heavy. . . . [I]f we demand the people to contribute excessively I fear that the masses will not have enough strength to hold out for the long term."[19]

While the decision to escalate the military struggle in 1964–65 is consistent with the main features of the strategic model, especially the desire to create turning points, many questions remain. This discussion has not, for example, dealt with the complex international situation and Vietnam's response to the Sino-Soviet split, which must have been a critical factor in influencing its decisions. This is clearly an area of Vietnam War history that would greatly benefit from a deeper understanding of the factors that underlay Hanoi's decision making during this period.

Response to U.S. Intervention

Perhaps the most difficult and complex period in Vietnamese strategy is the 1965–66 period, when Hanoi's planners tried to assess what the impact of the U.S. intervention would be, and debated the appropriate response to this new turn in the situation. The two elements that make this period difficult to analyze are (1) the fact that Hanoi's own assessment gradually evolved over an extended period of time during which it was apparently unsure of the ultimate extent of the U.S. buildup, and (2) the considerable debate about the most effective response, especially between the planners in Hanoi and the battlefield commanders in the South.

As the Johnson administration debated its course of action during the spring and summer of 1965, the military successes of the revolutionary forces convinced Secretary of Defense McNamara and others that the communists were shifting into a Maoist "Third Stage." Larry Berman observes that:

> The assumption by McNamara, Westmoreland, and the Joint Chiefs of Staff that the Viet Cong were about to abandon their successful guerrilla tactics in favor of more conventional regiment-sized confronations was pivotal to the reasoning of the July 28 decision. According to McNamara "the enemy clearly was moving into the third phase of revolutionary warfare, committing regiments and subsequently divisions to seize and retain territory and destroy the government's troops and eliminate all vestiges of government control."[20]

McNamara's contention was contested by Johnson's key civilian advisers, whose evaluation was summed up by a State Department report that concluded that there were no indications that the communists "have altered their traditional guerrilla strategy and tactics, despite occasional references to the development of conventional warfare in the South," and noted that Ho Chi Minh's stated resolve to go on for twenty years if necessary hardly suggested that "the DRV is pushing for an early victory by shifting to conventional warfare."[21] George Ball asserted that "we have no basis for assuming that the Viet Cong will fight a war on our terms"—a prophetic statement, but not entirely for the reasons that Ball and other critics of McNamara had in mind.[22]

Although the extent to which Hanoi's strategy would rely on small-scale guerrilla operations as opposed to large-unit attacks was an important issue, it did not get at their deeper strategic intent. In fact, McNamara's judgment was in many ways closer to the truth, as William Turley's account of the conflict suggests:

> As 1965 came to a close, the Communists could point to success in pushing Special Forces and CIDG camps out of the Ashau Valley, attacking the Danang airfield and mounting assaults against outposts all over the South. They also succeeded during the fall in grouping PLAF regiments to form two divisions (the 9th and the 5th) in the Mekong Delta and two more (the 3rd and the 2nd) in the midst of populous central provinces. But they had been unable to prevent U.S. forces from gaining a foothold in the highlands or from penetrating some areas where revolutionary forces had previously been safe from attack. The idea of dispersing into guerrilla formations gained support, forcing General Thanh to defend his strategy of preserving the initiative at any price. In a speech to COSVN cadres in mid 1966 Thanh admitted that the United States had only begun to tap its potential, but he maintained that big unit warfare was necessary if the revolution were to remain on the offensive. Dispersing the big units would be tantamount to defeat. "If we want to take the defensive position," he said, "we should withdraw to India."[23]

In short, General Thanh continued to pursue the big-unit approach he had implemented since 1964.

Preventing the revolutionary side from militarily defeating the Saigon forces would deny them an immediate victory, but this did not mean victory for the United States. What the Washington debate did not focus on was the crucial fact that ultimately Hanoi's strategy required only that it deny a decisive military victory to the United States. This was where Hanoi would dictate the terms on which the war would be fought. Whether this was done by guerrilla war or large-unit combat was a secondary question. Moreover, as the previous discussion of revolutionary strategy indicates, both levels of warfare were pursued simultaneously. They were regarded as mutually supporting, even though the exact mix between them was a matter of contentious debate throughout the war.

The issue of whether or not Hanoi had abandoned protracted war came closer to the mark. A protracted war strategy by definition would be one of denying a conclusive victory to an opponent. If an intensified military effort resulted in an attrition that would cripple the capacity to conduct protracted war or to hold on for an extended period of time, it would be self-defeating. But the large-unit tactics adopted by General Thanh were not incompatible with a denial strategy. The point that the Washington debate missed was that the intensification of the war was an attempt to send a message to the United States that if they intervened they would do so on the shaky foundation of a fatally weakened Saigon army and government. The continuation of big-unit battles after the American troops had come in did not, as will be argued below, reflect a strategy aimed at the military defeat of the U.S. forces, although there was clearly a difference of opinion among Communist strategists over the extent to which the major military effort should be directed at the Americans.

Following the introduction of U.S. ground forces in the spring and summer of 1965, Vietnamese strategic writings contained some ambiguity about when the Special War phase had actually ended. Resolution 9 of December 1963 had stated that the United States might keep its commitment at the November 1963 level, or increase it slightly. As a second possibility, also within the framework of Special War, the United States might send in several times the current level of troops and even combine them with some allied forces from SEATO. Even if this major escalation occurred, it would remain a Special War if the United States still relied primarily on the Saigon forces. Only if the United States took on the main burden of the fighting, or brought in SEATO troops along with it on a large scale, would the nature of the conflict shift to Limited War. As late as November 1965, when the scale of U.S. intervention was already clear, Le Duan guardedly concluded that while the United States had become the main combat force, the Saigon army remained "a large force with the very important political and military mission of providing the foundation for the puppet administration at the center and in the localities," and so the war in the south had "both the character of a 'Limited War' and of 'Special War.' "

This was no mere doctrinal quibble, because the clear transition from Special War to Limited War would dictate a greater priority for military efforts against U.S. forces and less attention to the Saigon military forces. Evidence presented by CIA analyst Patrick McGarvey in his book *Visions of Victory* suggests a vigorous debate among revolutionary military strategists on the appropriate response to the American escalation, involving apparent differences over the extent to which U.S. forces should be confronted in large-scale battles. This, in turn, was related to disagreements over the meaning of the changes in the balance of forces that the intervention had caused. Retrospectively, the official military history of the war asserts that Resolution 12 of December 1965 held that "Although the American imperialists have sent hundreds of thousands of expeditionary troops to the South, the balance of forces between us and the enemy still has not undergone great changes."[24]

Faced with a choice between giving priority to fighting U.S. troops or Saigon forces, Hanoi elected to focus on the latter, despite indications that some southern commanders would prefer to concentrate on the Americans. One of the most important and detailed documents on Vietnam's wartime strategic thinking, Le Duan's November 1965 letter to COSVN, the revolutionary headquarters in the South, noted that:

> At present *fighting the Americans and fighting the puppets are both important.* We completely agree with brother Nam Cong [Vo Chi Cong, at the time the party leader in Region V, that is, Central Vietnam] on this point. But we would like to reassert the point that in deploying on the battlefield, we must aim at annihilating the puppet army first, because of the enemy forces they are the weaker.
>
> In fighting the American troops we must try to select their weak points and situations where they are weak in order to annihilate them. With regard to the strong points or the situations in which they are strong we should temporarily avoid them—although this is not an unbreakable rule.[25]

At this time, Hanoi was still not certain of the extent of U.S. involvement, and still spoke of the certainty that Special War would be completely defeated, suggesting that it had not yet been, and that priority would still have to be given to neutralizing Saigon forces as an instrument of U.S. policy. In fact, Le Duan suggests that the phrase "seek out the Americans to fight," which was widely used in indoctrination of military and civilian supporters in the south was primarily for propaganda purposes.[26]

Le Duan's letter to COSVN of November 1965 offers a number of insights into Hanoi's strategic thinking. It confirms that Resolution 9 of December 1963 had anticipated that the United States might move to Limited War if defeated in Special War, and therefore that the possibility of provoking a U.S. intervention by stepping up the war had been taken into account. This, in turn, verifies that the "three-options" concept had become the dominant strategic framework by this time, if not earlier.

Additionally, Le Duan offered a definition of what "decisive victory" meant, which is of interest in connection with the later use of this term in the context of the Tet Offensive. Given the "serious crisis of the Special War," he argued, the revolutionaries had the prospect of "achieving a decisive victory in a relatively short period of time" but, significantly, said that this would be done "on the basis of protracted struggle." "Decisive victory" did not mean "complete victory," he added, and offered as an example the battle of Dien Bien Phu.

The extent to which a decisive victory could be achieved would depend on the ultimate number of U.S. troops sent to Vietnam. From the argument Le Duan presents, it appears as if he felt that the 1965 U.S. troop level of less than 200,000 would not conclusively turn the war into a Limited War; this would happen (second scenario) if 300,000–500,000 troops came in. In this case, "we believe that the United States cannot fight us for a long period of time; a protracted resistance will surely bring us final victory."[27] Although it is difficult to penetrate these debates over revolutionary strategy in 1965–66 and clearly understand the various positions taken, it does seem that the question of whether the conflict had definitively become a Limited War was in some way involved. The pseudonymous "Truong Son" (General Nguyen Chi Thanh) wrote from the southern battlefield that:

> We started fighting the U.S. troops at a moment when we were winning. The United States imperialists started their regional [i.e., "limited"] war . . . while they were being defeated. The fact that we started the fighting from a winning position gave us an advantageous combat position. . . . The fact that the U.S. imperialists started their war from a losing position increased the seed of defeat that the U.S. expeditionary forces brought along with them.[28]

This argument shows the importance attached to situational logic and strategic momentum as an element of the calculation of the balance of forces. It also contains a detailed exposition of the reinforcing elements of the strength that compensate for any military disadvantage in facing the U.S. forces. The coordination between the different battlefields and theaters of operations and between the different types of forces are discussed as well as the political and moral strengths that help compensate for any military disadvantage. Finally, the author concludes that the first dry season offensive served to underline the military failure of the United States and the "initial defeat" of the Limited War strategy. Truong Son concluded that the decision to move to Limited War constituted the third strategic error committed by the United States. The first had been to replace the French by supporting the Diem regime. The second was the "application of the Special War strategy."[29]

Understanding the significance of Limited War and its role in Hanoi's strategic thinking is essential for understanding the purposes of the Tet Offensive. From the very outset of the U.S. direct intervention the strategic task of Hanoi was not to strive for the military expulsion of the American forces but to try by all means to "limit the conflict with the enemy and defeat the enemy within those limits, inflicting many serious losses, and pushing him into a posture of become progressively more and more bogged down and seriously defeated," in which case "we will certainly gain a decisive victory in the South."[30]

General Tra observes that after the U.S. direct intervention "it was impossible to fight both the puppets and the Americans because the strength of the revolution was limited." Because of this the revolutionary side adopted what General Tra terms "a policy within a strategy" (*sach luoc trong chien luoc*) based on the recognition that both forces could not be simultaneously defeated. "We wanted to fight the Americans so that they would lose their aggressive will (*y chi xam luoc*) and would have to withdraw; we certainly did not rely on annihilating all the American troops in order to achieve victory."[31]

As General Tra has emphasized, "Revolution is the offensive, always being on the offensive in many different forms. Being on the defensive is dangerous. For this reason, throughout the war we used *the strategy of the offensive*."[32] (Italics in original.) This "strategy of the offensive" led many U.S. decision makers to conclude that the revolutionary strategy was purely military, aimed at a conclusive defeat of the U.S. forces. In fact, as General Tra also notes, the offensive would take many forms and be directed at many different targets, according to the stage and requirements of the revolution. Perhaps "maintaining the initiative" would be a more inclusive term. Or, as Truong Chinh put it in his early writings, "Our strategy is defensive, but our tactics and campaigning principles are constantly to attack."[33]

In response to the escalation of 1965, the main strategic task was to "bog down" the U.S. forces and create a stalemate. Much of Hanoi's efforts in 1966 and 1967 were expended in trying to convince the United States that the war was stalemated. This meant that Limited War had failed, because the war could not be won militarily within the limits observed during this period. Winning would require a substantial escalation of the war either in scope or in intensity, with all the costs and risks that would entail. The Tet Offensive was an effort to drive this point home to U.S. decision makers.

The Tet Offensive

Understanding Vietnamese revolutionary strategy is complicated by several factors. First, as any student of decision making will readily grasp, the idea that decisions are made by a "unitary actor" is misleading. Decisions reflect the inputs of a variety of sources, and are not always clear, unambiguous and consistent. The extent to which decisions specify the implementing measures can make a great difference. General orders can be interpreted in many ways, some not entirely consistent with the original intentions of those at the highest levels. For reasons of maintaining morale, decisions that are based on accepting heavy sacrifices may conceal the underlying calculation from those who will have to pay the price, and present the objectives in the most positive and encouraging manner. Finally, there are typically a range of goals sought, and fallback positions built in. Failure to achieve the maximum stated objective does not necessarily mean that the basic or minimum objectives were not met.

Nowhere is the evidence more difficult to assess than in the case of the Tet Offensive. There is much documentary evidence that suggests that the architects of this offensive expected that its most sweeping goals would be achieved. But if this event is examined in the framework of the strategic model outlined above, its ultimate purposes take on a different dimension.

The Tet Offensive was designed to highlight the failure of Limited War and force the United States to a decision point based on a recognition that its current policy would not work. An inherent risk of this action was that the United States would choose to escalate as they had in 1965. Hanoi was evidently convinced that Washington would select the only other option available, de-escalation and ultimate withdrawal. The fact that the actual military targets of the offensive were the Saigon forces suggests that a direct military defeat of the United States was not the main aim of the plan, which envisaged knocking the Saigon prop out from under the United States.

It could reasonably be argued, as General Westmoreland did in the wake of the Tet Offensive, that this all-out effort to bring the conflict to a head was a response to the losses that had been inflicted on the revolutionary side. Possibly Hanoi decided that since the argument that the war was stalemated had fallen on deaf ears in Washington some spectacular action would be required to make the point. To the extent that the losses of the Tet Offensive were greater than those that might have been incurred by simply maintaining the previous tempo of the war, this effort to "induce delivery" of a U.S. decision and unwillingness to wait for a natural delivery may have reflected some anxiety by Hanoi. Certainly the human and material costs that a protracted strategy would entail for the revolution were very great. Nonetheless, the fatal flaw of the U.S. strategy of attrition was that, in the words of one Johnson administration official, "Essentially, we are fighting a birthrate."[34] At no time, then or later, has there been any evidence that this was a price Hanoi was unwilling to pay.

Hanoi's planners concluded that the United States had boxed itself into a corner and Hanoi's official military history of the war reads:

> In June 1967 the party Central Committee met to evaluate the great victory of our people in defeating one very basic step of Limited War of the American imperialists. The enemy is shaken both militarily and politically. As for us, both in terms of strategic posture (*the*) and in terms of our strength (*luc*) we have made many advances. Because of this, taking advantage of a time that the American imperialists are confronted with a situation in which both advance and retreat are difficult, at a time when the United States is about to elect a president, we need to inflict a decisive blow, to win a great victory, creating a great leap forward in the strategic situation (*chuyen bien nhay vot*), forcing a military defeat on the United States.[35]

This account seems to indicate that the Tet Offensive was aimed at achieving a crushing military defeat of the United States. Moreover, this account cites a Politburo resolution of December 1967 which states:

> The basic point about the current situation is that we have a winning posture, a posture where we have the advantage and the initiative, while the enemy is in a posture of defeat, passivity and difficulty. This situation permits us to move the revolutionary war of our people in the South to a new era, an era of offensive and uprising and winning decisive victory. . . . The weightiest and most urgent mission we have is to mobilize the greatest effort of the entire Party, army and people of both regions to push our revolutionary war to its highest level of development, using the methods of general offensive and general uprising to achieve a decisive victory."[36]

Such language certainly suggests a picture of a grand terminating phase of the war based on a conclusive military victory.

It should be remembered, however, that "decisive victory" was differentiated from "complete victory" in the strategic lexicon of Hanoi's planners. As the military history points out, this maximum effort was aimed at "achieving the strategic objectives laid out." These objectives were a General Offensive and Uprising at a time that the opponent still had over a million troops and a great military potential. The purpose of the uprisings in the cities was to coordinate with the military attacks on the battlefield "with a tight and mutually supporting coordination of the general offensive and the general uprising in the three areas, cities, rural delta, and mountain and forest."[37]

This ambitious objective has been described as unrealistic by General Tran Van Tra, one of the key commanders entrusted with implementing the decision. General Tra writes that even though the Political Bureau recognized that the United States still had a formidable force in the field which still had the capacity of being reinforced:

> . . . the objective was defined as "annihilating and disbanding the larger part of the puppet army, overthrowing the puppet authorities at each level, and wresting the government into the hands of the people" as well as "annihilating a significant portion of the effectives and war materiel of the U.S." . . . This was really many times beyond the our realistic capabilities. To tell the truth, we really didn't have the strength—our military forces were only one-fifth those of the Americans and the puppets in infantry, and they had absolute air, naval and mechanized superiority. . . . So that to put forth the policy of general offensive and uprising to "put the entire government administration in the hands of the people," which our cadres and soldiers described concisely and simply as "going for all of it" (dut diem) was completely unrealistic and couldn't be accomplished. The general offensive could not annihilate the greater part of enemy forces, that is, we didn't have enough strength so that the masses couldn't possibly rise up strongly in a general uprising because they would be viciously suppressed by all the weapons the enemy had at his disposal.[38]

General Tra concludes that the Political Bureau was correct in its insight that the time was ripe for bringing the conflict into a new stage, but wrong in the concrete measures it selected for doing so, which overestimated its own strength and underestimated the capability and response of the United States. It might also be remembered that the Saigon army and administration also responded with unexpected determination. A general mobilization was ordered for the first time, and the Saigon forces became a significant military factor for the first time since their near collapse in 1965.

General Tra's analysis identifies the two key issues. First, from Hanoi's perspective, was the time ripe to make a major effort to change the strategic context of the war? Second, if it was, were the methods selected effective? On the first point there is little disagreement. Both the architects of the Tet strategy in Hanoi and those in the South like General Tra entrusted with carrying it out agree that the timing was right. So, in a sense, did key officials of the Johnson administration, who felt that the situation had reached a crossroads. This sentiment is documented by the *Pentagon Papers:* ". . . at every level of Government there is a sense that the conflict, if expanded further, can no longer be called 'a Limited War.' Officials acknowledge that any further American involvement carries serious implications for the civilian life of the nation—not only the call-up of military reserves and the enactment of a tax increase but problems with the budget, the economy and the balance of payments."[39]

If present policy was not working, escalation did not seem a promising alternative. Thus, if it could be proved that the policy was not working, Hanoi could reasonably expect a decision to change that policy that would be in its favor. Moreover, a presidential election year in the United States provided the occasion to challenge and re-examine policy.

Whether the means chosen to force this decision were the right ones is a more complicated issue. In order to evaluate this, however, it should be noted that the Politburo envisaged three possible outcomes of the Tet Offensive:

> One was that we would win a major victory on all the important battlefields, the offensive and uprising would succeed in all the big cities, the aggressive will of the enemy would be crushed forcing them to agree to negotiations to end the war in accordance with our demands. Second, although we might win important victories in many places, the enemy might still have many forces supported by big bases and would continue to fight. Third, the Americans might send in many more troops, and expand the conflict. We should make extraordinary efforts to gain the greatest victory in accordance with the first possibility, but we should be prepared to deal with the second possibility. The third possibility, while remote, still requires constant and active precautions.[40]

Thus a range of objectives was set out, and the possibility that the maximum objective might not be achieved was recognized, as was the possibility that bringing the issue to a head might produce an escalation rather than the reverse.

Le Duan's January 18, 1968, letter to COSVN and the Party Military Committee in the South on the eve of the Tet Offensive discusses the various outcomes on the battlefield in the South, ranging from victories in important rural and urban "key areas" to more limited victories in secondary areas, to the least successful outcome which would be similar to "high points" of military action in previous years (different only in that the 1968 "high point" would cover the entire South). If only this minimum result were achieved, it would have the impact of expanding liberated areas and bases in the rural deltas and mountain forest areas, so that the least successful scenario would still leave the revolution better off than before.[41]

Even the maximum objective, however, did not envisage driving the U.S. forces into the sea. Rather, it aimed at "defeating the aggressive will" of the opponent, and forcing the United States into negotiations on its terms. If those terms are defined as negotiations that accepted the NLF as an indispensible element of the negotiations, this objective was met. Whether convincing the United States that the war was stalemated and was unwinnable at the Limited War level of involvement could have been done in a more efficient and less costly manner is likely to be an important topic for future generations of Vietnamese historians.

Although it is not within the scope of this paper to analyze the U.S. debate over the Tet Offensive, a few points relevant to this controversy do emerge from the examination of Hanoi's strategic objectives in launching the offensive. First, both the U.S. and the Vietnamese sides agreed that a conclusive result could not be gained by the United States with its current strategy and level of commitment. Second, the purpose of Hanoi's planners was to convince U.S. decision makers that the war was at an impasse, and to force a reevaluation and change of policy. It was not, as has been alleged by some, designed for its propaganda impact on the American public. This reevaluation produced a consensus in Washington that the war was no longer worth the cost, because the original strategic context of Vietnam as the key link in containment and a test case of a feared wave of wars of national liberation had been changed by the Sino-Soviet split and China's absorption in the convulsions of the Cultural Revolution.

Hanoi did not foresee, however, that Johnson's successor might try to expand the scope of the war while at the same time limiting and reducing direct U.S. involvement. To this extent, the predictive value of the "three-options" framework was limited. Nonetheless, neither of these moves changed the ultimate outcome of the war.

From Cease-fire to Total Victory

In many ways the 1968–73 years constitute the most interesting challenge to the "three-options" strategic framework. Although it was no longer Limited War; the sporadic escalations of the incursions into Laos and Cambodia and the bombing of Haiphong and Hanoi did not constitute a "general war," in part because the international situation had changed since the early 1960s when Hanoi assumed that escalation beyond the borders of South Vietnam would bring a response from China or the Soviet Union. Nor was it a return to Special War despite the emphasis on "Vietnamization." Moreover, just as it was difficult to reverse course once the second or third stage of the Maoist "three-phase" strategy had been reached and return to an earlier phase, the "three-options" strategy seems to implicitly suggest that once an option has been foreclosed, it will not be available again.

During the post-1968 period, the main strategic problem was to sustain enough pressure on the battlefield to support the negotiations in Paris and definitively bring an end to the Limited War. As the "Vietnamization" strategy became the main focus of U.S. policy and withdrawal of American troops proceeded, the defeat of the Saigon forces became the main focus. While the purely military balance of forces had not been a major preoccupation of Hanoi during the period of greatest U.S. troop involvement (because to highlight this would only underline the U.S. advantage in purely military terms), the prospect of facing their internal opposition in a final showdown led the revolutionary strategists to consider the issue once again.

During the 1969–70 period the issue was what level of military activity was necessary to support the Paris negotiations and counter pacification and "Vietnamization" while waiting for the United States to complete its troop withdrawal. The military losses of Tet and the fierce combat of 1968–69 left the revolutionary forces, especially the southern forces, in a weakened condition. Turley's account succinctly summarizes the situation:

> The Communists felt the pressure. General Tran Van Tra recalled bitterly that in this period many local party organs and cadres were "lost." In heavily populated Long An province, the independent main force 320th regiment, sent to obstruct pacification, had to disperse into platoons and squads and take over the work of defunct political organizations. "Sending a concentrated main force unit to operate in such a dispersed manner," wrote Tra, "so that it could be said no longer to be a main force unit, was something we did reluctantly, but there was no alternative under the circumstances at that time." Lengthy articles by the PAVN's top brass in December 1969 obliquely acknowledged that the southern revolution was "temporarily" in a defensive posture.[42]

It may be that during the latter part of 1970 and throughout 1971 the strategists ordered a military "stand down," though how much of the quiescence was due to necessity rather than choice is uncertain.

The Spring Offensive of 1972 was aimed at rebuilding the military position of the revolution now that U.S. ground troops were nearly gone.[43] Particular efforts were devoted to reviving the guerrilla forces in the delta and coastal areas to restore the balance among the three zones and three types of forces that had been disrupted during the 1968–71 period. As the Tet Offensive had aimed to show the failure of Limited War the 1972 Spring Offensive aimed to prove that "Vietnamization" would not salvage Washington's objectives in Vietnam, and that a negotiated settlement establishing a cease-fire and confirming the U.S. withdrawal was inevitable.

Although the United States maintained a limited presence in South Vietnam after the 1973 Paris Agreement, the final outcome of the conflict would now depend primarily on the indigenous forces in Vietnam. At this point the "three-options" strategic framework became largely irrelevant to the conflict, oriented as it was to responding to U.S. plans and actions. American support for Saigon still remained an essential feature of Hanoi's problem, but the outcome sooner or later would hinge on a direct confrontation between the contending Vietnamese sides.

Hanoi's leadership was slow to recognize this basic change in the situation. Still preoccupied with influencing U.S. actions, Hanoi hoped that it could induce Washington to compel its Saigon ally to observe the cease-fire. Based on the assumption that the cease-fire would be honored, and the hope that the envisaged coalition government would come into being, Hanoi ordered a scrupulous adherence to the cease-fire.

In the eyes of some revolutionary commanders in the South this was a dangerous and illusory objective as Turley's account of this period reveals:

> Orders only to "defend the Agreement" seemed unwisely passive to some of Hanoi's field commanders, however. To older cadres in particular the strategy bore a haunting resemblance to the post-Geneva "political struggle" in which so many comrades had "drowned with blood." With the approval of COSVN's General Tra, the heads of Military Region 9, Vo Van Kiet and General Le Duc Anh, ignored orders and pushed the ARVN out of positions it had established before the Paris Agreements.[44]

General Tra offered this explanation of his decision:

> . . . the actions of the military forces of Region 9 were based on the view that there had been no agreement, that nothing had changed, and that it was necessary to keep on fighting. That was an incorrect understanding of the Paris Agreement and of the new strategic phase. But it correctly evaluated the obstinacy of the enemy just like the Geneva Accords period, and it was resolute in preserving the gains the revolution had won. It was consistent with the actual situation, not illusory or utopian. "Luckily," it was a distant battlefield, so upper echelon policies were often slow in arriving and rectification of errors was not prompt.[45]

Part of the hesitation in changing may have been the result of distance and communication difficulties. The greater problem seems to have been a mind-set habituated to formulating strategy with reference to U.S. actions and policies.

Not until November 1973 did Hanoi finally conclude that the Paris Agreement would not be implemented. This delay was not due to any naive illusions, but rather to a calculation that the revolution needed a breathing space because

the people of the South had been exhausted by war. In a letter to the revolutionary leaders in South Vietnam of August 1972, anticipating the cease-fire agreement, Le Duan ordered a strategy of rebuilding the political base of support for
the revolution, through reemphasis on such measures as land reform and by
"stabilizing the political situation in newly liberated areas":

> Our country has undergone 27 years of war. For the last 10 years the compatri-
> ots in the South have had to contend with an extremely fierce war of aggres-
> sion, have had to live under a barbarous fascist regime. There has been more
> pain, suffering, death, and degradation than we can recount. We must clearly
> understand the situation of our country and deeply sympathize with our com-
> patriots in order to find an effective remedy to reduce the people's misery.[46]

In addition to the humanitarian concern for the southern people's war weari-
ness, Le Duan also asserted that in the struggle with Saigon, victory would be
determined both in the near and far term, by popular support so that "we must
win over the majority of the people," possibly an implicit admission of how
much popular support for the revolution had slipped during the long war.

By November 1973 Le Duan had concluded that relying on implementation
of the Paris Agreement had failed. It had resulted in loss of some territory and
people in former liberated areas. "The main reason for this failure is that in the
party headquarters and in the army the leading echelon and the commanding
echelon *did not see the full extent of the enemy scheme after signing the Paris
Agreement. . . .* As a result there was hesitancy and a rightist tendency. . . ."[47]
(Italics in original.) General Tra's approach was retroactively vindicated.

Le Duan's 1973 instruction was to rebuild the balance among the three zones
and three types of force, with particular emphasis on rebuilding the guerrilla
movement and the local forces in the rural areas and revitalizing the liberated
areas. This strategy clearly envisaged a fairly long process of bringing about a
favorable strategic posture and balance of forces. By 1974, the timetable had
begun to change.

In a letter to Pham Hung, by then in South Vietnam, Le Duan presented his
views about the strategic direction for the next two years (1975–76). He noted
that, "In the end, defeat and victory in a revolution is determined by the balance
of forces."[48] After an extended discussion of the balance of forces at various
critical junctures of the revolution, and the reiteration that the balance must be
calculated "dialectically," not mechanically, Le Duan identified the new element
of the situation:

> The national people's democratic revolution in the South and the socialist
> revolution in the North are inextricably linked, but *the greatest and most
> decisive force is in the North, in the rear area.* As the war reaches the conclud-
> ing stage the decisive role of the rear area becomes even more obvious.[49]
> [Italics in original.]

The theoretical groundwork for a decisive military outcome with military support from the North tipping the balance had been laid.

After the Paris Agreement of 1973, the three-options strategic framework was no longer relevant to the situation in Vietnam. Was Hanoi still too much absorbed in an American-centered strategy to fully realize the fact that the final phase of the war would depend on the internal showdown rather than on the external factor? Was this a period of indecision or delayed adjustment to a new reality? Were there major alternatives to the policies followed and, if so, how seriously were they considered? How did Vietnamese strategic thinking evolve during this period? Was there a conscious recognition of the need to reconstruct a strategic framework for the final civil war phase of the conflict? Was this a period of indecision or delayed adjustment to a new reality? Were there major alternatives to the policies followed and, if so, how seriously were they considered?

Does this explain why there was no real strategy other than strict implementation of the Paris Agreement for nearly a year? Even then, the idea of concluding the war through a major military offensive and defeat of the Saigon government did not appear to take root until late 1974 with the collapse of Phuoc Long and the lack of a strong response from either Washington or Saigon, and seems to lie more appropriately within the old "three-phase framework" of moving from a strategic equilibrium to a general counteroffensive. Moreover, it involved the abandonment of the triangular architecture of the "model" that prevailed during the "three-options era" by largely ignoring the populated deltas and the guerrilla movement. Another element reminiscent of the "three-phase" model is the language used in describing the strategy of the final offensive:

> The rule of revolutionary warfare is to progress from small units to large commands of coordinated combat branches and to destroy the enemy's force on a large scale, and finally to attack the cities, attack the nerve centers and smash the enemy's administration.[50]

This sounds much like the fabled "phase three" that American planners had long anticipated but which, even in the Tet Offensive, was not the design of revolutionary strategic thinking during the American period of the Vietnam conflict. Indeed, General Dung wrote that by fall 1974, "The war had moved into its final stage. The balance of forces had changed."[51] Thus the history of Vietnamese strategic planning came full circle.

Notes

1. *The Pentagon Papers: The Defense Department History of U.S. Decision Making on Vietnam*, Senator Gravel Edition, vol. 4 (Boston: Beacon Press, 1971), 293.

2. In written comments on the first draft of this paper, General Tran Van Tra underlined his contention that Vietnam "never followed the strategic doctrine of Mao Zedong," and that to the extent that Vietnamese writings mentioned the three-stage approach it was

"simply a theoretical exercise not related to reality." In a sense this is true, since Vietnam's strategy was from the outset recognized as being different from China's both with respect to the small territory which dictated a different approach and with regard to a different type of enemy. Still, Truong Chinh's book *The Resistance Will Win*, originally written in 1947 and republished in 1960, devoted a chapter to the three stages of revolution and flatly asserted that the revolution would pass through these stages. Vo Nguyen Giap and others wrote at length on passing into the third stage in 1950. Vietnam differed from China even at that early stage, however, in the stress placed on a strategy of exploiting the inherent vulnerabilities of the enemy's position.

3. Le Duan, *La Thu vao Nam* [Letters to the South] (Hanoi: Su That, 1985), xv.

4. Ibid.

5. This point was confirmed by General Tra at the Columbia conference.

6. William S. Duiker, *The Communist Road to Power in Vietnam* (Boulder, CO: Westview, 1981), 206.

7. Le Duan, *La Thu vao Nam* [Letters to the South], 33.

8. Duiker, *Communist Road*, 207.

9. An excellent account of this complex issue may be found in George McT. Kahin, *Intervention* (New York: Knopf, 1986), 117–21. For a detailed account of the diplomacy of this period see Gareth Porter, *A Peace Denied* (Bloomington, IN: Indiana Press, 1975).

10. Le Duan, *La Thu vao Nam*, 54.

11. Ibid.

12. William S. Turley, *The Second Indochina War* (New York: Signet, 1986), 69.

13. Ibid., 72.

14. Duiker, *Communist Road*, 223.

15. Ibid., 227.

16. Ibid., 226.

17. Ibid.

18. Cf. David W.P. Elliott and W.A. Stewart, *Pacification and the Viet Cong System in Dinh Tuong: 1966–1967*, RM 5788 (Santa Monica, CA: Rand Corporation, 1969).

19. Le Duan, "Letter to COSVN," in *La Thu vao Nam*, 157.

20. Larry Berman, *Planning a Tragedy* (New York: Norton, 1982), 135.

21. Ibid., 136–37.

22. Ibid., 137.

23. Turley, *Second Indochina War*, 78.

24. Institute of Military History, Ministry of Defense, *Cuoc Khang Chien Chong My Cuu Nuoc 1954–1975* [The Anti-American Resistance War for National Salvation 1954–75] (Hanoi: Nha Xuat Ban Quan Doi Nhan Dan, 1988), 150.

25. Le Duan, *La Thu vao Nam*, 120.

26. Ibid., 127.

27. Ibid., 126.

28. "Truong Son on the 1965–66 Dry Season," broadcast by Radio Hanoi July 4–7, 1966, in Patrick McGarvey, *Visions of Victory* (Stanford, CA: Hoover, 1969), 78.

29. Ibid., 91.

30. Institute of Military History, *Cuoc Khang Chien Chong My*, 151.

31. General Tra's written comments on the first draft of this chapter.

32. General Tra's written comments on the first draft of this chapter.

33. Truong Chinh, *The Resistance Will Win*, reprinted in Bernard Fall, ed., *Primer For Revolt* (New York: Praeger, 1963), 147.

34. *Pentagon Papers*, vol. 4, 587.

35. Institute of Military History, *Cuoc Khang Chien Chong My*, 177.

36. Ibid., 178.

37. Ibid.

38. Tran Van Tra, "Thang Loi va Suy Nghi ve Thang Loi" [Victory and Thinking about Victory] draft of conference paper, 2.

39. *Pentagon Papers*, vol. 4, 586.

40. Institute of Military History, *Cuoc Khang Chien Chong My*, 178.

41. Le Duan, *La Thu vao Nam*, 193.

42. Turley, *The Second Indochina War*, 131.

43. For a more detailed discussion see David W.P. Elliott, "NLF–DRV Strategy and the 1972 Spring Offensive" (Ithaca, NY: Cornell University International Relations of Asia Project, Interim Report no. 4, January 1974).

44. Turley, *The Second Indochina War*, 165.

45. Ibid.

46. Le Duan, *La Thu vao Nam*, 328.

47. Ibid., 339.

48. Ibid., 363.

49. Ibid., 366.

50. Van Tien Dung, *Our Great Spring Victory* (New York: Monthly Review Press, 1977), 13–14.

51. Ibid., 12

5

Love, War, and Revolution: Reflections on the Memoirs of Nguyen Thi Dinh

Kristin Pelzer

The whole family loved to listen to Chan read the *Luc Van Tien* poem. When-ever we had nothing to do at night, we would gather around the oil lamp—my mother lying in the hammock, cradling her grandchild, my father sitting silent in front of a small tea pot, my sisters sitting around mending clothes. We all kept quiet and listened to my brother read the story fluently. As for me [a ten-year-old girl that year, 1930], although I had only learned to read printed letters, I sometimes replaced my brother and read for the whole family.

People in my neighborhood also loved to listen to the *Luc Van Tien* story. . . . So, in the evenings, as soon as my brother or I began to read, the neighbors would all come. Sometimes, when I reached the part of the story where Nguyet Nga, Van Tien and his young valet were harmed by the wicked people, I wept and the neighbors also wept. Once in a while, my father nodded his head in approval and commented:

—This story teaches people all the virtues they must have in life: humanity, kindness, filial piety, courage, determination, and loyalty.[1]

To show her agreement, my mother did not say anything but softly sang a few verses to lull her grandchild to sleep:

In the Netherworld, if your soul is blessed with power,
Mother, please be aware of your son's sincere feelings.
All around me, rivers have their sources and trees their roots,
You bore me in your womb for nine months,
And my gratitude and debt to you is boundless.

Gradually, in this manner, the beautiful images of Van Tien and Nguyet Nga filled my mind. I hated those in the old days who abused their power, position and wealth to harm honest people like Van Tien and Nguyet Nga. But

I did not know enough as yet to understand that I should also hate the wicked people who were bringing miseries and poverty to my family and other families at the time. On one occasion, the landlord in the village came to my house and demanded paddy in a threatening manner. My parents had to hastily prepare food and wine to regale him. We were out of chickens then, so they had to catch the hen about to lay eggs which I had been raising, and slaughter it for him to eat. When he finally left, his face crimson with all the drinking, I broke down and cried in anger, and demanded that my mother compensate me for the hen.
—*No Other Road to Take*, Memoir of Nguyen Thi Dinh[2]

In this passage from the opening pages of her memoirs, Nguyen Thi Dinh presents a tableau of close-knit family and community life suffused with poetry and philosophical reflection along with an analysis of the origins of her revolutionary political consciousness. *Luc Van Tien* is an epic poem by a leading nineteenth-century Confucian scholar, Nguyen Dinh Chieu. This infusion of culture in a village setting is not unusual; as historian Alexander Woodside has pointed out, "Vietnam is and always has been one of the most intensely literary civilizations on the face of the planet."[3]

When Nguyen Thi Dinh's memoirs first appeared in Vietnamese in 1968, she was deputy commander of the National Liberation Front Armed Forces in South Vietnam as well as chairman of the South Vietnam Liberation Women's Association. She was born and grew up in Ben Tre province in the Mekong Delta, an area of strong anticolonial sentiment throughout the French colonial period.

The memoirs describe Nguyen Thi Dinh's life, emotions, and involvement in the revolution during the three decades from the founding of the Vietnamese Communist Party in 1930 to the formation of the National Liberation Front in 1960. During the August Uprising of 1945, when the Vietnamese population under the leadership of Ho Chi Minh's Viet Minh rose up to seize power from the local Vietnamese agents of French and Japanese occupation, Dinh carried the revolutionary flag into the Ben Tre provincial capital. She played an important role in the Viet Minh anticolonial resistance. After the end of that war, she stayed in her native Mekong Delta to struggle for the implementation of the Geneva Agreements. However, she sent her only son north at this time so that he would be able to receive an education.

As detailed in other chapters in this volume, the years between 1954 and 1960 were a dark time for southern Vietnamese revolutionaries who were instructed by their leadership not to use armed struggle against repression by the Saigon government. They were to defend themselves by political means alone, without weapons. According to Dinh, these directives were obeyed, but not without great suffering, hardship, and impatience to fight back. When the policy changed, Dinh organized revolutionary supporters in three districts in Ben Tre province to attack Saigon guardposts virtually barehanded in order to seize weapons to equip a local armed force.[4] Thirty years after the date of the end of her memoirs, she was still active, and headed the Vietnamese Women's Union. She joined her ancestors in August 1992.

For readers interested in the origins and politics of the revolutionary move-ment in the South, Dinh's memoirs provide insights and historical information. While official Communist Party documents appear in American documentary histories of the war, which are often used as textbooks,[5] there is no comparable material available on the personal life of major political and military leaders, and little available on the formative period of the revolution in the South before 1960 or on the role of women in the revolutionary movement. In this respect, the memoirs are an ideal companion piece to the available historical accounts of the period such as George Kahin's *Intervention* and Carlyle Thayer's *War by Other Means.*[6]

One purpose of the memoirs was to convince the intended Vietnamese reader-ship of the correctness of the political choice Nguyen Thi Dinh had made: that there was "no other road to take" but the dangerous revolutionary path full of hardship and suffering; no alternative to following the leadership of the Vietnam-ese Communist movement in opposing French colonialism and its Vietnamese agents and later its heir, the American-backed Saigon government and its agents in the countryside. By this very fact, the memoirs are an introduction to Vietnamese revolutionary political discourse and political consciousness, with its tremendous emphasis on history, optimism, and the community. The memoirs were completed in November 1965 and published in 1968. However, the narra-tive ends on December 26, 1960, at the height of revolutionary optimism, with the introduction of the Ben Tre provincial National Liberation Front Committee to the people of that province at a large rally. Seeing that scene in her mind's eye, Dinh recalls:

> In the face of this enormous and imposing force of the people, I felt very small, but I was full of self-confidence, like a small tree standing in a vast and ancient forest. In struggling against the enemy, I had come to fully realize that we had to have the strength of the whole forest in order to be able to stay the force of the strong winds and storms. As I thought about the protection and support of the people . . . I felt more intimately bound, more so than ever before, to the road I had taken and had pledged to follow until my last days. . . . For me there was no other road to take. (p. 77)

It is remarkable that in this work completed in 1965 and published in 1968, the massive American military intervention of the time appears only as meta-phorical "strong winds and storms," which the "ancient forest," the Vietnamese people, will withstand.

Ironically, in the same year that the book was published, 1968, Ben Tre's provincial capital was discussed around the world when the commander of American forces that retook the province from revolutionary forces said, "We had to destroy the town in order to save it."[7] Nguyen Thi Dinh's memoirs provide a depth of Vietnamese political geography and personal history to con-textualize that remark.

Teachers who want to include the Vietnamese revolutionary viewpoint in their courses on the war most often choose one of several books by Vietnamese who had been on the revolutionary side (but not in the Communist Party) and who later broke with the revolution and came to the United States. *A Vietcong Memoir* by Truong Nhu Tang is probably the most frequently used.[8] A more recent book, by a Vietnamese woman who grew up in a contested village buffeted by both sides of the war, is Le Ly Hayslip's *When Heaven and Earth Changed Places*.[9] While there is much to learn from each of these texts about the viewpoint each author represents, they were written specifically for American audiences with the collaboration of American co-authors. They are thus tailored to American sensitivities. One of the interests of Nguyen Thi Dinh's memoir is that it was written in Vietnamese for a Vietnamese audience, but is available in English through an independent translation. English-speaking readers are thereby able to listen in on the dialogue—the "hidden transcript," to use Scott's term—of revolutionary Vietnamese.

Family, Poetry, and Revolution

At the beginning of her memoirs, Nguyen Thi Dinh recalls that as a ten-year-old she would wake up at 2:00 or 3:00 each morning to take fish by sampan to market to sell, carrying heavy baskets of shrimp on her head. "Seeing me, many women clucked their tongues, 'My, whose daughter is that skinny girl who can row a sampan so well.' " Vietnam's culture is highly oral; the memoirs make much use of the immediacy of such dialogue. The fact that neighbors gathered in her parents' house for readings of epic poetry indicated that her family was better off than many in the village, although still under the thumb of a landlord.

In one sense, the scene of the family reading poetry from *Luc Van Tien*, the literary work best known and loved by the southern Vietnamese population,[10] is familiar, archetypal, universal. A laconic father makes philosophical reflections; a mother cradles her grandchild and sings a lullaby; sisters mend clothes. It is an evocation of collective childhood nostalgia which makes the reader vicariously feel a part of an idyllic family scene. A feeling of warmth is created; the scene evokes an ordinary family suffused with both love and a deep connection with the nation's high culture.[11]

The father refers to well-known values associated with the patriarchal philosophy of Confucianism: filial piety and loyalty. His wife, "does not say anything," but to show "her agreement" with her husband, sings a lullaby about the power of the spirit of a mother and the boundless debt of a child to its mother: an evocation of pre-patriarchal Mother Right. While Confucian patriarchal dominance and Mother Right are usually thought of as polar opposites in conflict with each other, in this tableau the two elements are harmonious. The male and female discourses do not clash: the man is the expert on this life, and the woman is the connection with the "Netherworld" of the spirits.[12]

Nguyen Dinh Chieu, the nineteenth-century Confucian scholar and poet who wrote *Luc Van Tien*, went blind from crying in grief at the loss of his mother.[13] In the passage of his poetry that Dinh's mother sings as a lullaby, the lost mother is associated with water: "all around me, rivers have their sources." The child spent nine months in the water of the mother's womb. *Nuoc*, water, is also the word for country. In the Vietnamese popular imagination, the name of Nguyen Dinh Chieu is associated with extreme pain at both the loss of the mother (*mat me*) in death and loss of the country (*mat nuoc*) to foreign invasion and foreign military occupation. After the fall of his native province, Gia Dinh, to the French in 1859, Nguyen Dinh Chieu retreated to Ben Tre province to teach and refused to collaborate with the French despite repeated offers.

The idyllic scene of a family poetry reading in Nguyen Thi Dinh's memoirs is thus also deeply political. The year was 1930: Vietnam no longer existed as a nation and could not be found on any contemporary map. Officially, Ben Tre was in Cochinchina, a component part of French Indochina. The area had been under foreign occupation for over half a century, but the rural population preserved the poetry of an earlier generation of resistance, and parents taught their children the basic virtues and to remember their roots. Love of family and love of nation were one. The intimate scene of a family poetry reading does not fit the usual Western popular or academic image of Vietnamese "peasant" life. It is cut of a different cloth from the Western literature on peasants and peasant revolution. The family portrayed by Dinh is a human and cultured one. "Farmer," "citizen," or "civilian" are terms that would seem less alien than "peasant" and more fully human, since they are used to refer to people in American and other Western societies. As Polly Hill has pointed out in her incisive critique of development economics, "peasant is the semantic successor to *native*."[14] This cultural importance of poetry and moral philosophy for Vietnamese "peasants" is not familiar to Americans, who have seen countless Vietnamese "huts" burn and countless Vietnamese "peasants" shot in newsreel footage or fictional reenactment (e.g., the film *Platoon*). The American wartime journalistic cliché was that the peasants are apolitical and just want to be left to plow their farms in peace. In Graham Greene's *The Quiet American*, the cynical British journalist and "old Indochina hand" expressed a widely shared elitist view: "Thought's a luxury. Do you think the peasant sits and thinks of God and Democracy when he gets inside his mud hut at night?"[15] Such excerpts from *The Quiet American* were even read into the record by a congressman during hearings before the House of Representatives Select Committee on Intelligence as representing valuable cross-cultural insights relevant to the Vietnam conflict.[16] In fact, as Nguyen Thi Dinh's memoirs indicate, "peasants" do discuss religious and moral concepts and national and international politics in their homes. A respect for "peasant" intelligence would have been more valuable for American policymakers than "Intelligence." Nguyen Thi Dinh became a Communist revolutionary through family socialization, following in the footsteps of her admired older brother, Chan, who had taught her to read. Chan had joined the Indochinese Communist Party the year it was founded, 1930. Buddhism and communism were closely connected in Dinh's mind; in fact she initially thought that they were the same thing since several of her brother's comrades lived in a pagoda disguised as monks. Also, her parents were simultaneously strong supporters of the Communist movement and devout Buddhists who fasted six days a month. Initially, revolutionary activities were an extention of her duties for the family, including cooking for Communist meetings in her parents' house and hiding Communist leaflets under the fish she took to market, dropping them along the way. Although Dinh was drawn to the revolutionary movement by her family, conflicts arose when she reached puberty and began to spend a lot of time on more dangerous missions. The time she spent on revolutionary activities, which she refers to as her "work," conflicted with her family's need for her labor in cooking and working in the rice fields and in the vegetable garden. When she stayed out late on revolutionary missions, her parents worried for her virtue, and also thought that as a mere woman she would not be able to withstand torture and would betray the revolution, harming a lot of people, if she were caught. Her parents wanted her to limit her revolutionary activities and to marry, but she refused.

Courtship, Love, and Revolution

Dinh encountered little understanding of her desire to become a revolutionary rather than a wife. Tu Phat, one of the revolutionary "brothers" (a popular form of address in Vietnam not limited to family members) laughed at her desire to leave home for full-time revolutionary activity lest her parents force her to get married. "No matter where you go you'll have to get married eventually. Do you think you can run away from it?"[17] Her next line of defense was to say that she would only marry a revolutionary. Her appeal for support produced an unexpected result: an assignation, as a seventeen- or eighteen-year-old girl, with Bich, an admired, well-educated, and sophisticated revolutionary from the city some years her senior.

> —Bich asks you to go out and talk with him near the row of tangerine trees.
> —What does he want to talk with me about?
> Tu only smiled:
> —You'll find out when you go there.
> I felt thrilled and nervous. Perhaps Bich would allow me to leave and join the revolution. That afternoon, in great agitation, I went into the garden and headed straight toward the row of tangerine trees. Bich was already there, and was absorbed in admiring the dense clusters of ripe tangerines. Hearing a noise, he turned around. Suddenly I felt very awkward. He asked me calmly:
> —Miss Dinh, you talked with Tu Phat the other afternoon, didn't you?
> I answered in panic:
> —I didn't say much of anything.
> —Let me ask you truthfully, why do you want to marry a revolutionary?
> I plucked a few tangerine leaves and then said:
> —Because I want to leave and work for the revolution as you're all doing.

—In your opinion, what kind of man should your husband be?

I was so embarrassed I did not know what to say, but out of respect for him [I had to come up with a] reply:

—He must permit me to work for the revolution, he must treat my parents well and love me for the rest of my life.

He looked at me attentively, and then smiled and said:

—Is that all?

At that point, I became bolder:

—Actually, I don't want to get married yet, I only want to ask you and the other brothers to allow me to leave and join the revolution.

He asked me affectionately:

—Alright, have you really made up your mind?

I was overcome with joy and nodded my head. Bich seemed lost in thought. After a while, he looked straight into my eyes and asked to test me:

—If your husband is in the revolution, he might be killed, and sometimes he might even be jailed for nine or ten years, do you think that you can wait for him that long?

I lowered my eyes, my cheeks were burning with embarrassment, and then I said hesitantly:

—Yes.

That afternoon Bich asked me many questions. I answered him but did not ask him about anything. After we finished talking, I plucked a few tangerines for him to eat and then went back to the house. A thought crossed my mind: perhaps Bich wanted to. . . . But I chased it away, because I thought Bich was a famous intellectual and I was just a simple country girl. Mrs. Ba Theng had told me that the daughter of the man who owned the Ham Vang store at the market place—a beautiful rich girl—was running after him. However, she wanted him to become a Catholic, and he refused. After Bich left, my brother Chan called me over and told me in private that Bich wanted to marry me, and asked me what I thought of it. When I heard the news, I was both happy and embarrassed, and my face burned as though I had had a sunstroke. But I still had my doubts and wondered whether Bich really loved me.

My parents who had always been fond of Bich agreed immediately. From then on, Bich frequently came to the house. He loved to stay in the garden, so we often went and sat for hours under the tangerine trees to confide in each other. We got married at the end of 1938.

Dinh was proud of her husband, although she seldom got to see him; he was a busy, important man—the chair of several committees and a contributor to newspapers. He was delighted to learn, within a few months of their marriage, that she was pregnant. As with the vignette of poetry reading *en famille*, the preceding courtship scene has a universal, archetypal character: the minute attention to eyes, to looks, to tone of voice; the indirect conversation, the embarrassment, the doubts. Young man looks straight into young woman's eyes and asks whether she would be capable of being faithful; young woman lowers her eyes and turns scarlet, hesitates, answers yes. Afterwards, she is in agonies of doubt: he could not really be interested in me, he could not want to marry me, such a handsome intelligent man with a rich and beautiful girl in love with him, I wonder if he really loves me. But her family likes him, they spend hours and hours talking; marriage and baby follow.

Of course, there are regional and national variations to this scene of human courtship and the flowering of romantic love. If it were America, the courtship would have been by an apple tree. In Vietnam, the citrus is the Vietnamese tree and fruit of love; many rural women perfume their hair with the scent of grapefruit leaves. That the lives of Vietnamese "peasants," and Vietnamese revolutionaries include courtship and love comes as a surprise to American readers, partly because of the ethnocentric belief that romantic love was a European invention originating in the Medieval courtly love tradition. More specifically, it is a revelation to readers that a Communist Party leader and tough guerrilla commander would give such importance to the gentler emotions in her memoirs. The stereotype of the "hardened guerrilla fighter"—Dinh's identity as veteran fighter and second in command of the formidable "Viet Cong" armed forces at the time the memoirs were published—would seem to preclude attaching value and importance to the flowering of love.

Her husband Bich's concern about the hardships that faced the wife of a revolutionary were well-founded. At a time of repression and widespread arrests of revolutionaries he returned home to be with his wife when she gave birth, and was arrested three days after his son was born.[18] Her older brother and his comrades were arrested soon after, and she lost contact with the party, leaving her feeling isolated and helpless. "There was nothing I could do except try to support my child and wait for my husband's return."[19] At that moment of wifely passivity and despair a party leader got in contact with her.

> He comforted me a great deal and gave me a bit of advice so profound and ardent that I remembered it long afterwards:
> —Bich and the other brothers in jail are waiting for us to operate and bring them out, what do you think [we should do]?
> His voice was both stern and full of emotion. He did not utter a word of criticism to me but I was suddenly reminded of my mission, and felt that I was being too weak.[20]

Although she wanted to stay in her home area to carry out revolutionary activities so that she could take care of her baby, that was not possible because she was too well known there. She was able to see her husband in prison one last time, then was arrested herself and spent three years in prison camp. "When I thought of our situation—my husband in jail in one place, me in exile in another, and the baby separated from both his parents—my heart broke into pieces." She tried to keep these pieces together with simple acts. "Every time I made something, I made it for the three of us: I embroidered three pillow cases, made three pairs of chopsticks and sewed three handkerchiefs."[21] After three years in prison camp she was released to house arrest in her home village due to cardiac disorders. She learned that Bich had died at Poulo Condor, and she went out of her mind with grief for a month. The worst was not being able to tell her young son the truth when he asked when his father would be coming home.

In August 1945 she led thousands to take over the provincial capital of Ben Tre in the name of the revolution led by Ho Chi Minh. She does not expand on the details of this important historical event in her memoirs. A few days later, news arrived that the Poulo Condor prisoners had been liberated. "Though Bich had been dead for a long time, my heart was filled with excitement for I still nurtured the hope that he was still alive." Instead, one of his prison comrades advised her: "By continuing to work for the revolution and making progress, you're acting exactly in accordance with Bich's aspirations. If you love him, you must fight to avenge him."[22] There are echoes here of the legend surrounding Vietnam's first nationalist uprising against foreign rule led by the Trung sisters in 40 A.D. Vietnamese literary critic Dang Thanh Le has pointed out the strong association between patriotism and romantic love in Vietnamese culture dating back to the portrayal of Trung Trac as fighting both to avenge the death of her husband Tri Sach at the hands of the Han governor and to free her nation from foreign rule. Romantic love and patriotism have been closely associated in Vietnamese culture since at least the seventeenth century.[23]

In some respects, Nguyen Thi Dinh's memoirs bear a considerable resemblance to *Luc Van Tien,* the nineteenth-century epic poem evoked by Nguyen Thi Dinh at the beginning of her memoirs.[24] Both works contain a love story characterized by separation and intense loyalty, and much of each consists of a series of trials and tribulations in which the protagonists confront and ultimately confound the plots of evil people. *Luc Van Tien* begins with the happy scene of the sixteen-year-old hero, a talented young scholar, about to leave his teacher to take the imperial examination for entry into the mandarinate. Just after setting off with the youthful confidence that he will succeed in the imperial exam, Luc meets people fleeing in terror from a gang of bandits. He faces the bandits single-handedly; the bandits scatter, and it turns out that he has rescued a damsel in distress, Nguyet Nga, whose heart he has won by his courage. They have a brief conversation, including exchange of names, place of origin, and, of course, poems; they then each go their separate ways. On his arrival at the examination site, Van Tien learns that his mother has died and he must return home instead of taking the examination. His life for the following many years consists of a series of misfortunes along the road in which evil people, often for no apparent reason, try to kill him, and he is repeatedly saved, often with the help of supernatural forces.

Meanwhile the heroine, Nguyet Nga, has no further contact with or news of the hero, but paints his portrait and continues to love him loyally. Although they were never married, she considers him her husband, refusing all offers of marriage, even after believing him dead. One of the villains of the piece tries to convince her to marry before the spring coloring fades from her cheeks—an argument echoed by the corrupted landlord's daughter Nhi in Nguyen Thi Dinh's memoirs. At the end, virtue is rewarded: having refused to compromise, and having been tempered by their hardships, Luc Van Tien and Nguyet Nga's fortunes change. Van Tien takes the imperial examinations and wins first place; he and Nguyet Nga meet again and marry, and all their enemies are punished. The memoirs associate the traditional virtue of loyalty to husband with loyalty to the revolution. For example, Nguyen Thi Dinh expresses scorn for a neighbor, Nhi, a landlord's daughter who succumbed to pressure under the Diem regime and repudiated her "Viet Cong" husband who had gone North after the Geneva Agreements. This woman married a Saigon army officer and came back from a trip to the city "wearing a transparent and skintight nylon blouse and a bouffant hairdo which looked like an owl's nest"—mid-1950s imported Americana. Nhi's attitude was: "life is not very long. If we don't live it up we'll miss a lot of things and we'll grow old before we know it." Following American fashions and adopting an individualistic philosophy of life is thus connected with betraying both the revolution and traditional female virtue. In the traditional Vietnamese conception, love is associated with loyalty, and this is contrasted with individualistic love associated with Westernization. Nguyen Thi Dinh stresses that the faithless wife is the daughter of a landlord, and contrasts her to a faithful wife who is a poor peasant. This association of class and virtue is more than just a reflection of the Communist Party class line. In *Luc Van Tien*, the evil people who harm the hero and heroine are almost always from relatively wealthy and powerful families while those who save them include a poor fisherman, a poor woodcutter, and a poor old woman. Although as a high-ranking political leader and military officer Nguyen Thi Dinh was seen by Western feminists during the Vietnam War as exemplary of women's potential to succeed in roles traditionally reserved for men (whether in the United States or Vietnam), Nguyen Thi Dinh herself writes in the idiom of protecting and respecting tradition. In this respect, the memoirs are an excellent example of close association of revolution and tradition in Vietnam.

Democratic Republic of Vietnam; Independence, Freedom, Happiness

There are, unfortunately, no details in the memoirs on Nguyen Thi Dinh's role and experiences in organizing, in 1960, one of the first uprisings of what became known as "the Vietnam War." She does, however, give a fairly detailed account of her first major military mission, which took place during the Viet Minh Resistance against the French. Embedded in this passage is a detail on the process of institution building in the formation of the Democratic Republic of Vietnam, which the French were attempting to defeat in order to reestablish their rule over what they called "*Indochine Française*," French Indochina. The year was 1946, and she was just twenty-six. She had been entrusted with the job of transporting arms obtained from Ho Chi Minh to the Viet Minh organization in the South when her boat ran aground on a sand bank somewhere along the coast of Central Vietnam. Unable to budge the boat, she and one member of her small crew made their way to the nearest village, where they were promptly arrested by "five or six youths carrying sharpened sticks" who refused to answer her question: "Is this a French or a Viet Minh area, brother?" Instead, they interrogated her: "do you have any papers?"

> I pretended I was illiterate. A youth sat down in front of me and started to write the report. I continued to pretend weeping, but at the same time I stole a look to see what he was scribbling. The youth pulled out a fountain pen and wrote clumsily on the top line: "the Democratic Republic of Vietnam, Independence, Freedom and Happiness." I almost shouted with joy. I was about to spill out everything but checked myself. I asked the cadre in charge to go out into the yard with me. I pulled out my letter of introduction which I had hidden in my hair and showed it to him. After he finished reading, he jumped up and down with joy:
> —Heavens, this is sister Ba Dinh, brothers. We got the order to wait for you here a week ago, but the weather was stormy and we thought you couldn't make it.
> Suspicion suddenly gave way to trust. The comrades invited me inside the house, surrounded me and asked me all sorts of questions about our sea journey. The women immediately started to cook rice soup with duck broth.[25]

The next day the boat continued on and the mission was successfully accomplished. "I handed the weapons directly to Tran Van Tra who was then commanding the 8th zone."[26] As the scholar Paul Mus has pointed out, under French colonialism the words *Indochine Française* on the top of all official documents and papers were an affront to Vietnamese nationalist sensibilities.[27] After Ho Chi Minh declared Vietnam independent on September 2, 1945, beginning his speech with the words of the American Declaration of Independence, the government did not have the facilities and funds to produce and distribute new letterhead stationery. Instead, tens of thousands of Vietnamese, many of them newly literate, laboriously marked the name and aims of the country on the top of ordinary paper to create the "official documents" of the government which they recognized but which the United States and other foreign governments did not. Ho Chi Minh chose the phrase *Democratic Republic of Vietnam; Independence, Freedom, Happiness* in emulation of the American republic's revolution against colonial rule and monarchy: Life, Liberty, and the Pursuit of Happiness. Peasants who had seen the power of official documents and reports entitled *Indochine Française* in the hands of local officials firmly made their own letterhead in their own shaky but determined handwriting.

Reflections on Love and Hatred, War and Revolution

Frances FitzGerald, who has made one of the most sensitive attempts to understand and explain the dynamics of the Vietnamese revolution for American

readers in her book *Fire in the Lake*, has argued that the fuel for the revolutionary struggle came from mobilized hatred:

> Hatred was the beginning of the revolution, for hatred meant a clear break
> in all the circuits of dependency that had bound the Vietnamese to the West-
> erners, the landlords, and the old notables. Quite correctly the Party directive
> equated "hatred of the enemy" with the masses' "understanding of their own
> rights," for shame is anger turned against self.[28]

In the passage cited at the beginning of this chapter, Nguyen Thi Dinh partially confirms the validity of FitzGerald's insight. Dinh remembers that as a
little girl she was angry at the man who had been responsible for the death of her
chicken as well as enraged at the evil characters in the epic poem *Luc Van Tien*,
but she did not yet have political consciousness. "I did not know enough as yet to
understand that I should also hate the wicked people who were bringing miseries
and poverty to my family and other families at the time." However, it is love—of
family, poetry, community, and nation—rather than hatred that comes at the very
beginning of the memoirs and of Dinh's revolutionary consciousness. The origin
of this consciousness is Dinh's anger at those who harm the people whom she
loves; love is her primary emotion.

FitzGerald's discussion of the role of emotion in revolution is one-sided. In
the index to *Fire in the Lake*, one is referred to eight pages on the use of hatred as a
political tool by the Viet Minh and National Liberation Front. "Hatred: evocation of,
226–30; channeling of, 230–33." There is not a single entry for the evocation or
channeling of love. Perhaps this neglect of the role of love in revolution can be
partially explained by the fact that, for the American Left, the period of the Vietnam
War was marked by a great explosion of anger. The period was experienced on the
Left as "days of rage," to quote from the title of one book on the sixties,[29] and
antiwar protest was accompanied by the rise of the women's movement with its
anger at women's traditional roles in the family. It is crucially important to
understand the power of love as a political and military force on both sides of the
war. For the young American men who fought the war—many of them seventeen-
and eighteen-year-olds barely out of boyhood—answering their country's call had a
lot to do with the basic human need to love and be loved: they were motivated by
love of their country, the desire to win the love and approval of a father who had
served in World War II, and by the desire to win the love and admiration from
their home town, and of course all the pretty girls, when they returned to the
music of bands and welcome-home parades.[30] The American Vietnam veterans'
search for love and glory turned into a nightmare of rejection. Many received
"Dear John" letters in Vietnam. Back home, they faced criticism from anti-war
protestors, and, especially after the ignominious end in 1975, the scorn of World
War II veterans, who had won "their" war. Many combat veterans also suffered
self-hatred from feelings of guilt for killing Vietnamese civilians.

One Vietnam combat veteran diagnosed with severe post-traumatic stress disorder (PTSD) showed me a mug that for him summed up why he went to Vietnam. The mug had a drawing of a little boy, maybe five years old, in a cute sailor suit, looking out to sea beside his sailor father. This veteran was bitter at what he saw as the Veterans' Admini-stration's manipulation of the continued yearning of men destroyed by the war for the warmth of home and country. He showed me a matchbook he had picked up during his last stay in a VA hospital. It pictured the maternal, patriotic figure of Betsy Ross sewing the flag. The image played on the longing of bed-ridden veterans for the comforting ideal of family and nation that had been an important part of their motivation for participating in the war.

Nguyen Thi Dinh and *A Bright Shining Lie*

One of the most widely read books on America's involvement in Vietnam is former war correspondent Neil Sheehan's *A Bright Shining Lie*.[31] This best-selling account of the war is built around the life and death of John Paul Vann, a charismatic military-civilian strategist and notorious womanizer who was the hero of the American press corps in Saigon until, and after, his death in 1972. Vann served for a time as an American military adviser to ARVN troops in Ben Tre province in the early 1960s. The commanding "Viet Cong" general in the province was Nguyen Thi Dinh. Her name does not appear in Sheehan's massive study.

In an interview with Nguyen Thi Dinh in Hanoi, antiwar activist Don Luce raised the fact that she was not mentioned in the Sheehan book about Vann. Her reply:

> Oh, I understand. Men do not like to talk about women generals. Even Vietnamese men, and we have a history of famous women generals. . . . Yes, we knew Mr. Vann. It must be hard for his family. It is so hard for so many families.[32]

In this statement, Nguyen Thi Dinh expresses compassion for the family of a former enemy and recognizes the universality of suffering in war. This sentiment is shared by many American Vietnam War veterans who would like to return to Vietnam to do what they can to help heal the wounds of war. Now that the war is history, what remains is a tie of pain between Vietnamese and Americans who suffered in what Tran Van Tra has called "the war which should never have happened, and which should not have gone on so long." To suffer is human, and the Vietnam War is a painful experience that Vietnamese and Americans now have in common—a shared humanity.

Notes

I wish to thank Ruth Dawson, Alice Dewey, David Hunt, Le Thi Nham Tuyet, Mai Trang, Willie Nelson, Nha Trang Pensinger, Paul Shannon, Jayne Werner, and Marilyn Young for helpful comments on earlier drafts of this paper. Dialogue with students, and particularly Patricia Lane's thoughtful engagement with the text in a seminar paper, also enriched my reading of Nguyen Thi Dinh's memoirs. I am sad to write that Madame Dinh died in August 1992 as this book was going to press.

1. The Vietnamese terms for these virtues are: *nhan nghia, hieu, thao, tri, dung*, and *thuy chung*. Nguyen Thi Dinh, "Khong Con Duong Nao Khac," in Van Phac, ed., *Mot Mua Xuan Ruc Ro, Ky va truyen* [A Resplendent Spring: Memoirs and Stories] (Ho Chi Minh City: Nha Xuat Ban Van Nghe T.P. Ho Chi Minh, 1985), 67. *Nhan nghia*, translated here as humanity, is a complex concept virtually impossible to translate into one English term; dictionary translations include "benevolence and righteousness," "charity and righteousness," and even "love and righteousness."

2. Mai V. Elliott, *No Other Road to Take: Memoir of Mrs. Nguyen Thi Dinh* (Ithaca, N.Y.: Data paper number 102, Southeast Asia Program, Department of Asian Studies, Cornell University, June 1976). First published as *Khong Con Duong Nao Khac* (Hanoi: Nha Xuat Ban Phu Nu, 1968). Memoirs as recorded by Tran Huong Nam.

3. Alexander B. Woodside, *Community and Revolution in Modern Vietnam* (Boston: Houghton Mifflin, 1976), 2.

4. George McT. Kahin, *Intervention: How America Became Involved in Vietnam* (New York: Knopf, 1986), 111–12.

5. For example, Marvin E. Gettleman, Jane Franklin, Marilyn Young, and H. Bruce Franklin, *Vietnam and America: A Documented History* (New York: Grove Press, 1985).

6. Kahin, *Intervention*; and Carlyle A. Thayer, *War By Other Means: National Liberation and Revolution in Vietnam, 1954–1960* (Sydney: Allen and Unwin, 1989).

7. Marilyn B. Young, *The Vietnam Wars, 1945–1990* (New York: Harper Collins, 1991), 219–20.

8. Truong Nhu Tang, *A Vietcong Memoir* (New York: Harcourt Brace Jananovich, 1985). The title is misleading as the term Vietcong means "Vietnamese Communist" and the author was a non-Communist founding member of the National Liberation Front.

9. Le Ly Hayslip, *When Heaven and Earth Changed Places, A Vietnamese Woman's Journey from War to Peace* (New York: Doubleday, 1989).

10. Nguyen Dinh Chieu, *Luc Van Tien* [bilingual edition including French translation by Duong Quang Ham] (Hanoi: Editions Alexandre de Rhodes, 1945).

11. In the terms used in semiotic literary criticism, the scene evokes a "code" of emotional warmth and harmony associated with a blissful family scene. For an analysis of the importance of such codes for the understanding of poetry, see Jonathan Culler, *The Pursuit of Signs: Semiotics, Literature and Deconstruction* (Ithaca: Cornell University Press, 1981).

12. In Vietnam, as in many other cultures, spirit mediums are usually women.

13. Thomas Hodgkin, *Vietnam: The Revolutionary Path* (London: Macmillan, 1981), 147.

14. Polly Hill, *Development Economics on Trial: the Anthropological Case for a Prosecution* (Cambridge: Cambridge University Press, 1986), 9.

15. Graham Greene, *The Quiet American* (Harmondsworth: Penguin, 1962; first published in 1955), 95.

16. See U.S. House of Representatives, Select Committee on Intelligence, *Hearings*, 94th Cong., 1st sess., Nov. 4, 6, Dec. 2–17, 1975, part 5, 1706–7, cited in Loren Baritz, *Backfire: Vietnam—The Myths That Made Us Fight, the Illusions That Helped Us Lose, the Legacy That Haunts Us Today* (New York: Ballantine, 1986), 24.

17. Elliott, *No Other Road to Take*, 29.

18. Bich Thuan (transcribing the account by Nguyen Thi Dinh), *Nu Chien Si Rung Dua* [Female Warrior of the Coconut Grove] (Hanoi: Nha Xuat Ban Phu Nu, 1987), 243 pp. This untranslated second account is much longer than the earlier translated memoirs

and contains many more details about Dinh's life and feelings. *No Other Road* mentions only that Bich was arrested three days after his son was born, but not that he had stayed dangerously long in order to be with his wife and baby, thus risking arrest.

19. Elliott, *No Other Road to Take*, 32.
20. Ibid.
21. Ibid., 34.
22. Ibid., 36.
23. Dang Thanh Le, "Van hoc co voi nu anh hung Trung Trac," *Tap Chi Van Hoc* 5 (1969): 47–48, as cited in Keith Weller Taylor, *The Birth of Vietnam* (Berkeley: University of California Press, 1983), 335. According to research by Stephen O'Harrow, the argument that Trung Trac's motivation was to revenge her husband was an attempt by later Vietnamese Confucian historians to fit the Trung sisters into a properly feminine framework. According to Chinese historical texts, Trung Trac took the lead even when her husband was alive, and there is no mention of the Han governor executing her husband. Stephen O'Harrow, "From Co Loa to the Trung Sister's Revolt: Viet Nam as the Chinese Found It," *Asian Perspectives* 22, 2 (1979): 140–64.
24. Nguyen Dinh Chieu, *Luc Van Tien.*
25. Elliott, *No Other Road to Take*, 43.
26. Ibid., 44. This is the same Tran Van Tra whose contributions appear in this volume. Both Nguyen Thi Dinh and Tran Van Tra were invited to the conference for which this chapter was originally prepared; Tran Van Tra was granted a U.S. visa since he is now retired; Nguyen Thi Dinh's visa was denied since she was still working in an official capacity—as president of the Women's Union.
27. The term "*Indochine Française*," printed on coins, banknotes, stamps, and letterhead stationery, was an omnipresent sign of the country's subordinated status. Paul Mus, *Sociologie d'une Guerre* (Paris: Editions du Seuil, 1952), 265.
28. Frances FitzGerald, *Fire in the Lake* (New York: Vintage, 1972).
29. Todd Gitlin, *The Sixties: Years of Hope, Days of Rage* (New York: Bantam, 1987).
30. This is my conclusion from conversations with many veterans.
31. Neil Sheehan, *A Bright Shining Lie: John Paul Vann and America in Vietnam* (New York: Random House, 1988).
32. Don Luce, "The Search for a Final Absolution. Review of *A Bright Shining Lie: John Paul Vann and America in Vietnam.*" *Commonweal*, February 10, 1989, 83.

Part Two

The War from the American Side

6

U.S. Military Strategy
and the Vietnam War

George R. Vickers

*The first, the supreme, the most far-reaching act of judgment that the states-
man and the commander have to make is to establish . . . the kind of war on
which they are embarking; neither mistaking it for, nor trying to turn it into,
something that is alien to its nature. This is the first of all strategic questions
and the most comprehensive.*

—Clausewitz, *On War*[1]

More than fifteen years after the end of the Vietnam War, U.S. military analysts
remain divided over what lessons the war holds for future American military
involvement in third world settings. There is general agreement that American
military strategy in Vietnam was fundamentally flawed, but there is sharp disagreement over whether the failure was in *not applying* classical military principles or in applying the *wrong* principles for the kind of war Vietnam represented.

The disagreements are not solely a product of disinterested analysis, since
most of the key protagonists served as military officers during the Vietnam War
and have reputations or careers at stake in how that war is ultimately judged. The
military, as an institution, also has a good deal at stake in how its performance in
Vietnam is judged. Nor is the dispute simply about the past, since differing
conclusions imply changes in military doctrine or future military strategy. The
conduct of the war in the Persian Gulf was heavily influenced by "lessons"
drawn from the military's review of its strengths and weaknesses in the Vietnam
conflict.

There are sharp disagreements and subtle shadings of difference in military
analyses of U.S. strategy during the Vietnam War. There are also some common

themes. General Phillip Davidson has observed that, despite a tendency to frame analyses in terms of strategic and tactical concepts, the fundamental point of disagreement among military analysts concerns the very nature of the war: "The real question was *not* what was the proper strategy to guide the ground war in South Vietnam, but *what kind of war was the United States fighting in Vietnam at any given period.*"[2]

The closest thing to an "official" position is the view that the Vietnam War was, essentially, a *conventional* war in which North Vietnam sought to conquer South Vietnam through military force. According to this view, U.S. strategy erred by focusing on defeating a guerrilla insurgency in South Vietnam rather than developing a strategy aimed at defeating North Vietnamese aggression.

The alternative view is that the Vietnam War was a *revolutionary war* that required the United States to adopt a strategy aimed at denying the insurgents access to the population rather than a strategy aimed at seeking out and destroying main force units of the National Liberation Front (NLF) and North Vietnamese Army.

These perspectives are fundamentally opposed, yet both often utilize the same "facts" to support their position. While they differ over how much of the blame for U.S. failure belongs to military commanders as opposed to political leaders, both view the *actual* strategy employed as disastrous.

Vietnam as Conventional Warfare

Colonel Harry Summers, whose 1981 analysis *On Strategy* is widely used as a textbook in military academies and training schools, starts out by arguing that,

> One of the most frustrating aspects of the Vietnam War from the Army's point of view is that as far as logistics and tactics were concerned we succeeded in everything we set out to do. . . . On the battlefield itself, the Army was unbeatable.[3]

In a similar vein, General Bruce Palmer (a former army vice-chief of staff) maintains that

> The war was lost primarily at strategic, diplomatic, and domestic political levels, although the final defeat of the South Vietnamese forces on the ground was more tactical and military in nature.[4]

Summers emphatically rejects the notion that Vietnam was a revolutionary war,

> There are still those who would attempt to fit it into the revolutionary war mold and who blame our defeat on our failure to implement counterinsurgency doctrine. This point of view requires an acceptance of the North Vietnamese contention that the war was a civil war, and that the North Vietnamese regular forces were an extension of the guerrilla effort, a point of view not borne out by the facts. . . . [I]t was four North Vietnamese Army corps, not "dialectical materialism," that ultimately conquered South Vietnam.[5]

Summers and Palmer both argue that a fundamental weakness in U.S. policy in Vietnam was the failure to clearly define the *objective* of U.S. policy, and a corresponding failure on the part of political leaders to mobilize the national will in support of that objective. Summers complains that the rationale for U.S. actions in Vietnam shifted from "resisting communist aggression" to an emphasis on "counterinsurgency" to "preserving the integrity of American commitments," while the North Vietnamese maintained a singular focus on conquering South Vietnam.[6]

Both Summers and Palmer believe that the failure to define an attainable objective in Vietnam led to a failure of strategy and a violation of the principles of war as first articulated by Clausewitz and spelled out in U.S. Army training manuals. According to those principles, objectives must be achieved through offensive action that concentrates superior power at critical moments (the principle of *mass*) while using combat power prudently (the principle of *economy of force*) and by deploying troops and equipment in the most efficient and advantageous way (the principle of *maneuver*). They also argue that the U.S. effort was undermined by a failure to establish and maintain unity of command over the conduct of the war.

Summers complains that the United States wore itself out trying to conduct a counterinsurgency war against guerrillas in South Vietnam, while the real function of guerrilla units was to harass and distract "both the United States and South Vietnam so that North Vietnamese regular forces could reach a decision in conventional battles."[7] To support his claim that the Vietnam War was a conventional war, Summers cites North Vietnamese Chief of Staff General Van Tien Dung's account of the final offensive to conquer South Vietnam in 1975.[8] Summers argues that the final offensive was a classic example of the successful application of the principles of war by conventional forces to achieve complete victory.

The logical underpinning of Summers argument is what he calls "judgment by results"—the notion that because South Vietnam's final defeat was brought about by North Vietnamese regular units using conventional warfare, the North Vietnamese all along intended to dominate the South by conventional means.[9] For Summers the essential turning point of the war came in December of 1963, when North Vietnam made a decision to intervene directly with its own forces to defeat the South Vietnamese government.[10] From that point on, he argues, the war was no longer a revolutionary war but a conventional war between states.

Few military analysts go so far as Summers in arguing that the Vietnam War was solely a conventional war, but many agree with him that the key weakness in U.S. strategy was its failure to target North Vietnam as the main enemy and to take the offensive against North Vietnam. Colonel Rod Paschall, former director of the U.S. Army Military Historical Institute, argued in 1985 that "Asian Marxist Insurgent Doctrine" as developed by Mao Tse-Tung, Truong Chinh, and Vo Nguyen Giap aimed at combining conventional "mid-intensity conflict" (which he defined as "battle between regulars") with guerrilla warfare against regular troops to keep the enemy from concentrating superior firepower (or "low-intensity conflict").[11] Paschall compares Van Tien Dung's account of the final offensive in 1975 with that of Tran Van Tra[12] and concludes, "It is highly probable that the Vietnamese communists never even considered a campaign that was to be wholly conducted by guerrillas or one that was to be conducted solely by regulars. Their doctrine was clear—both were to be used, and used in concert."[13]

General Palmer agrees with Paschall that the Vietnam War strategy of North Vietnam combined mid-intensity and low-intensity features throughout. Summers, Palmer, and Paschall all suggest that U.S. strategy should have been aimed at isolating the battlefield in South Vietnam by going on the offensive against insurgent sanctuaries in Cambodia, Laos, and North Vietnam. Both Summers and Palmer argue that a strategy that employed U.S. forces to cut off North Vietnamese supply lines to the South while South Vietnamese armed forces concentrated on destroying insurgents in the South could have succeeded better than the defensive "war of attrition" actually conducted by General Westmoreland.

Vietnam as Revolutionary Warfare

Despite the widespread acceptance of Summers' analysis at top levels of the military establishment, the most detailed studies of U.S. and North Vietnamese military strategy and tactics in the Vietnam War challenge his characterization of the war as primarily conventional and governed by traditional principles of war. General Phillip Davidson, who served as chief intelligence officer for Military Assistance Command, Vietnam (MACV), from 1967 to 1969, agrees with Summers and Palmer that the United States did not have a clearly defined national objective in Vietnam, and he also agrees with them that U.S. strategy was incorrect, but he concludes that Vietnam was fundamentally a revolutionary war:

> This strategy of revolutionary war was the *key* ingredient of the Communist victory. . . . A critic might contend that other factors, such as massive aid from China and Russia, the use of the Cambodian and Laotian sanctuaries, the weakness of the South Vietnamese government and leaders, and the incredible martial spirit of the North Vietnamese soldiers were significant factors. And this is true, *but* the factor which welded and focused the Communist effort from first to last was the strategy of revolutionary war. Without it there would have been no Communist victory.[14]

What is "revolutionary war"? In the writings of U.S. military analysts who deny that Vietnam was a revolutionary war, the term is frequently used interchangeably with "guerrilla warfare" or "insurgency," and there is a tendency to analyze the Vietnam War in terms of a "Maoist model" of revolutionary war that begins in the countryside, gradually moves to surround the cities, and in the final stage conquers the urban areas.[15] This model treats insurgency as a relatively linear three-phase process:

Phase 1. In the first stage of "contention" or "guerrilla warfare," the insurgents emphasize political organization and proselytizing among the masses. Armed struggle is primarily defensive or harassing, aimed at keeping the opponent from concentrating force against the insurgents.

Phase 2. In the "equilibrium" or "mobile warfare" stage, regular armed units supplement guerrilla formations, and the insurgents establish base areas and control some of the population. In this phase larger-scale military actions take place, although the insurgents are highly mobile and avoid engaging the enemy except when they have a tactical advantage.

Phase 3. In the final "counteroffensive" or "positional warfare" stage the war resembles conventional war. Set-piece battles take place between insurgent regular forces and government forces, and the insurgent goal is to topple the government. Set-piece battles may be accompanied by a general insurrection of the populace.

This emphasis on stages of insurgency is misleading and confuses tactical doctrine with more central strategic features that distinguish revolutionary war from conventional war.[16] To the Vietnamese revolutionaries, however, it was not the tactics employed that defined the nature of their struggle; it was the very conception of war itself. General Vo Nguyen Giap called it "people's war," which he defined as:

> a *true revolutionary war, a war by the entire people, a total war.* A revolutionary war, because it was carried out on the basis of the mobilization and organization of the masses, with the aim of achieving a national democratic revolution. A war by the entire people, because it was a war in which a whole nation struggled in unity, each citizen becoming a combatant, a war in which our Party's correct revolutionary line succeeded in grouping all patriotic strata of the population in a broad front based on a strong worker-peasant alliance, and mobilizing them for the struggle. A total war, because armed struggle was frequently combined with political struggle, because at the same time as we engaged in a military struggle, we carried out reduction of land rent, land reform, political struggle in urban centers and enemy-occupied areas, and struggle in the economic and cultural fields.[17]

As Jeffrey Race observed in his excellent study of how the revolution developed in Long An province, Vietnamese insurgents saw revolutionary war as a political struggle to win over and mobilize the entire population in struggle against the government or foreign occupation.[18] He describes revolutionary war as an outgrowth of changes in the balance of forces in society between allies and opponents of the revolution. When the balance of forces is sufficiently favorable to the insurgent party, violence against the dominant power becomes a viable option, and the "three stages" of revolutionary war represent shifts in strategy to use greater military force as the balance of forces continues to shift in favor of the insurgents.[19]

Race notes that assessing the balance of forces at any given moment is the critical step in developing the appropriate strategic mix of political and military tactics by the insurgents. Similarly, alternative actions are constantly evaluated in terms of their likely impact on the existing balance of forces. The senior leaders of North Vietnam and the NLF were directly involved in this process of constant evaluation and reassessment,[20] and many of the Central Committee resolutions, COSVN directives, and party study documents reflect this process.[21]

General Davidson agrees with these characterizations. In his definition the key features of revolutionary war are: it is *political warfare* in that it is aimed at gaining political control within a state; it is *total war* because it mobilizes and uses all the people and almost every facet of power; it is waged with *total unity of effort* in the sense that all facets of power are employed with close coordination and tight control; it stresses *ambiguity* and attempts to confuse and misdirect the enemy; it is *protracted war* and tries to wear down the will and fighting capacity of the enemy over time; and it is *changing war* in that the tactics and the balance between political and military force change over the course of the struggle.[22]

Given the emphasis on mobilizing political support from the populace, access to the population was essential to a revolutionary war strategy. In a strategic and tactical sense, at any given moment insurgents would be less concerned about the ability of their regular military units to win set-piece battles than about their access to the population and their success in winning political support from the population.

From the perspective of revolutionary war, the central strategy of Vietnamese insurgents was to deepen their political influence over the South Vietnamese population and to build a political-military infrastructure capable of waging simultaneous political and military struggle. The objective was to gradually shift the emphasis toward military actions to overthrow the South Vietnamese government.[23] As the American military intervention grew after 1964, the strategy shifted to emphasize exacerbating contradictions between the United States and South Vietnamese forces with an interim objective of forcing a United States withdrawal.

Given this revolutionary strategy, U.S. military strategy should have been geared toward population security and denying the insurgents access to the population, rather than toward a war of attrition directed against insurgent main force units.[24] Those who view the war as a revolutionary war also argue that U.S. strategy should have emphasized pacification programs and cite isolated examples of successful pacification efforts in Vietnam.

What Kind of War Was Vietnam?

Starting with the Ia Drang Valley battle of 1965, and ending with the seventeen-division final offensive in 1975, regular unit warfare was a continuing feature of the Vietnam War. Analysts who argue that the Vietnam War was conventional emphasize the role of set-piece battles and claim that almost all major battles between regular units of the United States and the NLF or North Vietnamese, including the Tet Offensive of 1968 and the 1972 Spring Offensive of the North Vietnamese, resulted in heavy casualties for the insurgents. U.S. estimates of enemy casualties during the Tet Offensive range from 40,000 casualties to 58,000 deaths,[25] and President Nixon claimed that the North Vietnamese lost 100,000 dead during the 1972 Spring Offensive. Most of these analysts describe Tet and the 1972 offensive as major military defeats for the Vietnamese communists.

As Lieutenant Colonel Andrew Krepinevich has noted, however,

> in combating an insurgency, winning the big battles is not decisive unless you can proceed to defeat the enemy at the lower levels of insurgency operations as well, destroying his infrastructure and guerrilla forces as well as his main-force units.[26]

Prior to 1969, U.S. forces in Vietnam were seldom able to achieve such follow-up victories. The evidence suggests rather strongly that the insurgents controlled the timing and scope of battle.[27] For example, 88 percent of all the engagements in early 1967 were initiated by the insurgents. The monthly average of battalion-sized attacks dropped from 9.7 per month during the last quarter of 1965 to 1.3 per month in the last quarter of 1966. During the same period small-scale attacks increased by 150 percent.[28]

The casualty figures from large-unit battles are misleading in that they obscure the fact that the battles were generally initiated by the insurgents and broken off at their choosing. What is important about those battles is that they mostly occurred in remote areas away from heavily populated zones. Their major effect was to divert large U.S. units away from the populated areas where insurgent infrastructure was operative. General Westmoreland himself acknowledged that insurgent strategy sought to divert U.S. combat forces to remote areas:

> From the first the primary emphasis of the North Vietnamese focused on the Central Highlands and the Central Coastal provinces, with the basic aim of drawing American units into remote areas and thereby facilitating control of the population in the lowlands.[29]

The biggest example of large-unit warfare used to divert U.S. forces was the siege of Khe Sanh in 1968. The siege began in early January and involved more than three North Vietnamese Army (NVA) divisions in a remote area near the DMZ.[30] Five U.S. Marine battalions defended the base, supported by massive artillery and air support. The siege continued until March, when the NVA units were withdrawn. The NVA units took heavy casualties during the siege—U.S. estimates range from 3,000 to 15,000 NVA casualties.[31] Despite the diversionary effect of the siege, General Westmoreland and General Davidson, among others, still maintain that the siege was more than just a diversion. General Davidson believes that General Giap hoped to turn Khe Sanh into another Dien Bien Phu.[32]

While it would not be atypical of Vietnamese revolutionary strategy to have included in tactical planning for Khe Sanh flexibility to expand the siege if U.S. response and the situation on the ground demonstrated that a major military defeat of U.S. forces was possible, it seems unlikely that the North Vietnamese viewed this as a serious option. If Khe Sanh was intended as a major "Dien Bien Phu" battle, for example, it is strange that the NVA troops failed to attack the water supply for the base, which was outside the marine defense perimeter.[33] It is clear that the central focus of revolutionary planning at that time was the Tet Offensive and instigation of a general insurrection. The siege served to divert a large U.S. force and to occupy the major part of MACV's attention during January of 1968, while the insurgents were moving closer to cities in preparation for the Tet Offensive at the end of the month. Guenter Lewy has noted that the siege also drew marine Civil Action Patrol (CAP) units involved in successful pacification efforts away from population control and into the defense of Khe Sanh.[34] General Tran Van Tra, the commander of People's Liberation Armed Forces (PLAF) in southern South Vietnam, maintains that the siege was always and only intended as a diversion.[35]

While the insurgents controlled the level of fighting and generally avoided large-scale battles after 1965, they did fight when their access to the population was threatened. In 1967, 90 percent of all incidents of fighting in any given quarter occurred in the 10 percent of the country where eighty percent of the population lived.[36] Local government militia and regional forces, the units closest to the village level, bore the brunt of the fighting. Although they represented about 50 percent of all Saigon government armed forces from 1967 through 1971, they went from 52 percent of all government "killed in action" (KIA) to 60 percent of KIAs in the same period.[37] These units also accounted for 30 percent of the PLAF/NVA KIAs inflicted by the Saigon armed forces, although they represented only 20 percent of the armed forces budget.[38]

Prior to 1969, then, Vietnamese revolutionaries focused on maintaining and expanding their infrastructure in populated areas of South Vietnam and inflicting maximum casualties on Saigon government forces. NVA units were used to draw U.S. combat forces away from populated areas, while guerrilla forces sought to keep other U.S. units in static defensive positions while inflicting small but steady casualties.[39] What about the argument that casualties among southern revolutionaries during Tet were so great that, whatever the nature of the war up to that time, after 1968 the war was primarily one between North Vietnamese Army units and U.S. and South Vietnamese forces?

It certainly is the case that southern revolutionaries suffered severe casualties during the three phases of the Tet Offensive.[40] While significant North Vietnamese reinforcements were brought into the South, the southern revolutionaries were gradually put on the defensive. The United States began to move away from its prior emphasis on large-unit warfare, and smaller units began to pursue, and to maintain constant pressure on, revolutionary forces. The United States also began to pursue a very aggressive pacification campaign focusing on heavily populated areas. Both of these tactics placed great pressure on the revolutionary infrastructure at the village and hamlet level.[41]

North Vietnamese regular army units did play a more significant role in the South between 1969 and 1971, but this does not demonstrate that the nature of the war became conventional. General Davidson correctly points out that the insurgent leadership also had internal disputes over strategy and tactics, and there were periodic shifts in the emphasis placed on long-term versus short-term results, military versus political means, and main force versus small-unit warfare.[42] That there were serious disagreements is clear, and this includes differing evaluations about the wisdom and success of critical strategic decisions such as the Tet Offensive and the final offensive of 1975. General Tran Van Tra, for example, has argued that the revolutionary forces suffered greater losses than necessary during the Tet Offensive because "we did not correctly evaluate the specific balance of forces between ourselves and the enemy, did not fully realize that the enemy still had considerable capabilities and that our capabilities were limited, and set requirements beyond our actual strength."[43]

General Tra also argues, however, that the southern revolutionary infrastructure was entirely rebuilt to pre-Tet levels by the end of 1971.[44] While most U.S. military analysts cite the North Vietnamese Army conventional attack across the DMZ in spring 1972 as evidence to support the conventional war argument, the reality is that the offensive quickly became bogged down and most of the tanks employed were destroyed by U.S. air power. The North Vietnamese forces were extremely vulnerable, but hundreds of small attacks in urban areas and in the delta by southern revolutionary units prevented the United States and the South Vietnamese government from concentrating their forces against the NVA units.[45]

Although many North Vietnamese accounts of the final stage of the Vietnam War in 1975 ignore the role of southern revolutionaries,[46] General Tra claims that there were 10,000 sappers and 10,000 guerrilla commandos inside Saigon prior to the final North Vietnamese assault.[47] His account of the final phase of the war also indicates that the timing and strategy for the final offensive was the subject of extensive debate and disagreement between North Vietnamese and South Vietnamese revolutionary activists.[48]

It seems clear, therefore, that right up until the end the Vietnam War remained a revolutionary war that combined political and military struggle in an effort to mobilize the population of North and South Vietnam in a united movement to force a U.S. withdrawal and defeat the Saigon government. Gabriel Kolko summarizes the final collapse of the Thieu government forces in 1975:

> Throughout South Vietnam the end of the war saw a mixture of local militia and guerrillas complementing regional and main forces in ways indispensable to both. The local forces in many areas would surely have been destroyed had

it not been for the presence and imminent arrival of regular soldiers and their effect on RVNAF morale, but the main forces urgently needed the help of local fighters to take over policing and support operations, lest they themselves be diverted to less urgent tasks. In a conventional war that almost immediately became unconventional, the poorly armed local units performed a far greater function than they had at any other time since 1968, save in the Delta, where they played a primary role of immense strategic value.[49]

Win, Lose, or Draw?

There is a curious ambiguity in the final assessments by many military analysts of U.S. military performance in the Vietnam War. Summers, for example, bitterly criticizes political and military leaders who, he believes, wore out U.S. willpower and wasted precious time and resources by trying to fight a counterinsurgent war rather than a conventional one.[50] At the same time he asserts that *militarily* U.S. forces were capable of, and regularly succeeded in, defeating Vietnamese revolutionary strategy and tactics. Like Summers, Paschall argues that the U.S. military did not actually lose in Vietnam, because the military situation was effectively a stalemate when the United States withdrew from a direct combat role. As he puts it,

> by the time US combat forces entered, North Vietnamese regulars were being employed in South Vietnam in battalion-sized strengths. US ground forces thus began a conflict in which both guerrilla and main force units were being employed throughout the country. In 1973, at the negotiated close of this second conflict, the same situation prevailed. . . . The Republic of Vietnam still existed; the communists had not won, but they had not lost.[51]

By treating Vietnamese insurgent strategy as rigid and unchanging in response to the U.S. introduction of ground troops, this rather bizarre conclusion ignores the fact that the United States came and went, at a cost of 50,000 U.S. dead and $239 billion, without changing the balance of forces or the outcome of the war. When the United States began its massive buildup in 1965, the Vietnamese revolutionaries quickly changed their short-term goals. Rather than seeking a quick defeat of the South Vietnamese government, they began to use a combination of political and military tactics designed to embroil the United States in a protracted war and to defeat it at that level. This new strategy was formally approved by the Twelfth Plenum of the party in December, 1965.[52]

Summers' complaint that the United States wasted time and resources by trying to fight a "counterinsurgent war" ignores the evidence that, by and large, the United States did not prepare for or conduct a counterinsurgency war in Vietnam. Lieutenant Colonel Krepinevich has described in painstaking detail the failure of the army to prepare for counterinsurgency warfare prior to Vietnam, and its continued emphasis on conventional warfare once deployed to Vietnam.[53]

Indeed, those U.S. forces trained in counterinsurgency tactics were frequently redirected to conventional warfare tasks as the U.S. buildup began.[54] The U.S. military, with few exceptions, fought the Vietnam War as a "mid-intensity conflict" (i.e., a conflict between armies employing non-nuclear conventional weapons, with a direct combat role for U.S. troops).

When the United States did seriously implement pacification and counterinsurgency tactics, during the 1969 to 1971 period, they achieved greater success at weakening the revolutionary infrastructure in the villages than at any other point during the conflict.[55] Perhaps the most significant evidence that pacification was a threat to the revolutionaries are their own statements that they most feared expansion of those types of programs.[56]

Paschall maintains that U.S. leaders made a fatal error by allowing North Vietnam to remain a sanctuary for insurgents fighting in the South, and argues that nations that sponsor insurgency must be targets of offensive operations, "offensive ground operations within the contiguous sanctuary are particularly vital to the counterinsurgent. . . . The counterinsurgent must . . . go beyond the bounds of low-intensity conflict and into the realm of mid-intensity conflict. These operations may be wholly conducted by the nation beset with a foreign-sponsored insurgency, by US armed forces, or both."[57]

Summers and General Palmer agree that the United States never developed a strategy to deal with the real enemy—North Vietnam.[58] They believe that the United States could have isolated the battlefield and won the war by a tactical offensive involving sending five divisions to block the DMZ and create a defensive line through the Laotian panhandle all the way to the Thai border. This would have cut off North Vietnam's supply lines to the South and allowed remaining U.S. units and the South Vietnamese army to wipe out insurgents in the South.[59]

The blocking strategy proposed by Palmer and Summers is not a new idea. In late 1961, Walt Rostow suggested a smaller-scale version of the idea,[60] and in 1965 General Robert Johnson made a formal proposal for a four-division blocking force across the DMZ and Laotian panhandle to the Thai border. The army chief of staff commissioned a study of the proposal, but the idea was dropped when the study reported that the effort would be a logistical nightmare requiring at least 18,000 additional engineering troops plus large numbers of indigenous laborers.[61]

Even if the logistical problems could have been overcome, there is no particular reason to think the blocking strategy would have achieved the objectives of its proponents. On the one hand, why would the North Vietnamese not have simply done an end run around the blockade through Thailand? It might have caused delays and some temporary interruption, but there is little reason to think that the Thai military would have been any more willing or able to prevent the North Vietnamese from establishing a new route than the Laotians or Cambodians were. More importantly, *cutting the supply route would not have caused a critical shortage of manpower or supplies at that time.* In 1961 U.S. intelligence estimates were that 80 percent to 90 percent of the NLF/PLAF cadre were locally recruited in South Vietnam. In 1967 the CIA estimated that the vast majority of PLAF/NVA supplies used in South Vietnam were generated within the South.[62] Not until after the Tet Offensive in 1968 did North Vietnamese manpower and supplies become a decisive logistical issue.

The evidence suggests that the real failure of the United States in Vietnam was not a failure to perceive the conventional nature of the war and to develop a strategy aimed at North Vietnam, but a failure to understand and prepare for the revolutionary war we in fact encountered. As Lieutenant Colonel Krepinevich summed up the doctrinal failure of the army in Vietnam:

> [T]he Army's conduct of the war was a failure, primarily because it never realized that insurgency warfare required basic changes in Army methods to meet the exigencies of this "new" conflict environment. . . . In effect, MACV attempted to adapt what had been the low-risk strategy of attrition in a mid-intensity conflict environment to a low-intensity conflict in the hope of achieving similar results. The nature of insurgency warfare, however, made such a strategic approach a high-cost, high-risk option for MACV by mandating a quick victory before the American public grew weary of bearing the burden of continuing the war.[63]

Revolutionary War and U.S. Strategy

Those military analysts who view the Vietnam War as a revolutionary war have been actively involved in shaping a new military doctrine for "low-intensity conflict" situations.[64] This new doctrine accepts the fundamental argument of "counterinsurgency doctrine" that the key to defeating insurgents in a revolutionary war is to deny them access to the population. To do so requires that the threatened government assert control over the population, win the political support of the population, root out and destroy the insurgent infrastructure at the local level, and maintain a long-term physical presence of government in local villages to create confidence and security.[65] This implies that pacification efforts and protection of heavily populated areas should have been the chief priority for U.S. strategy in Vietnam, rather than attrition of insurgent main force units.[66]

Mere physical control of the population will not suffice, however. Insurgencies are rooted in genuine grievances and social inequality. The analysts argue that, to effectively counter insurgent appeals, the government must adopt structural reforms that eliminate some of the objective conditions on which insurgent appeal is based.[67]

The new doctrine argues that introduction of U.S. combat forces into third world conflicts should be avoided, except as a last recourse, since the foreign presence allows insurgents to appeal to nationalist sentiments in their proselytizing. The more desirable U.S. role is in training and equipping government forces.[68] Another reason for avoiding a direct U.S. role in combat is to reduce domestic opposition in the United States to the U.S. effort. In Vietnam, the insurgents skillfully appealed to an American audience to encourage domestic opposition to the war.[69]

In Vietnam, time aided the insurgents since U.S. will to continue wore down faster than insurgent ability to continue the struggle. That is the whole idea of protracted struggle. This need not be the case, however, according to low-intensity conflict doctrine. The very magnitude of U.S. material resources makes it possible for the United States to outlast and wear down a third world insurgency if U.S. leaders are able to maintain a clear objective and to keep domestic dissent at a manageable level.

Most of these "lessons" of Vietnam have been tested and refined in Central America during the last decade. The final verdict is not in (particularly with respect to El Salvador), but in general, the Central American experience provides support for the main theses of low-intensity conflict doctrine.

The most problematic of these lessons, in terms of whether it can actually be implemented, concerns the adoption and implementation of structural reforms by governments supported by the United States. In Vietnam, despite enormous financial and political leverage available to the United States, the United States had little success in getting the South Vietnamese armed forces to make even the most rudimentary reforms to improve its image or its behavior. The dilemma is that third world governments seeking U.S. assistance against insurgencies frequently are governed directly by elites benefiting from social inequality and the exploitation of a majority of the population.[70] These same elites generally control or include the officer corps of the military.

The experience in Central America, as well as in Vietnam, suggests that such elites are unwilling to make anything but "cosmetic" reforms, since to do more risks undermining the very basis of their power. Ironically, U.S. leverage to force more fundamental reforms is limited and perhaps insufficient because those elites perceive that in the midst of a revolutionary war, the United States often has no viable alternative to continued elite domination, except the revolutionaries. Unless it can force such reforms, however, the United States risks becoming bogged down in a very long-term commitment where the fundamental source of insurgent appeal remains unchanged.

The Vietnam War was a revolutionary war, and the failure of U.S. military strategy there reflected the military's lack of a strategy appropriate to the conditions of revolutionary warfare. Low-intensity conflict doctrine is an effort to develop such a strategy, but the Persian Gulf War also demonstrated that the U.S. military is applying lessons learned from Vietnam to conventional war situations. Just as Iraq hoped to wear down the U.S. public's support for the war by drawing out the conflict, U.S. military and civilian strategists sought a rapid and decisive victory and devoted major resources to controlling media access to information and shaping the perceptions of the nature of the war.

It may be that the U.S. victory in Iraq will eliminate the "Vietnam Syndrome" that has made Americans wary of military involvement in third world settings. But Sadaam Hussein was not Ho Chi Minh, and the Iraqi invasion of Kuwait was not a revolutionary war. An understanding of revolutionary war will be needed again, and controlling the media is not the most important lesson to be learned from the Vietnam War.

Notes

1. Carl von Clausewitz, *On War* (Princeton, NJ: Princeton University Press, 1976), 88–89.
2. Lt. General Phillip B. Davidson (Ret.), *Vietnam at War: The History 1946–1975* (Novato, CA: Presidio Press, 1988), 718–19.
3. Colonel Harry G. Summers, Jr., *On Strategy: A Critical Analysis of the Vietnam War* (Novato, CA: Presidio Press, 1982), 1.
4. General Bruce Palmer, Jr., *The 25-Year War: America's Military Role in Vietnam* (Lexington: University Press of Kentucky, 1984), 171.
5. Summers, *On Strategy*, 77–78.
6. Ibid., 90. Hugh Arnold describes twenty-two different U.S. rationales in "Official Justifications for America's Role in Indochina, 1949–67," *Asian Affairs* (September–October 1975).
7. Summers, *On Strategy*, 69.
8. General Van Tien Dung, *Our Great Spring Victory* (New York: Monthly Review Press, 1977).
9. Summers spells out this logic in "Defense without Purpose," *Society*, 21, 1 (November–December 1983).
10. Ibid. Summers is referring to a resolution adopted at the Ninth Conference of the Lao Dong Party Central Committee which directed a major effort to build up revolutionary military forces in the South. The resolution is quite clearly referring to a buildup of *southern* revolutionary military units, however. While it hints that more direct North Vietnamese involvement might be required if the United States directly intervenes by sending large numbers of troops, the resolution anticipates as more likely a defeat of the South Vietnamese regime by a "General Offensive and Uprising" led by the southern revolutionary forces. The document is part of the *Viet Nam Documents and Research Notes*, no. 96.
11. Colonel Rod Paschall, "Low-Intensity Conflict Doctrine: Who Needs It?" *Parameters: Journal of the US Army War College*, 15, 3 (Fall 1985). The definition of "low-intensity" and "mid-intensity" used by Paschall is fairly primitive, and there is much more than indicated here to those concepts.
12. Colonel General Tran Van Tra, *Vietnam: History of the Bulwark B2 Theatre*, vol. 5: *Concluding the 30-Years War* (Ho Chi Minh City: Van Nghe Publishing House, 1982). Published in the United States in *Southeast Asia Report*, No. 1247, Joint Publication Research Service (JPRS) 82783, February 2, 1983.
13. Paschall, "Low-Intesity Conflict Doctrine," 41.
14. Davidson, *Vietnam at War*, 717 (emphasis in original).
15. Paschall, "Low-Intensity Conflict Doctrine," for example, says that "The doctrine of the Asian insurgent is easy to understand and remained relatively unchanged from the 1930s until the 1970s. The prime oracles have been Mao Tse-tung, Truong Chinh, and Vo Nguyen Giap," 34.

16. In his classic *People's War: People's Army* (Hanoi: Foreign Languages Publishing House, 1961), for example, Vo Nguyen Giap made a distinction between the "strategic guiding principle" rooted in a careful examination of the balance of forces, and a "guiding principle of fighting" necessary to carry out that strategic guiding principle. The guiding principle of fighting in the war against the French involved moving "from guerrilla warfare to mobile warfare combined with partial entrenched camp warfare." The strategic guiding principle in that war involved "Facing an enemy who temporarily had the upper hand, our people were not able to strike swiftly and win swiftly but needed time to overcome its shortcomings and increase the enemy's weak points. Time was needed to mobilise, organise and foster the forces of Resistance, to wear out the enemy forces, gradually reverse the balance of forces, turning our weakness into strength and concurrently availing ourselves of the changes in the international situation which was growing more and more advantageous to our Resistance, eventually to triumph over the enemy."

17. Vo Nguyen Giap, "The Political and Military Line of Our Party," *Vietnamese Studies*, no. 7 (Hanoi, 1965).

18. Jeffrey Race, *War Comes to Long An* (Berkeley and Los Angeles: University of California Press, 1972).

19. Ibid., 146.

20. Gabriel Kolko, *Anatomy of a War: Vietnam, the United States, and the Modern Historical Experience* (New York: Pantheon, 1985), 182.

21. A 1965 Lao Dong Party Central Committee Directive, for example, states that, "In sum, our people in the South are in the posture of continuous offensive while the enemy is in the passive posture of reacting. The composition of forces between the enemy and us in the South is changing in our favor." "Lao Dong Party Central Committee Directive on the Reorientation Campaign for Spring 1965, January 2, 1965 [Extract]," in Gareth Porter, ed., *Vietnam: A History in Documents* (New York: New American Library, 1981), 291.

22. Davidson, *Vietnam at War*, 716–17.

23. Ibid., 141–209.

24. Ibid., 210–66. This is also the essential criticism by Lt. Colonel Andrew F. Krepinevich, Jr., in *The Army and Vietnam* (Baltimore, MD: Johns Hopkins University Press, 1986).

25. General Davidson, *Vietnam at War*, says there were 45,000 enemy casualties during Tet (427), while Colonel Krepinevich refers to MACV estimates of over 40,000 (248). George Donelson Moss cites the 58,000 figure several times in his *Vietnam: An American Ordeal* (Englewood Cliffs, NJ: Prentice Hall, 1990), and that figure has been used by several others. Ngo Vinh Long provides a detailed criticism of the higher estimate in "The Tet Offensive and Its Aftermath," forthcoming in Jayne Werner and David Hunt, *The American War* (Ithaca, NY: Cornell University Southeast Asia Publications Series). He cites Vietnamese estimates of "several tens of thousands" lost during all three phases of Tet.

26. Krepinevich, *The Army and Vietnam*, 268. Krepinevich was a Major when the study was published.

27. See, for example, Guenter Lewy, *America in Vietnam* (New York: Oxford University Press, 1978), 56–72.

28. Ibid., 188.

29. General William Westmoreland, *A Soldier Reports* (New York: Doubleday, 1976), 194.

30. Guenter Lewy and Colonel Krepinevich are among a number of analysts who mention only two North Vietnamese divisions encircling Khe Sanh. General Davidson says that the 304 and 325C divisions were directly employed, but that the 320 and part of the 324 were stationed nearby as reserves (495). General Tran Van Tra agreed with

General Davidson's estimate at the History of the Vietnam/Indochina War Seminar held at Columbia University, November 16–17, 1990.

31. Krepinevich, *The Army and Vietnam*, 252.

32. Davidson, *Vietnam at War*, 504–13. General Davidson is probably least reliable here, since he was General Westmoreland's chief intelligence officer (J–2) during the siege. His elaborate defense of the thesis cannot account for several curious actions by the NVA troops that are much more consistent with the diversion thesis.

33. Ibid., 509–10. Davidson's argument that probably "neither Giap nor the local NVA commander ever realized the vulnerability" of the water supply seems too incredible to warrant discussion.

34. Lewy, *America in Vietnam*, 116–17. Krepinevich also describes the marine CAP effort as one of the few successful pacification efforts in *The Army and Vietnam* (172–77).

35. He made this assertion very firmly in response to specific questions at the History of the Vietnam/Indochina War Seminar held at Columbia University, November 16–17, 1990.

36. Krepinevich, *The Army and Vietnam*, 188.

37. Ibid., 221.

38. Ibid.

39. William Duiker cites a November 1965 letter from Le Duan to Nguyen Chi Thanh (overall commander of Communist forces in the South), spelling out this strategy. See his chapter 2 in this volume.

40. See note 25 for a discussion of estimates of casualties during Tet. According to Ngo Vinh Long, "The Tet Offensive and Its Aftermath," the most severe casualties in terms of regional and local forces occurred during the third phase that began in August.

41. Ngo Vinh Long (ibid.) provides a detailed account of this period in Long An province.

42. Davidson, *Vietnam at War*. General Davidson tends to view these disagreements as an ongoing faction-fight within the Lao Dong Politburo between "North Vietnam firsters" and those who favored the liberation of South Vietnam and the reunification of the entire country as the highest priority. He also views North Vietnamese revolutionary strategy from 1960 through 1967 as something of a personal battleground between General Giap and Nguyen Chi Thanh.

43. Tra, *Vietnam: History of the Bulwark B2 Theatre*, 35.

44. Comments in response to specific questions during the History of the Vietnam/Indochina War Seminar at Columbia University, November 16–17, 1990. Ngo Vinh Long, "The Tet Offensive and Its Aftermath," supports this assertion based on his study of Long An province.

45. See Tra, *Vietnam: History of the Bulwark B2 Theatre*; and Long, "The Tet Offensive and Its Aftermath." Gabriel Kolko also stresses the continuing importance of the southern revolutionary forces in *Anatomy of a War*.

46. See, for example, Dung, *Great Spring Victory*. Ngo Vinh Long also cites an influential account by Le Duc Tho minimizing the contribution of southern guerrillas to the liberation of Saigon. See his chapter 13 this volume.

47. Comments made at the History of the Vietnam/Indochina War Seminar; see chapter 3 of this volume.

48. Ibid.

49. Kolko, *Anatomy of a War*, 536.

50. Summers, *On Strategy*, 81.

51. Paschall, "Low-Intensity Conflict Doctrine," 36.

52. See, for example, William J. Duiker's chapter in this volume.

53. Krepinevich, *The Army and Vietnam*.

54. Ibid., 70–74. For example, during late 1961 and through 1962 U.S. Special Forces Groups engaged in civilian pacification efforts with indigenous tribes in the Central Highlands. By the end of 1962 this program had "recovered" several hundred villages with a population of some 300,000 civilians. Local village patrols to guard against insurgent attacks involved some 38,000 civilian irregulars in these villages. The program was transferred from civilian control to DOD beginning in July 1962, and within the following year the Special Forces Groups had been transferred to offensive actions against NLF/PLAF base camps. With the transfer of the pacification effort to Saigon government control in 1963 the entire effort collapsed and the gains were reversed.

55. See, for example, Long, "The Tet Offensive and Its Aftermath." Krepinevich and Lewy also cite evidence that pacification might have been more successful than big-unit warfare.

56. See, for example, Tra, *Vietnam: History of the Bulwark B2 Theatre*, 32–33.

57. Paschall, "Low-Intensity Conflict Doctrine," 43.

58. Ibid.

59. Ibid., 111–12. See also Palmer, *The 25-Year War*, 182–86.

60. Cited in David Halberstam, *The Best and the Brightest* (New York: Random House, 1969), 150.

61. Krepinevich, *The Army and Vietnam*, 142–45.

62. Ibid., 187.

63. Ibid., 259.

64. In 1985, for example, the army initiated a Joint Low-Intensity Conflict Project, with a focus on Central America. The Vietnam experience was a critical source for ideas and reality-testing for this project, and many active participants in the project had their first combat experience in Vietnam. In 1986 the project issued a two-volume *Final Report* that focused on strategic and tactical implications of low-intensity conflict warfare.

65. Krepinevich, *The Army and Vietnam*, 10–16.

66. Ibid., 258–75; Race, *War Comes to Long An*, 210–66.

67. Race, ibid., 271–76.

68. Joint Low-Intensity Conflict Project, *Final Report*, vol. 1: *Analytical Review of Low-Intensity Conflict* (Fort Monroe, VA: United States Army Training and Doctrine Command, August 1, 1986), 9–1.

69. Davidson, *Vietnam at War*, 727–29.

70. Race, *War Comes to Long An*, highlights the centrality of social class and the notion of contradictions between social groups in the social analysis of Vietnamese insurgents (142).

7

History's Heaviest Bombing

James P. Harrison

The most astonishing question, and one of the most overlooked aspects of the American war in Vietnam, was how the Vietnamese Communists and their supporters could survive at all against the staggering firepower thrown at them. People heard of the free-fire zones, with death warnings given against million-pellet fragmentation, cluster (CBU), phosphorous-incendiary, and other antipersonnel bombs; of 15,000-pound, field-clearing "Daisy Cutters"; of infrared, and laser-guided "smart" bombs; of the chemical herbicides, tear and other gases; of oxygen-depriving, intense-fire napalm; and seemingly everything but the atomic bomb. Then people saw the statistics of bombardments that accumulated to over three times all those used in World War II, and rechecked the map to see if Vietnam (128,401 square miles) was indeed less than 1/25 the size of the United States (3,543,883 square miles), not to speak of the still greater differences in wealth and technological development. In fact, Vietnam is slightly smaller than the new Germany (137,931 square miles), although together Cambodia (69,898 square miles) and Laos (91,428 square miles) are slightly bigger than Japan (145,856 square miles). They are about the size of Iraq (167,924 square miles), and these days, it may be necessary to recall that Japan and Germany were America's enemies in the most destructive war in history, which they started and which cost over fifty million dead. Perhaps Vietnam should have devised a way to lose its war in 1975!* In any case, Vietnam will go down in history (hopefully!) as the country that—small as it is—suffered more bombardments than all others put together, in all previous wars!

---

*Would the United States then have ended its embargo, supplied reconstruction aid, and supplied maps of unexploded ordinance and mines left in Indochina? It demanded the latter of defeated Iraq in 1991, but reportedly refused to give the same for Vietnam after 1975.

Presumably, in Indochina most of the explosives went into the mud and dust. Some have argued that they would rather be on the ground shooting at a plane than be an airborne bombardier trying to target elusive enemies. But they do not suggest changing places, and one wonders how long the United States would have fought, had Vietnam had an air force capable of bombing our troops in a sustained and massive way.

The tunnel complexes, bunkers, caves, and intelligence about airplane movements must have helped the Communist forces. But still, to think of something like the northeast of the United States (163,474 square miles without Maine), or California (158,693 square miles), or much of France (213,072 square miles) pummeled by over three times the tonnage of World War II is stupefying. Can the Vietnamese give us some explanations of how they not only survived all those explosives, but how they went on to win? As Tran Van Tra told Jean Lacouture about the time of the 1975 victory, against "increased means we opposed increased skill."[1] Can we learn more details about those skills?

Here are some more descriptions of what went on, at least as analyzed from afar from diverse sources.

As if Washington believed that it was better to be dead than "red" in the years after 1961 (especially 1965–72), the United States unloaded over 15 million tons of explosives in Indochina, close to half from the air—the latter delivered, according to one source, by up to 5,226,701 sorties. That would amount to an average of close to a thousand flights of all sorts a day, but combat sorties in intense periods were more often at the rate of 400 a day. They escalated from 4,800 a month in June 1965 to 12,000 a month by late 1967. During "Operation Rolling Thunder," (1965–68), an average of 800 tons of bombs a day were dropped on the North, and several times as much on the South and Laos. In the eight years of heaviest warfare, the average tonnage of bombs dropped was close to 2,400 tons a day, accumulating to over 7 million tons.

Thus fell from the air on Vietnam and parts of Cambodia and Laos the seeming equivalent of something like 400 Hiroshima-style atomic bombs, which if magnified proportionately for the size of the United States would come to some 10,000 Hiroshimas minus the radioactivity! And the dry figures for Vietnam encompass the use of an estimated 400,000 tons of napalm and some 19.1 million gallons of herbicides (11.2 gallons of which were deadly dioxin). The bombs left over 25 million craters on an area about the size of New Mexico (121,666 square miles).[2]

Most of the bombs (about 4 million tons) and virtually all of the defoliants were dropped on our ally, South Vietnam (66,220 square miles), which is about two-thirds the size of Great Britain (94,226 square miles)—where the far smaller bombings (less than 100,000 tons) of World War II have long been greatly famous. In South Vietnam, over half of the forests and 9,000 of 15,000 hamlets were heavily damaged. In January 1969, up to a quarter of the South's then less than 20 million people reported bombings within three kilometers of their homes. Approximately another million tons of bombs were dropped on North Vietnam, 1.5 million on Laos, and over a half-millon on Cambodia.[3]

When did this crushing tonnage fall? The dropping of herbicides began in early 1962, and by 1964 there were already over 100 U.S. pilots flying combat missions, accompanied for cover by Vietnamese co-pilots. The first to be shot down was Captain Edwin G. Shank in May 1964. After the Tonkin Gulf incident reprisals against North Vietnam of August 1964, some eight sorties a week (called "Operation Barrel Roll") began December 14, 1964, against the Ho Chi Minh Trail in Laos. Then "Flaming Dart" sent strikes north after February 7, 1965, following a Viet Cong attack at Pleiku, killing eight American soldiers. That came despite the presence in Hanoi of the number two Soviet leader, Aleksey Kosygin, who predictably promised increased aid.

The most publicized bombing in history next commenced on March 2, 1965, with Rolling Thunder, which continued with eight pauses until 1968. "Linebacker I" resumed bombing the North with a vengeance from late spring to October 1972, and "Linebacker II" explosively closed the American side of the air war against Hanoi, December 18–29, 1972. The bombings never stopped on the South and Laos, and began secretly against Communists in Cambodia in 1969, and continued there with names like "Arc Light" and "Operation Menu" ("Breakfast," "Lunch," and "Dinner"!) until July 1973.

With mounting fury, the bombing and shelling escalated from over 300,000 tons in 1965 against all targets, to over 1 million tons in 1966 and over 2 million tons each year from 1967 to 1970 and close to that in 1971 and 1972. The peak year saw 2,966,548 bombs dropped by some 400,000 combat sorties in 1968. Other figures spoke of 300 pounds of explosives in peak years, and over 1,000 pounds throughout the war, for every man, woman and child. Costs have been estimated at $400,000 for every Viet Cong killed. At times, the figures were even more staggering, as in the use of seventy-three tons of explosives for every Communist killed in one fortified position; and in one area of Cu Chi in the single month of January 1969, of twenty-seven explosives per square meter! Another village in Long An province was battered by three tons of bombs per inhabitant in 1966. The heaviest single bombing in the history of warfare was the pulverizing of five square miles around Khe Sanh in the spring of 1968 by 100,000 tons of bombs. More devastating still were the strikes between December 18 and 29, 1972—the "Christmas" bombing in which about 2,000 combat sorties dropped over 20,000 tons of bombs on and around Hanoi.[4]

Such incredible bombardments continuing to 1973, and in lesser amounts to 1975, doubled by the ground fire, added up to over 1,269 pounds (577 kilograms) per inhabitant throughout the war! Another source states that the explosives used came to twenty-six times per soldier, those used in World War II, when the totals, including ground munitions, were about half of the more than 14 million tons exploded in Indochina.[5]

Comparable figures for other wars include the following. In World War I, some 16,000 tons of bombs were dropped from the air by the Entente Powers, and 27,386 tons by the Germans. In World War II, Allied forces dropped close to 2.7 million tons of bombs, 1,234,767 of them by Anglo-American bomber commands on Axis Europe, with some 70,000 tons on Berlin and over 147,000 tons on Japan in the last year of the war. Then 678,000 tons were dropped on Korea in 1950–53, less than one-tenth of the 7.8 million tons dropped from the air on Indochina. Such totals for Vietnam equal about five times the estimates of the bomb tonnage dropped by Anglo-American forces in World War II, as against the usual figure of three times, the latter perhaps derived from including Axis and Soviet bombing as well.* Totals for the bombing vary; from over 5 million tons on Vietnam, to 7.8 million tons on Indochina and Saigon's 2,000 combat planes added to these totals after 1972. An example of the greater accuracy and attempts to avoid civilian casualties there, however, might be shown by the contrast between the estimated 2,084 English killed by the less than 300 tons dropped on them in World War I; or, in World War II, the 60,000 English killed by 71,000 metric tons of German bombs, the 593,000 Germans killed by 1.25 million tons of Allied bombs, and the 330,000 Japanese killed by some 147,000 tons of U.S. bombs; with the perhaps 52,000 people killed by the 643,000 tons dropped by Rolling Thunder on North Vietnam.[6]

And in all the recent talk of terrorism, the biggest explosive I have heard of was the 2,000 pounds (or one ton) carried in the truck, which detonated to kill sixty-three U.S. Marines in Beirut on October 23, 1983. Most terrorist attacks have been far smaller. I recall an explosion outside the Soviet UN mission on 67th Street in Manhattan about a decade ago. It was on the order of ten pounds but blew out some windows about a block away at Hunter College where I teach.

Therefore, it hardly seems surprising that in Vietnam the bombings were killing thousands of civilians in addition to many thousands of combatants a month in all of Indochina by the late 1960s, adding up to some 1.9 million dead

---

*The figures for World War II given in this paragraph are from Clodfelter, *The Limits of Air Power*, 8ff.; and Edward Mead Earle in Eugene Emme. A total of 1,995,937 tons was dropped by U.S. planes, and 2,697,937 tons by all Allied bombing attacks. The Soviets dropped some 660,000 tons of bombs against German targets, while U.S. bombing reached a one-month maximum of 206,457 tons in the spring of 1945 (see endnotes 3 and 6).

In the Persian Gulf War, January 17 to February 28, 1991, at first tonnages were not given, but in March 1991 the Pentagon reported 88,500 tons dropped and also revealed that 70 percent of the bombs were off target, and only 7 percent of the bombs had been "smart" bombs. Others spoke of 110,000 sorties and estimated Iraqi casualties about 150,000. The United States lost some sixty-five aircraft and sustained about 146 combat deaths, thirty-five of them from "friendly fire," and some 395 wounded. The Allies reported seventy-seven killed and 830 wounded.[7] Most observers argued that the great accuracy of the high-technology bombing of Iraqi targets had limited civilian casualties, but incidents such as the hitting of a bomb shelter with great loss of life in Baghdad on February 13 by laser-guided 2,000-pound bombs dropped by the F–117 Stealth fighter bomber would seem inevitable given the 2,800 sorties flown that day (see endnote 7).

in the American war. Up to 800,000 died in the French war there before May 1954. Such figures would be the equivalent of over 12 million Americans killed and do not include the great numbers of wounded, as well as up to 300,000 Vietnamese MIAs. One source estimated 5 to 6 million Vietnamese casualties of all types in their thirty-year war, as well as over 10 million refugees and 362,000 war invalids.[8] The bombings also contributed heavily to history's most drastic, if temporary, urbanization, with the accompanying slums in Saigon and elsewhere.

Facing such an onslaught, many must have felt as did the Laotian survivor of the bombings of the Plain of Jars in Laos, whose culture "became the first society to vanish through automated warfare." He said " . . . our lives became like those of animals trying to escape their hunters. . . ." One could see why from the poem of an American soldier:

> We would find a V.C. village,
> and if we could not capture it
> or clear it of Cong,
> we called for jets.
> The jets would come in, low and terrible,
> sweeping down, and screaming,
> . . . dropping their first bombs
> that flattened the huts to rubble and debris.
> . . . And then the jets would come back once again, in a last pass,
> this time to drop napalm
> that burned the dust and ashes to just nothing.
> Then the village
> that was not a village anymore
> was our village.[9]

General Tran Van Tra, when asked in November 1990 how his side coped with such intensive bombing, stressed aspects of the "people's war" strategy that made use of the people's creativity at camouflage, dispersal, mobility, and tactical skills, such as "clinging to the belt" of the enemy to avoid "friendly fire."* He also stressed the use of secret locations, tunnels, and bunkers, and estimated that over two-thirds of the bombs were off target or produced no results.

Perhaps appropriately, another child of the bombardments, Le Ly Hayslip, has given one of the best descriptions ever of the wonder of flight. Describing her first airplane trip, from Danang to Saigon in the mid-1960s, she wrote:

> For me . . . the flight was much more than a thrilling ride. When we left ground and banked gently over the ocean, it was as if I was seeing my homeland for the very first time . . . and I felt my first true sense of peace. . . . In those few moments I soared above and beyond all the tragedies I had known. . . . That flight . . . brought . . . the simple feeling of hope.[10]

---

*"Friendly fire" caused an estimated 15 to 20 percent of American casualties in Vietnam, and perhaps 25 percent in the 1991 Persian Gulf War (see endnote 7).

Military pilots know the same feelings of peace and exhilaration from flying, but might read the books of people like Hayslip, Fred Branfman, and Marilyn Young, from which the above quotes were taken, to know some of the effects of their missions on the ground, thousands of feet below their speeding aircraft.

Although Washington's stated purpose for the bombing changed in mid-1965 from an effort "to break the will of North Vietnam" to "cutting the flow of men and supplies from the north to the south," and to support the increasing numbers of U.S. ground troops, most thought of the gigantic bombing rather as an effort to carry out Air Force General Curtis LeMay's advice of November 25, 1965, that "we should bomb them back into the stone age." And the "bleeding" of the Communists was to be measured by the number of dead, euphemistically surveyed by "body counts" in "meat-grinder" operations, which could be summarized in the hapless phrase about Ben Tre in March 1968, "we had to destroy it to save it."

The most feared bombings came from the giant, eight-engined B–52s, which dropped an estimated one-third of the bombing totals with some 126,615 sorties in all. Their runs obliterated almost everything within a "box" over a mile long and a half mile wide, and the 60,000 pounds of bombs in each B–52 were dropped from planes flying so high (up to 55,000 feet) they could not be heard. Even if there were no direct hits, deaths were caused by shock waves and deprivation of oxygen caused by exploding bombs, especially phosphorous bombs.

Truong Nhu Tang, the revolutionary government's minister of justice, stationed with the Central Office for South Vietnam (COSVN) during 1969–75, and author of *A Vietcong Memoir*, told me something of how A-frame–type reinforced underground bunkers developed after 1965 had been able to withstand the most destructive U.S. bombs if they did not fall too close. Nearly all the top leaders, using the tunnels and shelters and intelligence information, had been able to survive, although many others had been killed by the bombs, or by falling into water-filled craters. Tang agreed that the bombings were indeed "incredible and terrifying," so much so that on one occasion a group of visiting Russians had all "pissed in their pants" as the bombs fell. In *A Vietcong Memoir*, Tang spoke of the killing of the wife and children of the present prime minister, Vo Van Kiet, in a B–52 raid.[11]

And then there were the gunships, such as the AC–130, called "Puff the Magic Dragon," and the Huey Cobra helicopters, whose gun's sixteen barrels each fired at the incredible rate of 6,000 rounds a minute. They and the jets were guided to likely targets by "Forward Air Controllers" (FACs) flying small, relatively slow but maneuverable aircraft such as the OV–10 Broncos. The dropping of herbicides under "Operation Ranch Hand" was accelerated in 1964 with the motto, "only you can prevent forests." Indeed, as stated, over half of South Vietnam's forests were heavily damaged or destroyed along with some 9,000 of 15,000 hamlets.

Therefore, the seeming invulnerability of top leaders like Tran Van Tra and Truong Nhu Tang is amazing and calls for further documentation and analysis. Those who faced the bombs can obviously give the most convincing testimony, and some is now available. Front-line troops suffered most from the bombardments, but surprising numbers of them also survived, despite heavy losses. Nguyen Ngoc Hung, a veteran from Hanoi who fought below the 17th parallel for over six years before 1975, related during a 1990 tour of the United States how they used intelligence sources, reinforced bunkers, and constant movements in the jungle and mountains to avoid most of the bombing, even as they suffered great hardship and numerous casualties.

In the air-to-air war, the United States achieved "only" about a 2.6-to-1 kill ratio in fighter combat, as against about a 10-to-1 ratio in the Korean War. Vietnamese aces Nguyen Van Bay and a Colonel Tomb (a nickname?) shot down a dozen or so U.S. planes. By 1967, the approximately two thousand (at any one time) American F–4s, F–105s, and other aircraft were going against some 115 MiG fighters, and later against 204, including 93 Mach 2 MiG–21s. Surface-to-air (SAM) missiles from some 300 sites also downed U.S. aircraft, 115 of them by 1971. The United States lost 171 aircraft in 1965, 280 in 1966, 326 in 1967, and some 918 in all the Rolling Thunder strikes. According to U.S. figures for the entire war, over 3,339 fixed-wing aircraft, including seventeen B–52s, and over 4,800 helicopters were lost, the great majority to ground fire.[12] Some 2,000 U.S. pilots lost their lives in the war and another 1,400 were listed as MIAs.

U.S. pilots criticized the Rules of Engagement (ROE) or restrictions that were imposed on them, mainly out of concern to prevent Chinese or Russian intervention; this despite dropping over three times the tonnage of bombs of all of World War II on a relatively small, poor country. Such criticisms nonetheless form an important part of the "revisionist" argument that "the brass" prevented the proper use of superior U.S. force to win the war, as "political limits placed on targeting and tactics prevented dealing with the source of supply."[13] But given the statistics above, such arguments seem literally incredible, though one can always talk about timing and target selection—or atomic bombs as implied by the "madman strategy." A recent book stated, "Nixon wanted the North Vietnamese to think that he was a bit deranged, an unstable personality who, in a moment of extreme frustration, might act capriciously, ordering in the B–52s with H-bombs to do what negotiations could not do."[14]

Fortunately, that did not occur, but then came the massive bombings of Iraq beginning January 17, 1991, ominously signaled two months before by maneuvers named "Imminent Thunder," and target areas labeled "killing zones." At first, well over 2,000 sorties a day, about half of them combat missions, were flown in an attempt to settle the Gulf War by quick massive bombings, as hawks and revisionists argue should have been done in Vietnam from 1965. General Westmoreland remarked after the first week of the 1991 war, "one can only speculate what would have happened [in Vietnam] if we had used that kind of bombing after our military victory at Tet [sic]. The outcome of the war could have been very different," if the United States had not waited until 1972 for unrestricted bombing.[15] Combat missions in the 1991 Gulf War were often three or more times as numerous per day as they had been in Indochina, but since the latter war mercifully ended after six weeks on February 28, the total of 88,500 tons of bombs dropped on Iraq came to only about one-eightieth the over 7 million tons dropped on Vietnam, Laos, and Cambodia.

Given what the senior Vietnamese leaders had already survived for over forty years—for example, an average of seven years in French prisons, the comeback of southern resistance fighters by the early 1970s, the effects of Tet on U.S. opinion and politics, and the nature of jungle warfare—the outcome in Vietnam surely would only have been further delayed by even more massive bombardments. After close to thirty years of devastating war, the leaders of the Vietnamese Revolution undoubtedly would have continued to fight for their country's complete independence, as they repeatedly affirmed, whatever Washington ordered up after 1965. After all, they did survive by far the heaviest bombing in history for three years to force the turnaround of 1968, then an additional four long years of more of the same to force the American withdrawal two years before their final victory.

Notes

1. Cited in James P. Harrison, *The Endless War: Vietnam's Struggle for Independence* (New York: 1982, 1990), 29, 310.

2. Myra MacPherson, *Long Time Passing: Vietnam and the Haunted Generation* (New York: 1985), 693, 697. Regarding U.S. weapons and bomb totals, see: Mark Clodfelter, *The Limits of Air Power: The American Bombing of North Vietnam* (New York: 1989), 134ff., 166ff., 194; Jeffrey L. Levinson, *Alpha Strike Vietnam: The Navy's Air War, 1964–73* (New York: 1989), 53 ff., 353; Raphael Littauer and Norman Uphoff, eds. *The Air Ward in Indochina* (Boston: 1972); Bernard C. Nalty et al., *Air Power and the Fight for Khe Sanh* (Washington, D.C.: 1973); William Momyer, *Air Power in Three Wars* (Washington, D.C.: 1978); Marilyn Young, *The Vietnam Wars* (New York: 1991), 191, 271; Guenter Lewy, *America in Vietnam* (New York: 1978), 243ff.; Harrison, *The Endless War*, 192ff., 254ff., 259, 270, 301, 339, fn. 16.; John Morrocco, *Rain of Fire* (Boston: 1984), 177ff; James William Gibson, *The Perfect War: The War We Couldn't Lose and How We Did* (New York: 1986), 319ff., 495; Frank Harvey, *Air War—Vietnam* (New York: 1967); Drew Middleton et al., eds., *Air War, Vietnam* (Indianapolis: 1978); Robert Dorr, *Air War: Hanoi* (London: 1988); and Dorr, *Air War: South Vietnam* (London: 1990), 46; and many of the other sources cited below.

3. Eugene Emme, *The Impact of Air Power: National Security and World Politics* (Princeton: 1959), 107, 221, 225; William S. Turley, *The Second Indochina War: A Short Political and Military History* (New York: 1987), 152; and Harrison, *The Endless War*, 287ff.

4. M. Clodfelter, *The Limits of Air Power*, 194, 287ff.; and Harrison *The Endless War*, 194ff., 260ff., 287ff.

5. Nguyen Khac Vien, in *Le Courrier du Vietnam*, July 1980, 14; Gabriel Kolko, *Anatomy of a War* (New York: 1986), 189ff.; and Harrison, *The Endless War*, 192ff.

6. Emme, *The Impact of Air Power*, 107, 225, 432; M. Clodfelter, *The Limits of Air Power*, 8, 22ff.; Meldon Smith, "The Strategic Bombing Debate: The Second World War and Vietnam," *Journal of Contemporary History* 12 (1977): 180ff.; L. Goldstein, *The*

Flying Machine and Modern Literature (Bloomington, IN: 1986), 75ff.; Ngo Vinh Long, "Vietnam: The Real Enemy," *Bulletin of Concerned Asian Scholars*, no. 4 (1989): 6; John Morrocco, *Rain of Fire*, 177ff.; Harrison, *The Endless War*, 269ff., 291ff., 301ff., 339, fn 16; C.H. Gibbs-Smith, *Flight through the Ages* (New York: 1974), 125; John W.R. Taylor, *A History of Aviation* (New York: 1976); Robin Higham, *Air Power: A Concise History* (London: 1972); Rober E. Bilstein, *Flight in America, 1900–1983: From the Wrights to the Astronauts* (Baltimore: 1985), 133ff.; *US Air Force Museum* (Dayton, OH: 1983), 92; Neil Sheehan, *A Bright Shining Lie: John Paul Vann and America in Vietnam* (New York: 1988), 618ff.; *The Soviet Air Force in World War II: The Official History* (New York: 1973), 380; Lee Kennett, *A History of Strategic Bombing* (New York: 1982), 25, 122, passim; Kennett, *The First Air War, 1914–1918* (New York: 1991), passim; Michael Sherry, *The Rise of American Air Power* (New Haven: 1987), 204–5, 209, 260, 284, 314–15; and Ben Mackworth-Praed, *Aviation: The Pioneer Years* (London: 1990), 216.

7. *New York Times*, February 7, March 20, 24, May 30, June 3, 5, 11, 22, August 15, and December 9, 1991; *Time*, March 5, May 20, 27, June 5, 17, 1991; *Newsweek*, November 18, 1991; *Le Monde*, June 5, July 24, 1991.

8. *Indochina Newsletter*, January 1989, 76ff., and September 1990. 3; Gibson, *The Perfect War*, 319; and Nguyen Khac Vien, *Vietnam Ten Years After* (Hanoi: 1985), 6.

9. Cited respectively in Fred Branfman, *Voices from the Plain of Jars* (New York: 1972), 20, 35; and Young, *The Vietnam Wars*, 175–76. For a sadly contrasting statement of a navy A–4 pilot's indifference to the victims of his bombs, see Levinson, *Alpha Strike Vietnam*, 79–80. For intelligent if official discussion of people's war techniques, see especially Vo Nguyen Giap, *The Military Art of People's War* (New York: 1970); and General Giap, *People's War agaist U.S. Aeronaval War* (Hanoi: 1975).

10. Le Ly Hayslip, *When Heaven and Earth Changed Places: A Vietnamese Woman's Journey from War to Peace* (New York: 1989), 114.

11. Truong Nhu Tang, *A Vietcong Memoir* (New York: 1985), 261, 294ff.; Gibson, *The Perfect War*, 357ff., 372ff.; and *Time*, January 13, 1992, which reported that the killings were by helicopter.

12. Marshall Harrison, *A Lonely Kind of War: Forward Air Controller Vietnam* (Novato, CA: 1989); Jack Broughton, *Thud Ridge* (New York: 1969); Kolko, *Anatomy of a War*, 189ff.; N. Sheehan, *A Bright Shining Lie*, 618ff.; Turley, *The Second Indochina War*, 107; Harrison, *Air Force* (New York: 1984), 16ff.; Jerry Scuts, *Northrop F–5/F–20* (London: 1986), 90ff.; Ivan Rendall, *Reaching for the Skies* (New York: 1989), 264; M. Clodfelter, *The Limits of Air Power*, 131, 165, 194ff.; and Levinson, *Alpha Strike Vietnam*, 353. The president of Vietnam Airlines in the early 1990s, Nguyen Hong Nhi, was said to have downed several American aircrafts *(New York Times*, December 26, 1992).

13. J.B. Nichols and B. Tillman, *On Yankee Station* (Annapolis, MD: 1987), 163. See also Jack Broughton, *Going Downtown: The War against Hanoi and Washington* (New York: 1988); Levinson, *Alpha Strike Vietnam*, 54ff., 353; Smith, "The Strategic Bombing Debate," 177ff.; Rene Francillon, *Vietnam: The War in the Air* (New York: 1987); R.L. Mason, *Chickenhawk* (New York: 1983); Jay and David Groen, *Huey* (New York: 1984); Joseph Buttinger, *The Unforgettable Tragedy* (New York: 1977), 95; Gibson, *The Perfect War*, 319ff.; and T.D. Boettcher, *Vietnam: The Valor and the Sorrow* (Boston: 1985), 205ff., 254ff. See also *Indochina Newsletter*, especially September–October 1990; Col. J.M. Drew, *Rolling Thunder, 1965: Anatomy of a Failure* (Maxwell AFB, AL: 1986); J.C. Thompson, *Rolling Thunder: Understanding Policy and Program Failure* (Chapel Hill, NC: 1980); T. Mangold and J. Pennygate, *The Tunnels of Cu Chi* (London: 1985); John Clark Pratt, *The Laotian Fragments* (New York: 1974); C. Berger, ed., *The USAF in Defeat: Vietnam in Retrospect* (San Rafael, CA: 1978); Major W.A. Buckingham, *Opera-*

tion Ranchhand: The Air Force and Herbicides in Southeast Asia, 1961–71 (Washington, D.C.: 1982); Caroline Harnly, *Agent Orange and Vietnam: A Bibliography* (Metuchen, NJ: 1988); T. Whiteside, *Defoliation* (New York: 1970); Harrison Salisbury, ed., *Vietnam Reconsidered* (New York: 1984); and Jonathan Schell, *The Real War: The Classic Reporting on the Vietnam War* (New York: 1988); Robert Dorr, *Vietnam: The Air War, 1945–75* (New York: 1991); Hy V. Luong, *Revolution in the Village: Tradition and Transformation in North Vietnam, 1925–1988* (Honolulu: 1992); and F. Quirielle, *Sous les bombes américaines à Hanoi: 1966–9* (Paris: 1992).

14. James S. Olson and Randy Roberts, *Where the Domino Fell: America and Vietnam, 1945–1990* (New York: 1991), 112, 224.

15. *New York Times*, January 25, 1991.

8

The Strange "Dissent" of Robert S. McNamara

George C. Herring

Perhaps more than any other single individual, Robert Strange McNamara personified the American commitment in Vietnam. He was "the can-do man in the can-do society, in the can-do era," David Halberstam has written; "he was American through and through, with the American drive, the American certitude and conviction."[1] During the Kennedy and early Johnson years, McNamara managed U.S. policy in Vietnam almost as a desk officer. Whether slogging through Vietnam in army fatigues, spewing out statistics to demonstrate progress, or presiding at press conferences, map on the wall, pointer in hand, he epitomized what came to be called McNamara's War. He exuded a confidence that seemed to ensure ultimate success whatever the difficulties of the moment.

In McNamara's case, the public image of confidence far outlasted the emergence of deep private skepticism. His doubts about American success in Vietnam developed much earlier and went much deeper than is generally recognized. Yet such was his commitment to the commitment and such was his sense of loyalty to the president that he did not act decisively on his own steadily growing skepticism. He repeatedly fought off military proposals for drastic escalation, to be sure, but he did not follow his own doubts to their logical conclusion. For nearly two years, he waged a war he felt could not be won. Only in 1967 did he reveal to President Lyndon Johnson the full range of his doubts and make policy proposals that squared with them. And when the president rejected his advice and kicked him downstairs, he left quietly, refusing from that day forth to discuss Vietnam. McNamara's strange "dissent," his unwillingness to act on his convictions, constitutes one of the truly tragic chapters in an epic story of tragedy.

McNamara's disillusionment began within six months after the major U.S. troop commitment of July 1965. He, more than any other single individual, had defined the administration's response to General William C. Westmoreland's 1965 request for major increments of combat troops, a carefully hewn middle ground between the military proposals for major escalation and Undersecretary of State George Ball's recommendations for withdrawal. The deployment of these troops, especially the First Cavalry Division (Airmobile) in the Central Highlands in late 1965, more than anything else triggered McNamara's initial doubts. In a series of engagements in the Ia Drang Valley, the 1st Cavalry went head-to-head with three regiments of North Vietnamese regulars. Both sides suffered heavy losses. By U.S. count, the North Vietnamese lost 3,000 dead in three weeks of action. American losses totalled more than 300, roughly half of them coming in a bloody ambush on November 17 in which an entire company was wiped out, causing consternation in the 1st Cavalry and at Westmoreland's headquarters.[2]

The engagements in the Ia Drang had a profound impact on McNamara. He went out to Vietnam shortly after the battle and talked to the officers and men of the 1st Cavalry. The manner in which the North Vietnamese had fought and the losses they had been willing to absorb and had inflicted on the United States seem to have disabused him of earlier notions that U.S. goals could be achieved in a reasonable time and at acceptable cost. While McNamara was in Vietnam, moreover, Westmoreland admitted in a briefing conducted specifically for the secretary of defense that U.S. officials had underestimated the enemy and overestimated the South Vietnamese. We "should take a good hard look at our future posture," the general added, and shortly after he requested substantial additional troops.[3] McNamara's memoranda of the time appear not to convey the full depth of his emerging doubts. Almost twenty years later, however, under intense questioning by attorneys in the Westmoreland/CBS Trial, he admitted that in November 1965 he had concluded that the war could not be won militarily.[4]

It is equally clear that the secretary of defense could not act on his growing doubts. In part, no doubt, his inability to follow them to their logical conclusion reflected the depth of his personal entanglement in, responsibility for, and commitment to U.S. Vietnam policy. A man for whom success had become a way of life and for whom lionization was routine and expected, McNamara could not admit to himself the bankruptcy of the policies he had done so much to create.

Moreover, his own profound—perhaps perverted—notions of loyalty made it impossible for him to join George Ball in the role of dissenter. "I don't believe the government of a complicated state can operate effectively," McNamara once said, "if those in charge of the departments of the government express disagreement with decisions of the established head of that government."[5] Whenever someone dissented, it made more difficult the attainment of the larger group goals. Ball himself later recalled that McNamara treated his dissenting memos like "poisonous snakes." He was "absolutely horrified" by them, considered them "next to treason."[6] Thus, although he was deeply concerned by his belated realization of the potential cost of the war and increasingly persuaded that it was not winnable, McNamara's own personal code of conduct prevented him from following his instincts.

His memoranda to the president on November 30 and December 6, 1965, reveal his ambivalence. In each case, he warned ominously of "dramatic new changes" on the "military side," most notably increased North Vietnamese infiltration and increased willingness to stand and fight. He predicted that U.S. casualties would reach 1,000 per month. And even with the deployment of 600,000 men by the end of 1966, there was no guarantee of success. The "odds are about even," he concluded, "that . . . we will be faced in early 1967 with a military standoff at a much higher level . . . with any prospect of military success marred by the chances of an active Chinese intervention."[7]

Yet even with these gloomy predictions, McNamara urged plunging ahead. In his November 30 memorandum, he outlined two options, a compromise solution with a less than favorable outcome, or a dramatic escalation of both ground and air wars. Admitting again that additional deployments of troops might well gain nothing more than a " 'no-decision' at an even higher level," he added, incongruously, that "the best chance of achieving our stated objectives" lay in expanding the war.[8]

Unwilling to follow his doubts to their logical conclusion, McNamara sought what turned out to be expedients. Shortly after returning from Vietnam in December 1965, he began pushing for an extended bombing pause over the Christmas holiday. He justified the pause as necessary to build public support for subsequent escalation of the war. But he may also have hoped, although there was little to support it, that a pause might produce a diplomatic breakthrough that would avert further escalation and provide the United States a way out. He pushed the pause with great vigor, eventually persuading a skeptical Lyndon Johnson of its value. Aware, as Johnson put it, that the Joint Chiefs of Staff (JCS) "go through the roof when we mention this pause," McNamara made an end run around them, in effect excluding them from the decision-making process.[9]

Failure of the bombing pause merely heightened his dilemma. When the diplomatic breakthrough did not occur, McNamara was forced to go along with the escalation he had hoped to avert. He had imposed the pause upon a skeptical Johnson and it had produced nothing. The president's resistance to further pauses thus hardened, and from this point McNamara's stock began a steady decline and that of the JCS a steady rise.

Throughout the rest of 1966, McNamara's private doubts grew. At the Honolulu Conference in February, journalist Stanley Karnow noted the change in his appearance. "His face seemed to be grayer and his patent leather hair thinner," Karnow recalled, "and his voice lacked the authority it had once projected when he would point briskly to graphs and flip-charts to prove his rosy appraisals." In a private briefing, he confided to Karnow and a few other journalists that the bombing had not worked and could not end the war.[10]

In May, during the height of the Buddhist protests in South Vietnam, he privately spoke the heretical words "coalition government." Speculating that the Saigon government would grow weaker and weaker, he advised Averell Harriman that the United States would do well to let the South Vietnamese decide their own future, even if it meant a coalition government with the Viet Cong, which, he added, might or might not take over South Vietnam. He insisted that "a political settlement, not a military settlement, is the only way to end the fighting." He pressed Harriman to get in touch with the National Liberation Front (NLF) and discuss the possibility of a coalition government. He claimed to be flexible on what sort of deal might be arranged with the North Vietnamese on mutual de-escalation of the war, provided that there was some mutuality, that North Vietnam gave some concession in return for the U.S. stopping the bombing.[11]

Yet his formal recommendations to President Johnson were still ambivalent. After another trip to South Vietnam in October 1966, he reported himself a "little less pessimistic" than a year before and added that the United States had "done somewhat better militarily than I had anticipated." It had at least denied the enemy victory. But his basic conclusion remained the same as in November 1965. Despite enormous losses, enemy morale showed no signs of breaking, and the losses in fact had been replaced. The North Vietnamese and Viet Cong appeared ready to wait the United States out, taking advantage of its impatience. Thus the secretary of defense concluded, "I see no reasonable way to bring the war to an end soon."

Again struggling for alternatives, McNamara proposed a new approach that might be less costly in blood and treasure and that the United States "credibly would maintain indefinitely—a posture that makes trying to 'wait us out' less attractive." He urged stabilizing ground forces at 470,000 troops and the "Rolling Thunder" bombing program at its present level. To reduce the cost of the war and prepare for the long haul, he proposed revitalizing the long-stalled pacification program. As a substitute for the bombing and to reduce the costs and dangers of the ground war, he also recommended the construction of an elaborate barrier across the demilitarized zone (DMZ), what became known—contemptuously in some quarters—as the "McNamara Line." Finally, in notably ambiguous terms, he urged a new emphasis on negotiations. The bombing should be stopped as an inducement to Hanoi to negotiate. And without using the phrase "coalition government," he spoke of trying to split the NLF from North Vietnam and permitting a role for it in negotiations, in the government of South Vietnam, and in the postwar life of the country.[12]

The McNamara Line and pacification offered no more hope of a way out than the earlier bombing pause. The military remained hostile toward the idea of an electronic barrier and pursued the plan halfheartedly. And while the administration in late 1966 and again in 1967 reorganized the administrative machinery for pacification, U.S. officials quickly perceived that real progress would require years, not months.

Increasingly concerned about the war, McNamara in the spring of 1967 went far beyond his earlier positions, for the first time carrying premises he had arrived at in 1965 to their logical conclusion. By late March, David Lilienthal observed a "harassed and puzzled look on the no longer sprightly" secretary of defense, and McNamara virtually conceded to Lilienthal that his exercise in crisis management had failed. "We have poured more bombs onto North Vietnam than in the whole of World War II," he said, "and yet we have no sign that it has shaken their will to resist."[13]

More important perhaps, in mid-March, apparently certain that McNamara's influence was on the wane and the winds of war were shifting in their favor, the JCS and Westmoreland struck out for drastic escalation.[14] They called for mobilization of the reserves and urged expanding the troop commitment by an additional 200,000 men. They asked for authority to go into enemy sanctuaries in Laos, Cambodia, and North Vietnam. And they pressed for expansion of the bombing and for bombing and mining North Vietnam's ports. In short, they sought to gird the nation for an all-out effort to win the war. On April 27, JCS chairman General Wheeler and Westmoreland met alone with the president and in words no doubt deliberately chosen to appeal to the political animal that was Lyndon Johnson warned that unless such measures were taken the war might go on for an additional five years.

Shaken by the military proposals, McNamara drafted a memorandum for the president that went much further than what his most dovish civilian advisers urged and advanced positions the authors of the *Pentagon Papers* accurately described as "radical."[15] For the first time, in fact, his proposals came close to harmonizing with his inner doubts. The war was acquiring a momentum of its own, he urgently warned, and it must be stopped. He expressed grave doubt that the JCS proposals would produce victory, and by provoking conflict with the Soviet Union or China they might lead to a "national disaster." Giving Westmoreland an additional 200,000 troops would create "irresistible pressures" to expand the war, and mobilization of the reserves would spark a "bitter debate" in Congress.

As an alternative, McNamara sketched out a complex politico-military "strategy" that raised the possibility of compromise and even hinted at extrication. The bombing of North Vietnam should be cut back to the area around the 20th parallel. Additional troop deployments should be limited to 300,000 men, after which a firm ceiling should be imposed. While keeping military pressure on the enemy, the United States should more actively seek a political settlement. McNamara insisted that Vietnam must be considered in its larger Asian context. Pointing to the defeat of the Communists in Indonesia and the current turmoil from the Cultural Revolution in China, he advised Johnson that events in Asia were running in favor of the United States, thus reducing the importance of South Vietnam. He proposed a scaling down of objectives, indicating that the United States should not be obligated to guarantee an independent, non-Communist South Vietnam. He spoke frankly of a compromise, even "involving, inter alia, a role in the

South for members of the VC." He even called for a National Security Action Memorandum "nailing down" the new policy and without naming names proposed "major personnel changes within the government."[16]

The JCS responded immediately. Unaware that McNamara had shown the Draft Presidential Memorandum (DPM) to Johnson on May 19, they urged the secretary not to forward it to the president. Privately denouncing his proposals on the air war as an "aerial *Dien Bien Phu*," they advised that such steps would only encourage Hanoi's will to resist. The "drastic changes" proposed by McNamara would "undermine and no longer provide a complete rationale for our presence in Vietnam or much of our effort over the past two years." The DPM badly underestimated the significance for the free world of U.S. failure in Vietnam. With understatement, General Wheeler advised Admiral U.S. Grant Sharp at Pacific Command Headquarters that McNamara's views "were at considerable variance with our own thinking and proposals" and advised him to "batten down for rough weather ahead."[17]

Johnson refused to resolve the debate between his subordinates or even confront the fundamental issues. He continued to fear that adoption of the JCS program might provoke a larger war. On the other hand, like his adviser Walt Rostow, he felt that McNamara's proposals went "a bit too far" to the other extreme. Consensus was for him a way of life and controversy anathema, and he was undoubtedly concerned with what Rostow described as the "dangerously strong feelings in your official family." He sought, like his national security adviser, a "scenario" that could hold his administration together in ways that looked "after the nation's interest and made military sense."[18] Characteristically, he delayed a decision, and when he decided he did so on a piecemeal basis, carefully avoiding the larger issues. He approved an expansion of the bombing, but stopped well short of mining North Vietnamese ports. He refused to approve expansion of the war into Laos, Cambodia, and North Vietnam. He agreed to deploy only an additional 55,000 ground troops, but he refused to set a ceiling and scrupulously avoided discussion of the larger issue of how and for what purposes they would be used.

Johnson's non-decisions satisfied no one, and the debate that could not take place in his administration moved into the halls of Congress in the late summer of 1967. In August, the JCS mounted for Vietnam the closest thing to a MacArthur-like challenge to civilian authority, taking their case for an expanded air war to the hawkish John Stennis's Senate Preparedness Subcommittee. Alarmed by reports of McNamara's May recommendations, the committee, on its own or with the encouragement of the JCS, announced in late June its intention to conduct hearings on the air war. Its aim was to "get McNamara," administration officials speculated, and, more important, to put pressure on the White House to authorize the military to do what was necessary to win the war.[19]

Ironically, McNamara saw hearings designed to "get" him as an opportunity to combat pressures for expanding the war without violating his own rigid standards of loyalty to the president. By the late summer of 1967, the secretary of defense was a man "visibly in torment."[20] He was more than ever convinced, as he told Harriman on August 22, "that the only way to settle this is by having a coalition government."[21] Although painfully aware of the growing gap between his own views and those of the White House, he retained a powerful—indeed crippling—sense of loyalty to Johnson. At the same time, he was completely disillusioned with the war that had once borne his name, and he feared that its further expansion would result in a "national catastrophe."[22] To convince the executive branch, the Congress, and the public that further escalation would be ruinous, he determined to analyze the air war publicly as he had not done before. The Stennis hearings gave him the chance to do so, building a foundation for partial or total cessation in the future and heading off pressures for expansion while defending the president's basic policy.[23]

In a strange, almost surreal way, the Stennis hearings thus became the forum for a debate that could not take place within the inner councils of the executive branch. Military officials prepared their case with the utmost care, and for two weeks top brass paraded before a sympathetic committee.[24] They insisted that the air war against North Vietnam was an indispensable element of the overall military effort, inflicting heavy damage on the enemy and significantly restricting his capacity to fight in the South. A partial or total bombing halt, they warned, would be a "disaster." The military muted their arguments somewhat, refraining from outright advocacy of expanding the air war. But their witnesses did insist that the effectiveness of the bombing had been limited by gradualism and by restrictions that had posed "severe handicaps which were contrary to military principles." The slow pace of escalation had given the enemy time to adapt and adjust and develop a highly effective air defense system. Important targets remained unstruck.

McNamara spent the entire day of August 25 before the committee, and gave, by friendly accounts, perhaps the performance of his career. He bombarded the committee with statistics, hard facts, and cold logic, and made and remade his essential points in numerous different ways. He seemed to concur with the JCS that the bombing had been effective, and, to a point, he minimized his differences with the military. Privately, he admitted to Dean Acheson that he was not telling the whole story and was providing a "loyal treatment putting the best face on a poor situation."[25] Still, in a move that for him approached heresy, he tried to destroy the case for expanding the air war, thus making public the sharp differences between himself and the JCS. He vigorously defended the restrictions that had been imposed on the bombing. Most important, he warned that no amount of bombing could totally interdict the flow of men and supplies to the South or break the will of the North. The air war against the North could not be a substitute for the ground war in the South. "You cannot win the war on the cheap with bombing," he said. It was, according to those close to him, a do-or-die performance on McNamara's part, with President Johnson and the nation as much his intended audience as the committee.

Curiously, while waging the battle of his life, McNamara in top-level meetings doggedly persisted in the role of team man. By the time of the Stennis hearings, the stalemate he had predicted as early as November 1965 had become a topic of public and press speculation, causing great alarm in the White House and Pentagon. At a meeting on July 12, however, McNamara emphatically proclaimed: "There is not a military stalemate."[26] Years later, the secretary described the Stennis hearings as "an extraordinarily trying ordeal" for him personally, spoke of a "very, very painful dispute" with the military, and admitted that during this period he "went through hell."[27] At a meeting with the president on August 19, however, he praised his adversary General Wheeler for a "helluva good job" before the committee and observed that the differences between himself and the JCS were largely "worked out."[28]

McNamara appears to have won the battle or at least *a* battle—and lost the war. Johnson did not expand the air war as the JCS had urged. Nor did he authorize mobilization of the reserves and escalation of the ground war. On the other hand, more than ever before, an increasingly nervous president in late 1967 tilted toward the military. To mute criticism from the JCS and the hawks in Congress, he authorized a handful of new bombing targets. For the same reasons, he literally ordered a reluctant McNamara to initiate an antiballistic missile system. As if to symbolize McNamara's waning influence, General Wheeler for the first time was formally brought into the administration's Tuesday lunch policy meetings.

Most important, McNamara himself was kicked downstairs to the World Bank. Precisely how the secretary came to leave the Pentagon will probably never be known. He recently admitted that he himself does not know to this day whether he quit or was fired.[29] By one account, when McNamara deliberately chose not to clear his Stennis committee testimony with the president, he was summoned to the White House to receive the "full blast of presidential anger."[30] By another account, he discussed it with the president, both became "quite hot," and Johnson made clear that henceforth McNamara was on his own.[31]

The truth seems much more complicated. The secretary's influence had undoubtedly waned by the time of the Stennis hearings, and his testimony does appear to have sealed his fate. McNamara has also admitted that "tremendous tension" had developed between him and Johnson over Vietnam. He quotes the president as complaining, "Why in the hell, McNamara, are you being so goddamn difficult?"[32] He also notes, however, that to the end, he and Johnson loved each other deeply. By some accounts, Johnson feared that his secretary of defense was on the verge of cracking and might go the way of his predecessor, James Forrestal. To save a dear and loyal friend, therefore, he assigned him to a position he had long coveted. When an exhausted McNamara departed the Pentagon, a genuinely appreciative president praised him as "this intensely loyal, brilliant and good man" and "just about the textbook example of the modern civil servant."[33] McNamara openly wept.

Lame duck McNamara made one last effort to change U.S. Vietnam policy. At the Tuesday lunch on October 31, he warned that continuation of the present course "would be dangerous, costly in lives, and unsatisfactory to the American people." The following day, he handed the president a long memorandum he had not cleared with National Security Adviser Walt Rostow, Secretary of State Dean Rusk, or Wheeler. As so often in the past when he had the president's ear, he urged Johnson to authorize him to discuss the memo with other advisers and submit formal proposals. He warned again that continuation of the present course would not end the war, and he added that a further erosion of public support would generate dangerous new pressures for withdrawal or drastic escalation. He retreated from his May 19 advocacy of a political compromise and coalition government. On the other hand, he went beyond his earlier proposals in advocating an indefinite bombing halt and the stabilization of ground operations by publicly fixing a ceiling on force levels and by a searching review of the ground strategy with the object of reducing U.S. casualties and turning over more responsibility to the South Vietnamese.[34]

Johnson was unmoved. Like McNamara, he continued to fear the risk of an expanded war, and he rejected simultaneous JCS proposals to escalate the air war. But he was equally dubious that McNamara's proposals would bring results. "How do we get this conclusion?" he scrawled on the memo where McNamara had predicted that a bombing halt would lead to peace talks. "Why believe this?" he noted, where McNamara had noted a "strong possibility" that North Vietnam would stop military activity across the DMZ after a bombing halt.[35] He submitted the McNamara memo to old friends and trusted advisers, people like Maxwell Taylor, Clark Clifford, and Abe Fortas, and to validate his own approach he brought to Washington for a review of Vietnam policy the "Wise Men," a group of establishment figures occasionally called upon for advice. Buoyed by their general support for his middle-of-the-road policy, he rejected McNamara's proposal for a bombing halt and would go no further than privately commit himself to conduct a full review of the ground strategy at some undetermined point in the future. To the shock of the nation, at the end of November he announced McNamara's departure from the cabinet and his appointment to head the World Bank.

The war over the war took a heavy toll on Johnson's advisers. The once proud and indomitable McNamara left office in February 1968 a depleted and dispirited man.[36] The JCS also departed exhausted and embittered. The Chief of Naval Operations later admitted his shame for going along with policies he deeply disapproved.[37] "I'm sick of it. . . . I have never been so goddamn frustrated by it all," General John McConnell, Air Force chief of staff, privately complained in 1967.[38] When Admiral Thomas Moorer arrived to assume the position of JCS chairman, a "very distraught" General Wheeler, face in hands, warned his successor, "You'll never survive."[39]

Yet in their public demeanor, loyal to the end, the president's men bravely maintained the facade of unity. In the immediate aftermath of the Stennis hearings, McConnell spoke publicly in terms completely at odds with his private lament, dismissing as an "erroneous conception" the notion that there were "fundamental disagreements" between the president and the JCS.[40] After leaving office, McNamara, through his wife, expressed to the Joint Chiefs great pride at the "amazing display of restraint and mutual respect" and the "dignity" with which they had worked together despite their differences.[41] No one wrote a better epitaph for a badly flawed decision-making process than its architect, the man who had imposed his own "Macy's window" variety of loyalty on a badly divided administration. "There have been no divisions in this government," President Johnson proudly proclaimed at a National Security Council meeting at about the time McNamara's departure was announced. "We may have been wrong but we have not been divided."[42] The comment reflected a curious sense of priorities. And of course it was not true. The administration was both wrong and divided, and the fact that the divisions could not be worked out or even addressed may have contributed to the wrong policies, at huge cost to the men themselves—and especially to the nation.

For McNamara, the most loyal of the president's men, the same principles that had muted his dissent during much of the war bound him to silence after his departure from government. It was "sad," *New Republic* columnist TRB* lamented, that the obviously dissident secretary of defense did not "speak plainly upon leaving. . . . If McNamara really does think the war is another Edsel, it would be good to hear him say so and recommend that it be junked."[43] Such was not his style, however. Not only did he refuse to speak out upon leaving, he stubbornly refused to speak about Vietnam later, even after he had reemerged into the public eye as an advocate of nuclear restraint and responsibility. Indeed, in a recent interview, he admitted that he never even talked to his children and closest friends about the war.[44]

He first broke his silence at the time of the Westmoreland trial, again, out of a strange sense of loyalty, emerging to defend a man he admitted having fought "like hell" over issues of policy during the war. In his deposition and in the actual court proceedings he admitted to his early private doubts, but he tried to wriggle free from charges that for two years he had waged a war he saw no hope of winning. "It was a huge price to pay for me to go up there," he later admitted. "It was painful as hell. I cannot go before the American people and be forced to talk about Vietnam without a lot of pain and personal embarrassment. It's humiliating, frankly. But I did it and it's over and so the hell with it."[45] And having done his duty, he retreated once again into silence.

He surfaced again in early 1991, shortly after the outbreak of the Persian Gulf War, speaking briefly to Carl Bernstein about the mistakes of Vietnam. He blamed his wife's death partially on the trauma of the war—"she was with me on occasions when people said I had blood on my hands." He also confided the obvious, that his

---

* This colunmist was known only by these initials.

own personal torment "went on for a long time—months, if not years."[46]

It is pointless, of course, to speculate on the might-have-beens. And even if McNamara had acted on his doubts in late 1965 when he retained considerable influence, he probably would not have been able to persuade Johnson to accept a less-than-satisfactory settlement when the military option remained untested. He undoubtedly persuaded himself, as well, that only by remaining in government could he exert influence on policy, and that by departing he would open the field to the military and drastic escalation of the war. Still, while perceiving the flaws in the policies he had done so much to create, he could not accept the reality of defeat and failure. His inability to follow his growing doubts to their logical conclusions, his distorted notions of loyalty, and his subsequent silence served the nation poorly.

Notes

1. David Halberstam, *The Best and the Brightest* (New York: Harper and Row, 1972), 215.

2. George C. Herring, "The First Cavalry and the Ia Drang Valley," in Charles E. Heller and William A. Stofft, eds., *America's First Battles, 1776–1965* (Lawrence: University of Kansas Press, 1986), 300–86.

3. Westmoreland History Notes, November 29, 1965, William C. Westmoreland Papers, U.S. Army Military History Institute, Carlisle Barracks, PA, Box 27.

4. Paul Hendrickson, "A Man Divided against Himself," *Washington Post Magazine* (June 12, 1988), 31.

5. Quoted in Henry Trewhitt, *McNamara* (New York: Harper and Row, 1971), 237.

6. George Ball oral history interview, Lyndon Baines Johnson Library, Austin, TX.

7. McNamara memoranda for the president, November 30, December 6, 1965, Lyndon Baines Johnson Papers, Lyndon Baines Johnson Library, National Security File, Country File, Vietnam, Box 75.

8. Ibid.

9. Notes on meetings, December 17 and 18, 1965, Johnson Papers, Meeting Notes File, Box 1. Wallace M. Greene, "The Bombing 'Pause': Formula for Failure," *Air Force Magazine* (April 1976), 36–39.

10. Stanley Karnow, *Vietnam: A History* (New York: Viking, 1983), 498.

11. See Harriman memoranda of converations with McNamara, May 14 and 28 and June 23, 1966, all in W. Averell Harriman Papers, Manuscript Division, Library of Congress, Washington, D.C., Box 486.

12. McNamara memorandum for the president, October 14, 1966, Johnson Papers, National Security File, National Security Council Meetings, Box 2.

13. David Lilienthal Journal, March 21, 1967, in *The Journal of David Lilienthal*, vol. 6 (New York: Harper and Row, 1964, 1983), 418.

14. See, for example, Wheeler backchannel cables to Admiral U.S. Grant Sharp and Westmoreland, February 18 and March 6, 1967, Backchannel Messages, Westmoreland/CBS Litigation File, Record Group 407, Federal Record Center, Suitland, MD, Box 20.

15. Indeed, it was sometime during this period that he ordered the compilation of the *Pentagon Papers* project, later explaining that he had concluded that the United States could not achieve its objectives in Vietnam and had ordered the study to determine why and to learn what alternatives might have been pursued. See Carl Bernstein, "On the Mistakes of the War," *Time* (February 11, 1991), 71.

16. McNamara draft presidential memorandum, "Future Actions in Vietnam," May 19, 1967, Johnson Papers, National Security File, Country File, Vietnam, Box 75.

17. Neil Sheehan et al., *The Pentagon Papers as Published by the New York Times* (New York: Bantam Books, 1971), 538–39; Wheeler to Sharp, May 26, 1967, Back-channel Messages, Westmoreland/CBS File, Box 20.

18. Rostow memoranda, May 19 and 20, 1967, Johnson Papers, National Security File, Country File, Vietnam, Box 75.

19. Robert Ginsburgh memorandum for the record. August 14, 1967, Johnson Papers, National Security File, Name File/Col. Ginsburgh, Box 3.

20. Walter Isaacson and Evan Thomas, *The Wise Men: Six Friends and the World They Made* (New York: Simon and Schuster, 1986), 675.

21. Harriman memorandum of conversation with McNamara. August 22, 1967, Harriman Papers, Box 486.

22. Phil Goulding, *Confirm or Deny* (New York: Harper and Row, 1971), 178.

23. Ibid., 179–80.

24. For the preparations, see Wheeler to Westmoreland, August 10, 1967, Back-channel Messages, Westmoreland/CBS Litigation File, Box 20.

25. Isaacson and Thomas, *Wise Men*, 683, quoting letter from Acheson to Anthony Eden, August 27, 1967.

26. Tom Johnson notes on meeting, July 12, 1967, Johnson Papers, Tom Johnson Meeting Notes, Box 1.

27. McNamara deposition on Westmoreland trial, copy in Johnson Library, 113, 176, 322.

28. Notes on LBJ meeting with McNamara, Wheeler, Rusk, and Rostow. August 19, 1967, Johnson Papers, Meeting Notes File, Box 1.

29. Bernstein, "On the Mistakes of the War," 72.

30. Halberstam, *The Best and the Brightest*, 643–44.

31. Trewhitt, *McNamara*, 272.

32. Bernstein, "On the Mistakes of the War," 72.

33. Press releases, February 27, 29, 1968, Harriman Papers, Box 486.

34. McNamara to LBJ, November 1, 1967, National Security File, Country File, Vietnam, Box 75.

35. Johnson handwritten notes on McNamara to LBJ, November 1, 1967, Johnson Papers, National Security File, Country File, Vietnam, Box 75.

36. Trewhitt, *McNamara*, 275, 287–88, 297.

37. Admiral David McDonald to Hanson Baldwin, July 20, 1967, Hanson Baldwin Papers, Yale University Library, Box no. 8[5]; and David McDonald Oral History Interview, Naval Historical Center, Washington, D.C.

38. Quoted in Halberstam, *The Best and the Brightest*, 646–47.

39. Moorer interview with author, Washington, D.C., July 14, 1987.

40. Rostow to LBJ with attachments, September 13, 1967, Johnson Papers, National Security File, Name File, Col. Ginsburgh Memos, Box 3.

41. Margy and Bob McNamara to JCS, April 12, 1968, copy in John McConnell Papers, Air Force Historical Center, Maxwell AFB, AL.

42. Notes on NSC meeting, November 29, 1967, Johnson Papers, Tom Johnson Notes on Meetings, Box 1.

43. Undated clipping in Richard Dudman Papers, Manuscript Division, Library of Congress, Washington, D.C., Box 7.

44. Bernstein, "On the Mistakes of the War," 70.

45. Quoted in Henrickson, "Divided against Himself."

46. Bernstein, "On the Mistakes of the War," 71–72.

9

"How Do You Know If You're Winning?": Perception and Reality in America's Military Performance in Vietnam, 1965–1970

Ronald H. Spector

The American war in Vietnam, 1965–1975, has frequently been compared to other "unconventional wars" such as those in Greece and Malaya in the 1940s and 1950s and, of course, to the First Indochina War between the French and the Viet Minh. A number of writers have also recently compared it to the Korean War as well.[1] This chapter suggests, however, that World War I is a far more appropriate model or "paradigm" for Vietnam than any of the wars to which it is usually compared. At first sight, this appears an outrageous comparison, yet I believe that a close look at the dynamics of the Vietnam War will highlight the critical similarity between these two apparently disparate conflicts.

Some fifteen years after the last American soldiers left Vietnam, confusion and controversy still rages over the nature of the war they fought there, the degree of their success or failure, and their role in the ultimate U.S. defeat in Indochina. "The defeat of the U.S. in Vietnam was above everything else a military defeat, a defeat for the U.S. military art," declared a senior People's Army of Vietnam (PAVN) officer, writing ten years after the Fall of Saigon.[2] Gabriel Kolko reaches a similar conclusion in *Anatomy of a War*. According to Kolko, the Vietnam War demonstrated the "ability of a determined, able revolutionary force to defeat immensely richer Americans." American forces had superior firepower and more sophisticated war machines, but American forces were pinned down everywhere by the necessity to defend the large bases and enclaves that they established all over the country.

> The key to the Communist party's maintaining the strategic initiative was its ability to keep U.S. and ARVN forces dispersed. . . . The strategic initiative on the battlefield always rested with the Revolution. . . . [T]he American military to some extent always had to respond to its challenges. . . . [B]y early 1967 everyone important in Washington knew from CIA and Pentagon reports that American strategy was failing.[3]

This has not, needless to say, been the predominant view among senior American military men. Colonel Harry Summers, whose book, *On Strategy: The Vietnam War in Context,* has had enormous influence within the military profession, declares on page 1, "On the battlefield itself, the Army was unbeatable. . . . In engagement after engagement, the forces of the North Vietnamese and Viet Cong were hurled back with terrible losses."[4] Similarly, General Bruce Palmer, former army vice-chief of staff, finds "American direction and conduct of the war and the operational performance of our armed forces, particularly during the period 1962–69, generally were professional and commendable."[5] Two studies by military professionals which take a much more critical view of American military performance and the appropriateness of U.S. strategy and tactics, Andrew F. Krepinevich, *The Army and Vietnam,*[6] and Mark Clodfelter, *The Limits of Air Power,*[7] are by very junior officers. They have not enjoyed anywhere near the influence and popularity of the books by Summers and Palmer. (Copies of Summers' book were issued to every student at the Army War College and Command and General Staff College.[8]

Let's start with the statement that the army was never defeated on the battlefield. (There are similar claims by admirals and generals for the naval and marine components.) In one sense, the statement is perfectly true. If we compare the Vietnam War with the Korean conflict, the differences are clear and striking. On at least two occasions during the Korean War, American defeats on the battlefield confronted American leaders with the likelihood that the United Nations forces in Korea might be forced off the peninsula or even annihilated. On these occasions the United States and its allies faced the grim possibility of having to choose between negotiating a disguised surrender or widening the war to the point of risking world conflict and nuclear confrontation.

Nothing remotely like this occurred in Vietnam. American forces there were never in danger of annihilation. The closest that Washington leaders ever came to confronting a genuine military emergency in Vietnam occurred in the wake of the Tet Offensive when the Joint Chiefs of Staff (JCS) chairman, General Earle Wheeler, in a bureaucratic ploy to win presidential approval for a reserve call-up, recast General William Westmoreland's request for 200,000 additional troops from a proposal to take the offensive against a badly weakened enemy into a call for help to stave off defeat.[9]

In another sense, however, the assertion that U.S. forces "were never defeated on the battlefield" is absurd. Most of the "battles" in the Vietnam War were not ponderous collisions of divisions and corps as in World War II or Korea, but short, sharp clashes between units of company-, platoon-, or even squad-size which lasted a few hours and often only a few minutes.[10] There were thousands of these encounters in the course of the Vietnam War and to characterize all of them as U.S. victories not only strains credibility, but runs contrary to the clear evidence in the admittedly incomplete historical records we have about these minibattles. That evidence strongly suggests that in at least a few of these encounters, the U.S. platoons or companies involved were virtually wiped out.

Some sense of how varied and confused the pattern of ground combat was in Vietnam can be gained from a study prepared for the Advance Research Projects Agency on Marine Operations in a single province of Vietnam by a single U.S. division during 1968 and 1969. The study reviewed all types of operations ranging from patrols to major offensive operations. The researchers found wide variations in the effectiveness of the operations, the tactics employed by the U.S. and Communist forces, and the terrain involved. The costliness of these operations in terms of U.S. casualties also varied widely.[11]

In addition, the causes of the casualties differed markedly from one operation to another:

> In two operations, about 26 percent of total U.S. mortalities occurred during attacks on enemy bunkers. In two other operations, about 26 percent of total U.S. mortalities resulted from U.S. ordnance. Mortalities from mines ranged from one to 30 percent of total cost. In still another operation, 45 percent of U.S. mortalities occurred while U.S. units were resting either in a temporary base or in bivouac.[12]

The only sustained attempt to systematically examine the whole pattern of ground combat in Vietnam was, strangely enough, the product of a group of civilians. They were the young systems analysts in the Defense Department, who, General William C. Westmoreland complained, "constantly sought to alter strategy and tactics with naive, gratuitous advice."[13] General Westmoreland notwithstanding, a reader of the system analysts' successive studies, entitled "Southeast Asia Analysis Reports" cannot but be struck by how little the analysts appear concerned about strategy and tactics or other general questions about the effectiveness of U.S. leadership and operation art. What they are concerned about are casualties—U.S. and enemy.

In the context of the time, this is perfectly understandable. During 1965 to 1968, the principal U.S. strategy in Vietnam, so far as the United States could be said to have a strategy, was one of imposing crippling losses on the enemy through gradual attrition of his forces to the point where he would be unable or unwilling to continue the struggle. From 1969 on, the U.S. aim was to minimize American casualties in order to minimize domestic pressure for a rapid U.S.

withdrawal and allow President Nixon maximum time and freedom of action to implement his policy of Vietnamization, diplomatic and military pressure on Hanoi and gradual troop withdrawals. In neither period was there any particular interest in operations, strategy, or tactics except insofar as they related to casualties.

The analysts conducted four studies between May 1967 and May 1969, and found that in "the real war" of platoon- and company-size fights, the Americans were not exactly undisputed masters of the battlefield. Their earliest study analyzed 56 firefights and found that 79 percent had been initiated by the enemy.[14] A second study in December of 1967 reviewed 165 engagements and found that the enemy held the initiative in 73 percent of these actions.[15]

A 1969 study reviewed 68 engagements occurring over a two-year period from October 1966 to May 1968 and involving all U.S. Army divisions and all areas in Vietnam. Of the 68 engagements, 68 percent were initiated by the enemy. Strangely enough, successful ambushes by either side were relatively rare (five for the U.S. and eight for the Communists). By far the most common type of engagement occurred either when the Communists attacked a U.S. defensive perimeter or a U.S. unit assaulted the enemy in a well-prepared defensive position. In about half of the engagements against Communist defensive positions, the U.S. unit had blundered unaware into a well-dug-in, alert enemy.

The systems analysts' studies naturally raised serious questions about the logic of pursuing a U.S. strategy based on attrition in a war in which the enemy held the initiative in most engagements and retained the option to disengage whenever necessary by withdrawing to his Laotian and Cambodian sanctuaries. Moreover, the enemy could, when he wished, increase the tempo of the fighting and thus increase U.S. casualties. In other words, the enemy could not only control his own casualties but, to a larger extent, those of the United States as well.

Nevertheless, before concluding, as more than a few writers have, that U.S. soldiers and marines were simply hapless pawns flailing away blindly and ineffectively against the wily and subtle Viet Cong, it is well to look again at some of the other findings of the systems analysts. Their data showed, for example, that regardless of who held the initiative, Communist units lost one-third to one-half of their strength every time they engaged a U.S. unit.

Both systems analysts in Washington and grunts in Vietnam agreed that the Viet Cong and North Vietnam Army (NVA) forces excelled in defense and in a wide variety of carefully prepared ambushes. An often-employed Communist tactic was to allow an American unit on a patrol or sweep to blunder on to carefully prepared field fortifications such as the formidable bunkers repeatedly encountered by U.S. Marines around Khe Sanh. A captured North Vietnamese officer expressed the view that "The American infantry units are weak," because they "cannot take or destroy a machine gun position in a properly prepared bunker except by calling for air or artillery. However, the NVA can destroy any American bunker with its B–40 rockets."[16]

"They were masters at aligning weapons with fields of fire," recalled a former company commander with the First Air Cavalry Division. "They were superb at masking their true position. The Americans would move up, you would kill a couple and the rest would run and it was a natural tendency to take off after them. . . . In close terrain against enemy like the North Vietnamese that will get you your nose bloodied. . . . They were absolute masters at choosing the right terrain at the right place at the right time to blow your crap away."[17]

Although the Communists' skill and tenacity in defense inspired awe and respect, their performance on the offensive was often weak and ineffective. Their supporting fires were almost always weaker than the Americans, and they often lacked the ability to coordinate anything larger than company-sized attacks. A Defense Department study found that Communist-initiated attacks on U.S. positions, though they often achieved surprise, still cost the Communists an average of five soldiers for every U.S. casualty. On the infrequent occasions when Communist units were taken by surprise, they often proved incapable of rapidly adapting to the situation, frequently suffering heavy losses and sometimes disintegrating in panic. Communist losses in U.S.-initiated ambushes averaged more than twenty-five times those of the American units opposing them.[18]

American fire power in the form of artillery and air strikes was usually capable of making any but the briefest type of encounter a deadly one for the enemy. Communist-initiated attacks on U.S. positions, for example, though often achieving surprise, nevertheless cost an average of five Communist soldiers for every U.S. casualty.[19] Even in Communist-initiated ambushes, enemy losses were generally higher than those of their victims, while in the minority of cases where a U.S. unit held the initiative in an ambush or a well-prepared attack, the results were catastrophic for the Communists.

An example of the Communists' continued inability to carry out successful coordinated attacks was an assault on the American base complex at Long Binh by elements of the Fifth Viet Cong Division in February 1969. Five different regiments of the Fifth Viet Cong Division totaling over 8,000 men were assigned to attack the Long Binh–Bien Hoa military complex. The Fifth Division's plan called for simultaneous attacks against the air base, the town of Bien Hoa, and the U.S. Army headquarters at Long Binh.

In the event, only the 274th Viet Cong Regiment carried out its attack. The Thirty-third North Vietnamese Army Regiment was hit by a B–52 strike and was caught in an ambush by South Vietnamese Marines and American armored cavalry elements while the 174th North Vietnamese Regiment was scattered by intense artillery fire as it attempted to cross the Dong nai north of Bien Hoa. The Ninety-fifth North Vietnamese Army Regiment failed to reach the staging area in time for the attack.

The 274th's attack began with a mortar and rocket barrage but a full-scale ground attack never developed, perhaps because the First and Third Battalions were late getting into position. The two battalions dug in and waited for darkness to renew their attack. But, with the coming of daylight, the Americans counter-attacked and caught the two battalions deployed in their attack position. The First Battalion had the unwelcome honor of being the first Communist troops to face the new U.S. Army "Sheridan" armored personnel carrier. The Sheridan's powerful 152mm main gun firing deadly flechette rounds—projectiles filled with hundreds of steel darts—took a heavy toll on the Viet Cong. The First Battalion left 88 bodies on the battlefield.[20]

By 1969, the systems analysts were concluding "that the military initiative had shifted" since mid-1968. Prior to that time the Communists were able to inflict significantly higher losses on U.S. forces simply by increasing their level of attacks. After May 1968, the Communists largely lost this ability, although they retained much of their ability to control their own casualties.[21] In other words, the statistics now seemed to suggest that the Americans were getting a little better at the job of finding and killing the enemy while the enemy's ability to hurt the Americans simply by raising the level of combat was declining.

The analysts attributed this change to the fact that "the U.S. has changed its tactics" and also to heavy Communist losses of "trained VC/NVA over the past five years particularly during the 1968 offensives [which] may have lowered the Communist aggressiveness and effectiveness."[22] The 274th Viet Cong Regiment, which had carried out the unsuccessful attacks on Long Binh, for example, was constantly on the move during the latter half of 1969 and into 1970, chronically short of food and supplies, and harried by allied patrols and aircraft. By the end of 1970, U.S. intelligence analysts believed that the regiment had been obliged to devote all its efforts simply to feeding itself and obtaining adequate munitions. Its units had been forced to disperse and two of its battalions had been reduced to less than 70 men.[23]

The conclusions of the systems analysts are generally supported by evidence that has since become available from the Communist side. In March 1969, Ho Chi Minh reportedly complained to Major General Le Tung Tin [ed. note: sic], commanding the Communist forces in the Quang Tri and Thua Thien area, that "no progress had been noted in the overall situation for several months due to various difficulties."[24] A study outline for party cadres directed that though "the revolution was still in the General Offensive/General Uprising stage, complete military victory is now impractical."[25]

At this point, it may prove enlightening to turn from the abstract and quantitative views of the battlefield provided by the systems analysts and intelligence reports and to consider the subjective and impressionistic views of the combatants themselves. Students of organizational behavior are agreed that for an organization to be successful it must, above all, believe that it is succeeding. Did the soldiers and marines of 1965 to 1970 feel that they were succeeding in their mission in Vietnam?

The answer, as any aficionado of Vietnam movies or readers of the now-massive collection of Vietnam novels and firsthand accounts would agree, is, appar-

ently, a resounding "No!" As one of the more perceptive students of the experience of Vietnam GIs has observed,

> [F]rom the outset of America's war in Vietnam, U.S. troops encountered evi-
> dence that undermined every effort to perceive the war a meaningful and
> worthwhile cause. . . . Those who believed that the war should be fought were
> most appalled by the absence of meaningful measurements of military success
> and a clear view of what would constitute victory. Those who questioned the
> legitimacy of our involvement focused more on the senselessness and futility
> of the war.[26]

"I feel as if I've been used," a soldier with the First Infantry Division told a
reporter in 1969. "Nothing I've seen or heard about the way we've been doing
things and why makes any sense."[27] Over 10 years later, two career army officers reviewing their experiences in Vietnam reached much the same conclusion.
"I didn't understand why I was in Vietnam very clearly, I really didn't," recalled
a former company commander with the Fourth Infantry. "And in free moments
when we didn't have a lot to do, those personnel that were close to me were
struggling for the same kind of explanation and that created a lot of problems."[28]
"I'm not really sure that anybody in the higher up levels knew what we were
supposed to be doing," recalled another officer. "I'm like I say, like my troops, I
just wondered, you know, ok if we do all this, what's going to happen, what are
we doing, what's the goal of the whole thing?"[29]

One of the most troubling aspects of the war for most American combatants
was the problematic role of the South Vietnamese. Although the official rationale for the war stressed the American aim of helping and protecting the
civilian population of South Vietnam from the Communists, most GIs found
the attitudes of the Vietnamese villagers to be frustrating and confusing at
best, hostile and treacherous at worst. Charles C. Moskos found that the
soldiers he interviewed in 1969 "have little belief that they are protecting an
outpost of democracy in South Vietnam. . . . [T]he soldier definitely does not
see himself fighting for South Vietnam. Quite the contrary, he thinks South
Vietnam a worthless country."[30]

Among many GIs, it was taken as axiomatic that most villagers secretly
aided and protected the Communists while lying to and misleading the Americans. An American general reported:

> The Viet Cong in this area are experts in the use of explosives for booby traps
> and mines. We have had approximately 300 booby traps and mines explode
> during our operations. . . . Apart from casualties the booby traps are very bad
> psychologically for our young paratroopers and commanders in that the men
> develop a sometimes bitter hatred for the local villagers. The men have every
> reason to believe, and are sometimes correct in the belief that the booby traps
> are made by the very people they see living in the villages. The situation is

worsened by the fact that the Viet Cong use certain other tactics that frustrate my men. When our troops receive fire from a hut in a village and prepare to return fire, women and children burst out of the entrance to the hut and smile and wave their hands, because they know the soldiers will not fire. While this is happening the enemy escapes through a tunnel complex.[31]

Equally troubling to many GIs was the feeling that they were being handicapped by unreasonable rules and constraints imposed by higher headquarters or "the politicians." While pacification experts deplored the excessive and counterproductive use of firepower by most American units, many of the combatants believe they were being unreasonably handicapped by whatever rules of engagement the higher command managed to impose. "If we're going to fight we ought to fight and not play around with a lot of sanctuaries and lulls and pauses," declared one soldier.[32]

Throughout the war, soldiers and marines continued to voice such sentiments. Yet I believe there is nevertheless an important difference between the way the war was perceived in 1965–1968 period and the period from 1968–1971. In the absence of systematic polling data, evidence about personal attitudes must always be fragmentary and uncertain, yet there is strong, indeed, overwhelming, evidence to suggest that the attitude of the GIs toward the war they were fighting in Vietnam was even more pessimistic, disillusioned, and confused during the 1969–1972 period, when they were apparently winning, than during the earlier period when the Communists had the initiative. The differences between the two periods can easily be exaggerated and it is well to keep in mind that throughout the war, the most widespread attitude among combat troops was a desire to survive and see one's comrades survive. All other motivations were at best secondary. "I guess my standard of success was keeping my soldiers alive," recalled a former company commander with the 3rd of the 503rd Infantry.[33] It was a standard that would have been readily endorsed by almost all small-unit leaders in Vietnam (and probably many other wars).

Nevertheless, there are many indications in the contemporary interviews and later first-hand accounts of the early period of the war that, despite the frustrations and confusion, many soldiers in the early years of the Vietnam conflict could still believe that they were performing a meaningful task and one which would ultimately lead to success for the United States. As one former company commander recalls, "Morale . . . was really, really super. In '65 we really felt we were winning, felt we were making great progress."[34] "Nobody wanted to be known as a coward, nobody wanted to be known as not carrying his share of the load," recalled another former company commander of the 1967–1968 period. "The war was young. It was the only war they knew."[35] "A feeling of invincibility really weighed on that company," recalled an armored cavalry leader of the same period. "It was a source of pride to them the casualties they took. It was a source of pride that they were as tough as they were . . . the harder they fought, the higher their morale and esprit."[36]

The Tet Offensive is widely believed to have destroyed this relative optimism and to have inaugurated a period of increasing disillusionment and indifference. As one soldier recalled,

> There was this thought that if we persevere, you know, we'll win. That was the sort of collective consciousness that we had as GIs. But Tet taught us that wasn't so; you know, that these people were determined to kick our ass! It was not immediate . . . but the message was there and we got it. In different ways and on different levels.[37]

Yet the psychological effects of the Tet Offensive on GI morale were far more varied than such observations suggest. While many soldiers recall that the Tet battles, with their increased hardship and loss, brought home to them the fact that they still faced a determined and far from defeated enemy; many also recall that they emerged from the ordeal with increased confidence in themselves and their unit. The same soldier who saw Tet as a sign of enemy determination "to kick our ass" also recalled with pride "a different aspect of Tet. We all pulled together, did what we were supposed to do as a group of people . . . because we were a motley undisciplined rag tag group of clerks. . . . I would never have thought we had the ability to function cohesively as a military unit."[38] The commander of an aviation maintenance detachment recalled that during Tet, "when a fire fight would happen, these guys would run and get their weapons and want to go out and mix it up with the enemy. . . . It got so bad one time during Tet, they were standing on top of CONNEX boxes cheering the guys on the perimeter and just causing all manner of hell, just like a football game."[39]

If the Tet Offensive did not completely destroy American morale in Vietnam, why then did it decline so precipitously in 1969–1972, the period in which the military situation was actually more favorable to the Allies. In other words, if the United States was winning the war, why didn't American soldiers perceive themselves to be winning?

One reason was that the war still lacked tangible, easily understandable measures of progress. Even in World War II, the last "good war," the capture of features on a map often held little enough meaning for a soldier in combat. "That river was our objective last week, this hill here is our objective today, and beyond it lie other hills and other rivers, each with its toll of sacrifice."[40] Nevertheless, army psychologists noted that during the rapid advance of the Allied armies through France and Belgium in August and September 1944, "combat troops sometimes exhibited an almost 'civilian' optimism." Moreover, the capture of a hill or a town could mean greater safety, comfort, or even (in the final days) war booty.[41] Few of these factors were ever present in Vietnam.

By contrast, in Vietnam, hard-won terrain was often abandoned almost as soon as it was secured, leaving GIs with a feeling of frustration and confusion. In one of the most dramatic and successful attacks of "Operation Pegasus" in May

1968, troops of the Third Battalion, Twenty-sixth Marines seized Hill 881 North near Khe Sanh. A few days later a squad leader commented, "I'd like to say I feel this operation was successful. But it was needless, due to the fact that after we had taken our objective we just left it. . . . We ran them off the hill and they came right back and reoccupied the position."[42]

In addition, the improvement in U.S. military posture was only a relative one. Even at the lowest point of their effort in South Vietnam, probably 1970 and 1971, the Communists were still able to mount attacks by fire and increasingly effective sapper attacks on U.S. bases and successfully defend their own base areas in such places as the Ashau Valley near the Laotian border and the An Hao basin of the Quang Nam province which the Americans were only able to enter sporadically and at considerable cost.[43] Most important of all, the Communists continued to successfully elude the Americans. As late as March 1970, a senior officer on General Abram's staff pointed to the U.S. "continued inability to develop a detailed understanding of the Viet Cong capability to evade, withdraw, and escape at will, even at this stage of the war."[44]

The war also retained its frustration and confusion, a confusion simply compounded by the introduction of Vietnamization in 1969. Above all, President Nixon's troop withdrawals, once begun, served as an unambiguous signal that there would be no decisive military outcome to the war so far as American GIs were concerned. Morale and motivation plummeted. "There was no doubt that people didn't see a mission over there," recalled a company commander of the 1971–72 period. "It led to not doing a lot of things that would put you in a dangerous light. At least our battalion C.O. indicated to us 'look, we didn't want to get committed.' "[45] "Like nobody had hopes of winning the war. Everybody knew that the war was a loss," recalled a former infantryman of that period. "Everybody felt like they were outcasts."[46]

What conclusions can we draw from all this? First, that easy generalization about Americans "winning all the battles" or conversely floundering blindly at the mercy of a wily enemy bear little resemblance to the reality of combat operations in Vietnam and to the complexity and variety of the thousands of small unit clashes that make up "the war."

Second, that we know relatively little about the nature of military operations in Vietnam compared to World Wars I and II. Even the systems analysts and other data collectors and evaluators had only a sketchy and generalized idea of the meaning of the information they were collecting. The analysts often noted they lacked sufficient detailed information on the tactics employed in each operation, the enemy units engaged, and the terrain and population of the operational area to offer more than generalized observations on those operations.[47]

The absence of such detailed knowledge of actual operations could sometimes lead to ludicrous results. One OSD analysis used kill-ratios and "friendly fatalities" to prove that sergeants were better recon team leaders than lieutenants, a conclusion that the marine reconnaissance troops found highly amusing since they were aware that lieutenants were given the more difficult patrols and sergeants generally given the less demanding missions.[48]

A third conclusion is that there are radical and striking differences between the subjective perceptions of the war by the American combatants and the strategic picture of the war presented by the system analysts and intelligence experts. This is particularly true of their perceptions of "winning" or "making progress." The possibility that armed forces can feel like "winners" when they are losing and "losers" when they are winning may sound odd, but it is far from unique in military history. It is especially common in protracted, repetitive kinds of warfare. In the Battle of Britain, for example, German pilots could see little signs of progress and often felt themselves to be losing at times when the British, in fact, were in a desperate situation. Conversely, the British never thought they were losing even when they were.

Finally, there is overwhelming evidence that the Vietnam War was, in fact, what many of its critics claimed it was, a stalemate. But a stalemate for the Communists, as well as the Americans. In this sense, it may be enlightening to compare it with World War I. "When war broke out in Europe in August 1914," Michael Howard reminds us, "every major power at once took the offensive."[49] As in World War I, neither side could accept the fact of stalemate and each side always conceived its opponent to be near the breaking point. So, caught between an American government which could never quite make up its mind and a Communist government which refused ever to change its mind, thousands of brave and dedicated young men and women gave up their lives for no good purpose.

Notes

1. Cf. John Halliday and Bruce Cumings, *Korea: The Unknown War*(New York: Pantheon, 1988) and Max Hastings, *The Korean War* (New York: Simon and Schuster, 1987), especially chapter 18.

2. Nhuan Vu, "Black Page in the History of the U.S. Military Art," *Tap Chi Cong San,* no. 12 (December 1984): 51–53.

3. Gabriel Kolko, *Anatomy of a War* (New York: Pantheon, 1985), 176, 179–180.

4. Harry Summers, *On Strategy* (San Rafael, California: Presidio Press 1982), 1.

5. Bruce Palmer, Jr., *The 25-Year War: America's Military Role in Vietnam* (Lexington: University of Kentucky, 1984), 314.

6. Mark Clodfelter, *The Limits of Air Power* (Baltimore: Johns Hopkins University Press, 1986).

7. Andrew F. Krepinevich, *The Army and Vietnam* (New York: Free Press, 1989).

8. Bob Buzzanco, "The American Military's Rationale Against the Vietnam War," *Political Science Quarterly* 101 (1986): 560.

9. The literature on this episode is extensive; cf., John B. Henry, "February 1968," *Foreign Policy,* no. 4 (fall 1971): 3–34; Herbert Y. Schandler, *Lyndon Johnson and Vietnam*, 95–117; Townsend Hoopes, *The Limits of Intervention* (New York: McKay, 1969), 159–162.

10. Pentagon systems analysts who studied ground engagements in Vietnam during 1966 to 1968 found that between 75 and 83 percent involved units of smaller than

battalion size. In the course of the war they identified over 11,000 actions initiated by the Communist side alone which involved units smaller than a battalion; see "Tactical Initiative in Vietnam," *Southeast Asia Analysis Report (May 1969)*, 7; Thomas C. Thayer, *War Without Fronts: The American Experience in Vietnam* (Boulder, CO: Westview Press, 1985) 45–46.

11. M.E. Arnstein and F.J. West, Jr., "A Tabular Method for Comparing Friendly and Enemy Casualties: A Case Study of Marine Mortalities Resulting from Patrols and Six Offensive Operations in Quang Nam Province" (RM–6378-ARPA December 1970), iii–iv. Copy in J.R. Chaisson Papers, Box 19, Hoover Institute Archives.

12. Ibid.

13. William C. Westmoreland, *A Soldier Reports* (New York: Dell), 115.

14. "The Strategy of Attrition," *Southeast Asia Analysis Reports* (January 1969). Copy in U.S. Army Center of Military History.

15. Cited in "Tactical Initiative in Vietnam," 7.

16. "A Monograph of 2d Lt. Nguyen Van Thong, 320th Regt. 1st NVA Div.," September 1968, Records of I Field Force, G–2 Section. Copy in Center of Military History.

17. Lt. Col. Thomas G. Rhame interview, "Company Command in Vietnam" series, U.S. Army Military History Institute, Carlyle, PA.

18. "Tactical Initiative in Vietnam," 9.

19. Ibid., 11.

20. Combined Intelligence Center, Vietnam, "History of the 274th Viet Cong Regiment," 12, 30. Copy in MACV J–2 files, MACV Records, National Archives.

21. "Military Initiative in South Vietnam: A Follow-Up," *Southeast Asia Analysis Reports* (January 1970): 35–36.

22. Ibid., 37.

23. Combined Intelligence Center, "History of the 274th Viet Cong Regiment," 30.

24. "Personal Notebook of NVA Commanding General Tri Thien-Hue Military Region" (CDEC Document 10–1327–60, October 7, 1969).

25. "Study by Sub Region Six of Long An Province for Use of Sub Region Party and Group Member" (CDEC Document 6028–2926–291, August 2, 1969). Copy in Race Papers, Center for Research Libraries, Chicago, IL. See also the discussion of similar documents in William J. Turley, *The Second Indochina War* (New York: New American Library, 1987), 130–131.

26. Christian G. Appy, "A War for Nothing: Attitudes of American Soldiers in Vietnam," 3–4. Paper presented to the 1985 annual meeting of the SHAFR.

27. Arnold Abrams, "South Vietnam: Everybody, USA," *Far Eastern Economic Review* (February 12, 1970).

28. Interview with Major 5351, former Commanding Officer, "E" Company, Eighteenth Infantry, Fourth Infantry Division, March 1982, 2. "Company Command in Vietnam" series, Oral History Collection, U.S. Army Command General Staff School.

29. Interview with Major 5341, former Commanding Officer, "E" Company, 3rd of the 503rd, February 1982, 42. "Company Command in Vietnam" series, Oral History Collection, U.S. Army Command and General Staff School.

30. Charles C. Moskos, *The American Enlisted Man* (New York: Russell Sage, 1970), 148–149.

31. Interview with Brigadier General Richard J. Allen, October 9, 1969, Vietnam Interview Tape 151, U.S. Army Center of Military History.

32. B. Drummond Ayres, "Many G.I.s Disillusioned on War," *New York Times*, August 4, 1969.

33. Ibid. See also Jim Heiden interview, 31–32. Winter Soldier Collections, Columbia University LTC G.A.L. interview, 61. Oral History Collection, U.S. Army Command

and General Staff School; Robert Santos interview in Al Santoli, ed., *Everything We Had,* (New York: Ballantine, 1982), 20, 22.

34. Interview, Lieutenant Colonel E.O., "Company Command in Vietnam" series, Oral History Collection, U.S. Army Command and General Staff School.

35. Interview, Lieutenant Colonel J.L., "Company Command in Vietnam" series. See also interview, Major J.H., 3–7. "Company Command in Vietnam" series, Oral History Collection, U.S. Army Command and Staff School.

36. Interview with Lieutenant Colonel A.R.W., November 12, 1982, 82. "Company Command in Vietnam" series, Oral History Collection, U.S. Army Command and General Staff School.

37. Bob Hood, Oral History Interview, 17–18. Winter Soldier Collection, Columbia University.

38. Ibid., 16.

39. Interview with Colonel P.E.B., 26. "Company Command in Vietnam" series, Oral History Collection, U.S. Army Command and General Staff School.

40. S.A. Stouffer, et. al., *The American Soldier: Combat and Its Aftermath* (New York: Wiley, 1965), 170.

41. Ibid., 170–171.

42. Corporal Glenn R. Horne interview, Tape 2776, Marine Corps Oral History Collection. See also P. Goldman and T. Fuller, *Charlie Company: What Vietnam Did to Us* (New York: Ballantine, 1984), 254.

43. See the frequent and bloody engagements in the An Hoa area described in Charles R. Smith, *U.S. Marines in Vietnam* (Washington, D.C.: Historical Divisions, U.S. Marine Corps, 1988) 80–125 and Graham A. Cosmos and Terence P. Murray, *U.S. Marines in Vietnam, 1970–1971* (Washington, D.C.: Historical Division, U.S. Marine Corps, 1986) 42–43, 47–51.

44. Colonel E.O., Memo for General Abrams, sub: End of Tour Report and Appraisal, March 11, 1970. Copy in Abrams Papers, Center of Military History.

45. Interview with Lieutenant Colonel J.L., "Company Command in Vietnam" series. Oral History Collection, U.S. Army Command and General Staff School.

46. Jim Peachin interview, 85. Winter Soldier Collection. I have discussed the question of declining morale and motivation in the latter years of the war at greater length in my essay "The Vietnam War and the Army's Self-Image," in John Schlight (ed.) *Second Indochina War Symposium Proceedings* (Washington, D.C.: U.S. Army Center of Military History, 1986), 1169–187.

47. M.E. Arnstein and F.J. West, Jr., "A Tabular Method for Comparing Friendly and Enemy Casualties."

48. F.J. West, "Problem Recognition and Organizational Adaptation in a Counter-Insurgency Environment," unpublished paper. Copy in John R. chaisson Papers.

49. Michael Howard, "Men Against Fire: the Doctrine of the Offensive in 1914," in Peter Paret, ed., *Makers of Modern Strategy* (Princeton, NJ: Princeton University Press, 1986), 510.

10

Direct and Indirect Effects
of the Movement against
the Vietnam War

Paul Joseph

During the Vietnam War, millions of U.S. citizens not only opposed the policies of their government but mobilized themselves in a conscious effort to stop it. What effect did these activities have? What was the influence of the antiwar movement on policymakers? What legacy, if any, was left to society? Despite a new generation of scholarship on the Vietnam period, we are not even close to achieving consensus on these questions. Significantly, the disagreements cross cut ideological and occupational positions.

Former antiwar activist and now sociologist Todd Gitlin holds "the movement against the Vietnam War the most successful movement against a shooting war *in history*" (1984: 71; emphasis in original). However, Sam Brown, another former leader of the antiwar movement, finds that "although the antiwar movement had strategic goals (sometimes simply the cessation of the bombing, sometimes the ending of imperialism, but mostly something in between), it accomplished very little of what it set out to do. The reasons for its failure are rooted in the history of the movement itself; they led directly to its isolation and ultimate failure" (1976: 121).

Scholars also disagree. Gabriel Kolko's critical treatment of U.S. intervention assesses the influence of the movement this way: "no one of the antiwar efforts was important, but combined they became very significant. . . . At a minimum, it fixed to the war an unprecedented social price for the status quo after a sustained postwar era of apathy" (1985: 174).[1] Guenter Lewy's interpretation of Washington's decisions comes from another part of the political spectrum, yet he also finds that "the antiwar movement had a significant impact on both the Johnson and Nixon administrations. . . . [This] impact was enhanced by the widely publicized charges of American atrocities and lawlessness" (1978: 434). On the other hand, in Leslie Gelb's influential treatment of the impact of domestic politics on Vietnam decision making, the organized antiwar movement virtually disappears. Dissent is reduced to public opinion polls, electoral campaigns, and organized elite viewpoints (1979).

Among actual decision makers, the antiwar movement is not, with one exception, granted much influence. Presidents and secretaries of state and defense repeatedly claim that they were immune to public pressure. Their assistants tend to back them up. For John Roche, an adviser to President Johnson, "the protest movement as such had only marginal influence on American policy, though they were naturally accused of hindering negotiations, giving aid and comfort to the enemy and similar sins" (1976: 136). In 1969, moratorium protesters picketed the White House. Richard Nixon made sure everyone knew that he spent the afternoon watching the Washington Redskins play football on TV (Zaroulis and Sullivan 1984: 286). For decision makers, the exception to the finding of minimal influence is the impact that the movement is said to have on the leadership in Hanoi and the morale of the revolutionary forces who fought against the Saigon government. Former Assistant Secretary of State John McNaughton reflects this attitude when he wrote in May 1967, for internal government consumption, that "the state of mind in the U.S. generates impatience in the political structure of the United States. It unfortunately also generates patience in Hanoi" *(Pentagon Papers,* vol. 4: 478). Melvin Small's recent study also finds leading government officials concluding that the antiwar movement encouraged Hanoi and the southern resistance (1988).

The remainder of this chapter offers an assessment of the impact of the movement against the war in Vietnam. I develop nine criteria by which movement influence, both direct and indirect, can be measured. In so doing, I find that the antiwar movement had considerable influence, certainly more than that accorded it in prevailing academic treatments, which tend to discount its impact. The tendency in academia is to claim that the policymaking process, especially for foreign policy and defense, is either "autonomous," or influenced only by the interplay among international states or a relatively narrow range of bureaucratic pressures operating largely within government itself. "Domestic politics" can have an impact upon policy, but are conceived only as the interplay among competing congressional factions, as presidential interests, or as organized interest groups. In this view, popular forces have little to no effect.[2]

Definition and Characterization of the
Vietnam Peace Movement

Any discussion of the impact of the peace movement must start with a clear definition and classification of its practices. For example, some of the variation in the assessments offered above can be attributed to implicit differences in the characterization of the antiwar movement itself. Without a clear definition and broad sense of possible avenues of influence, the tendency will be to limit possible impact to direct policy decisions made by governmental authorities. This is, of course, a crucial measure of the success of the peace movement. But as the activities and goals of the peace movement were quite varied, both a definition and a sense of the diversity of goals and strategies is required. We need to measure both the direct impact of social movements on policy, and more oblique patterns of influence that are mediated by third parties and refracted through altered social contexts. We need to peer behind the contradictory voting pattern of a congressman, the businessman who complains about the improper management of the economy, the editor who finally agrees to run the reporter's more critical story, and the quickening pace of negotiations. To explore and fully appreciate the varied forms of influence stemming from the mobilization of the public, I will introduce several concepts that illuminate the dynamics of indirect forms of influence.

The antiwar movement can be characterized *as an effort to transform U.S. strategy that:*

1. presented ideas and policy options that went beyond the boundaries of elite policy discourse;
2. conveyed a sense of urgency in its opposition to prevailing policy;
3. employed influence strategies combining efforts within existing institutions, such as lobbying and coalition building, with activities encouraging direct popular participation in protest, such as demonstrations and civil disobedience; and
4. attempted to speak for and mobilize a broader, unorganized constituency than the formal members of the organizations themselves.

As such, the movement against the war in Vietnam was a particular type of peace movement that drew upon important predecessors during the twentieth century (Chatfield 1988; DeBenedetti 1973, 1980, 1990; Wittner 1984). In turn, these peace movements are examples of social movements which, as defined by Tilly (1984: 313), are "sustained interactions in which mobilized people, acting in the name of a defined interest, make repeated broad demands on powerful others via means which go beyond the current prescriptions of the authorities." This concept of an antiwar movement distinguishes among organized and mobilized social protest, and other important forms of domestic dissent such as public opinion, or the views of the "attentive elite."

Peace Movement Effectiveness

The effectiveness of the movement against the Vietnam War can be measured by the following nine criteria:

1. The classic measure of movement success is forcing an actual change in policy goals. Government officials either accommodate the demands of the peace movement, or accept the challenging group as a legitimate constituency to the policymaking process with the goal of changing policy as the result.[3]

The movement against the war in Vietnam, though its members numbered in the millions and it developed a wide range of organizations and strategies, cannot be considered a success in this sense. The movement did not force either the Johnson or Nixon administrations to change the overall goals of U.S. intervention in Vietnam. These goals were both regional and global. Within Indochina, Washington sought a non-Communist government, first throughout all of Vietnam and, after 1954, in South Vietnam itself. Globally, the effort demonstrated a commitment that the United States would not permit a revolutionary movement from coming to power, and that this commitment would include, if necessary, the direct use of military force. The antiwar movement did not succeed in modifying these goals, either by forcing a unilateral withdrawal from Vietnam, or by forcing Washington to negotiate a political settlement that permitted the possibility that either the National Liberation Front or, later, the Provisional Revolutionary Government, might come to power through a fair election. In fact, as the war progressed, most of the antiwar movement became still more narrowly focused on opposing specific military measures. No effective leverage against the underlying premises that led the United States to intervene in Vietnam in the first place was developed. Despite the movement, Washington's goal of preserving an anti-Communist government in Saigon remained intact.

2. Peace movements may block the specific programs and strategies that are necessary for government officials to implement a policy. Overall goals do not change, but the measures necessary to carry out policy are denied. Government officials are forced to adjust. The result is a contradictory or ambivalent situation that contains both the impact of the oppositional movement and the continued efforts of authorities to pursue traditional policy objectives, although now through a different strategy. The strength of the blocking measures may be sufficient to create an impasse.

By this criterion, the movement against the war in Vietnam was increasingly effective. Washington's strategies, particularly those related to the use of military force, were continually changed due to domestic pressure. Before opposition emerged, Washington was relatively free to define its strategies. After World War II, diplomatic and military aid was given to the French. After the Geneva Accords, covert action was used against the North, military and economic assistance propped up Ngo Dinh Diem and a small privileged elite in the South, and a growing number of U.S. military advisers were sent to train the South Vietnamese Army. After the reorganization and increasing success of the revolutionary forces in the South and the turmoil following the Diem coup in 1963, the United States used ground troops in "search and destroy" missions and began sustained bombing of the North under "Rolling Thunder." These two military strategies were vital for U.S. goals as, after 1963, a political solution along lines that Washington found acceptable was simply impossible to achieve.

After 1965, the movement against the Vietnam War gradually imposed constraints on U.S. strategies. U.S. troops were confined to South Vietnam.[4] After March 1968, a ceiling was placed on the number of troops that could be used in South Vietnam.[5] Also in 1968, a partial and then a total bombing halt was enforced over North Vietnam. Under these circumstances Washington could not win. By the time Richard Nixon assumed the presidency, it had become a political necessity to withdraw troops from South Vietnam regardless of who was in office. As a result, Washington's military position on the battlefield and Kissinger's negotiating leverage in secret talks in Paris were undermined. Nixon resumed air strikes over North Vietnam because these were essential to demonstrate to Hanoi that he could exercise military force. But these strikes were only symbolic expressions of intent. They caused destruction but did not have significant strategic impact. Nixon never reestablished domestic political support for renewed bombing.[6] The means necessary to keep the bombing secret eventually backfired in the Watergate scandal that subsequently undermined the entire U.S. effort in Indochina as well as Nixon himself. In short, by denying the strategic means to achieve long-standing policy objectives, the antiwar movement severely constrained the ability of government decision makers to achieve their goals.

3. Peace movements also try to educate or otherwise affect two kinds of attitudes: those held by what has been called the "attentive elite," and those held by the general public as a whole. In several theories of social change, especially of foreign and defense policy, the views of the attentive elite are especially important. Theories of the impact of general public opinion are broader and include perspectives that stress its importance as well as those that dismiss its role entirely. The issue here is the impact of peace movements on these two types of attitudes.

Measuring the impact of the movement against the Vietnam War on either segment of the public is far from simple. Examining the general public first, we do know that support for the war declined significantly over time. We also know that the strength of the antiwar movement increased between 1964 and 1969 (its relative strength from 1970 on is a matter of dispute). At issue is the relationship between these two facts. Most of the academic literature argues that the connection is incidental. John Mueller (1973), for example, believes that declining public support reflects the duration of the war and its consequent casualty levels, not the influence of the antiwar movement itself. Mueller maintains that every time casualties increased by a factor of ten, support for the war declined by 15 percentage points.[7] Similarly, Schreiber (1976: 228) argues for the impact of duration, and even offers a formula whereby support for the war declines at roughly 1 percent every two months.[8] The argument that the active antiwar movement had at best a minimal impact on the views of the rest of the public is further supported by studies indicating that the political culture of the United States carries significant disapproval of most forms of even nonviolent activism such as demonstrations (Schreiber 1976: 230).

An alternative approach is to trace the indirect impact of the organized antiwar movement on public attitudes. Visible forms of protest may simply *force* the public to consider an issue, even while individuals claim that their (shifting) opinions are not derived from the movement itself. In this sense, the movement may contribute to a form of cognitive dissidence whereby individuals disavow the source of their modified opinion even while accepting the substance of their argument.[9] In addition, the inconclusive battlefield results that produce public frustration are themselves a reflection, in part, of restrictions on military force imposed by the movement, and by the anticipation of leading decision makers that the movement would grow still further if additional increments of military power are adopted.[10] Finally, the public, even while not accepting the moral arguments against the U.S. role in Vietnam that constituted the main thrust of active movement opposition, may at the same time be more inclined by the presence of that movement to accept pragmatic arguments regarding the impossibility of winning.[11] These indirect forms of possible influence on the part of the organized movement on public opinion cannot be measured systematically. Yet there exists the strong possibility that the two not only interact but combine to affect policymakers and Congress. Burstein and Freudenburg (1978: 99), for example, find that "cumulative war costs, public opinion, and antiwar demonstrations all had significant effects on Senate roll call outcomes, but they were so highly intercorrelated that their separate effects could not be disentangled." Methodological difficulties that accompany circuitous forms of impact remain, but should not blind us to the nuances of the interaction between the movement and public opinion.

The impact of the antiwar movement on elite opinion is also difficult to trace, although it is possible to argue that overall influence was considerable. Between 1965 and 1968, much of the campus protest was focused at elite universities whose faculty began to publish articles, write op-ed pieces, and use their own influence channels to lobby policymakers. The connections between Harvard faculty and the civilian staff of the Department of Defense were particularly critical in this regard. Vietnam policymakers were well aware that support for the war effort was dissipating among the educated elite (Small 1988). In fact, it was the readers of the *New York Times* who were affected by the antiwar movement and translated the emotion and anger that accompanied it into opposition that policymakers found more legitimate.

4. Peace movement effectiveness is also measured by its impact on third parties or *mediated agents*. In the case of the Vietnam War these included (a) experts in the field, (b) the press and media, and (c) other social movements.

In this case, experts can be defined as scholars of foreign and defense policy and the staff of policy-oriented think tanks. Accompanying the growth of the antiwar movement was a profound intellectual change among many members of both groups. Opposition to the war undermined the virtual consensus that then existed toward U.S. armed intervention and the efficacy of military force. While revisionist accounts of the Cold War preceded the escalation of the Vietnam War, much of the reinterpretation of key post–World War II events was prompted by more immediate opposition to the Vietnam War itself. As a result, a central element of opposition to the war was the creation of a more permanent and broader ranging debate among those identified as experts in national security.

The Vietnam movement also had a significant impact on press and media coverage. The emergence of a "credibility gap," or the difference between what the government said was happening in Vietnam and what the press and media reported was happening in Vietnam, can be traced back to Washington's desire to avoid public debate over the costs of the war effort and its expected duration. During the escalation of the war in 1965, Johnson and McNamara could not tell the public what their advisers were reporting in private, namely that the war could not be won in a short period of time (Gelb 1979: 371). The result, they feared, would be a loss of public support. Deception, in the form of overly optimistic projections of victory, was the only possible answer. The press was *not* quick to criticize the government on this count. Examples of more accurate and pessimistic reporting before 1968 are relatively rare.[12] Not until the Tet Offensive did the mass media offer coverage that was both more complex and negative. In this respect, the press and media did not abandon their professional norms and practices, but only altered their coverage by presenting a broader range of views regarding progress of the war than had previously been the case. In effect, the press and media *appeared* more oppositional by including in their stories legitimate critics who took up the arguments of the antiwar movement. "Illegitimate" critics from the movement itself continued to be ignored (Hallin 1984). The press and media did not create the critical coverage, but instead boosted the opposition that stemmed from other sources. A critical press did emerge. But their principal concern, inflated government optimism regarding progress in the war, can be traced back to the false expectations of a relatively quick victory that were promised by official spokesmen. These promises were themselves induced by the anticipated loss of public support that more realistic assessments would produce. The press and media thus conveyed popular opposition in a manner that legitimized some of its arguments, while simultaneously trivializing the legitimacy of the movement itself (Gitlin 1980). This interpretation differs from both the thesis of a disloyal and oppositional press, as well as from the thesis of a press that is fully subservient to the foreign policy elite (Chomsky and Herman 1988; Parenti 1986).

Peace movements may also contribute to the growth of other social movements that collectively communicate a strong sense of constraint to policymakers. The experience of participating in a movement may encourage some individuals to initiate or join new movements.[13] In fact, the movement against the war in Vietnam was itself partly inspired by another form of social activism, the civil rights movement. In turn, opposition to the Vietnam War was at least partly responsible for the emergence of the women's movement,[14] the environmental movement, and other movements for reform. Opposition to the war was also intertwined with the transformation and radicalization of the civil rights movement (Gill 1990). Many of these "new" social movements are a product of recent economic and social change and, had there been no war in Vietnam, would have emerged in some form anyway. Yet the antiwar movement lay at the core of the broader sense of collective animation that there was something deeply wrong in the world, and also that there was a possibility of creating something much better. Measurement of this general mood is difficult if not impossible, as is tracing its precise impact on Washington's policies. Yet it is safe to say that beyond the antiwar movement itself, policymakers were affected by the emergence of a broader array of social movements, and that specter formed one motivation for reducing the economic and political impact of the war.

5. Peace movement effectiveness is also measured by its ability to maintain an oppositional organizational culture. Movements need to create and maintain the resources that permit participating individuals to feel that their actions are contributing, even if in the long run, to a better life. The form of this expression varies from bearing "moral witness" in the case of the Quakers to experiencing "empowerment" or other forms of personal growth in movements influenced by feminist perspectives. Here an important aspect of peace movements is creating and then sustaining feelings of affiliation, social connection, belonging, and participation (Parkin 1988). The cultivation of human networks and appreciation of the links between local and global developments create a sense of dedication that surpasses success and failure on particular issues. Participation in grass-roots initiatives, cultivation of affinities, and direct action produce a vision that sustains local actions on the one hand, and feelings of membership in a global community on the other. Here effectiveness is the creation of a sense of collective identity that transcends individualism. A sense of spirit and so-

cial consciousness is created that leads to added commitment to work for peace. The challenge is to develop tactics that permit this expressive function of political participation to coexist alongside and even to enhance the more instrumental function of influencing policy change.

In this respect, the record of the antiwar movement is mixed. Much has been written about the cultural changes that accompanied the movement against the war, including both its liberating elements and its self-destructive excesses (Breines 1979; Gitlin 1980; Miller 1988). The cultural dimension of the antiwar movement raised enormous possibilities, most of which were denied or co-opted (Baritz 1985). In this sense, the long-run impact of the movement on the political culture of the United States, and its own ability to maintain internal cohesiveness, was at best limited. The most important failure of the antiwar movement was its inability to claim victories for itself and its constituency, even if the impact of its activities remained ambiguous.[15] On the other hand, the antiwar movement left an important organizational legacy, namely a core of activists who participated in other efforts for social change including the environmental movement of the 1970s, the peace movements of the 1980s, and the rapid development of opposition to the Persian Gulf War in 1991.

6. Peace movements can contribute to the formation of internal cleavages within the political elite. In general, policymakers do not regard peace movements and their leaders as legitimate. However, the influence of these movements may raise policy costs, which in turn prompt those more sensitive to the constraints of popular pressures to distance themselves from prevailing orthodoxy, some privately, others in public. The official dissenters command status and are respected by the press, media, and specialized journals of opinion. Unlike movement leaders, these views "count." Elite opposition receives special attention and may even encourage a new round of popular dissent. A term for this might be *fractionalization*, or the emergence of significant disagreement among well-established authorities as a mediated expression of more deep-seated social protest.

The existence of elite disagreement over the conduct of the Vietnam War is now well documented. President Johnson received advice that questioned the advisability of his large-scale troop commitment to Vietnam in early 1965 (Ball 1990: 234–36; Clifford 1979: 371). By 1966, Secretary of Defense Robert McNamara had become privately skeptical of Washington's ability to exert its will against Hanoi (*Pentagon Papers*, vol. 3). Yet these disagreements did not carry political weight. Dissenters did not yet feel a special urgency to break fundamentally with Johnson, or to use unorthodox influence channels to affect Johnson's decision making. The opposition was only an "opinion" of whether the policy would be effective. At this time, no significant social force stood behind the dissenting opinion. The cost of ignoring the skeptical arguments was "only" to be wrong (unfortunately, the ongoing cost of thousands of American and Vietnamese lives were not considered a factor in these deliberations). No political liability had yet been created. In this sense, the opposition remained loyal. No internal critique of Vietnam policy could be detected by the public. While McNamara's growing skepticism was known within the administration, true elite opposition to Johnson's Vietnam policy did not emerge until 1968, after the Tet Offensive, and after continued domestic opposition made it impossible to conduct the war in the same manner. In March of that year, the so-called "Wise Men," a group of businessmen and former government officials gathered by new Secretary of Defense Clark Clifford, conveyed directly to President Johnson their newfound judgment that the war could not be won (Joseph 1988: 267–73).[16] Johnson took their advice and began to de-escalate the war. One could even say the "Wise Men," and Clifford's own transition from hawk to dove, were the critical elements in Johnson's reversal. Yet the reasons cited by the elite for the need for a change in strategy, including the war's economic cost, urban unrest, the depth of public opposition, and recognition of the ability of the Vietnamese to stalemate almost any conceivable level of military commitment, had more to do with the indirect restriction imposed by domestic dissent than by the ethical or intellectual inclinations of the "Wise Men" themselves.

Argument over the failure to win the Vietnam War eventually solidified into more broadly based intra-elite disagreement concerning the role of military force and the use of U.S. power in the world arena. Of special interest is the post-Vietnam emergence of a liberal face to the U.S. policy debate under such labels as "managerialism," "post–Cold War internationalism," and "trilateralism."[17]

This debate produced, in turn, a reaction from supporters of the need of the United States to continue to threaten military force. Henry Kissinger argued that Americans "have been traumatized by Vietnam as we were by Munich" (quoted in LaFeber 1985: 280). For some, Vietnam represented both a loss in military capabilities and, even more significantly, a loss in the psychology of power. Writing shortly after the end of the war, former Secretary of Defense James Schlesinger argued that "growing instability reflects visible factors such as the deterioration in the military balance, but also, perhaps more immediately, such invisible factors as the altered psychological stance of the United States, a nation apparently withdrawing from the burdens of leadership and power" (quoted by Klare 1981: 3). An attempt to overcome the Vietnam Syndrome was one motivation behind the commitment of U.S. troops in Grenada and Panama, and the deployment and eventual engagement of the military in combat during the Gulf crisis. President George Bush made this connection explicit when he proclaimed in the immediate aftermath of the military defeat of Iraq: "We've defeated the Vietnam syndrome once and for all" (*Boston Globe*, March 2, 1991).

7. Another criterion for effectiveness is a more accommodating stance on the part of governmental authorities toward the challenging group. Gamson (1990: 32) defines four indicators of a more positive relationship: (a) "consultation" in which the views of members of selected peace movement organizations are actively solicited; (b) "negotiations" where a government agency enters into discussions on a continual basis with a peace movement organization; (c) "formal recognition" in which the government recognizes the challenging group as a legitimate representative of a constituency; and (d) "inclusion" in which some members of the challenging group become members with authority in the government organizational structure.

The movement against the war in Vietnam was not very effective in gaining the acceptance of government authorities. Negotiations, formal recognition, and inclusion were never real possibilities. The only consultation came between more moderate representatives of the movement and some members of Congress. Nor did most of the movement even put much thought into the question of how greater acceptance from the executive branch of government might be achieved.

8. Peace movements can have an indirect effect on policy by transforming surrounding social conditions which may in turn influence the process of policy formulation. There is something of an *ad hoc* quality to this dimension of peace movement effectiveness, for no theory can predict the precise ways that the original protest emanating from the movement will reverberate throughout other institutions. Methodologically, it becomes extremely difficult to isolate and measure a precise impact for the movement. Instead, peace movements and government policy coexist within a changing social context in which each influences and is influenced. The challenge is to detect the role of social movements behind the intermediate filters.

The case of Vietnam is particularly interesting this regard. While a full exploration of the indirect influence of the antiwar movement would take us too far astray, one can identify the following examples:

A. The economic cost of the Vietnam War, while considerable, was never more than 1 percent of the gross national product. Many economists feel that the additional cost of the war could have been managed with a tax increase. Yet, the fear of exacerbating domestic dissent that would have followed the scuttling of the Great Society programs, themselves required by the pressure of the civil rights movement, led President Johnson and Secretary of Defense McNamara to deceive Congress and the public about the war's true costs. The absence of a tax increase contributed to inflation, a severe weakening of the dollar, and tremors throughout the international financial system. These factors, in turn, annoyed businessmen who communicated their fears regarding the economic impact of the Vietnam War directly to Johnson during the March 1968 meeting of the Wise Men. In this case, deteriorating economic conditions affect policy, but it is also the fear of actual and potential public opposition that leads policymakers to adopt suspect measures of economic management in the first place.

B. By 1967, Johnson's declining popularity among the public reflected both dovish and hawkish sentiment. Much support for dove presidential candidate Eugene McCarthy's strong showing in the March 1968 New Hampshire primary came from those believing that the United States should actually escalate in Vietnam. However, the antiwar movement, and fear of a possible Soviet and Chinese response, ruled out any dramatic military steps. In this particular context, hawks expressing dissatisfaction with the Vietnam War and with Johnson's performance as president in effect had only *a dovish impact on decision making*. Hawkish sentiment commanded attention from the press and media, and contributed to growing pressures for some kind of a change in policy. However, since their preferred direction was rejected (or, more accurately, judged impossible to follow), and a policy of more-of-the-same was no longer tenable, the net result of hawk pressure, in these particular circumstances, was in the direction of de-escalation.

C. Protest against the Vietnam War occurred against the background of an increasingly radicalized black power movement and racial disturbances that followed the assassination of Dr. Martin Luther King. Many political authorities shared a perception of widespread urban decay. As U.S. commitments in Indochina deepened, several advisers to President Johnson, including much of the military, wanted to mobilize the strategic reserve (including the National Guard). This step, they felt, would both provide additional manpower and help redirect, through the sense of urgency that this move would invoke, public opinion back toward the administration. However, fear of the broad range of social movements that then existed in the United States prompted the state governors to oppose this measure. The National Guard was needed in U.S. cities, not Vietnam. Thus, political and pragmatic opposition to sending the troops considered necessary to preserve domestic tranquility contributed to the judgment of Vietnam decision makers that they were operating under severe constraints. Pressure against further escalation was the result.

D. By 1968, many decision makers feared that Vietnam was leading toward the degeneration of the postwar domestic consensus. The antiwar movement contributed significantly to a diffuse yet powerful sense of chaos that swirled around the leading decision makers of the Johnson and Nixon administrations. As a result, a major imperative of the moment was to avoid political and cultural breakdown, and this motivation also operated against further escalation of the war. In retrospect, the United States was far from a political breakdown. Yet the perception that events were moving beyond control seems to have affected a considerable number of decision makers. On a personal level, each rejected the countercultural themes of the movement, even while they felt the accompanying pressure of an emerging alternative. A significant number of officials later acknowledged the impact of political transformations among their own children or close relatives in creating an impression that the world could be slipping beyond their control (Small 1988). Very few of us are comfortable with havoc and we try to reduce its disconcerting impact.

E. The Watergate scandal was both the downfall of the Nixon administration and a weakening of commitment to a non-Communist South Vietnam. Its roots are normally traced to Nixon's personality and his predilection for dirty campaigning. What is less often recognized is that the "plumbers squad" who engineered the break-in at the headquarters of the Democratic Party was formed to stop "leaks" to the press of the secret bombing of Cambodia. Nixon and Kissinger feared that this information would interfere with their ability to demonstrate to Hanoi that they could still use significant military force without answering to the American public (who thought that the war was "winding down"). The need to avoid still more domestic opposition was responsible for the imperative of controlling information, which in turn was partly responsible for the political scandal that ended the U.S. effort in Vietnam.

F. Finally, as a political and cultural force, the antiwar movement had a impact on the armed forces themselves. By 1969, a significant proportion of the ground troops in Vietnam had, in effect, ceased fighting. Resistance spread in the U.S. Navy as well, particularly among black sailors (Cortright 1975, 1989).

It may be possible to trace other indirect effects of the antiwar movement and generalized public opposition on the overall context that affected Vietnam decisions. The channels that have been described are contained in the figure that appears on the next page.

9. The last criterion for measuring peace movement effectiveness is the degree to which conditions for a long-term change in policy have been established. In this case, the targets of influence are deeply ingrained institutional practices and ideological assumptions regarding the nature of national security. Examples of partial success might include, at the levels of both public and intellectual discourse, a deeper understanding of the roots of war and the emergence of coherent alternatives to prevailing concepts of security and defense. Policy formation over relatively long periods may also be affected by latent public opposition, or the potential for renewed mobilization against government decisions. Even where the visible strength of a social movement has receded, decision makers can be deterred from the commitment of military force by the *anticipation* of a new period of opposition. In this manner, social movements may continue to affect policy formation even where the most visible manifestations of influence—large-scale demonstrations, fund-raising, petition drives, lobbying efforts, and membership in social movement organizations—are in apparent decline.

Indirect Influence of Domestic Dissent on Policymakers

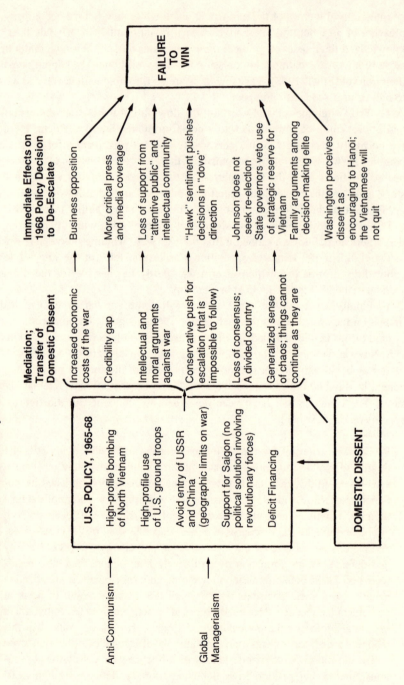

The classic example of the latent power of a peace movement is the "Vietnam Syndrome," or the reaction to the defeat of the U.S. government in South Vietnam in April 1975. Both popular and elite disgust over Washington's failure prevented the executive branch from sending U.S. ground troops into sustained combat when they might suffer more than the most minimal casualties.[18] Manifestations of the Vietnam Syndrome include the War Powers Act and other legislative limitations on the arbitrary use of military force by the president, restraints on covert operations by the Central Intelligence Agency (exemplified by the Clark Amendment prohibited U.S. military involvement in Angola), statements by leading politicians disavowing the role of the United States as a world policeman, and (more temporarily) a reluctance to establish military alliances with regional and repressive leaders such as the Shah of Iran or Somoza in Nicaragua. The constraints against U.S. military force under the Vietnam Syndrome were not absolute. Since the end of the war, naval and air power have been exercised on several occasions. The Vietnam Syndrome did not rule out short-term commitments of ground troops without the significant loss of U.S. life such as the invasions of Grenada and Panama. Different types of covert action were also possible. Nonetheless, the policy impact of the Vietnam Syndrome until the Persian Gulf War was a significant restriction on the use of military force.

The impact of the Vietnam Syndrome on public attitudes has been particularly striking. Poll after poll has indicated a strong desire to avoid another Vietnam debacle. A 1983 *New York Times* poll showed only 14 percent of the population thinking "the U.S. did the right thing in Vietnam, as opposed to 77 percent who thought the U.S. should have stayed out." For most of the 1980s, the possibility that the United States might intervene directly in El Salvador or Nicaragua was the lightning rod for the Vietnam Syndrome. Thus, in 1981 only 3 percent favored sending U.S. troops to El Salvador, and only 26 percent favored sending U.S. military advisers (Gallup, 1981). A 1983 Gallup poll found 72 percent of the public fearing that U.S. intervention in El Salvador could turn into another Vietnam (Gallup, 1983), and by a roughly two-to-one ratio the population disapproved of a plan to double the number of U.S. advisers. A 1985 poll found Americans agreeing by 48 percent to 14 percent that the Vietnam experience has made it less likely that the nation will again go to war (*Washington Post*/ABC 1985). A 53 percent to 39 percent majority oppose aiding anti-Communist groups and governments in the third world if that means "sometimes supporting dictators and others who do not believe in democracy" (Center for Foreign Policy Development 1988). Negative reaction to U.S. involvement in Vietnam reached a record high in 1990 (Gallup, 1990).

Beyond public opinion polls, the cultural debate over the Vietnam experience has proven critical for how the United States looks toward the future, defines its past, and feels about its present (see chapter 17 by Marilyn B. Young in this volume). The outcome of the debate over how to define the lessons to be learned from the Vietnam War would determine the long-term legacy of that conflict, as well as how Washington would react when faced with future possibilities of military intervention. During the six months leading up to the Gulf War, Vietnam metaphors, albeit different ones, were used both by supporters of the Bush administration and by antiwar activists. From the perspective of Washington policymakers, perhaps the greatest lesson of Vietnam was the need to control domestic dissent. Timely information, images of the human cost of war, forthright discussion of the historical context, and future consequences of large-scale military commitments were all sacrificed in order to preserve support for the actions of the Bush administration. In this manner, the political and military leaders of the United States gave oblique support to the thesis that the level of support from the population remains the most central element in their prosecution of military actions. At this writing, in the immediate aftermath of the military victory over Saddam Hussein, it remains unclear whether the U.S. public will support future military intervention that carries the prospect of significant loss of (U.S.) life. While initially reluctant to endorse the initiation of war against Iraq, the public became more willing to support the military effort than would have been predicted by the polls of the late 1970s and the 1980s. We do not yet know whether public support was simply the product of the well-managed control of information, a reflection of a war with a relatively small loss of U.S. life, a temporary phenomenon based upon a need to celebrate the United States rather than the war itself, or a genuine and significant shift in attitude. Comprehensive polling carried out by the Americans Talk Security Foundation does *not* support the thesis that the public is now more hawkish (*Americans Talk Security*, vol. 16, 1991). The constraints against the future use of military force may remain unchanged, with support for such action in the Persian Gulf War reflecting particular circumstances. The Vietnam Syndrome is an uncertain legacy.[19]

I have made a case for both the direct and indirect influence of the antiwar movement during the Vietnam War. While that movement did not succeed in transforming the goals of U.S. foreign policy in general, or the specific purposes of U.S. intervention in Vietnam, the mobilization of popular sentiment against the war did manage to block and/or reduce the scale of military strategies that were necessary to achieve those objectives. The result was an ambivalent or contradictory context for decision making. After 1965, Washington's decisions reflected both continued commitment to the goal of a non-Communist South Vietnam and constraints imposed by domestic opposition to that goal and the ineffective means that were chosen to achieve it. The efforts of the antiwar movement contributed significantly to the fractionalization of the decision-making elite and created a social impulse that was carried or mediated by other influential actors such as the media and expert opinion. Both during and after the war, decision makers anticipated the potential opposition to more militarist policy options that they were actively considering and moderated their decisions as a result. The prevailing political culture of the United States tends to view success or failure in black-and-white terms. While a direct impact can be noted on the scope and scale of Washington's military strategies, we have yet to appreciate the muted but still-powerful forms of influence generated by the antiwar movement. An important corrective is to understand the roots of ambivalent decision making, fractionalization of the elite, the impact of mediating agents, and the anticipation of still further dissent.

Notes

1. Kolko's assessment also contains a more critical side. For example: "The consequent outpouring, including its highly visible proportion of egoist politics, existential intellectual posturing, and sectarianism among religious bodies, bourgeois leftists, or simply people with growing anxieties, nonetheless created a large critical mass which produced one decisive effect: social disorder."

2. For example, neither Berkowitz (1973) nor Schreiber (1976) find a consistent, dramatic, or lasting effect of antiwar demonstration size, or other operational measures of peace movement strength, on either public opinion or different military indicators such as troop strength or size of the defense budget.

3. Successful examples of social movement influence in this sense include the civil rights movement, which forced a change in the role of the federal government in redressing racial discrimination, and the labor movement in the 1930s, which succeeded in establishing the right of collective bargaining and pro-labor goals for a new wave of legislation.

4. U.S. Special Forces did operate within Cambodia but these operations were relatively small-scale and indecisive. In 1970, U.S. troops entered Cambodia but withdrew shortly thereafter, in no small measure because of the hostile response within the United States.

5. Even before 1968, domestic opposition to the war caused Secretary of Defense McNamara to scale down the number of troops recommended by the military as necessary to produce a win.

6. In fact, the November 1969 Moratorium demonstrations may have blocked Nixon's planned "savage blows" against Hanoi (Small 1988).

7. In Mueller's view, increased casualties also explain rising public disenchantment with the Korean War where there was no oppositional movement on the scale of Vietnam.

8. Schreiber also maintains that duration explains declining public support among the French for intervention in Indochina in the early 1950s.

9. There do not appear to be any studies on this question.

10. Other elements include fear of either a Chinese and/or a Soviet response, the adoption of self-defeating military and political tactics, and the resilience of the Vietnamese themselves.

11. For more on the distinction between moral criticisms of the Vietnam War and pragmatic disillusionment over the possibility of winning it, see Schuman (1972).

12. David Halberstam's reportage in the New York Times is an exception.

13. On the one hand, the potential exists for a broader range of allies and coalitions who may work together in opposition to government policy. On the other, different social movements may work at cross-purposes creating not coordination but relatively disorganized chaos that undermines overall effectiveness. Even in this situation, however, the specter of a broader array of movements may produce a sense of crisis sufficiently acute to force government authorities to modify their position.

14. The first leaders of the women's movement were motivated less by overall social inequities and more by the pervasiveness of sexism that existed within the ranks of the antiwar movement itself (Evans 1979).

15. Because influence channels are varied and indirect, it sometimes appears that participants in peace movements themselves do not appreciate the impact of their efforts. Unambiguous victories occur only rarely. Even where peace movements do succeed in mobilizing significant support, the short- and medium-term result is not a clear-cut victory for the peace movement or for government. During these periods, influence becomes more fluid with decisions reflecting contradictory impulses. As Nigel Young has argued: "With peace movements, as with other social movements, the results of public activity are always ambiguous. Like other great social change or social protest campaigns, they have both latent and manifest consequences. They may actually prolong the wars they aim to stop. They may alienate public opinion. Their relative success or failure always depends on other independent or external factors, not just the degree or level of activity achieved" (1986: 210).

16. Several months earlier, in the fall of 1967, the Wise Men had endorsed the conduct of the war.

17. Using the somewhat different terms of "Containment Militarism" and "Managerialism," Sanders (1982) also describes heightened debate within the policymaking elite following the Vietnam War.

18. Fixing the exact threshold for "sustained" and "minimal casualties" is difficult. For the 1980s, I would place "sustained" at more than one week, and "minimal casualties" at one hundred. Arguments can be made that the thresholds of concerted opposition are in fact longer and higher. However it is defined, the projected costs of overthrowing the government of Nicaragua, placed by one source at five thousand deaths over six months of fighting (CDI 1988), was clearly beyond the threshold. As a result, a major commitment of U.S. forces against the Sandinistas was impossible.

19. These issues are explored in more depth in Joseph (1993).

References

Americans Talk Security. 17 volumes. 1988–91.

Ball, George. "George Ball Dissents, 1965." In *Major Problems in the History of the Vietnam War*, Robert McMahon, ed. Lexington, MA: D.C. Heath, 1990.

Baritz, Loren. *Backfire: A History of How American Culture Led Us into Vietnam and Made Us Fight the Way We Did.* New York: William Morrow, 1985.

Berkowitz, William. "The Impact of Anti-Vietnam Demonstrations upon National Public Opinion and Military Indicators," *Social Science Research* 2 (1973): 1–14.

Breines, Wini. *The Great Refusal: Community and Organization in the New Left, 1962–1965.* New Brunswick, NJ: Rutgers University Press, 1979.

Brown, Sam. "The Defeat of the Antiwar Movement." In *The Vietnam Legacy*, Anthony Lake, ed. New York: New York University Press, 1976.

Burstein, Paul, and William Freudenberg. "Changing Public Policy: The Impact of Public Opinion, Antiwar Protest, and War Costs on Senate Voting on Vietnam War Motions," *American Journal of Sociology* 84 (July 1978): 99–122.

Center for Defense Information (CDI). "Special Issue on the Possibility of a U.S. Invasion of Nicaragua," 1988.

Center for Foreign Policy Development. "The Public, the Soviets, and Nuclear Arms," A Joint Project of the PUblic Agenda Foundation and Center for Foreign Policy Development, Brown University. Providence, RI, 1988.

Chatfield, Charles. *Peace Movements in America.* New York: Pantheon, 1988.

Chomsky, Noam, and Ed Herman. *Manufacturing Consent*. New York: Pantheon, 1988.

Clifford, Clark. "Letter to Lyndon Johnson," May 17, 1965. In Leslie Gelb with Richard Betts, *Irony of Vietnam: The System Worked*. Washington, D.C.: Brookings Institute, 1979.

Cortright, David. *Soldiers in Revolt*. New York: Doubleday, 1975.

————. "Black GI Resistance during the Vietnam War." Unpublished manuscript, 1989.

DeBenedetti, Charles. "On the Significance of Citizen's Peace Activism, 1961–1975," *Peace and Change* 9 (Summer 1973).

————. *The Peace Reform in American History*. Bloomington: Indiana University Press, 1980.

————. *An American Ordeal: The Antiwar Movement of the Vietnam Era*. New York: Syracuse University Press, 1990.

Evans, Sara. *Personal Politics: The Roots of Women's Liberation in the Civil Rights Movement and the New Left*. New York: Knopf, 1979.

Gallup Report. "Three in Five 'Informed' Americans Fear 'Another Vietnam' in El Salvador." April 1981.

————. "Afraid of 'Another Vietnam,' Americans Continue to Oppose Greater United States Involvement in Central America." July–August 1983.

————. "Negative Reaction to U.S. Involvement in Vietnam Reaches Record High." May 1990.

Gamson, William. *The Strategy of Protest*. 2d ed. Belmont, CA: Wadsworth Publishing, 1990.

Gelb, Leslie, with Richard Betts. *The Irony of Vietnam: The System Worked*. Washington, D.C.: Brookings Institute, 1979.

Gill, Gerald. "From Maternal Pacifism to Revolutionary Solidarity: African-American Women's Opposition to the Vietnam War." Unpublished manuscript, 1990.

Gitlin, Todd. "Home Front Resistance to the Vietnam War." In *Vietnam Reconsidered*, Harrison Salisbury, ed. New York: Harper and Row, 1984.

————. *The Whole World is Watching*. Berkeley: University of California Press, 1980.

Hallin, David. "The Media, the War in Vietnam, and Political Support: A Critique of the Thesis of an Oppositional Media," *The Journal of Politics* 46 (1984): 2–24.

Joseph, Paul. *Cracks in the Empire*. New York: Columbia University Press, 1988.

————. *Peace Politics: The United States Between the Old and New World Orders*. Philadelphia, PA: Temple University Press, 1993.

Klare, Michael. *Beyond the Vietnam Syndrome*. Washington, D.C.: Institute for Policy Studies, 1981.

Kolko, Gabriel. *Anatomy of a War*. New York: Pantheon, 1985.

LaFeber, Walter. "Review of the Vietnam Revisionists," *Democracy*, 1985.

Lewy, Guenter. *America in Vietnam*. New York: Oxford University Press, 1978.

Miller, James. *Democracy in the Streets: From Port Huron to the Seige of Chicago*. New York: Simon and Schuster, 1988.

Mueller, John. *War, Presidents, and Public Opinion*. New York: John Wiley and Sons, 1973.

Parenti, Michael. *Inventing Reality*. New York: St. Martin's Press, 1986.

Parkin, Frank. *Middle Class Radicalism: The Social Basis of the British Campaign for Nuclear Disarmament*. New York: Praeger, 1988.

Pentagon Papers. Gravel Edition. Boston: Beacon Press, 1972.

Roche, John. "The Impact of Dissent on Foreign Policy: Past and Future." In *The Vietnam Legacy*, Anthony Lake, ed. New York: New York University Press, 1976.

Sanders, Jerry. "Elites, Public Opinion, and Empire: On Lions, Foxes and Mass Politics in the Post-Vietnam Era," *Alternatives* 8 (1982): 1–23.

Schreiber, E.M. "Antiwar Demonstrations and American Public Opinion on the War in Vietnam," *British Journal of Sociology* 27, 2 (June 1976): 225–36.

Schuman, Howard. "Two Sources of Antiwar Sentiment in America," *American Journal of Sociology* 78, 3 (1972): 513–36.

Small, Melvin. *Johnson, Nixon, and the Doves*. New Brunswick, NJ: Rutgers University Press, 1988.

Tilly, Charles. "Social Movements and National Politics." In *Statemaking and Social Movements: Essays in History and Theory*, Charles Bright and Susan Harding, eds. Ann Arbor: University of Michigan Press, 1984.

Washington Post/ABC. April 14, 1985.

Wittner, Lawrence. *Rebels against War: The American Peace Movement, 1933–83*, Philadelphia, PA: Temple University Press, 1984.

Young, Nigel. "The Peace Movement: A Comparative and Analytical Survey," *Alternatives* 11 (1986): 185–217.

Zaroulis, Nancy, and Gerald Sullivan. *Who Spoke Up?* New York: Doubleday, 1984.

Part Three

The War in the South and Cambodia

11

Civil-Military Relations in South Vietnam and the American Advisory Effort

Jeffrey Clarke

The assistance of the United States was vital both the establishment and to the survival of the Republic of Vietnam. Without American support, the early Saigon government of Ngo Dinh Diem might have easily succumbed to internal chaos. Nevertheless, although American military advice and materiel ensured the regime's survival, they had little influence over Diem's domestic plans and policies. American influence over South Vietnam's internal politics was, in fact, problematic throughout the war. During Diem's early tenure, the U.S. Military Assistance Advisory Group (MAAG) supported the creation of a conventional army capable of halting a Korean War–style attack from the North. The South Vietnamese president, however, preferred a weaker, more fragmented military force, one less likely to challenge his own political power and one that was counterbalanced by a large paramilitary force whose loyalty was more assured. Their different outlooks regarding the shape and role of Saigon's military forces established a pattern that was to continue until 1975.

The assassination of Diem in November 1963 threw the structure of Saigon's military apparatus into further disarray. The political vacuum left by Diem's death was rapidly filled by Saigon's heavily politicized senior officers, who then proceeded to militarize the entire civil administration. At the time, the centralization of American military support in a single headquarters, the Military Assistance Command, Vietnam (MACV), helped rationalize the U.S. assistance effort, but had little effect on the South Vietnamese Army's expanding venture into both national and local politics. One result was the presence of U.S. military advisory teams throughout both the military and the political structure of the southern republic. A second was the incremental commitment of U.S. combat forces to support Saigon's failing war effort. Together these changes ought to have given American political and military leaders greater control over their sometime troublesome ally. Nothing, however, could have been further from the truth.

The South Vietnamese

Under American tutelage, Diem and his successors had created a Western-style military and civil apparatus. In Saigon, for example, ministries for agriculture, education, commerce, and so forth drew up plans and policies in their areas of interest and supervised their execution by some forty-four appointed province chiefs and their subordinate district heads. For the armed forces, a ministry of war and a joint staff, with all the requisite bureaus, offices, and directorates, stood above a conventional field army organized into corps, divisions, regiments, and battalions, buttressed by a small air and naval force, and further reinforced by the normal cast of signal, engineer, quartermaster and other service units. A small marine corps and airborne reserve based on the outskirts of the capital completed the illusion of a conventional defense establishment. Outfitted with American-made equipment and American-style dress, the South Vietnamese soldiers seemed to be carbon copies of their American benefactors.[1]

Elaborate American "wiring diagrams" of the South Vietnamese politico-military structure provided few clues as to how it actually worked. The four regional corps commanders, for example, ran both political and military affairs in their respective zones with little direction from Saigon. Under them, division commanders and province chiefs often acted as semi-autonomous vassals, whose own relationships with their nominal superiors and subordinates had little to do with rank or position. By 1965 appointments and promotions within the South Vietnamese military as well as within the militarized civil service depended primarily on personal loyalties, family connections, and financial blandishments. Many province and district seats could be had for a price, while military administrators routinely supplemented low government salaries with a wide variety of extralegal practices, such as the sale of draft deferments, land titles and other licenses; the levy of protection fees for various commercial activities; and the general diversion of government monies and materiel into private hands. In fact, as American troops began to take over an increasing share of the war effort after 1965, these activities became one of the primary preoccupations of the Saigon officer corps.[2]

A parallel development was the officer corps' almost complete immersion in military politics. Saigon's American-equipped forces were, in fact, a greater threat to one another than to the local insurgents and the growing number of North Vietnamese troops who were moving south to assist them. The leading

South Vietnamese commanders were often little better than medieval warlords whose power and position depended on the number of troops loyal to them. The recurrent coups and countercoups at the national level in 1964 and early 1965 only obscured the deeper divisions within the government and military bureaucracy and the danger of open civil war. This continued state of affairs ensured both the ineffectiveness of Saigon's forces and also their continued fragmentation among many competing centers of power. Province and district chiefs headed small armies of local territorial troops; division commanders controlled nominally loyal regiments and battalions; corps commanders kept their own Ranger, armor, and artillery reserves close at hand; and the national level generals depended on the airborne and marine forces to anchor the more critical national-level military cliques. Although with fewer bayonets at their disposal, South Vietnamese Air Force and Navy officers had the ability to move troops rapidly in and out of Saigon, while their control over the nation's sea and air terminals offered many opportunities for financial gain. For similar reasons Saigon's paramilitary national police constituted another independent power center, as did the Army's Special Forces service, although, with most of its units operating with Americans along the country's western borders, the attractiveness of the latter component was somewhat minimal.[3]

In mid-1965, following the arrival of the first contingents of American ground combat troops, senior South Vietnamese officers made several important decisions to stabilize their rather shaky politico-military establishment. Under the provisions of the Convention of June 19, 1965, they agreed to establish a formal "Committee for the Direction of the State" (shortened to the Directory), consisting of ten leading general officers. General Nguyen Van Thieu, the former III Corps commander, became both Directory chairman and "chief of state," while his rival, Air Marshal Nguyen Cao Ky, agreed to serve as "prime minister," or premier of South Vietnam. In these capacities, Ky supervised the national-level government ministries in Saigon while Thieu represented the interests of the senior army generals. Other Directory members included General Nguyen Huu Co, the former I Corps commander and now minister of war, General Le Nguyen Khang, the Marine Corps commander, and the four Army Corps commanders who also served as regional governors.[4] In practice these senior generals, whatever their formal position, dealt with one another as equals, each jealously guarding his own prerogatives and each anxiously watching for any aggrandizement in power by his compatriots.

One of the Directory's first acts was a series of decrees that somewhat systematized the existing dispersion of power. These measures carefully apportioned authority for the nomination and approval of all significant officer appointments and promotions. Under their provisions, for example, the army chief of staff in Saigon approved the appointment of all division commanders while the corps commanders in the field controlled the selection of deputy division commanders; the appointment of province and district chiefs and their deputies was handled in a similar manner.[5] The senior generals also continually opposed American recommendations to abandon the stiff educational entrance requirements to the officer corps, ensuring that the corps remained dominated by the upper echelons of South Vietnamese society.[6] All of these measures greatly improved the internal stability of the Saigon politico-military regime, but in the long run they made it highly resistant to change and action.

Examples, large and small, of the deep impact these arrangements had on Saigon's war effort were common throughout the war. The results of the competition between the military cliques surrounding Thieu and Ky during the Directory period were typical. Thieu's power base in Saigon rested primarily on the airborne force under an ally, General Du Quoc Dong, and the troops of the nearby 5th Division headed by General Pham Quoc Thuan. Ky retained control of the air force, and could count on Khang's marines and the troops of General Phan Trong Chinh's 25th Infantry Division also based in the capital area. American leaders were habitually frustrated by the practice of Chinh and Thuan of keeping at least half of their troops on the outskirts of Saigon to counter possible coups, but could do nothing to change the situation.[7] Similarly, General Cao Van Vien, the chief of South Vietnam's joint staff and the nominal head of the armed forces, found it difficult to dispatch the requisite number of airborne reserve units to danger spots in the countryside without ensuring that a like number of marine units were also deployed out of the Saigon area.[8] Again, the carefully maintained military balance of power improved political stability in Saigon, but did little for South Vietnamese military effectiveness. Moreover, the army's more serious deficiencies in these areas were often obscured by the widespread corruption and confusion that had characterized its original assumption of political responsibilities.

The precarious nature of South Vietnam's internal stability was clearly demonstrated by the revolt in the northern I Corps zone during the spring of 1966.[9] Outwardly an expression of Buddhist discontent over the delayed restoration of constitutional government, the crisis was actually sparked by Saigon's unilateral dismissal of General Nguyen Chanh Thi, the I Corps commander. The action led to an immediate uprising of local army and territorial units under Thi's control, including the Hue-based 1st Infantry Division and the separate 51st Regiment at Danang. Buddhist organizations used the incidents to demand an end to military government, the creation of an elected, constituent assembly, and the return of civilian rule. American leaders saw the entire affair as a Communist plot but could produce no evidence to support the allegation. All parties sought to influence the turmoil, which appeared to have no center of focus.

The fracas lasted for several months and was highlighted by demonstrations through South Vietnam. More ominous was the series of military confrontations and even fighting between rebel and loyal (government) troops in Danang and Hue, and the general reduction of the war effort in the northern zone that resulted. U.S. Marines and Army advisers were often caught in the middle, sustaining a few casualties and some damage to their facilities. Although the conflict was formally resolved in Saigon's favor several months later, its political legacy was dubious. South Vietnam's political stability seemed more fragile than ever, and American leaders more reluctant to do anything that might disturb the delicate balance of power in Saigon.

The crisis in the northern I Corps area strengthened the Ky–Thieu government, but it did little for the country's long-term politico-military health. General Hoang Xuan Lam, a weak but loyal commander, took over the I Corps zone, while Ky strengthened his position by making Khang the III Corps commander and another close supporter, General Nguyen Ngoc Loan, head of both the Military Security Service and the National Police. The appointment of two other Ky supporters, Generals Linh Quang Vien and Nguyen Duc Thang, to head the Ministries of Security and Revolutionary Development, respectively, further solidified Air Marshal Ky's power in Saigon. To their credit Thieu and Ky also had an appointed constituent assembly draw up a fairly liberal constitution that was ratified by a popular vote that fall and that called for general elections the following year. But with a weak political infrastructure, the prognosis for a working democracy in the South was poor.

Throughout the spring and summer of 1967, the Directory generals debated incessantly over the constitutionally mandated presidential elections scheduled for the fall. Would there be a military candidate and if so who would receive the blessing of the Directory? American advice was generally limited to lecturing them on the dangers of a divided military ticket or a weak civilian candidate.[10] Much to the relief of U.S. officials, the Directory generals decided to make Thieu the army's presidential candidate with Ky as his vice-presidential running mate—perhaps the ambitious Air Marshal Ky had grown too powerful in the eyes of the army generals—and the American nightmare of a destructive Ky–Thieu political contest was thus avoided. Thieu's electoral victory in 1967 further pleased his American advisers and in the following years led to the gradual eclipse of the more excitable Ky. Slowly, one by one (and sometimes at a faster pace) his supporters were replaced by officers seen to be more loyal to Thieu. However, Thieu's own constituency was never large enough to provide him with an independent base of support, and his second electoral victory in 1971 appeared to be a much more contrived affair.[11] In the end, the military's continued domination of the nation's political process brought a degree of continuity to South Vietnam's war effort, but never produced the benefits of participatory democracy that the Americans had hoped for.

The Americans

From the beginning, the South Vietnamese politico-military environment constituted a unique and difficult challenge to the American MACV commanders and their field advisers. Following the integration of the early MAAG headquarters into MACV, the advisory effort had been sharply divided between the field advisory teams in the countryside and the command and staff advisory effort in Saigon. By 1965, the former consisted of several hundred cellular teams spread throughout South Vietnam, including those serving with combat and support units, those at South Vietnamese training camps and schools, those assigned to province and district seats, and still others with the South Vietnamese air and naval components, and the technical support depots and installations located generally in the Saigon area. The U.S. Army Special Forces teams, operating nominally as advisers to a variety of paramilitary ethnic and religious minority programs in the interior, constituted another, almost autonomous advisory effort. Although many of these teams, some with no more than three or four soldiers at full strength, fell under the general supervision of the corps senior advisers, they operated generally with little daily supervision or support.[12]

In Saigon MACV's primary advisory tasks centered around assisting the Vietnamese joint staff; drawing up national-level operation plans and organizational and training programs; and providing materiel and supply support to Saigon through the U.S. Military Assistance Program, a broad effort designed to strengthen American military allies throughout the world. Within MACV, functional staff sections directly advised their South Vietnamese counterparts, while above it the American chain of command stretched eastward through the Pacific Command in Hawaii and on to the Joint Chiefs of Staff, the secretary of defense, and the president of the United States.

By the end of 1965, the evolution of the war had produced profound changes in Westmoreland's central headquarters. Most evident was the rapid transition of MACV from a advice and assistance command to a military theater headquarters as increasing numbers of U.S. troop units arrived in South Vietnam. The advisory functions of both Westmoreland and his staff were quickly eclipsed by the exigencies of daily combat operations and the long-term need to create a logistical support base in what military planners termed an "austere environment." In the field, a similar transition occurred with American corps-level military commanders assuming the additional and almost incidental duty of senior adviser to the four South Vietnamese corps commanders. In the remote interior even the U.S. Army Special Forces teams felt the impact of these changes as their operations were brought under the direct control of senior U.S. field commanders, and the focus of their activities changed from organizing part-time security forces to providing full-time reconnaissance commando units to track down an elusive enemy. Searching for a military victory on the battlefield, MACV had, in the jargon of the times, put its advisory responsibilities "on the back burner."

Amid this transition was another, even more significant change that went almost unnoticed by outsiders—the growth of MACV's political responsibilities. The domination of South Vietnam's national-level politics by Saigon's generals and the entrenchment of the officer corps in the country's civil administration transformed American advisers, from Westmoreland on down, into political counselors whether they welcomed or were prepared for the role or not. The steady increase of U.S. military resources available in South Vietnam accelerated this trend. The huge U.S. logistical base and the growing number of troops greatly enhanced the prestige and potential political influence of the local American military community at the expense of the U.S. ambassador and his small staff who theoretically had primary responsibility for such matters. A belated recognition of this state of affairs came in April 1967 when the entire U.S. civilian advisory effort was transferred to MACV, organized into a military hierarchy, and placed under U.S. military commanders.[13] Whatever the ultimate success of this reorganization, it reflected a situation in which the U.S. assistance effort was being pulled in two directions, with its political responsibilities always constituting a secondary concern.

Not surprisingly, the American pacification advisory effort in both Saigon and the countryside focused on security and stability. The general military situation and the American hope for a battlefield decision meant that much less attention was paid to political, economic, and social development and reform. Progress in these areas was difficult to measure and even then significant results took place only after years rather than weeks or months of effort: the tempo was just too slow for the action-oriented Americans whose one-year tours in South Vietnam gave a sense of immediacy to all of their activities. Nevertheless, Westmoreland and the American ambassadors were probably correct in pushing at least the return of constitutional government in Saigon. Although the national elections of 1967 were cosmetic, never resulting in the restoration of true civilian rule or in a more effective government at the local levels, perhaps little more could have been expected at the time.

In the field, the evolution of the military advisory effort was also profound. As early as 1965, MACV considered changing the name of its tactical advisory teams to "combat support teams" to reflect their actual duties.[14] Most regarded their most critical function as providing U.S. support to their counterparts or serving as conduits for the various American aid programs at the province, district, and installation levels. The scattered field advisers, numbering 6,000 to 9,000 individuals at various times, were also charged with rating their counterparts, monitoring all their activities, and attending to their own administration and housekeeping. Competition with U.S. troop units for skilled, experienced, and able personnel also reduced the overall quality of advisers, making it difficult for them to work with veteran South Vietnamese officers who were often senior to them in service, age, and of course political experience.[15]

The U.S. Army Special Forces advisory cells dealing with ethnic minority groups along the western borders presented a special case. There the U.S. Army had organized the Highland Montagnard tribes into a variety of paramilitary organizations collectively known as the Civilian Irregular Defense Corps (CIDG). Later, the program was expanded to include Cambodians, Laotians, and

Chinese along with members of the Hoa Hao and Cao Dai religious sects. This force, about 20,000 to 30,000 strong, was only nominally under the control of South Vietnamese authorities, with U.S. Army Special Forces teams responsible for recruiting, training, equipping, leading, and even paying the salaries of its members. Not surprisingly, many CIDG units felt little loyalty to Saigon, reflecting the deep historical animosity between the minorities and the ethnic Vietnamese. In some cases, the tension resulted in open rebellion with the advisers again being caught in the middle. Although the CIDG program provided an invaluable adjunct to U.S. forces operating in the remote border regions (without the program the minority populations might have been conceded totally to the revolutionaries), it was never successfully integrated into the South Vietnamese military apparatus, and both militarily and politically remained a separate entity throughout the war.[16]

The Special Forces experience was unique. The average field advisers had little control over the South Vietnamese military units or the provincial and district military administrations to which they were assigned. With no authority, or "leverage," over their counterparts, they had little to say about what South Vietnamese commanders did or did not accomplish. Yet American advisers continually criticized South Vietnamese military capabilities and the effectiveness of their units. These complaints routinely traveled up the advisory chain of command to Westmoreland and his successors but, in the interests of political stability, little of substance was ever done. The entire advisory effort was thus characterized by a tremendous frustration on the part of the action-oriented Americans from the beginning. Even at the highest levels neither Westmoreland nor his successor in mid-1968, General Creighton Abrams, nor the American ambassadors were ever able to make a significant impact on the composition of the senior Vietnamese military leadership, or even on the selection of the lesser commanders and staff officers in the field. Nevertheless, American leaders continued to hope that the decentralized advisory effort would still have a salutary effect on South Vietnam's political and military leaders, if only by dint of an individual adviser's own personality, dedication, and persistence. But such expectations were unrealistic and contributed only to the false sense of optimism that seemed to permeate almost all official American evaluations of the war.

In practice the one-on-one adviser–counterpart approach worked no better in the field than it did at MACV headquarters. Since advisers were often judged by the perceived effectiveness of their counterparts, the numerical ratings which they periodically assigned to their charges were not surprisingly inflated, while those whose relationships with the Vietnamese were less than satisfactory were often reassigned to other tasks. The adviser's ability to establish "rapport" with his counterpart became a byword at MACV headquarters, with attention paid to how such rapport might be used to improve weak Vietnamese leaders, many of whom had little desire for a military career, or had simply burned out after long tours in the field, or who had personal, political, and economic interests remote from the ongoing war effort. In any case, if the war was ultimately to be decided on the battlefield by superior American firepower and mobility, the mental state of the Vietnamese officer corps did not seem especially critical.

Throughout the war, American advisers cited the poor quality of South Vietnamese military leadership. Their low evaluations included not only the senior political generals, but also officers at all levels and within all components of the armed forces; those serving within the civil administration were rated lower than those following their normal trade. Both principal MACV commanders, Generals Westmoreland and Abrams, freely admitted the fact in their many reports to Washington but had no solutions.[17] Westmoreland had considered establishing some sort of combined U.S.–South Vietnamese theater headquarters in early 1965, which would have given him much greater authority over South Vietnamese commanders and their operations. But control over the South Vietnamese military would have given MACV de facto political control over South Vietnam itself, and the measure was thus rejected by both American and South Vietnamese leaders.[18] Nevertheless, Westmoreland's subordinates continued to suggest more creative solutions such as establishing generous trust funds for each Vietnamese general officer on the condition that he avoid political involvements and reduce his interest in monetary affairs.[19] However impractical, such proposals reflected the real dilemmas facing the entire American assistance effort.

Intermittent changes in South Vietnamese military leadership were more the result of political infighting between the bickering officer cliques than a product of American influence. Most dismissals had little to do with the affected officer's fighting or administrative ability. Thi, for example, the I Corps commander ousted in 1966, had been considered an extremely capable officer by the senior U.S. military officer in the zone, General Lewis Walt (USMC).[20] On the other hand, Generals Chinh and Thuan managed to retain their divisional commands for over four years despite continuous American recommendations for their immediate dismissal, and even then their long-awaited reliefs were ultimately followed by appointments to higher levels of authority. The same could be said of General Doan Van Quang, the IV Corps commander and Thieu ally who was dismissed for corruption in 1967 (engineered by Ky), only to reemerge several years later as one of President Thieu's primary "military" advisers.[21]

In the meantime, Thieu himself found it necessary to retain the services of Marine General Khang, one of Ky's principal supporters, until 1972 because, according to Thieu, Khang was one of his few senior officers who knew how to fight.[22] Rarely, in fact, was any South Vietnamese officer forced to leave the service, and most rotated between military and political assignments based on their political connections. The poor quality of South Vietnamese military leadership thus bedeviled the American advisers throughout the war. In 1972, prior to his departure from South Vietnam, General Abrams could only shrug his shoulders when asked about the matter by one of his contemporaries, saying "we've done what we can."[23] Privately, he remarked many times to his aides that American leaders had far less control over their South Vietnamese counterparts than anyone ever realized.[24]

Reviewing his experiences as commander of the Eighth Army in the Korean War, General Matthew Ridgway was puzzled by the lack of American leverage over Saigon's military leaders. Ridgway noted that his strong personal relationship with South Korean President Syngman Rhee had made it relatively easy for him to have poor Korean military commanders relieved immediately and without fuss.[25] But the two situations were not comparable. After the demise of President Diem no political leader of any stature emerged in South Vietnam comparable to Rhee. Indeed, strong support by both American political and military leaders for the Thieu–Ky presidential ticket only assured the military's continued domination of South Vietnam's political process despite the trappings of a democratic constitution. At the time, American leaders believed that a civilian government would lack the backbone to continue the war effort with vigor, leading to confusion and chaos. They may have been correct. Nevertheless, the continuation of military rule undermined both Saigon's claim to political legitimacy and the ability of its armed forces to fight effectively.

Notes

Guide to Abbreviations

CMH: U.S. Army Center for Military History
Copy CMH: denotes copy of the source
 (not the original) found at CMH
DNG: Da Nang
JCS: Joint Chiefs of Staff
MAC: Message eminating from MACV
MACV: U.S. Military Assistance Command

MHD: Military History Detachment
Msg: Message
NHT: Nha Troug
RG: Record Group
Sgn: Saigon
sub: Subject
WNRC: Washington National Records
 Center

1. For general surveys of the South Vietnamese armed forces, see James L. Collins, Jr., *Development and Training of the South Vietnamese Army, 1950–1972*, Vietnam Studies (Washington, D.C.: Department of the Army, 1975); and the Vietnamese authored Indochina Monograph series published by the U.S. Army Center of Military History (CMH), especially Dong Van Khuyen, *The RVNAF* (Washington, D.C., 1980); Ngo Quang Truong, *Territorial Forces* (Washington, D.C., 1981); and Cao Van Vien, *Leadership* (Washington, D.C., 1981).

2. For details, see Vien, *Leadership*, 117–23.

3. An early appraisal is Allen Goodman, *An Institutional Profile of the South Vietnamese Officer Corps* (Santa Monica, CA: Rand, 1970).

4. For organizational details, see JCS, *Southeast Asia Military Fact Book*, January 1967, in MACV Microfilm files, Reel No. 1, Record Group (RG) 334, Washington National Records Center (WNRC).

5. Khuyen, *The RVNAF*, 54–55, 87.

6. For discussion, see the author's *Advice and Support: The Final Years, 1965–1973*, The U.S. Army in Vietnam (Washington, D.C.: CMH, 1988), 467–68.

7. For one adviser's comments, see Col. Donald A. Seibert, "The Regulars" (draft manuscript), 1035–91, Seibert Papers, Military History Institute (MHI), Carlisle Barracks, PA.

8. For comments on the General Reserve, see MFR, Col. Francis E. Naughton (senior airborne adviser), January 8, 1966, sub: Airborne Brigade Personnel Status (Officers), History file, 3C2, Westmoreland Papers, CMH; and interview, author with LTC Donald C. Wells (airborne adviser, 1965–66), March 25, 1975.

9. For a detailed treatment, see Clarke, *Advice and Support: The Final Years,* 127–44.

10. Msg, Lodge Sgn 16463 to Secretary of State, January 25, 1967, History file 12D9; and Msgs, Bunker Sgn 26674 and 26779 to Secretary of State, May 25 and 26, 1967, History files 17B3 and 17B4, all in Westmoreland Papers, CMH.

11. In 1971, both Ky and Duong Van Minh ("Big Minh"), a popular retired general, dropped out of contention; and Truong Dinh Dzu, the well-known peace candidate of 1967 remained jailed, as did Deputy Tran Ngoc Chau, one of Thieu's prominent critics, despite his legislative immunity and the decision of the South Vietnamese Supreme Court overturning the results of his questionable trial.

12. For treatments, see Collins, *Development and Training of the South Vietnamese Army;* Vien et al., *The U.S. Adviser,* Indochina Monographs (Washington, D.C.: CMH, 1980); the annual MACV Command History, 1964 through 1972–73; and for the Army's Special Forces as advisers, Francis J. Kelly, *U.S. Army Special Forces, 1961–1971,* Vietnam Studies (Washington, D.C.: Department of the Army, 1975).

13. Detailed in Thomas W. Scoville, *Reorganizing for Pacification Support* (Washington, D.C.: CMH, 1982).

14. Memo, MACV, sub: Meeting—100830 March 1965: Advisors in the Support Role, History file 14–28, Westmoreland Papers, CMH.

15. See Gerald Cannon Hickey, *The American Military Advisor and his Foreign Counterpart: The Case of Vietnam* (Santa Monica, CA: Rand, 1965); Report, Military History Branch, MACV, April 1966, sub: Report on Interview Program with U.S. Army Advisers in Vietnam, CMH.

16. General works treating the CIDG program are Kelly, *U.S. Army Special Forces;* Charles M. Simpson, III, *Inside the Green Berets: The First Thirty Years* (Novato, CA: Presidio, 1983); Shelby L. Stanton, *The Green Berets at War: U.S. Army Special Forces in Asia, 1956–1975* (Novato, CA: Presidio, 1986); and a 21st MHD historical study, Encl to Transmittal Ltr, Aaron, HQ, 5th Special Forces Group (Airborne), 1st Special Forces, May 24, 1969, sub: Vietnamese Special Forces (VNSF), copy CMH.

17. E.g., see Msg, Westmoreland, MAC 8875 to McConnell (acting CJCS), September 20, 1967, History file 22A16, Westmoreland Papers; and Msg, Abrams MAC 04039 to Laird, 020443 May 71, Abrams Papers, both at CMH.

18. Clarke, *Advice and Support: The Final Years,* 85–93.

19. Memo, MACV, sub: Meeting—100830 March 1965: Advisors in the Support Role, History file 14–28, Westmoreland Papers, CMH

20. Jack Shulimson, *U.S. Marines in Vietnam: An Expanding War, 1966* (Washington, D.C.: USMC History and Museums Division, 1982), 8.

21. History, Notes of January 1, May 2, November 11 and 21, 1966, History files 3B, 6B, 11C, Westmoreland Papers, CMH.

22. Msg, Bunker Sgn 27359 to Sec State, 151125 May 68, Bunker Papers, State Department Archives.

23. Interview, author with Gen. William B. Rosson, March 16, 1984.

24. Interviews, author with MG James N. Ellis, January 1983; and Col. James Anderson, June 23, 1983.

25. Ridgway interview in Department of Defense/International Security Affairs (DOD/ISA), Southeast Asia Analysis Report, October 1969, 44–63, copy CMH.

12

The Seven-Point Proposal of the PRG (July 1, 1971) and the U.S. Reaction

Luu Doan Huynh

In 1971, the Nixon administration had to face new difficulties concerning its "Vietnamization of the war" strategy and its scheme to isolate South Vietnam's revolution: the fiasco of the operation on Route 9 (in southern Laos) and a number of setbacks on the Cambodian battlefield. It also faced additional difficulties in the United States and in the world, but was trying to promote détente with the USSR and China.

In the same year, the people and armed forces of Vietnam scored initial successes in frustrating the Vietnamization strategy, and grass-roots revolutionary bases in the countryside of South Vietnam were being restored. On the whole, the relations of forces on the South Vietnamese battlefield had not yet changed substantially.

At the same time, however, the political struggle in the urban areas of South Vietnam was alive and well: the withdrawal of U.S. troops and the removal of Nguyen Van Thieu were demanded, and protest against the forthcoming general elections occurred. In particular, inside the Saigon establishment, Thieu was subjected to increased criticism following military setbacks in southern Laos and Cambodia.

Since 1969, the Nixon administration had been holding negotiations in Paris with a view to contributing to the success of Vietnamization of the war, that is, the United States would withdraw all its troops but the Saigon regime would remain stable. In 1971 President Nixon used the POW question to arouse U.S. public opinion while evading the issue of specifying a concrete deadline for the complete withdrawal of U.S. troops. Opposing this evasion, the U.S. antiwar movement and public opinion laid stress on the return of the POWs and brought pressure on Nixon to set a date for the final withdrawal of all U.S. troops. A private meeting between the Vietnamese delegation and Kissinger in Paris on May 31, 1971, gave a hint that a solution might be reached in 1971. In that meeting, Kissinger expressed U.S. willingness to finalize the date for the complete withdrawal of troops and the release of all prisoners, and, remarkably, he failed to reiterate the demand for withdrawal of North Vietnamese troops from South Vietnam. To some Vietnamese officials, this was indeed an indication that the U.S. side seriously intended to reach an agreement. What was not clear was whether Kissinger's assurances were an indication of his zeal to reach an agreement or were an expression of the true position of the Nixon administration.

Following two private meetings in Paris on March 31 and June 26, 1971, the Provisional Revolutionary Government (PRG) of the Republic of South Vietnam came out with a Seven-Point Proposal, of which Points 1 and 2 were the most important. (The text of the PRG's Seven-Point Proposal can be found in Gareth Porter, *Vietnam: The Definitive Documentation of Human Decisions.* Vol. 2. New York: Coleman Enterprises, 1979, pp. 556–58.) These two points demanded respectively that the United States set a date for the withdrawal of all its troops coupled with the release of prisoners, and that the United States put an end to its support for the maintenance of power of the Thieu group; and the South Vietnamese people be allowed to set up an administration favorably disposed to peace and national reconciliation that the PRG would be willing to negotiate with.

The broad objectives of the seven points were:

• to get the Nixon administration to set a date for complete troop withdrawal and the return of POWs (the PRG's proposed date of December 31, 1971, coincided with what was requested by U.S. public opinion);
• to get the Nixon administration to join in also addressing the political aspect of the Vietnam War (the Nixon administration wanted only to solve the military problem while the political problem would be left to direct talks among North Vietnam, the PRG, and the Thieu administration).

More concretely, Point 2 was aimed at achieving a solution of the internal aspect of the South Vietnamese problem—in parallel or almost in parallel—with a complete withdrawal of U.S. troops. To this end, the PRG tried to have an impact on the forthcoming elections of the Saigon regime. It was hoped that public opinion and political circles in South Vietnam—including members of the Saigon establishment and the U.S. government—would take advantage of the elections to discard Thieu and promote the necessary conditions for the emergence of a new Saigon government favorably disposed to peace and national reconciliation (that the PRG could talk to with a view to establishing a coalition government).

The best-case scenario, in view of Vietnamese officials, would be the acceptance of Points 1 and 2 by the United States. In the event that no agreement could be reached on those points, it was hoped that at least the Seven-Point Proposal and the debate and struggle around it at the negotiating table in South Vietnam and in the United States would result in the further exacerbation of differences: inside the Saigon establishment; between the latter and the Nixon administration; and between the South Vietnamese people and the Saigon regime. This would further weaken the Thieu group and expose the bellicose character of the Nixon administration to U.S. and world opinion, resulting in an increased struggle by the American people for an end to the war.

The discussions among Vietnamese officials over the chances of success of Point 2 focused on three possible scenarios:

1. The Nixon administration would not bring about any change in the Saigon regime, and would not discard Thieu.
2. The Nixon administration would bring about a partial change in the Saigon regime.
3. The United States would bring about a change in the Saigon regime, roughly in keeping with the desire of South Vietnamese revolutionary forces, thus making it possible to have an internal solution in parallel with a complete U.S. troop withdrawal.

The discussions showed the danger of reading too much into Kissinger's proposal of May 31, 1971, and the acrimonious debate inside the Saigon regime in the wake of the southern Laos fiasco (Route 9). This might result in too much optimism about scenarios 2 and 3. But if the relation of forces on the South Vietnamese battlefield and our difficulties in restoring grass-roots bases in the countryside were taken more into account, this would lead to the assumption that the Nixon administration would balk at anything that might harm the Vietnamization strategy and therefore reject the Seven-Point Proposal, particularly Point 2. Furthermore, having seen how "ping-pong diplomacy" could reduce U.S. public pressure on the Nixon administration after the Route 9 debacle, some felt that an early agreement with the United States would be welcome but were apprehensive that a new diplomatic move by Vietnam could be weakened by further moves on the China–United States normalization front.

During the first week that followed its publication, the Seven Point Proposal did indeed have a powerful impact.

The Nixon administration was driven into a passive position: It did not officially reject the proposal and would only admit that there were some positive elements in it but also some elements that it found difficult to accept, and intended to ask the Vietnamese side to clarify these points; it also made a comment that the United States could never accept any arrangement that would hand over 17 million southern Vietnamese to the Communists. That comment reflected the true feelings of the Nixon administration.

We remarked earlier that in the United States, the press, the antiwar movement, and opposition political figures expressed views that were favorable to the Seven-Point Proposal but focused more on Point 1 (a deadline for complete troop withdrawal and the return of POWs) and gave less attention—or not enough attention—to Point 2. Professor George Mc T. Kahin was one of the few Americans who focused a great deal of attention on Point 2.[1]

But the public pressure that had steadily built up in the United States over the seven points quickly faded following the reported visit of Kissinger to Peking and the U.S.-Chinese agreement on President Nixon's future visit early in 1972. By the end of 1971, U.S. public opinion again criticized the Nixon administration for the mishandling of negotiations in Paris. The public demanded that the administration respond to the Seven-Point Proposal. Partly because of this, Nixon had to come out with an Eight-Point Plan in January 1972 to calm public opinion. But it was obvious from this plan that the Nixon administration rejected the PRG's seven negotiating points and that the first breakthrough in U.S.-Chinese relations had impacted negatively on those in the United States who were in favor of the seven points and, therefore, incited Nixon to greater stubbornness.

In terms of by-products, the Seven-Point Proposal did create some tension between the Nixon administration and the Saigon regime. Kissinger, who was scheduled to visit Saigon on July 5, 1971, had to move up his arrival to July 3; Nixon sent Thieu a message assuring him that the United States would continue to support the Saigon administration but mentioned that the United States was being pressured into withdrawing troops from Vietnam.

The proposal also had a strong impact on the Saigon establishment: Nguyen Cao Ky continued public criticism of Thieu; more people began trying to distance themselves from Thieu, while certain opposition groups openly demanded that the United States set a date for troop withdrawal. A number of people's organizations continued to demand that the United States withdraw all troops by the end of 1971; that it stop supporting Thieu; that Thieu resign. The groups also kept up their criticism of rigged elections. In short, the anti-United States–Thieu front did broaden in the occupied areas of South Vietnam.

In hindsight, one can make the following observations. Some clear-sighted Americans could see that while the relation of forces on South Vietnam's battlefield was still unfavorable to the National Front of South Vietnam, an agreement reached in 1971 would be more beneficial to the United States and the Saigon regime. At the same time, Vietnamese officials also wanted to see an early agreement to ensure that the Vietnamese war of resistance would be less subject to the negative impact from the forthcoming détente among the superpowers. They also hoped that if a political breakthrough could emerge, the NLF would have more of an opportunity to win the broad allegiance and support of the people in South Vietnam.

However, the Nixon administration could not accept this proposal, because:

1. Its real aim mainly was to solve the military aspect of the war and leave the political problems to discussions between North Vietnam and the PRG on one

side, and the Thieu regime on the other. Therefore, in the administration's view, no move should be taken to remove Thieu. Previous experience might also have strengthened this reluctance to move against Thier: the liquidation of Diem brought about serious confusion inside the Saigon administration as reflected in the successive coups against the generals that succeeded him and in the end, the United States had to prohibit further coups d'état; if Thieu were discarded, there would be as much or more confusion, and North Vietnam and the PRG would be tempted to take advantage of this. Also, removing Thieu at this juncture might jeopardize any chance of success of the Vietnamization strategy.

2. Ultimately, the Nixon administration would have to set a final deadline for a U.S. troop withdrawal and the return of POWs. The timing of this, however, should not endanger the Thieu regime. The announcement of a date prior to elections, particularly the date of December 31, 1971, would result in a further lowering of the morale of Thieu's troops and the Saigon establishment, and if these two elements became too unstable or chaotic, then the United States would have had no more legal basis for its presence and actions in South Vietnam. (One can see that both items involve the notion of "a decent interval" for U.S. decisions on withdrawal from South Vietnam.)

3. Further, the initial euphoria in the United States over the prospects of normalization of relations with China did help Nixon evade, for some time, the pressure of U.S. opinion against the Vietnam War.

While actively taking advantage of new opportunities to promote a settlement, the Vietnamese leadership always bore in mind that the Nixon administration could be very stubborn in negotiations. The best case would be if success-scenarios 2 and 3, mentioned earlier, could materialize. But in war, one also has to be prepared for the worst. Therefore, this lost opportunity did disappoint us, but did not disarm us. In fact, preparations were made in 1971 for a new wave of large-scale attacks in 1972, the objective of which was to promote a solution to the war. In the wake of these attacks in 1972, Vietnam and the Nixon administration started a new round of talks which showed that the U.S. side was interested in reaching a settlement, to which Vietnam actively contributed. Yet, new delays and new incidents intervened, crowned by a very destructive series of air attacks, and only in January 1973 could a solution finally be reached.

Note

1. See George McT. Kahin, "Nixon and the PRG's Seven Points," in Jayne Werner and David Hunt, eds., *The American Way* (Ithaca, N.Y.: Cornell University Southeast Asia Publication Series, forthcoming).

13

Post–Paris Agreement Struggles and the Fall of Saigon

Ngo Vinh Long

Misunderstanding and misinterpretations of the post–Paris Agreement period have perhaps created more recrimination than any other period of the entire war in both the United States and Vietnam.

In the United States, the groundwork for recrimination has been laid in part by repeated assertions on the part of former American policymakers, Saigon expatriates, and revisionist historians that reduction of aid to the Thieu regime after the signing of the Paris Agreement led to the "loss" of South Vietnam. Soon after the war ended, Henry Kissinger, for example, appeared in a television interview with Barbara Walters of NBC on May 6, 1975, and blamed Congress for having made it impossible for the United States to "enforce" the Paris Peace Agreement. He said that Congress had cut aid to South Vietnam by 50 percent each year and that not even spare parts had been sent to Thieu's armed forces. He also blamed the Soviet Union for having "caused the Vietnamese to bring the tragic situation about," reminding the viewers, however, that while "[i]t is true that Soviet arms made the conquest of Vietnam possible, it is also true that the refusal of American arms made the conquest of South Vietnam inevitable." Later on, Kissinger expounded on this assertion at greater length in his memoirs.

Many other Americans and Saigon expatriates, however, have extended this stab-in-the-back theory to include the "liberal" American press and the American peace movement as being ultimately responsible for the defeatist attitude of Congress. While this theory might have served to justify the American policy of punishing Vietnam in every way possible since the end of the war (as well as to intimidate Congress and the American people into allowing the White House to maintain highly destructive ventures elsewhere, such as support of the Nicaraguan contras and military aid to El Salvador), we will see later in this chapter that it has little factual basis.

Connected to this aid-cut-off/stab-in-the-back theory is the overemphasis by former American policymakers and revisionist historians on military matters, especially in the last few months of the war, to show that the liberation of the southern part of Vietnam was purely a military takeover by the "North" Vietnamese. Therefore, the roles of the southern revolutionary fighters of the former National Liberation Front (NLF) and the southern urban opposition have been largely ignored, if not dismissed as being insignificant or irrelevant. The social, economic, and political problems of the Saigon regime as contributing factors to its downfall have also been de-emphasized. It should be added that the stress on a military takeover by North Vietnam has also been of special importance to former Saigon leaders who are now trying to rally and control the close to one million Vietnamese expatriates in the United States. Since the majority of these expatriates either had immediate family members or close relatives who fought with the National Liberation Front (NLF), it would have been difficult to organize them against the present government in Vietnam by directing their hatred against the southern revolutionaries.

In Vietnam, the dominant official view has also tended to emphasize the role of the northern People's Army of Vietnam (PAVN) in the liberation of southern Vietnam. An example of one of the latest, and one of the most subtle, arguments along this line is contained in Mr. Le Duc Tho's article published in the March 1988 issue of *Tap Chi Lich Su Quan Su* (Journal of Military History).[1] Mr. Tho was at that time still considered by many to be the most powerful man in Vietnam. He admitted in the article that there had been a number of problems after the signing of the Paris Agreement. One problem was that both the Soviet Union and China cut off all military aid to Vietnam and that China, for ulterior motives, also cut off all economic aid. Another was the fact that "some high [northern] cadres who went to the South to explain the situation had placed too much emphasis on maintaining a peaceful stance for the sake of reconstruction. . . . Therefore, at that time there were many cases in which our [southern] brothers simply withdrew from, or at best tried to maintain, the areas attacked by the enemies but did not fight back." Tho continued that it was not until after the southern revolutionary fighters had fought back in many areas, in spite of orders to the contrary by the northern cadres, that the Central Committee was forced to meet in October 1973 and authorized the revolutionary fighters in the South to strike back against encroachments by Saigon. However, Tho went on to explain that the liberation of Saigon was made possible only by large contingents of regular forces in coordination with regional forces and sapper units, which, of course, had already been in place in the city. And while Mr. Tho conceded that "political forces" did play a limited role in aiding military operations in the Mekong Delta and other rural areas throughout the southern region of Vietnam, he considered the urban opposition as only a minor irritant to the Saigon regime and not much else.

In a sense, therefore, the revisionist American view and the dominant official Vietnamese view on the role of the NLF and the southern struggles during the post–Paris Agreement period have converged. This is one of the many instances of increasing convergence that I think are very insidious. I have argued elsewhere that the recovery of the southern revolutionary forces was crucial to the military successes in 1972 that led to the Paris Agreement and finally to liberation in 1975. I will not repeat myself here since the fifth volume of General Tran Van Tra's opus, which was secretly printed in Ho Chi Minh City in 1982 and is available in an English translation done by the CIA, has confirmed this analysis in great detail.[2] I would like to add a personal note here. After interviewing hundreds of southern revolutionary fighters intermittently for the past 10 years I have learned that many of them have felt frustrated and slighted by the fact that the struggles of the people in the South have not been appropriately recognized in official accounts. Moreover, many of those who operated in the urban areas— especially in Saigon—have told me that after the war they have been regarded with suspicion and have been marginalized, in part because of the incorrect official assessment of the role of the urban opposition during the war years. In my opinion, this has created a certain resentment which in turn has made political accommodation and integration in postwar Vietnam that much more difficult.

Incorrect assessment of the role of the urban opposition—and hence of political support for the revolution in the southern towns and cities—has also had other consequences. In early 1980, during a long and intimate interview with Hoang Tung, at that time editor-in-chief of *Nhan Dan* (People, the official daily newspaper of Vietnam) and the person in charge of the Department of Party Propaganda and Education, I was told that one of the reasons for Vietnam's striking back at Pol Pot was because his incessant attacks so close to Ho Chi Minh City could have created the conditions for a takeover of the city by reactionary elements there. Saigon, according to Hoang Tung, was the weakest spot in the body politic of Vietnam. The same analysis might have contributed to the arrest and detention, on sedition charges, of progressive Catholic priests Father Chan Tin and Father Nguyen Ngoc Lan, and a number of other former peace activists and Third Force personalities in March and April of 1990.

It seems to me that in order to heal the wounds of war both in the United States and in Vietnam, as well as to lay the groundwork for improved relations between the two countries, the least one should do would be to set the record straight. To this end, a number of recent efforts by American writers have been laudable. For the period under discussion, Part Six of Gabriel Kolko's *Anatomy of a War* is particularly good on the overall analysis of the military, political, social, and economic problems facing the Saigon regime and how it would have been impossible for Saigon to survive even with increased aid.[3] I have also argued in some detail elsewhere, looking at the situation both in the rural as well as urban areas, that the system created by the United States to prop up the Saigon regime would collapse from its own weight.[4]

For our purpose here I will reiterate only two simple observations: One is that too much, and not too little, aid from the United States to the Thieu regime, especially after the signing of the Paris Agreement, plus an explicit verbal guarantee given to Thieu by Nixon that the United States would reenter the war (at least with air power) to bail him out if worse came to worse, encouraged Thieu to sabotage the agreement by attacking areas controlled by the Provisional Revolutionary Government of Vietnam (PRG) and to carry out repression against Third Force groups. The other observation, a corollary point, is that Thieu's actions forced a military confrontation with the PRG as well as a rise in urban opposition. The military and political struggles of the southern revolutionaries and the urban opposition together weakened the Saigon regime to such an extent that by the beginning of 1975, it was already an overripe fruit that would fall at the slightest touch. In my opinion, debates on fine military points aside, Saigon could have been taken by any means. It was only a question of timing.

U.S. Aid and Thieu's Aggression

It should be remembered that although both the United States and the Thieu regime were forced to sign the Paris Agreement, both believed that carrying out the agreement to the letter might lead to the eventual political takeover by the Vietnamese revolutionaries. Therefore, in spite of the fact that the Paris Agreement established two parallel and equal parties in South Vietnam—the Saigon regime and the PRG—and that the two parties were supposed to reach a political settlement under conditions of full democratic rights without U.S. interference (Articles 1, 4, 9, and 11), the United States and Thieu consistently denied the PRG any political role in South Vietnam. Article 12 of the Paris Agreement also stipulates that a "National Council of National Reconciliation and Concord" would be created with "three equal segments."

The third segment was supposed to be composed of non-aligned "neutralists" or the "Third Force" as it was then known. But as soon as the Paris Agreement was signed, Thieu reiterated, with American acquiescence—if not outright support—his Four No's policy: no recognition of the enemy, no coalition government, no neutralization of the southern region of Vietnam, and no concession of territory. Later on, in an interview published in the July 15, 1973, issue of *Vietnam Report*, an English-language publication of the Saigon Council on Foreign Relations, Thieu stated: "The Vietcong are presently trying to turn areas under their control into a state endowed with a government, which they could claim to be the second such institution in the South. . . . In the first place, we have to do our best so that the NLF cannot build itself into a state, a second state within the South." In the same interview Thieu also ruled out any role for the third segment, branding all Third Force people as pro-PRG. In a November 13, 1974, speech, Thieu said that all government means had to be used to prevent the creation of a Third Force.[5] He ordered his soldiers to "use clubs to beat up a bothersome minority in the National Assembly" and said that if the opposition legislators fought back physically, he would bring in tanks to dissolve the assembly.[6]

Thieu's bellicose stance was certainly encouraged by the fantastic amounts of military aid given to him by the United States. After the signing of the Paris Agreement the United States supplied the Thieu regime with so many arms that, as Major General Peter Olenchuck testified before the Senate Armed Services Committee on May 8, 1973, "We shortchanged ourselves within our overall inventories. We also shortchanged the reserve units in terms of prime assets. In certain instances, we also diverted equipment that would have gone to Europe."[7] In fiscal year 1974, Congress gave Saigon $1 billion more in military aid. Saigon expended as much ammunition as it could—$700 million worth. This left a stockpile of at least $300 million, a violation of the Paris Agreement which stipulated that equipment could only be replaced on a one-to-one basis. For fiscal year 1975, Congress again authorized $1 billion in military aid, but appropriated $700 million—about what was actually spent in 1974.

Meanwhile, according to the report entitled "Vietnam—A Changing Crucible," issued by the House Committee on Foreign Affairs on July 15, 1974, "Hanoi faces uncertainty over the level of Soviet and Chinese support . . . there is no evidence that Hanoi's allies are prepared to mount a 'massive' resupply operation to the extent believed necessary for an all-out attack. In recent briefings to troops and cadres in the south, the Communist high command . . . has accused Moscow and Peking of having cut back aid and of having opposed certain North Vietnamese objectives." This cut of military aid from the Soviet Union and China, as confirmed by Le Duc Tho in the article quoted earlier, might have influenced the cautious attitude of the Vietnamese policy makers, resulting in their defensive posture during the post-agreement period.

In any case, Thieu was certainly encouraged by the American military aid and immediately carried out so-called "military operations to saturate the national territory" *(hanh quan tran ngap lanh tho)* through indiscriminate bombings and shellings as well as ground assaults on PRG-controlled areas. The February 16, 1974, issue of the *Washington Post* quoted Pentagon officials as saying that the Thieu armed forces were "firing blindly into free zones [i.e., PRG-controlled areas] because they knew full well they would get all the replacement supplies they needed from the United States." A study by the U.S. Defense Attache Office in conjunction with the Saigon Joint General Staff and the U.S. Pacific Command revealed that "the countryside ratio of the number of rounds fired by South Vietnamese forces [since the signing of the Paris Agreement] to that fired by Communist forces was about 16 to 1. In Military Regions II and III, where South Vietnamese commanders have consistently been the most aggressive and where some U.S. officials said that random 'harassment and interdiction' fire against Communist-controlled areas was still common, the ratio was on the order of 50 to 1."[8] In addition to the shellings, on the average about 15,000 bombs were dropped and 10,000 different military operations were conducted into the countryside every month. A classified study by the province of Long An, which is immediately south of Saigon, has documented the fact that in the post–Paris Agreement period every village under the control of the NLF was bombed four or five times and struck by an average of 1,000 artillery shells per day. Repeated assaults by large forces which sometimes involved up to several divisions were conducted and, as a result, from May to August 1973 the revolutionary forces in the province had to battle the Saigon troops 3,300 times.[9]

On the basis of this aggressiveness, the Thieu regime and its American supporters sought to persuade congressional delegations to Vietnam that the regime itself had finally matured militarily and, therefore, more aid should be given to it. One such delegation was moved to write in a report entitled "United States Aid to Indochina" issued by the House Committee on Foreign Affairs in July 1974 that "the Viet Cong infrastructure has become almost completely destroyed and there are no local units worthy of the name." According to the House Committee on Foreign Affairs report of July 15, 1974, "Vietnam—A Changing Crucible," this military aggressiveness actually enthralled many congressional supporters of the war because

> The GVN has fared well during the post-ceasefire maneuvering: Since January 1973 it has added 770 hamlets to the list of those over which it has dominant control, and it has reportedly reduced the number of disputed hamlets by well over a third. . . . In fact, our Embassy estimates that the GVN has maintained "dominant access" to roughly 93–94 percent of the population since the ceasefire. . . .

However, the Saigon regime's military aggressiveness also inflicted untold death and suffering on the civilian population as well as exposed Saigon's own armed forces to danger and death. As early as August 30, 1973, the respected French newspaper *Le Monde* reported that the Saigon high command had stated that about 41,000 of its troops had been killed and 4,000 were missing since the signing of the Paris Agreement. Saigon was never known for inflating its own casualty statistics; and the casualty rate climbed continuously as Thieu increased his attacks on the rural areas.

Economic Blockade and Consequences

Worse still, because of the increase in economic aid to the Thieu regime in 1973 and 1974,[10] it felt confident enough to carry out an "economic blockade" designed to inflict hunger and starvation on the PRG areas.[11] Thieu was frequently quoted as exhorting his armed forces to do their utmost to implement the "economic blockade" in order to defeat the "Communists" by starving them out.[12] This blockade, which was also known as the "rice war" in the American press at the time, included prohibitions on the transport of rice from one village to another, rice-milling by anyone except the government, storage of rice in homes, and the sale of rice outside the village to any except government-authorized buyers. Widespread hunger and starvation were the results. According to reports by Saigon deputies and Catholic priests, up to 60% of the population of the central provinces were reduced to eating bark, cacti, banana roots, and the bulbs of wild grass. Children and the aged were the first victims. In some central Vietnam villages, deaths from starvation reached 1 to 2 percent of the total population each month.[13] On September 30, 1974, *Dai Dan Toc* (The Greater National Community) quoted official reports to the National Assembly by a number of deputies as saying that in four districts of Thua Thien province alone, 21,596 persons had died of hunger by mid-1974 out of a total population of half a million. In the same issue of this newspaper there are also heart-rending excerpts from official reports of deputies from the provinces of Quang Tin, Quang Ngai, Phu Yen and Binh Dinh on the acute problem of hunger and starvation there.

Hunger became so widespread that even in the wealthiest section of Saigon itself, the Tan Dinh district, a poll conducted by Catholic students in late summer 1974 disclosed that only 22 percent of the families had enough to eat. Half of the families could only afford a meal of steamed rice and a meal of gruel per day; the remainder went hungry.[14] And in the once rice-rich Mekong Delta, acute rice shortages became commonplace in many provinces.[15]

The conditions facing refugees in the camps were even worse. These people not only did not receive relief prescribed under the terms of U.S. economic aid programs, but they even had to pay the Saigon authorities to live in the refugee camps. For example, in the village of My Chanh in Binh Dinh province, 560 families complained that they were starving because they had only received 100 piasters (about eighteen U.S. cents) each when they first arrived there, while 300 families had to pay 3,000 piasters each to have a roof to live under.[16] In the province of Binh Tuy, the 18,000 refugees who had been resettled from Dong Ha had to pay 3,000 piasters to be officially legalized and 30,000 piasters for one-half of a house lot. Since the refugees could not pay such bribes, they had to trade in their refugee cards to rich and enterprising people from Saigon who swarmed up to Binh Tuy. Each card brought 30,000 piasters. Subsequently, every time rice was distributed, beautifully dressed strangers, wearing expensive jewels and driving shiny cars, came to receive the rice.[17]

As for the economy, Thieu's policies precipitated a major depression. On February 25, 1974, *Hoa Binh* (Peace, a conservative Catholic daily newspaper in Saigon) quoted Deputy Premier Phan Quang Dan as complaining that there were from three to four million unemployed persons in the Saigon-controlled areas alone. Throughout Thieu's Vietnam, firms were firing workers in droves. The owners frequently mistreated and insulted their workers to force them to quit. Even foreign companies, which enjoyed many special privileges such as exemption from all income taxes, had to cut back their work force by 30 percent.[18]

Hunger and unemployment increased crimes, suicide, and demonstrations throughout the areas under Saigon's control. On September 11, 1974, *Dien Tin* (Telegraph, a Saigon paper published under strict censorship) commented on the problem of suicide as a result of hunger and unemployment with the following words:

> Faced with these kinds of suicides, people expect the government, especially the Department of Social Affairs, to express some kind of positive attitude. On the contrary: beyond ignoring the whole thing, they bad-mouth these dead people. . . . What are we waiting for? Why not organize a movement for aiding the miserable—a movement to save people from hunger?

A Committee for Hunger Relief was created partly as a result of this call, but the Minister of the Interior immediately outlawed this organization for fear that it might become a rallying point for the hungry and the frustrated.[19] The Saigon regime saw this Committee for Hunger Relief as such a threat that it repeatedly carried out repression against it and consistently prevented it from giving food to the hungry in all parts of the country.[20] The corruption and callousness of the Saigon regime caused *Dong Phuong*, a conservative Saigon daily, to write the following in an editorial on September 27, 1974:

> We are told that the South Vietnamese population is hungry and that many families have died while several million people in the central provinces are hanging on with a meal of rice and a meal of roots. Many people have even died from the grass and cacti they had to eat. . . .
>
> The hunger and suffering of several million inhabitants of South Vietnam have occurred beside rice bins which are filled to the top and within sight of the abundance, wealth, callousness, and festivities of the majority of officials who are corrupt, who speculate and hoard rice, and of a minority who enrich themselves on the war and on the blood of the soldiers. . . .
>
> Therefore, the most pressing responsibility facing us is not just to promote a movement of hunger relief. The entire people must also struggle hard for the eradication of corruption, the elimination of injustices, the implementation of democratic freedoms, the establishment of peace, and the decapitation of those who have created so many tragic situations for our people.

Demonstrations demanding jobs and food occurred almost daily. Here are a few random examples taken from a single Saigon daily to illustrate the intensity of the urban struggles by August and September of 1974. The August 30, 1974, issue of *Dien Tin* reported that 1,000 disabled veterans and other inhabitants of Do Hoa village in Thua Thien province blockaded the streets with barbed wire, demanding that the government provide them with food and jobs. Later, on September 19, 116 trade unions in Saigon and Cholon met to demand food and clothes and an end to mistreatment and unwarranted layoffs *(Dien Tin,* September 20, 1974). Two days later, on September 21, the whole work force of Saigon, Cholon, and Gia-dinh demonstrated for food, clothes, and temporary relief *(Dien Tin,* September 22, 1974). While this was going on, huge numbers of workers in Danang, the second largest city in South Vietnam, marched in the streets and then went on a mass hunger strike *(Dien Tin,* September 22 and 24, 1974).

The demonstrators were met with selective but extremely harsh repression. On November 1, 1974, for example, Father Nguyen Ngoc Lan, a progressive Catholic priest, and a number of deputies were severely beaten in a demonstration in the streets of Saigon.[21] The next day, disabled veterans were also beaten in a demonstration.[22] In a demonstration in the Chanh Tam district of Saigon on the following day, Thieu's police forces fired into the crowd, killing one person and wounding many others. These forces also burned houses and destroyed religious shrines. When the people of the area and religious leaders protested, the Thieu regime simply said it was conducting a regular military operation against the Communists in the area.[23]

The NLF Strikes Back

The death and suffering caused by Thieu's military attacks and economic blockade not only intensified the general population's hatred of the Thieu's regime, they also forced the PRG to fight back. In the summer of 1974, the PRG's counterattacks forced Thieu's armed forces to make one tactical withdrawal after another. Even in the heavily defended delta provinces, Saigon was forced to abandon 800 firebases and forts in order to increase mobility and defense.[24] The northern half of Long An province, which was considered the gateway to the Mekong Delta, was largely liberated and Saigon forces could travel on the main roads only from six o'clock in the morning until four o'clock in the afternoon. The province of Kien Tuong, which was immediately west of Long An and southwest of Saigon, was largely liberated.[25] Kolko is certainly correct in making the following conclusion:

> The RVN was by mid-1974 politically and economically brittle. The volume of aid in no way explains its political weaknesses; its real economic dilemma was intrinsic in the countless structural distortions the United States had built into the RVN system over a decade. Its military fragility was the consequence of a collapsing army, underpaid and without morale, which traumatized the peasants, who increasingly turned against the RVN and toward the Revolution. Given also the other American dilemmas, it was certain that the balance of forces in Vietnam by the summer of 1974 had tilted overwhelmingly against the RVN, and it would not take much more to shatter its institutional layers and create fatal political traumas and economic upheavals.[26]

But instead of drawing some lessons from the whole experience and responding to the demands of the PRG as well as the general population of Vietnam to return to the Paris Agreement, both the Thieu regime and the Ford administration resorted to trickery to obtain more aid from Congress to shore up the already hopeless situation. For its part, the Ford administration tried to set in motion a plan it had long held in reserve. This was the replacement of Thieu by a right-wing coalition capable of winning more aid from Congress and keeping some control of the country. High-ranking CIA agents were sent in droves to South Vietnam in September and October 1974.[27] The U.S. embassy in Saigon publicly encouraged a coalition of conservative forces within the Catholic, Buddhist, Cao Dai, and Hoa Hao churches to give the appearance of widespread popular backing for Thieu's successor regime.[28] The whole rightist Catholic opposition to Thieu was based on six specific charges of corruption, and called itself the Anti-Corruption Campaign. Father Tran Huu Thanh, the campaign's chairman, was quoted by the *Washington Post* as saying that the reasons for the Catholic actions were that "South Vietnam also needs a clean government so our allies will trust us and will send foreign aid and investment."[29]

On November 19, 1974, Colonel Vo Dong Giang, PRG spokesman at the two-party Military Commission in Saigon, held a press conference in which he criticized Father Thanh and his campaign for trying to maintain the Thieu regime, for following American policy, and for refusing to move toward peace as called for by the Paris Agreement and the Vietnamese people. The colonel warned that unless the United States heeded the aspirations of the Vietnamese people and returned to the Paris Agreement, there would soon be an uprising by the Vietnamese people. The next day, the *New York Times* reported this press conference and chided the colonel for bragging and for being arrogant.

Perhaps impressed by the show in Saigon and by the Ford administration's promise that there would soon be a regime worth supporting, on December 17 and 18, Congress authorized $450 million in economic aid to Saigon for fiscal year 1975, which represented a $100 million increase over the amount authorized for fiscal year 1974. The PRG evidently interpreted this action by Congress as a renewed commitment to the Saigon regime. In response, they increased their counterattacks against Thieu's aggressive military stance, and by early January 1975, eight districts and a province had fallen into the PRG's hands. But the administration and Saigon used this opportunity to accuse Congress of having weakened South Vietnam militarily by its reduction of aid requests and clamored for supplemental appropriations.

"The More the Aid, the Quicker the Collapse"

It was already clear to most Saigon observers, however, that more aid would at best only prolong the agony, if not cause the Saigon regime to collapse that much quicker. Following are a few excerpts from statements made by the more conservative public opinion makers in South Vietnam:

Huynh Trung Chanh, a deputy in the Lower House, wrote the following in an editorial in the January 17, 1975 issue, of *Dien Tin:*

> The leaders of the Republic of Vietnam are now spreading the view that the present deteriorating situation is due to the lack of aid. But the reality of the situation is that the difficulty is not because of a lack of aid but because of *lack of support of the people* [emphasis in original]. In previous years, aid was overly abundant and yet what was ever solved? Now, if there were supplemental aid in order to meet this military situation, then the difficult period will only be prolonged and in the end nothing will be solved.

Dong Phuong, another Saigon daily which had been very conservative, also wrote the following in its January 13, 1975, issue:

> The United States has poured several hundred billion dollars into this country to feed the flames of war! It has also poured in many billions more in so-called military and economic aid. This great amount of money has been justified by the American leadership as necessary for creating a "Peace With Honor."
> But what has become of South Vietnam now? What has become of its economy? What does a several-hundred-billion-dollar "Peace With Honor" mean? And what do people think they can do now if they beg a few hundred million dollars more?

An appropriate answer to the above question would show people the solution to the Vietnam question and the real value of American dollars with regard to this war.

Finally, even Father Nguyen Quang Lam, an ultraconservative Catholic priest, wrote the following in the February 10 issue of *Dai Dan Toc:*

> Yesterday I wrote that whether there is an additional $300 million or $3,000 million in aid, South Vietnam will still not be able to avoid collapse. . . . In the afternoon, a reader called me up and said that I should have put it more strongly. I must say that the more the aid, the quicker the collapse of South Vietnam. All I had to do was to take a look at our society. . . . Come to think of it, the reader has a point there. The American dollars have really changed our way of thinking. People compete with each other to become prostitutes, that is to say, to get rich in the quickest and most exploitative manner. . . . No wonder whenever our soldiers see the enemy they run for their lives, even though they might have a basement full of ammunition which they could presumably fire till kingdom comes.

It is clear from the above Saigon editorials by even the more conservative and anti-Communist Saigon elements that there was no longer a mood for any kind of military confrontation. But neither the Saigon regime nor the United States would take the hint and pushed even harder for the supplemental aid requested. Meanwhile, perhaps in a last-ditch effort to get Congress to vote for the supplemental aid, CIA agents were sent in mid-January 1975 to Capitol Hill to brief many of the senators about a "Heartland" policy. They maintained that the Saigon army had high morale, was well trained and fully equipped, but overextended. They recommended abandonment of some central highland provinces and withdrawal to the coastal areas to preserve the strength of the Saigon troops. This would also help provide tighter control of populated areas, making it possible to conduct and manage the upcoming elections so as to create the impression that a future Saigon regime indeed had overwhelming popular support. Therefore, when the PRG and DRV were forced to mount an offensive in early March to try to get the United States and Saigon to come back to the Paris Agreement, Thieu withdrew his forces from the central highlands and caused a stampede as one province after another fell with hardly a fight.

Thieu has often been blamed for making the fatal military mistake of withdrawing from the central highlands. But it seems that Thieu might have listened too well to his American advisers. The *Far Eastern Economic Review* reported on April 25, 1975, that

> The United States knew in advance of Saigon's plans to withdraw its troops from part of the north of the country, according to a report from Tokyo. Japan's financial leaders were reportedly told by sources close to U.S. Secretary of State, Henry Kissinger, in early February that the Americans were prepared to condone a South Vietnamese military "redeployment" from the north in order to form a new, stronger defense perimeter near Saigon.

But this is merely a footnote to show how puppets are usually made strawmen by their masters. The end of the Saigon regime did not begin with the attacks by the DRV forces on Ban Me Thuot, Kontum, and Pleiku that forced Thieu to carry out hastily the American "Heartland" policy. It began much earlier than that—perhaps as early as the first massive infusions of American dollars into the body politic of South Vietnam.

Notes

1. "Dong Chi Le Duc Tho noi ve mot so van de tong ket chien tranh va bien soan lich su quan su" [Comrade Le Duc Tho Discusses a Number of Questions on the General Assessment of the War and the Writing of Military History], *Tap Chi Lich Su Quan Su* [Journal of Military History] (March 1988): 1–10.

2. Tran Van Tra, *Vietnam: History of the Bulwark B2 Theatre*, vol. 5: *Concluding the 30-Years War* in *Southeast Asia Report,* No. 1247, Joint Publication Research Services (JPRS) 82783, February 2, 1983.

3. Gabriel Kolko, *Anatomy of a War: Vietnam, the United States, and the Modern Historical Experience* (New York: Pantheon Books, 1985), 457–558.

4. For examples, see the issues of my monthly newsletter *Thoi Bao Ga* (Vietnam

Resource Center, Cambridge, MA) for the period from January 1973 to April 1975 and the article entitled "Agrarian Differentiation in the Southern Region of Vietnam" in the *Journal of Contemporary Asia*, no. 3 (1984).

5. *Chinh Luan* [Official Discussion, a very conservative Saigon daily newspaper which was accused by others as having a CIA connection at the time], November 14, 1974.

6. *Dien Tin* [Telegraph, a Saigon daily], November 14, 1974.

7. *Fiscal year 1974 Authorization for Military Procurement, Research and Development, Construction Authorization for Safeguard ABM, and Active Duty and Selected Reserve Strengths*, hearings before the Committee on Armed Services, United States Senate, 93rd Congress, pt. 3, Authorizations (Washington, D.C.: U.S. Government Printing Office, 1973), 1383.

8. *Vietnam: May 1974*, Staff Report Prepared for the Use of the Committee on Foreign Relations, United States Senate (Washington, D.C.: U.S. Government Printing Office, August 5, 1974), 22.

9. *Bao Cao Dien Bien 21 Nam Khang Chien Chong My va nhung Bai Hoc ve Toan Dan Danh Giac cua Long An* [Report on Developments in 21 Years of Resistance against the Americans and the Lessons of the Entire Population Fighting the Enemy in Long An] (Long An: Ban Tong Ket Chien Tranh Tinh Long An [Committee on Overall Assessment of the War in Long An Province], August 1985), 127–30.

10. Economic aid to the Thieu regime during the same period was also increased and channeled through various programs such as the Foreign Assistance Act and "Food for Peace." For example, on December 17 and 18, 1974, Congress passed the Foreign Assistance Act, authorizing $450 million in economic aid to Saigon. This was $100 million more than the amount authorized by Congress in fiscal year 1974. According to the January 16, 1975, issue of *Dien Tin* [Telegraph]—a Saigon paper published under Thieu's strict censorship—90 percent of U.S. economic aid to the Thieu regime had been used to maintain the war.

11. See the *Congressional Record*, May 20, 1974, and June 4, 1974, for detailed reports on the economic blockade and its impact.

12. *Dai Dan Toc* [The Greater National Community, a Saigon daily run by a group of deputies in the Lower House], August 8, 1974.

13. For details see the August 30, 1974 issue of *Dai Dan Toc* and the 1974, issues of *Thoi Bao Ga*, especially numbers 45, 46, 47, and 48.

14. *Chinh Luan*, November 5, 1974. [Official Discussion, a conservative Saigon daily newspaper.]

15. *Dien Tin*, September 6, 20, 22, and 24, 1974; and *Dai Dan Toc*, September 30, 1974.

16. *Dien Tin*, November 10, 1974.

17. *Dai Dan Toc*, November 19, 1974.

18. *Dien Tin*, September 20, 1974.

19. *But Thep* [Iron Pen, an extremely conservative Saigon daily], October 7, 1974.

20. This was reported frequently in the Saigon press. For examples see *Dai Dan Toc*, November 19, 1974; and *Dien Tin*, November 22 and December 16, 1974.

21. *Chinh Luan, Dong Phuong,* and *Song Than* [Tidal Waves], November 2, 1974.

22. *Dien Tin*, November 3, 1974.

23. *Song Than, Dong Phuong,* and *Chinh Luan*, November 7, 1974.

24. *Chinh Luan*, September 25, 1974.

25. *Bao Cao Dien Bien 21 Nam*, 131–32.

26. *Anatomy of a War*, 502.

27. *Washington Post*, November 2, 1974.

28. *Hoa Binh*, September 27, 1974.

29. *Washington Post*, October 7, 1974.

14

The Impact on Cambodia of the U.S. Intervention in Vietnam

Ben Kiernan

Background

In 1975, the "Khmer Rouge," a Communist organization led by Pol Pot, came to power in Cambodia for four reasons. First, a Khmer Communist movement had emerged in reaction to French colonialism's attempt to reassert control of Cambodia after its declaration of independence at the end of World War II. This new intrusion frustrated and radicalized Khmer nationalist sentiment and provoked thousands of Cambodian peasants and Buddhist monks to join with Vietnamese Communists against the common colonial enemy. The Vietnamese helped build a grass roots Cambodian Communist organization in the fight for independence. It ran probably the largest mass organization in the country's history.[1]

Later, rivalry between Vietnamese and Chinese Communists provided openings for younger Cambodian Communists of largely middle-class backgrounds, like Pol Pot, to rise to the top of the party, exchange Vietnamese patrons for Chinese ones, and take the movement in a new direction. After France withdrew from Cambodia in 1954, Pol Pot rose within the local Communist movement. In 1962 he became party leader after his predecessor, a former Buddhist monk, was mysteriously killed. The leadership of the Cambodian Communist Party had been rural, Buddhist, moderate and pro-Vietnamese, but it now became dominated by a group that was urban, French-educated, extremist, and anti-Vietnamese.

This changing of the vanguard was facilitated by the repression launched by the country's first independent ruler, Prince Norodom Sihanouk. While Pol Pot criticized party members who supported Sihanouk's neutral foreign policy, the prince's increasingly brutal autocracy in the 1960s drove such veterans of the country's independence struggle back into dissidence, where the young party elite subjected them to its plan for a new rebellion.

Finally, although it was indigenous, Pol Pot's revolution would not have won power without U.S. economic and military destablization of Cambodia, which began in 1966 after the American escalation in next-door Vietnam, and peaked in 1969–73 with the carpet bombing of Cambodia's countryside by American B–52s. This was probably the most important single factor in Pol Pot's rise.

An earlier U.S. impact had also reinforced the other factors. At least from 1950, the United States had backed French efforts to re-establish colonial rule in Vietnam and Cambodia. In 1954, U.S. attempts to partially encircle China had aggravated differences between Vietnamese Communists (who wished to fight on to certain victory) and their Chinese allies (who feared continuing war would bring American troops to their southern border). From 1960, U.S. escalation of the war in Vietnam made Sihanouk's neutrality increasingly precarious, provoking him to lean toward Hanoi and Beijing in foreign policy while taking ever more repressive measures against the grass-roots and rural domestic left. This cleared the field for the urban, middle-class, pro-Chinese party elite, which was almost untouched by the repression until 1967.

In 1963, Cambodia had a record rice harvest. In 1964, that record was broken. Rice exports soared, and the country's balance of trade was positive for the first time since 1955. The year 1965 saw another good crop, and National Bank deposits recovered from a long decline.[2]

But in the same year, the United States escalated the Vietnam War next door. American troop levels rose from 20,000 to 300,000 by mid-1966,[3] and Saigon forces also increased in number. In response, recruitment and conscription by the National Liberation Front (NLF) opposition quadrupled. The 1964 level of 45,000 new recruits increased to 160,000 in 1965.[4] All these additional soldiers had to be fed and, more importantly, were doing greater damage than ever to Vietnam's rice production. Large amounts of Cambodian rice now began to be smuggled across the Vietnamese border to the armies of both sides.

Prince Sihanouk's Cambodia depended for its revenue on taxing rice exports. It now plunged toward bankruptcy. In December 1965, U.S. intelligence noted that Sihanouk was already complaining privately about "considerable loss of revenue" as a result of "the illicit traffic in rice from Cambodia to Vietnam."[5] Over the next year, taxable rice exports fell by two-thirds, from 490,000 metric tons in 1965 to only 170,000 in 1966 (later figures are not available). About 130,000 metric tons of rice, 40 percent of rice exports for 1966,[6] were smuggled to Vietnam, both to communist agents and to black-market circles in Saigon.

Equally important, the Vietnamese Communists were resorting increasingly to the use of Cambodian territory for sanctuary from American attack. At the end of 1965, according to the U.S. intelligence report, they had established "clandestine and probably temporary facilities" there, but that year there had already been "eight instances of fire fights between Cambodian border forces and the Viet Cong." Meanwhile, Sihanouk's emissary, Prince Norindeth, on a visit to Australia in 1966, protested against U.S. bombing and strafing of the Cambodian border areas, claiming that "hundreds of our people have already died in these attacks."[7]

The U.S. intervention in Vietnam also produced a wave of Khmer refugees. From the early 1960s, ethnic Khmers born in Vietnam began fleeing to Cambodia to escape the Saigon government's repression in the countryside. In 1962 a Khmer Buddhist monk who had fled the Diem regime with 400 others claimed: "Our schools have all been closed. . . . With the slaughter of our people, the destruction of our villages, the repression of our culture and language, it seems our people are to be exterminated." In 1965–68 over 17,000 Khmers, including over 2,300 Buddhist monks, fled South Vietnam for Cambodia.[8]

Since the early 1960s, U.S. Special Forces teams, too, had been making secret reconnaissance and mine-laying incursions into Cambodian territory. In 1967 and 1968, in Operation Salem House, about 800 such missions were mounted, usually by several American personnel and up to ten local mercenaries, in most cases dressed as Viet Cong. One Green Beret team "inadvertently blew up a Cambodian civilian bus, causing heavy casualties." The code name of the operation was changed to "Daniel Boone," and from early 1969, the number of these secret missions doubled. By the March 18, 1970, coup against Sihanouk, over a thousand more had been mounted. In a total of 1,835 missions, twenty-four prisoners were taken and an unknown number of people were killed or wounded by the "sanitized self-destruct antipersonnel" mines which Daniel Boone teams were authorized to lay up to 30 km. inside Cambodia.[9]

Another U.S. Special Forces operation in Cambodia was the highly secret Project Gamma, which was formally listed as Detachment B57 but not mentioned under either name in an official army history of the Green Berets. Unlike Salem House and Daniel Boone, Project Gamma, according to a former member, "utilized only ethnic Cambodians in its operations, which were designed to gather tactical intelligence from deep inside Cambodia."[10]

Starting exactly a year before the coup (on March 18, 1969), over 3,600 secret B–52 raids were also conducted over Cambodian territory. These were code-named "Menu," and the various target areas were called "Breakfast," "Snack," "Lunch," "Dinner," "Dessert," and "Supper."[11] About 100,000 metric tons of bombs were dropped; the civilian toll is unknown. The U.S. aim was to destroy the Vietnamese Communist forces in Cambodia, or drive them back into Vietnam. But in September 1969, Lon Nol reported an *increase* in the number of communist troops in the sanctuaries, which he said was partly "motivated by the cleaning-up operation" of the U.S.-Saigon forces. He added ominously, "In this period, nothing suggests that these foreign units will soon leave our territory."[12] Like the failing economy, this was one of the major issues in Sihanouk's downfall at Lon Nol's hands. Both issues were exacerbated (if not caused) by the U.S. escalation of the Vietnam War.

Thus, by 1970 Cambodia's frontier with Vietnam was breaking down. It was unable to withstand the pressure exerted by the two mighty contending forces which had been expanding and straining against one another in the limited space of southern Vietnam ever since the U.S. escalation of the war in 1965. The pressure on Cambodia's frontier was economic and demographic as well as political and military. Cambodia's rice crop drained into devastated Vietnam, while both Khmers and Vietnamese fled into Cambodia, with the U.S. military and air force pursuing them.

The 1970 Coup

Prince Sihanouk has long claimed that the CIA "masterminded" the coup against him. Henry Kissinger, on the other hand, has stated that it "took us completely by surprise"; the United States, he claims, played no role, "at least not at the top level."[13] There is little evidence of CIA involvement in the 1970 Lon Nol coup, but a good deal of evidence points to a role played by sections of the U.S. military establishment and the Army Special Forces. The Australian security specialist Richard Hall made this point in *The Secret State*:

> Although the overthrow of Sihanouk is generally attributed to the CIA, I have heard that disputed in both Canberra and Washington. The counter-story has it the CIA was prepared to live with Sihanouk, who at the time of his overthrow was tilting towards the West and had cut back the movement of supplies through his port, Sihanoukville, to the Viet Cong. But for years the American military had portrayed Sihanouk as an ogre. The existence of an old boy network of Cambodian officers trained in the U.S. enabled the coup to be organised with American army support by-passing the CIA.[14]

The CIA had already attempted to intervene in Cambodia. Prom Thos, a senior Minister in the post-1970 Lon Nol regime, told me in an interview that he knew of no evidence of U.S. involvement in the coup, but he recalled that in 1965 another of the coup leaders, Long Boret, had told him that he had been approached by an American CIA agent and invited to work for Sihanouk's overthrow. Boret confided to Prom Thos that he had then approached Lon Nol for his cooperation in such a plan. Lon Nol's reply in 1965, according to Boret, was neither "yes" nor "no," but he had asked Boret to "maintain his contacts with the agent."[15] By early March 1970, the secretary of Lon Nol's own cabinet was also an American intelligence agent. As it turned out, Lon Nol was in contact with a third U.S. intelligence operative, "a Cambodian merchant of Chinese ancestry who regularly travelled between Saigon and Phnom Penh." This man's case officer was an American working under cover as an Agency for International Development adviser to the Saigon customs service.[16]

The most informed account of U.S. involvement in planning the 1970 coup is that of Navy Yeoman Samuel R. Thornton, who says he was "the first person the case officer spoke to after his debriefing of the agent." Thornton worked from May 1968 to May 1969 as an intelligence specialist at the U.S. Navy Command in Saigon.[17] Thornton has told journalist Seymour Hersh that he had gained intimate knowledge of coup preparations as early as late 1968. It was at that point, Thornton says, that Lon Nol approached U.S. military intelligence, through the Cambodian merchant, for a commitment to provide him with military, political, and economic support after his proposed overthrow of Sihanouk. The U.S. government was prepared to go further, however. It proposed, according to Thornton, to infiltrate in advance Special Forces–trained Khmer Kampuchea Krom (KKK) troops into "key Cambodian Army units stationed in Phnom Penh in order to support the first stages of the coup," and also "to insert a U.S.-trained assassination team disguised as Viet Cong insurgents into Phnom Penh to kill Prince Sihanouk as a pretext for revolution." The aim was to establish a new regime which would "issue a public request for U.S. military intervention." Thornton says: "I was present at some of the discussions which resulted in this plan, helped prepare the proposal to use Khmer Kampuchea Krom elements, and personally delivered this portion of the proposal to the action office of the MACV [the U.S. Military Assistance Command, Vietnam] intelligence staff."

Thornton recalls that this proposal, at first code-named "Dirty Tricks" and then rebaptized "Sunshine Park," was given "blanket approval" by "the highest level of government" in Washington in February or March 1969. Washington, Thornton says, authorized "any and all measures" to overthrow Sihanouk. However, Lon Nol rejected the plan to assassinate Sihanouk as "silly," a case of "criminal insanity." This part of Thornton's account is corroborated by Prom Thos, a leading member of the Lon Nol government from 1970 to 1973. Thos told me in 1980 that planning for the overthrow of Sihanouk had begun "a year before" the March 1970 coup, i.e., in March 1969, when, he said, Prince Sirik Matak had argued for the assassination of Sihanouk, but Lon Nol had opposed it.[18]

Lon Nol made a counterproposal to Washington. He wanted, Thornton recalls, "to lead a coup when Prince Sihanouk left the country on one of his periodic rest cures . . . in the south of France. [It] was felt by the general and his advisers that by confronting the Prince with a fait accompli when he was cut off from direct access to his resources they could discourage him from attempting to mount a countercoup. . . ."[19]

Lon Nol renewed his original request for "overt United States military support for a possible coup." He wanted weapons, ammunition, and money. The "response," Thornton recalls, "was surprisingly cool considering the original carte blanche authorization." But Lon Nol was then told "unofficially" (by back channels) that "he could in fact expect the requested support." However, the message went on that Lon Nol "must understand that the U.S. was sensitive to international criticism on this point, so that he must be prepared for a show of vacillation and great reluctance on our part to his initial, public requests for military assistance." According to Thornton, Lon Nol "indicated an understanding of this problem and an eagerness to go forward on these terms." Agreement was then reached with Lon Nol on the infiltration of the KKK units into Cambodia.[20] In May 1969, indeed, 640 Khmer Krom troops "surrendered" to the Sihanouk government. Their commander became a captain in Lon Nol's army, and fourteen others were appointed as officers.[21]

In August 1969, Lon Nol became Prime Minister of Cambodia. The next month he made secret contact with Son Ngoc Thanh, a U.S.-supported leader of the Khmer minority in South Vietnam, "and began tentative discussions about overthrowing Sihanouk." But only in February 1970 did Thanh assure Lon Nol of material aid, in the form of the Khmer Special Forces troops still on the U.S. and South Vietnamese payrolls.[22] The next year Son Ngoc Thanh told T.D. Allman that, through him, "Lon Nol had requested, and the CIA had approved, a U.S. pledge to send the Khmer Krom troops to support Lon Nol in the event he overthrew Sihanouk."[23] It was in February 1970 that U.S. Secretary of Defense Melvin Laird visited South Vietnam and authorized "clandestine South Vietnamese ground attacks across the border to begin at once."[24] Also in February 1970, according to Forrest B. Lindley, a Green Beret captain operating near the Cambodian border, "I was told there would be a change of government in Cambodia." The source was higher up the U.S. Special Forces command system. Two companies of Khmer Special Forces troops were then sent into Cambodia. It may have been these KKK units which took part in the sacking of the two Vietnamese Communist embassies in Phnom Penh on March 16, two days before the coup.[25] Sihanouk was undergoing a rest cure in France.

While Thornton's allegation that the highest level of the U.S. government was party to the coup plans remains uncorroborated, it is clear that Lon Nol carried out the coup with at least a legitimate expectation of significant U.S. support. William Colby, former director of the U.S. CIA, told William Shawcross that in 1970, "Lon Nol may well have been encouraged by the fact that the United States was working with Son Ngoc Thanh." Colby added: "I don't know of any specific assurances he was given, but the obvious conclusion for him, given the political situation in South Vietnam and Laos, was that he would be given United States support."[26] Son Ngoc Thanh himself told T.D. Allman: "Only after I was able to provide assurances that the U.S. would send the Khmer Krom troops, did Lon Nol act." Lon Nol's brother, Lon Non, told Allman: "We would not have done what we did, had we not been absolutely sure President Nixon would support us."[27]

The Bombing

Nixon's May 1970 invasion of Cambodia (undertaken without informing Lon Nol) followed simultaneous invasions by Saigon and Vietnamese Communist forces. It created 130,000 new Khmer refugees, according to the Pentagon.[28] By 1971, 60 percent of refugees surveyed in Cambodia's towns gave U.S. bombing as the main cause of their displacement.[29] The U.S. bombardment of the Cambodian countryside continued until 1973, when Congress imposed a halt. Nearly half of the 540,000 tons of bombs fell in the last six months.[30] In the ashes of rural Cambodia arose a Communist Party of Kampuchea (CPK) regime, led by Pol Pot. It went on to kill or starve to death over a million Cambodians from 1975 to 1979.

Pol Pot's CPK (known as the Khmer Rouge) had profited greatly from the U.S. bombings. It used the devastation and massacre of civilians as recruitment propaganda and as an excuse for its brutal, radical policies and its purge of moderate Communists and Sihanoukists. This is clear from contemporary U.S. government documents, released to me under the Freedom of Information Act, and from interviews in Cambodia with peasant survivors of the bombing.

In the early years of the Cambodian War, Sihanoukists, moderates, and pro-Vietnamese Communists predominated in a factionalized insurgency. The CPK "Center," as the Pol Pot leadership was known, admitted it still needed to "get a tight grasp, filter into every corner."[31] Before defeating Lon Nol, it needed to eclipse its revolutionary rivals and allies.

In 1973 the United States withdrew its troops from Vietnam, but switched its air arm to Cambodia. The secretary of the air force later said that President Richard Nixon "wanted to send a hundred more B–52's. This was appalling. You couldn't even figure out where you were going to put them all, you know. . . ."[32] The early bombing had been disastrous enough. In 1970 a combined U.S. aerial and tank attack in Kompong Cham province had taken the lives of 200 people. When another raid killed seven people nearby, a local peasant recalls, "some people ran away . . . others joined the revolution."[33]

In 1971, the town of Angkor Borei in southwest Cambodia was heavily bombed by American B–52s and Lon Nol's U.S.-supplied T–28s. It was burned and leveled. Whole families were trapped while hiding in trenches they had dug for protection underneath their homes. Over 100 people were killed and 200 houses destroyed, leaving only two or three standing, local residents say. In the same year, Sihanouk's former adviser Charles Meyer, in his book *Derrière le sourire khmer*, accused the U.S. Air Force of "systematic pillage" of "peaceful and captivating villages, which are disappearing one after another under bombs or napalm," and ended with a prescient observation:

> According to direct testimonies, peasants are taking refuge in forest encampments and are maintaining their smiles and their humour, but one might add that it is difficult to imagine the intensity of their hatred towards those who are destroying their villages and their property. Perhaps we should remember that the Cambodians have the deserved reputation for being the most spiteful and vindictive people in all Southeast Asia, and this should in any case hold the attention of President Nixon.[34]

U.S. intelligence soon discovered that many "training camps" on which Lon Nol had requested air strikes "were in fact merely political indoctrination sessions held in village halls and pagodas." Lon Nol intelligence noted that "aerial bombardments against the villagers have caused civilian loss on a large scale," and that the peasant survivors of the U.S. bombing were turning to the CPK for support.[35]

One young Khmer joined the Communists a few days after an aerial attack took the lives of 50 people in his village. Not far away, bombs fell on O Reang Au Market for the first time in 1972, killing 20 people,[36] and twice more in 1973, killing another 25 people, including two Buddhist monks.[37]

When bombs hit Boeng village, it was burned to the ground, and according to peasants, many people were caught in their houses and burned to death. Nearby Chalong village lost over twenty people. An inhabitant told me:

> Many monasteries were destroyed by bombs. People in our village were furious with the Americans; they did not know why the Americans had bombed them. Seventy people from Chalong joined the fight against Lon Nol after the bombing.[38]

B–52s scored a direct hit on Trapeang Krapeu village. At least twenty people died. Anlong Trea was napalmed and bombed, killing three people. "Over sixty people from this village then joined the Khmer Communist army out of anger at the bombing," locals recall.[39]

In March 1973, the bombardment spread west across the whole country. Around Phnom Penh, 3,000 civilians were killed in three weeks. UPI reported at the time:

> Refugees swarming into the capital from target areas report dozens of villages . . . have been destroyed and as much as *half their population killed or maimed* in the current bombing raids.[40]

Days later, the U.S. bombardment intensified, reaching a level of 3,600 tons per day.[41] As William Shawcross reported in his book *Sideshow: Kissinger, Nixon and the Destruction of Cambodia*, the "wholesale carnage" shocked the chief of the political section in the U.S. embassy, William Harben. One night, he said, "a mass of peasants" went out on a funeral procession and walked straight into a bombing raid. Hundreds were slaughtered. And Donald Dawson, a young air force captain, flew twenty-five B–52 missions but refused to fly again when he heard that a Cambodian wedding party had been razed by B–52s.

As one Cambodian villager put it in April 1973: "The bombers may kill some Communists but they kill everyone else, too." In May 1973 the *New York Times* reported that "extensive" destruction had wiped out "a whole series of villages" along the main highway, including seven villages in the east of the country, with many people killed. Nothing was left standing for miles: "a few people wander forlornly through the rubble, stunned by what has happened, skirting the craters, picking at the debris." Correspondent Sidney Schanberg noted: "The frightened villagers uprooted by the bombing have a great deal to say." One refugee requested politely, "I would be very glad if the Government would stop sending the planes to bomb," while a Buddhist monk pleaded with the U.S. government, "Don't destroy everything in Cambodia."[42]

But in July and August 1973, the Southwest Zone of Cambodia was carpet-bombed. It was the most intensive B–52 campaign yet. The impact of this bombing in the Southwest was not simply to destroy many more civilian lives. Politically, it tipped what had been a delicate CPK factional balance there,[43] in favor of Pol Pot's "Center" group.

This political effect of the U.S. bombardment reached the highest level of the CPK in the Southwest Zone, its ruling Party Committee. In 1973–74, four of the six leaders of this zone committee were purged. Two of these CPK moderates were murdered by Pol Pot's warlord ally Mok. The other two were killed after 1975, when the Southwest became the stronghold of the Pol Pot regime, and Mok went on to purge all other zones in the country.

During the 1973 bombing, a similar process occurred at the local level. In one village in the Southwest, eighty people died when B–52s hit the village and its pagoda.[44] Nearby Wat Angrun village was annihilated; a single family survived, and 120 houses were destroyed in the air raid, peasants told me.

This part of the Southwest was one of the strongholds of the CPK Center. In 1973, Mok's son-in-law, the local deputy CPK secretary, was promoted to become chief of a new Southwest Zone Brigade, and his wife became district chief.[45]

The CPK were now able to recruit many peasants by highlighting the damage done by U.S. air strikes. The CIA's Directorate of Operations, after investigations in the Southwest Zone, reported on May 2, 1973, that the CPK had launched a new recruiting drive:

> **They are using damage caused by B–52 strikes as the main theme of their propaganda.** The cadre tell the people that the Government of Lon Nol has requested the airstrikes and is responsible for the damage and the "suffering of innocent villagers." . . . The only way to stop "the massive destruction of the country" is to . . . defeat Lon Nol and stop the bombing.
> This approach has resulted in the successful recruitment of a number of young men. . . . Residents . . . say that **the propaganda campaign has been effective** with refugees and in areas . . . which have been subject to B–52 strikes.[46]

Mam Lon, a CPK cadre in the Southwest, says that when T–28s and B–52s bombed his village, more than 100 people were killed and wounded. "The people were very angry at the imperialists," he adds. Soon afterward the CPK's political line hardened, and a number of cadres, including Lon himself, were dismissed.[47]

Early in 1973, the CPK began a new purge of Sihanoukists, pro-Vietnamese Communists, and other dissidents. Mok rounded up hundreds from all over the Southwest Zone. They were forced to perform hard labor before being executed.[48]

In the Northern Zone of the country, where Pol Pot himself was based, B–52s struck Stung Kambot village one morning in February 1973. They killed 50 villagers and seriously wounded 30 others. Then in March, B–52s and F–111s bombarded an ox-cart caravan in the same district, killing 10 peasants. One local man recalls that "often people were made angry by the bombing and went to join the revolution."

A peasant youth, Thoun Cheng, says B–52s bombed his village three to six times per day for three months. Over 1,000 people were killed, nearly one-third of the population. Afterward, Cheng says, "there were few people left . . . and it was quiet."[49]

Chhit Do was a CPK leader near Angkor Wat in northern Kampuchea. In 1979, he fled the country. Australian journalist Bruce Palling asked him if the Khmer Rouge had made use of the bombing for anti-U.S. propaganda:

Chhit Do: Oh yes, they did. Every time after there had been bombing, they would take the people to see the craters, to see how big and deep the craters were, to see how the earth had been gouged out and scorched. . . . The ordinary people . . . sometimes literally shit in their pants when the big bombs and shells came. . . . Their minds just froze up and they would wander around mute for three or four days. Terrified and half-crazy, the people were ready to believe what they were told. . . . That was what made it so easy for the Khmer Rouge to win the people over. . . . It was because of their dissatisfaction with the bombing that they kept on cooperating with the Khmer Rouge, joining up with the Khmer Rouge, sending their children off to go with them. . . .
Bruce Palling: So the American bombing was a kind of help to the Khmer Rouge?
Chhit Do: Yes, that's right. . . . Sometimes the bombs fell and hit little children, and their fathers would be all for the Khmer Rouge. . . .

On August 3, 1973, U.S. aircraft bombed the hill village of Plei Loh, home of Montagnard tribal people. An American agent reported after a follow-up mission that "the village was totally destroyed, with 28 civilians and five VC guerrillas killed."[50] The next day, B–52s attacked nearby Plei Lom village, "killing twenty people, including children."[51] On August 10, Plei Lom was bombed again, killing 30 Montagnards.[52] On the same day B–52s struck nearby Plei Blah village: 50 died. The U.S. Army report on this noted that "the Communists intend to use this incident for propaganda purposes."[53]

Another report to the U.S. Army in July 1973 stated that "the civilian population fears U.S. air attacks far more than they do Communist rocket attacks or scorched-earch tactics."[54] Up to 150,000 civilian deaths resulted from the U.S. bombing campaigns in Cambodia from 1969 to 1973.

In 1991, accused of not having been very candid about the 1969–70 bombings, former U.S. Secretary of State Henry Kissinger replied: "My quick response is that journalists keep saying 'bombing Cambodia.' We were bombing four Vietnamese divisions that were killing 500 Americans a week."[55] In a longer response, Kissinger made the sarcastic claim, "We destabilised Cambodia the way Britain destabilised Poland in 1939."[56] His memoirs state, "It was Hanoi—animated by an insatiable drive to dominate Indochina—that organised the Khmer Rouge long before *any* American bombs fell on Cambodian soil."[57]

Kissinger's view *at the time* was more perceptive. In a 1974 cable to Phnom Penh's U.S. embassy, he had pointed out that in areas like southwest Cambodia, the Vietnamese were actually in conflict with Khmer Communists, who "not only had little training abroad but probably resent and compete with the better-trained men from North Vietnam." "The Khmer Communists, such as Saloth Sar [Pol Pot]," he said with prescience, "are probably xenophobic . . . when it comes to Vietnamese."

In 1974, Kissinger was unsure if the Cambodian insurgency was "regional" and "factionalized" with only "a veneer of central control," or whether "the real power" lay with Pol Pot's central presidium.[58] The tragedy is that the former had been largely true in 1972, the latter was largely true in 1974, and Kissinger and Nixon were largely responsible for the change. Attempts on their part to rewrite the record are not surprising.

CPK cadres told young peasant victims of the bombing that "the killing birds" had come from Phnom Penh (not Guam), and that Phnom Penh must pay for its assault on rural Cambodia.[59] On the day the bombing ended, CPK propaganda leaflets found in bomb craters attacked the "Phnom Penh warriors" who were, they vowed, soon to be defeated.[60] The popular outrage over the U.S. bombing, predictably manipulated by the CPK, was as fatal for the two million inhabitants of Phnom Penh as it was for moderate Khmer Rouge and for Lon Nol's regime.

In April 1975, when CPK troops took the country's second largest city, Battambang, they headed straight for the airport. There they found two T–28 tactical bombers of the defeated Lon Nol air force. They tore the planes apart, with their bare hands, according to a witness. "They would have eaten them if they could," he added.[61] When they forcibly evacuated Battambang and Phnom Penh, CPK forces told the urban population that the exodus was necessary because American B–52s were about to bomb the city. The second phase of the Cambodian tragedy had begun.

Notes

1. See Ben Kiernan, *How Pol Pot Came to Power* (New York: Routledge, Chapman, and Hall, 1985), chaps. 3 and 4.
2. Laura Summers, "Introduction," in Khieu Samphan, ed., *Cambodia's Economy and Industrial Development* (Ithaca: Cornell University Southeast Asia Program Data Paper No. 111, 1979), 13.

3. Michael Maclear, *Vietnam: The Ten Thousand Day War* (London: Methuen, 1981), 129–30.

4. Noam Chomsky, *American Power and the New Mandarins* (London: Chatto & Windus, 1969), 221, note 11, citing "official Pentagon figures." See also Maclear, *Vietnam*, 130, for another U.S. estimate that guerrilla strength in 1965 had shown "an increase of thirty-three percent over 1964."

5. See Kiernan, *How Pol Pot Came to Power*, 228.

6. Rémy Prud'homme, *L'Economie du Cambodge* (Paris: P.U.F., 1969), 255, table 12, note *a*.

7. Kiernan, *How Pol Pot Came to Power*, 228–29, 285.

8. Ben Kiernan, "Put Not Thy Trust in Princes: Burchett on Kampuchea," in B. Kiernan, ed., *Burchett: Reporting the Other Side of the World, 1939–1983* (London: Quartet, 1986), 252–69.

9. William Shawcross, *Sideshow: Kissinger, Nixon and the Destruction of Cambodia* (London: Deutsch, 1979), 65, 24; and Seymour M. Hersh, *The Price of Power: Henry Kissinger in the Nixon White House* (New York: Summit Books, 1983), 177–78.

10. Hersh, *The Price of Power*, 178–79.

11. Shawcross, *Sideshow*, 27.

12. Kiernan, *How Pol Pot Came to Power*, 286.

13. Norodom Sihanouk, *My War with the CIA* (New York: Penguin, 1973), 56; Kissinger, quoted in Hersh, *The Prince of Power*, 180, and in T.D. Allman, *Unmanifest Destiny: Mayhem and Illusion in American Foreign Policy from the Monroe Doctrine to Reagan's War in El Salvador* (New York: Doubleday, 1984), 342. Kissinger's credibility on such matters is undermined by the memorandum of a December 18, 1975, meeting, in which he lambasted his staff for committing to writing their interpretation of U.S. law concerning arms support for the Indonesian invasion of East Timor: "that will leak in three months and it will come out that Kissinger overruled his pristine bureaucrats and violated the law. ... You have a responsibility to recognize that we are living in a revolutionary situation. Everything on paper will be used against me . . . it will be a national disaster." See "Minutes of the Meeting: The Secret Life of Henry Kissinger," *Nation*, October 19, 1990, 473, 488–93.

14. Richard Hall, *The Secret State: Australia's Spy Industry* (Sydney: Cassell, 1978), 133. Hall adds: "If this is true it might explain why the Australian MO9 head of station was away on leave. . . . Australia maintained two MO9 agents in the [Phnom Penh] embassy and they carried out a variety of tasks for the Americans, although they were not part of the coup operation—indeed the senior MO9 man was out of Cambodia on leave when the coup occurred. His number two was a fairly junior man, certainly not experienced enough to have helped play a major role in a coup." MO9 operations in Cambodia specifically included "assisting the CIA" (8). Another Australian organization, the Australian Secret Intelligence Service, was apparently credited by George Bush with having performed "unique operations" for the United States in Cambodia. Canberra denies any ASIS role in Sihanouk's overthrow. ASIS reportedly "provided a vital link with the Australian Embassy in Cambodia during the 1970 coup." Brian Toohey and Marian Wilkinson, *The Book of Leaks* (Sydney: Angus and Robertson, 1987), 117, 121.

15. Author's interviews with Prom Thos, Paris, February 12 and June 3, 1980. In 1959, a 471-page study entitled "Psychological Operations: Cambodia" had been commissioned by the Pentagon to identify groups "susceptible" to American influence, but found that Cambodians "cannot be counted on to act in any positive way for the benefit of U.S. aims and policies." Shawcross, *Sideshow*, 55.

16. Hersh, *The Price of Power*, 179.

17. Much of the following is from Allman, *Unmanifest Destiny*, 337–39 (letters from Thornton cited on page 438); and Hersh, *The Price of Power*, 179–81.

18. Author's interviews with Prom Thos, Paris, 1980.

19. Hersh, *The Price of Power*; and Allman, *Unmanifest Destiny*; see note 17 above.

20. Allman, *Unmanifest Destiny*, 337–39; and Hersh, *The Price of Power*, 179–81.

21. Kiernan, *How Pol Pot Came to Power*, 301.

22. Milton Osborne, Melbourne *Age*, January 12, 1971.

23. T.D. Allman, *Unmanifest Destiny*, 339.

24. Shawcross, *Sideshow*, 117.

25. Hersh, *The Price of Power*, 178, 181.

26. Quoted in Allman, *Unmanifest Destiny*, 342.

27. Ibid., 342–43.

28. Hersh, *The Price of Power*, 202.

29. George C. Hildebrand and Gareth Porter, *Cambodia: Starvation and Revolution* (New York: Monthly Review Press, 1976), 109, note 83. They cite interviews conducted with Khmer refugees in 1971 by the General Accounting Office, Congressional Record, April 18, 1973, S7812.

30. A longer, fully documented version of this section appears in "The American Bombardment of Kampuchea, 1969–1973," in the inaugural issue of *Vietnam Generation* 1, 1 (winter 1989): 4–41, available from 2921 Terrace Drive, Chevy Chase, MD 20815.

31. See Kiernan, *How Pol Pot Came to Power*, 323, for the full quotation.

32. Shawcross, *Sideshow*, 218–19.

33. See Kiernan, *How Pol Pot Came to Power*, 349–57, for further details.

34. Charles Meyer, *Derrière le sourire khmer* (Paris: Plon, 1971), 405–6.

35. "Cambodia: Can the Vietnamese Communists Export Insurgency?" *Research Study*, Bureau of Intelligence and Research, U.S. Department of State, September 25, 1970, 4, 6.

36. Author's interviews with Som Yan and others, O Reang Au, October 6, 1980.

37. Ibid.

38. Author's interviews with Chin Chhuon, Chhai Chhoeun, Khim Veng, and Yem Yiem, at Ampil Tapork, October 6, 1980; and author's interview with Sang, O Reang Au, October 6, 1980.

39. Author's interviews with Song Rus and others, Prek Chrey, October 7, 1980.

40. United Press International dispatch, *Boston Globe*, April 1, 1973 (emphasis added).

41. Dana Adams Schmidt, *Christian Science Monitor*, April 5, 1973.

42. *New York Times* reports of April 11 and May 24 and 27, 1973, quoted in Edward S. Herman and Noam Chomsky, *Manufacturing Consent: The Political Economy of the Mass Media* (New York: Pantheon, 1988), 277–78.

43. Kiernan, *How Pol Pot Came to Power*, chap. 8, esp. 314 ff., 331 ff., 340–47.

44. Author's interviews with Kus villagers, July 16, 1980.

45. Ibid., and author's interview with Ieng Thon, Tram Kak, July 16, 1980.

46. "Efforts of Khmer Insurgents to Exploit for Propaganda Purposes Damage Done by Airstrikes in Kandal Province," Intelligence Information Cable, May 2, 1973, three-page document declassified by the CIA on February 19, 1987 (emphasis added).

47. See Kiernan, *How Pol Pot Came to Power*, 354–55, for references.

48. Nou Mouk, interview with the author, Oudong, August 26, 1981.

49. Author's interview with Thoun Cheng, Ubon, March 13–14, 1979. For the full account of Cheng's experiences, see Ben Kiernan and Chanthou Boua, eds., *Peasants and Politics in Kampuchea, 1942–1981* (London: Zed, 1982), 330–34.

50. U.S. Army Bomb Damage Assessment, August 20, 1973.

51. U.S. Department of Defense, Intelligence Information Report, No. 2 724 2014 73, dated August 16, 1973.

52. U.S. Department of Defense, Intelligence Information Report, No. 2 724 2083 73, August 23, 1973.

53. Ibid., and U.S. Department of Defense, Intelligence Information Report, No. 2 724 2116 73, August 27, 1973.

54. "Effectiveness of U.S. Bombing in Cambodia," U.S. Army document dated August 21, 1973, 2. Declassified April 7, 1987.

55. Kissinger in reply to a query by UPI's Helen Thomas, on Cable News Network TV, Bill Moyers Program, "The Press Goes to War," January 26, 1991. Kissinger immediately added: "And we were informing major leaders of Congress of that event. And we were waiting for somebody to protest, so that we could ask for a UN investigation."

56. Bruce Page, "The Pornography of Power," in Anthony Barnett and John Pilger, *Aftermath: The Struggle of Cambodia and Vietnam* (London: New Statesman, 1982), 43–53, at 51.

57. Quoted in Page, "The Pornography of Power," 45.

58. "Emergence of Khmer Insurgent Leader Khieu Samphan on the International Scene," cable from Secretary of State to U.S. Embassy, Phnom Penh, April 1974, 4 pp.

59. Staffan Hidlebrand, personal communication.

60. U.S. Department of Defense, Intelligence Information Report, "Bomb Damage Assessment, Cambodia," No. 2 725 1716 73, August 22, 1973, 2.

61. David P. Chandler, Ben Kiernan, and Muy Hong Lim, *The Early Phases of Liberation in Northwestern Cambodia: Conversations with Peang Sophi* (Clayton, Australia: Monash University Centre for Southeast Asian Studies, Working Paper No. 10, 1976), 3.

Part Four

Retrospective and Postwar Issues

15

The War That Should Not Have Been

General Tran Van Tra

Eighteen years have elapsed since the end of the prolonged and atrocious U.S. war in Vietnam. But it is hard to know how long its political, economic, social, and moral consequences will continue to be felt in Vietnam and in the United States. It is usually said in the East that bitter fighting will bring about better understanding and mutual affection. What is harmful for our two nations is that so far, the friendship between us has not yet been restored.

Undoubtedly, the war originated from the wrong U.S. perception that identified many postwar liberation movements with communism. The war was also the product of President Harry Truman's Cold War policy against the USSR and against China after 1949.

By the end of 1949, the aim of the U.S. administration was to check the further expansion of communism in Asia and, therefore, Indochina immediately became an important front. Assistance was given by the United States to France for intensifying its colonial war starting with $110 million, and that sum rapidly increased until it accounted for 70 to 80 percent of French military expenditures in Indochina. When France became conscious of the inevitability of its defeat and began to negotiate a peace agreement in Geneva, it came up against the firm opposition of the United States, which demanded that France continue the war to keep Indochina within the Western orbit. The U.S. National Security Council then stated that the U.S. aim was no less than a military victory. Therefore,

Originally entitled "The War Which Should Not Have Broken Out, that Should Not Have Gone on So Long and Could Have Ended Differently than Was the Case."

233

Vietnam, a small, poor, and backward country, ruled by colonial France for nearly 100 years, now became a victim of the Cold War.

Vietnam is a nation with several thousand years of history marked by a great determination to defend its independence and freedom. It carried out a successful revolution in August 1945, but was subsequently compelled to fight a difficult war for nine years. On several occasions, during this conflict, Vietnam had to make concessions for the sake of peace: the Preliminary Agreement of March 6, 1946; the Modus Vivendi of September 14, 1945; and then the 1954 Geneva Agreements. Even so, Vietnam could not escape the calamities heaped on it by the big powers.

After other Vietnamese political parties had failed as a result of French repression, President Ho Chi Minh and the Communist Party of Vietnam assumed the mission of national salvation and enjoyed the confidence and solidarity of the entire people. The Party and President Ho Chi Minh's line, which was a combination of patriotism and socialism—advocating the happiness and dignity of human beings—elicited a strong positive response from the whole nation. This positive energy, brought about by the will and determination of a whole nation, was translated into a material power: the readiness to sacrifice everything for independence and freedom.

However, the leaders of the American administration at the time did not understand the strength of Vietnam's nationalism as reflected in Vietnam's age-old history, particularly by the defeat inflicted by the Vietnamese people on Yuan Mongolian invaders in three successive wars (within 30 years) during the thirteenth century. At that time, Vietnam, known as the Dai Viet Kingdom, had a population of barely six million, but defeated nearly one million enemy troops from an empire with an army that had conquered most of Europe and half of Asia, and that was preparing to invade Southeast Asia and India in a bid to become the master of the world.

In 1954, the Dien Bien Phu victory was a great encouragement to the Vietnamese people, giving them justified confidence in their own strength and the wise leadership of the Vietnamese Workers' Party and President Ho Chi Minh, and in their hope for an independent, free, and unified Vietnam that would build its own happy future.

Shortly afterward, the leaders of the U.S. administration brought to power Ngo Dinh Diem, a feudal mandarin who had served the French colonialists and then the Japanese militarists; this arrangement was designed to set up an administration that would serve the U.S. purpose of making South Vietnam a separate, anti-Communist state within the orbit of the West. The United States also provided Diem with a well-equipped army of 150,000 and put South Vietnam under the protection of the Southeast Asia Treaty Organization (SEATO) bloc.

Obviously, U.S. policy did not take into account the age-old burning aspiration of the Vietnamese for freedom. This oversight contains in itself the fundamental cause of the U.S. defeat. Should we ascribe this negligent attitude of U.S. leaders to their arrogant overconfidence in material power, modern weaponry, and wealth of a superpower—both in human and material resources? Was it also those leaders' arrogance that caused them to treat small, backward, and poor Vietnam with contempt, riding roughshod over public opinion both in the world and in the United States (a nation known for its traditions of justice and democracy)?

A policy that goes counter to the wishes of the people can in no way win victory, only temporary success, if any. The wishes of the Vietnamese people are peace, national independence and unity, general welfare and happiness. The Geneva Agreements of 1954 recognized these wishes and fixed July 1956 as the date for nationwide elections for the purpose of national reunification. If all parties had respected this international commitment and allowed the Vietnamese people to decide their fate for themselves, the war would not have raged for another twenty-one years. This war ultimately led to the realization of the long-held national aspirations of the Vietnamese people, that is, to achieve peace, independence, unity, and territorial integrity. Yet, tens of thousands of Americans and millions of Vietnamese had to die and the country had to suffer massive devastation before a post-1975 Vietnam could return to a situation that should have prevailed as early as 1956. This situation would have occurred much earlier if the Geneva Agreements had been observed.

The Geneva Agreements were disavowed and the general elections canceled. Furthermore, a dictatorial family rule, under Ngo Dinh Diem, was imposed on the people of South Vietnam. It was a government that tried to maintain its rule by force of arms, jails, and bloody repression (including the use of mobile scaffolds). It even murdered those who opposed its views, labeling them Communists. All these actions constituted acts of war by the United States and Ngo Dinh Diem against the Vietnamese people. We in Vietnam described that period as the period of unilateral war because we acted in accordance with the appeal of President Ho Chi Minh, who called for strict adherence to the Geneva Agreements, by waging only political and peaceful struggles in our demand for general elections, and not to resort to armed struggle. This policy was also reflected in numerous statements and appeals made by the government of the Democratic Republic of Vietnam and letters sent by the latter to the governments concerned.

It is hard to describe accurately how a nation angered to the extreme by the ruthless and barbarous repression of the Diem government could abide strictly by the instruction of President Ho Chi Minh and the leadership of the Vietnam Workers' Party. At that time, those who resorted to arms to defend themselves were disciplined by the Party for erratic behavior, while those who refrained from violence were captured and/or killed. It was clear that the Vietnamese side, both in North and South Vietnam, tried its best to maintain peace and ensure a correct implementation of the Geneva Agreements, but all these efforts were of no avail because of the U.S. policy of preventing Southeast Asia from falling into the Communist orbit.

It was only long after the expiration of the date specified for holding general elections under the Geneva Agreements that an increasing number of South Vietnamese, on their own initiative, resorted to the use of guns. This demonstrated that the situation had developed beyond the limits of self-restraint. South Vietnamese officers and soldiers who went to the North under the Geneva Agreements demanded that they be allowed to return to the South in order to defend the people. The minds and feelings of tens of thousands of these soldiers constantly focused on their families and friends being subjected to massacres in the South. This spiritual mood of "living in the North during the day, but dreaming about the South at night" spread quickly to the people of North Vietnam who naturally nurtured deep feelings for their fellow countrymen in the South. A whole nation stood up for the right to live and maintain their dignity as human beings.

It was amidst this pressure from a whole mass movement that, in 1959, the Workers' Party of Vietnam adopted Resolution 15 which resulted from an analysis of actual conditions prevailing in the country. The analysis concluded that only the path of mass revolution could solve the situation, since peaceful and legal struggle had proved to be ineffective. Thus, the people of South Vietnam could take the initiative in staging an uprising and soldiers born in the South could return there without any hindrance.

When a whole nation, under wise leadership, resolutely stands as one for independence, freedom and unity, no force however powerful and modern in weaponry can prevent it from fulfilling its aim. With this situation, the people would be creative enough to provide themselves with all the necessary means, methods, and forms of struggle in order to survive and emerge victorious. But it was the policy of the United States to win by military means, using the "flexible response" strategy to counter any form of struggle of the people.

The war started and developed in this way. It was an American war designed to counter world communism but it was imposed on the Vietnamese people and fought on Vietnamese soil.

Such a war could have been avoided if due respect had been given to the right of human communities for freedom and democracy, to the aspirations of each nation to live its own way.

Any type of war (including nuclear war), any political theory, any culture, or any political institution cannot be imposed successfully—and would sustain a devastating defeat—if it runs counter to the interest of the overwhelming majority of the people.

The mass uprising in South Vietnam brought about the birth in 1960 of the National Front for the Liberation of South Vietnam (NLF) headed by a lawyer, Nguyen Huu Tho. The NLF was the inevitable product of the revolutionary mass movement in the country, and comprised all strata of the people, regardless of their political predilections. The NLF advocated an independent, democratic, peaceful and neutral South Vietnam that would be ruled by a national and democratic coalition government and would establish diplomatic relations with all countries, regardless of their social regimes. National reunification would be carried out step-by-step and peacefully.

These policies enjoyed very broad support among the people of South Vietnam and gained approval of the people in North Vietnam. The policies were welcomed by progressives throughout the world.

Another valuable opportunity could thus be seized to quell the flames of war and bring about peace in Vietnam and Southeast Asia by recognizing the NLF and its correct policies. At that moment, a new administration assumed power in the United States, led by President John F. Kennedy. The realities in South Vietnam were these: the Diem administration had become a family dictatorship, owing its continued existence to U.S. dollars and arms; the regime had enriched itself on the blood of the people and had been rejected and opposed by the people; and the NLF had emerged as a force enjoying the broad support of the whole of Vietnam, advocating moderate and reasonable policies. In view of this situation, the new U.S. administration should have adopted more realistic policies involving the return to the Geneva Agreements or the encouragement of some other approach that might help restore peace and friendship. There was indeed a reasonable chance for the war to end in 1961. Instead, the new American administration went on with its policy of war and deeper intervention in Vietnam, making use of the "flexible response" strategy of General Maxwell Taylor. This strategy was none other than the continuance of the Cold War policy against the USSR and the liberation movements of oppressed nations. Following an inspection tour by Vice President Lyndon Johnson to South Vietnam in May 1961, the United States decided to commit troops to combat operations. Thus, the unilateral war had become a war between two opposing sides: a war of aggression waged by the United States, and a war of liberation mounted by the people of South Vietnam. The immense U.S. war machine rolled on, with increasing intensity, motivated by the determination to achieve military victory and the U.S. aim—as once interpreted by Diem—to extend the U.S. frontier to the 17th parallel in Vietnam.

Successive U.S. administrations ordered their armed forces—considered the mightiest in the world, equipped with the most modern arms and composed of troops that had never suffered defeat—to come tens of thousands of miles to a foreign land in order to wage a war unlike any other war. It was neither a full-fledged guerrilla war nor a conventional one. It had no front line, no rear. U.S. troops had to fight an invisible enemy, about whom they knew very little. They had to wander through the countryside, forests, and hills to "search and destroy" the enemy—an ever-present foe who could be found even in the most important rear base areas and who could even take the initiative in attacking U.S. command headquarters. Furthermore, the objectives of the war were not clear. They were not in the interest of the American people; they were neocolonial in character, and therefore could not elicit the support of peace- and justice-loving people of the world, including the majority of the American people.

Under these conditions, it was impossible for the United States to be victorious. Yet, President Johnson chose to fight communism, to oppose Soviet and Chinese communism by fighting the Vietnamese Communists in their homeland, thinking perhaps that this fight would be easy and would certainly result in victory. When he was vice president, Johnson did tell President Kennedy that the fight against communism in Southeast Asia should be prosecuted with vigor and with the determination to win victory. Johnson assumed the presidency when a number of opportunities had presented themselves that could have been advantageous to any effort to bring about peace and avoid a local war that would be most atrocious and costly to the United States and Vietnam in material resources and human lives.

At the end of 1963 and in early 1964, the NLF called on Duong Van Minh, who had replaced Diem as president, to start negotiations with the NLF to organize free elections. President Ho Chi Minh also sent a message to President Johnson proposing peace talks. French president Charles de Gaulle was willing to act as an intermediary to help bring about compromise and peace. UN Secretary-General U Thant also proposed that Washington support a coalition government in South Vietnam. The new president of South Vietnam, General Duong Van Minh, also expressed a desire for talks, free elections, a neutral policy, and a coalition government in South Vietnam. The Buddhist and student movements in South Vietnam strongly protested against the war and demanded a solution involving neutralization of South Vietnam.

Having suffered greatly from the prolonged war, almost all Vietnamese, and all the opposing parties in Vietnam, including the two opposing sides in the South, earnestly desired peace talks, coalition and neutrality.

The world and the UN secretary-general supported the wishes of the Vietnamese people, but the United States stood alone in ignoring these desires, preferring instead to continue and intensify the war with the unyielding desire to make South Vietnam an anti-Communist state. President Johnson rejected all peace talks and all neutralist tendencies. He instructed Ambassador Henry Cabot Lodge to crush any talk of neutrality the moment it surfaced. Duong Van Minh was then replaced by Nguyen Khanh who truculently called for "a march to the North." With the massive commitment of troops to the war effort, the United States launched a local war in southern Vietnam as the second rung of the "flexible response" strategy while conducting a destructive air war against North Vietnam.

Thus, a golden opportunity to put an end to the war and restore peace was callously discarded in favor of intensifying the war. This was indeed a very unrealistic, mistaken, truculent and arrogant approach to resolving the conflict in Vietnam.

The events involving the General Offensive–General Uprising during Tet 1968 constitute a decisive turning point in a ferocious war that had gone on too long and finally brought the contending parties to the negotiation table in Paris. But no armistice was signed; the peace talks were inconclusive. These were fighting-cum-peace talks. Under such conditions, the developments on the battlefield impacted heavily on the talks. War was still raging in South Vietnam, while the air war against North Vietnam also went on—though more limited in scope. Even while seated at the negotiation table, the United States still wanted to proceed from a position of strength. The talks therefore dragged on without results, but both sides tried to keep the talks and contacts going on as a prime necessity.

The Tet events did inflict losses—much heavier than before—on the U.S. and Thieu forces, but they were quickly replaced and provided with more equipment; the number of troops reached its highest level of the war. The "search and destroy" strategy was replaced by one of "sweep and hold." With increased troop strength and equipment, the U.S. armed forces launched massive "sweep" operations coupled with an accelerated pacification program and the notorious Phoenix Project. The result was a marked U.S. superiority on the battlefield from 1969 to 1970. The liberation forces sustained so many losses (much heavier than during any previous period) that they could not be replaced fast enough to carry out normal operations. They also had to face extremely arduous conditions under repeated enemy assaults. A large portion of the guerrilla units mobilized to attack the cities during Tet had also sustained losses that could not be made up in time for new operations. These grass-roots units also had to deal with the enemy's new pacification schemes and the Phoenix program.

During this same period, the U.S. administration thought that victory was near at hand. The extension of the war to Cambodia in 1970, following the overthrow of Sihanouk, and the operation against Route 9 in southern Laos in 1971 were designed to completely surround and destroy the Viet Cong, thus ending the war with a total victory for the United States and Thieu. Under these conditions, the Paris talks would have to wait for new developments on the battlefield before concluding an agreement. During this period, we in Vietnam had to do our utmost on the battlefield not to sustain further reverses, while we strove to replenish and build up our strength and enhance our fighting capacity. In 1972, we took the initiative in launching new attacks which resulted in numerous victories in Quang Tri province, in *Sa-thay* (the High Plateau area), and in Loc Ninh (north of Saigon). Again the developments on the battlefield impacted heavily on the negotiation table and in October 1972, both sides came to an agreement. But it was only after the failure of the most ruthlessly destructive air raids of the U.S. Air Force against Hanoi and Haiphong (twelve days and nights of continuous attacks in December 1972) that the Paris Agreement could be concluded.

The United States did properly implement the provisions of the Paris Agreement on the complete withdrawal, within sixty, days of U.S. troops, as well as those from other countries. However, U.S. equipment, including modern weaponry such as the F5E aircraft and CBU bombs were given to the Thieu army. Moreover, a large quantity of arms and ammunition was ferried to South Vietnam, thus providing the Thieu regime with huge stocks of war material. All this was designed to help the Thieu army successfully continue Washington's "Vietnamization of the war" strategy, that is, to bring about the gradual annihilation of the Viet Cong and therefore cause the war to fade away from view. South Vietnam would thus be maintained as a viable state within the Western orbit, an objective which many years of war had failed to achieve. Therefore, the United States condoned and supported Thieu in all his attempts to break the Paris Agreement. Indeed, Thieu refused to enforce a cease-fire, continued mopping-up and land-grabbing operations, set up thousands of new military posts and strongholds in areas that the Thieu troops could invade and occupy under their so-called "Ly thuong Kiet" [ed note: the eleventh–century Vietnamese general] program of operations.

As for the forces of the Revolution, both the NLF and the government of North Vietnam committed mistakes. After 1954, we were too confident that the Geneva Agreements would be abided by and implemented. After January 1973, we again were under the illusion that the Paris Agreement would be adhered to. The only difference was that after 1954, we continued the peaceful struggle and waited for that agreement's implementation (five years) before taking action. But the waiting period only lasted five months in the case of the Paris Agreement, since we learned from our experiences in the 1950s. It was clear that both international agreements were not implemented.

I was instructed to withdraw from combat and come to Saigon on January 28, 1973—the day the cease-fire would take effect—in order to take part in the work of the Four-Party Joint Military Commission and discuss measures for the proper implementation of the Paris Agreement. I was also given the task of exploring the establishment of a three-party coalition government for a peaceful and neutral South Vietnam. Such an historic mission filled me with genuine joy and I felt confident that this task could be carried out successfully.

Meanwhile, liberation forces on the battlefields received their orders: establish contacts with the opposing forces in a spirit of conciliation; do not fire upon moving enemy troops or those located in these bases; withdraw all forces from areas controlled by the enemy and bring them back to our areas for resupply and regroupment, as well as to avoid military confrontations. Because of this, Thieu's army enlarged its occupation zones by invading new territories as the liberation forces, who did not want to be accused of violating the Paris Agreement, chose to withhold their fire and withdrew.

Perhaps the United States and Thieu truly understood our genuine desire to abide by the peace accords, as reflected in actions which involved the rearrangement of forces for the purpose of a strict implementation of the agreement. But it was also quite certain that the theme of the "exhaustion" of the Viet Cong and North Vietnamese was very much on the minds of the other side, who clung to the idea of winning a complete victory. They had set out since the beginning of the war to attain this objective. Thus a wrong assessment of oneself and of the adversary will inevitably lead to error and danger.

History would surely have reserved many surprises for us if Thieu had not so truculently violated the Paris Agreement after 1973 and if the United States had not carried on its Vietnamization policy. Indeed, we can catalog more what-ifs that would have altered the course of history: If the withdrawal of U.S. troops had not been coupled with the maintenance of the Thieu regime and a strong army; if the implementation of the 1975 and 1976 plans designed by the Defense Attache Office (DAO) to cause a fade-out of the war by driving the Viet Cong into fifteen isolated base camps had not been carried out; and if those same planners had never wanted to annihilate the liberation forces to give Thieu a total victory in 1977 or 1978—if all these things had never taken place, the history of Vietnam might certainly have taken a different course. The prospects would have been numerous: the restoration of peace in South Vietnam as early as 1973; a three-component coalition government in power; the possibility that the United States would shift from a military assistance program to one of economic aid; and, in the end thereafter, gradual reunification of Vietnam by peaceful means. Of course, what could have stopped the war and brought peace to Vietnam early in 1973 was dismissed and the bloodshed had to continue for two more years before an end could be put to it in 1975.

Such a peace would certainly have brought honor to all sides; there would have been no victors or losers. Justice would have been the sole victor. One could add that the Vietnam War certainly would have been assessed in a different way, and the modern history of Vietnam could have been written quite differently from how it is today.

The Vietnam War started in 1945 as an attempt by France to recover a lost colony and continue its rule of Vietnam. The same war was given continuance and a new character from 1954 onward: It was part of a policy to check the advance of Chinese Communists southward (as part of an extreme anti-communism ideology and the Cold War). Vietnam became a test site for the "flexible response" strategy and various modern weapons. The Vietnamese people had to suffer from callous injustice and ruthless terror during the war, just because they wanted to have an independent, free and unified country. Young men from the United States and other allied countries did not shed their blood in the interest of their own people; indeed, they died fighting against a people that held no enmity whatsoever for their country.

For humanity, war is immoral. The war waged against the Vietnamese people was even more immoral because it did not serve the interests of either of the two belligerents; its only aim was to impose the domination of one nation over another, impose the ideology (way of thinking and way of life) of one group on another. Many opportunities arose for putting a reasonable end to the war, in the interest of peace and honor for all sides, but they were not taken advantage of.

Let us allow each and every nation to think and act in the way they think best for their homeland. It is our firm view that revolution can never be exported and that the ideology and culture of one nation cannot be imposed on another nation. Peace must be safeguarded by all means and friendship among nations must be promoted throughout the world. This is the aspiration of humanity as a whole, particularly in the nuclear age.

Because of the suffering and extreme losses suffered during the war, the Vietnamese people appreciate the value of peace all the more and deeply aspire to live in harmony with other nations. These feelings and aspirations are certainly shared by freedom- and justice-loving Americans, particularly the families that have lost their kith and kin in the war. Given their experiences in the war, American and Vietnamese veterans can better understand the value of peace and would never like to see such a war break out again in any part of the world.

16

The American War in Vietnamese Memory

Luu Doan Huynh

The liberation of South Vietnam in 1975 was greeted by the Vietnamese people with joy, relief, and pride. Of course, this feeling has been somewhat eroded among people who now feel that their contribution to the national cause was not duly recognized or who are depressed by various economic difficulties.

The peasantry and the laboring people proudly believe that Vietnam, a small and poor country, defeated U.S. imperialism—sometimes they simply say "America" instead of "U.S. imperialism." But sophisticated people make a clear distinction: Vietnam could not defeat the United States because we had neither the will nor the capacity to land troops on her shores; furthermore, since we considered the American people to be our friends, how could we talk about defeating them? Therefore, one can only say Vietnam defeated a war of aggression waged against it by the U.S. government, by U.S. imperialism.

As time went by, our victory was overshadowed by new problems. Many sections of the population came to the realization that this great victory was now a matter of history and that the present task was to develop the economy—a task of decisive importance for the future and happiness of Vietnam—a criterion by which the leadership and the present generation will be judged.

That the history of war is solely written by the victors is an erroneous bit of conventional wisdom. Vietnamese historians do not think they can write history as they like, taking liberty with the facts. Indeed, the past few years have been marked by controversies and debates concerning the various military plans and maneuvers during the war and the role of various forces (both military and political) in winning the war. I am looking forward to the day when contacts and exchange of opinions can be carried out between military and diplomatic historians of both the United States and Vietnam for the benefit of a more balanced account and analysis of the Vietnam War. This will help promote a rapprochement between the two peoples.

As is known, the war brought to the Vietnamese people a great amount of suffering, far greater than for the American people, in terms of devastation, casualties, and so forth. Overcoming these consequences involved far greater difficulties for Vietnam in view of the poverty of the country.

Vietnam has a large number of war veterans, wounded and disabled soldiers whose lives are affected not only by war-inflicted wounds and the aftereffects of toxic chemicals but also by economic difficulties and the distress caused, in many cases, by the inability of their children to have an adequate education. We also have a large number of widows and missing persons as a result of the war, much larger than the number of U.S. MIAs. Furthermore, undetonated bombs and mines continue to kill and wound many peasants and woodcutters.

The government and people of Vietnam have to cooperate in overcoming or at least alleviating these consequences. The respect and affection of the population is an important source of comfort to our veterans and their families, as reflected, among others, in the provision of "houses of affection."* Further, I cannot but touch on the devotion of our women for their husbands, the veterans. I met a soldier who, having lost both legs in the war, married and now has two children. Every afternoon, his wife carries him to the bridge over the pond in their village, so that he can bathe.

Since 1975, many families have never given up in their efforts to find and bring back the remains of their sons killed on various battlefields for burial in the home cemeteries and all without requesting any help from the government. In Ho Chi Minh City alone, there are 37,000 known cases of Vietnamese MIAs of this type, and so far the remains of some 20,000 have been recovered. Also, many families have been trying, through ads in the newspapers and television, to find out the whereabouts of their relatives missing since 1945: fathers fighting in the regular army, mothers arrested for revolutionary activities in enemy-occupied areas, children left to the care of other people.

What is remarkable to me is that all these efforts have been accompanied by virtually no anti-American outbursts.

I would be less than frank if I concealed the fact that during the war we all hated the U.S. government and its leaders. I met a peasant woman soon after an air raid that killed her husband. She told me that she had four sons in the army and would ask her youngest one to go to the front when he was old enough to avenge his father.

But now, a decade after the end of the war, a change in thinking has taken

---

*"Houses of affection" are homes built by the community and provided free to veterans or parents of dead soldiers.

place. To many, the war is over, and it is now time to build up new ties. More knowledgeable people argue that Vietnam is now independent and reunified, and there is no longer a reason to consider the United States as the enemy. There is no particular contradiction in terms of national interest between the two nations.

Many officials and ordinary people still blame the U.S. government for adopting a hostile attitude toward Vietnam. The July 18, 1990 statement of Secretary of State James Baker on opening a dialogue with Vietnam was welcomed by some and treated with suspicion by others. But with regard to the American people, everyone in Vietnam adopts a friendly attitude as testified by the warm welcome given to American visitors. Why is this so? Because of the old habit of making a distinction between the U.S. government (the bad guys) and the American people (our friends) on account of the U.S. antiwar movement. Perhaps it is also because the very fact that Americans visit is, in our view, a mark of solicitude.

We in Vietnam love French films for their wit and sense of fun. For a few years now, some American films, among them "Platoon," have been shown on television. Some people like them more, some less, but their screening has not caused any anti-American comments.

What may become a problem for relations between our two peoples is that many Vietnamese do not understand U.S. internal politics and the agonizing debate in the United States about the Vietnam War. Also, a number of officials and ordinary people are still apprehensive about CIA-aided attempts at subversion.

During the war, we in Vietnam felt deep sympathy and gratitude for the antiwar movement in the United States and other countries but were reminded by our leadership that while antiwar movements were a great help to us, our own efforts and sacrifices should be the decisive factor in attaining victory.

The antiwar movement in the United States has struck me in many ways. The Anglo-Saxon world has been notorious for its saying, "my country, right or wrong. . . ." Yet the American people went out of their way and treated the war in Vietnam with fairness: many felt that justice is on the side of the Vietnamese people. The Quaker ship bringing medical supplies to Vietnam in spite of the Seventh Fleet, the poems of Barbara Beidler, the sit-ins, the demonstrations, all spoke of a spontaneous movement, feelings coming from the heart. The resignation of high officials in protest against the war; the presence of priests and businessmen in the protest movement; all these are, to my mind, indications of a great nation.

And now, many years after the end of the war, many Americans are still discussing, pondering over the Vietnam War, with nearly 7,000 books published on this topic. This shows that the American people are a responsible nation, seriously trying to draw lessons from past experience in order to formulate a better path for the future.

I still remember the names of some U.S. statesmen who have committed grave crimes against my people: Johnson, McNamara, Dean Acheson, Dean Rusk,

Cabot Lodge. To be fair and objective, however, I must say that these persons, once they recognized the futility of their attempts, were willing to steer a different course, as testified by the decision of President Johnson and his "Wise Men" in March 1968. They did not openly acknowledge their error, but at least they, in effect, renounced their criminal course of action. Of course, that was the result of the valiant struggle of the Vietnamese and American people, but the final action of these men somehow reflects an important feature of the American nation: that is, not to stubbornly cling to what is wrong and doomed to failure. We now have good relations with France, but I must say that France had to form a new government, with a completely new set of leaders and military commanders, to be able to come to terms with Vietnam after Dien Bien Phu.

While making clear my personal admiration for the fairness and honesty of the American people, particularly with respect to the war that ravaged my country, I cannot fail to mention the bad losers in the United States. We also have to deal with our own bad winners. I believe, however, that both of these groups do not represent the main and long-term trends of the two nations.

Therefore, I think that now we should and can forget the past bitterness engendered by the war, overcome its consequences in Vietnam and in the United States, and make the most of the positive elements that these years of suffering have created or evidenced:

• The strength of Vietnam's nationalism should be acknowledged.
• The humanity, honesty, and fairness of the American people should be recognized.
• The war greatly harmed relations between our two countries. These relations had been peaceful and friendly since the nineteenth century and ought to have been so since 1945. The war has brought the two nations closer, and the day will come, I hope, when the American people will agree that an end to the Vietnam War was indeed a victory for both nations.

We will try to convince the Vietnamese people that at present there is no basic contradiction in terms of national interest between our two countries, and we hope that America will no longer regard Vietnam as its enemy.

I believe that after the normalization of relations, U.S. policy on Vietnam will no longer run the risk of failure because the United States will be dealing with a self-respecting nation, genuinely attached to its independence and to relations of cooperation with all nations on the basis of equality and mutual benefit. Also, perhaps the United States now has a better understanding of the Vietnamese people. Above all, it is my hope that in the next five or ten years, both nations and their governments shall refrain from any act or statement that might give rise to new misunderstandings or hatreds.

Overcoming the sufferings and bitterness left over by the war, developing a consensus on diversifying foreign relations, and focusing efforts on national development and welfare are the general objectives now taking shape in Vietnam. While not going into the reasons for such a mood, I will only stress that the iron is now hot, and that is a positive fact, for both nations.

I am happy to share with you some of my thoughts and feelings, as I appreciate the constructive attitude of Americans seeking to understand the war.

17

The Vietnam War in American Memory

Marilyn B. Young

I recently asked my students what images they had of the Vietnam War. The heat, one said; the smell, said another, and a third, the noise. They were eighteen- and nineteen-year-old Americans who went to movies about Vietnam as if to the country itself and remembered the movies later as would one a trip to another country. They remembered hearing the soft whoosh of helicopter blades from *Apocalypse Now* and their eyes stung from the dust and heat of the opening scene of *Platoon*. Young Americans have little difficulty inserting themselves into these movie memories because, like most of the novels and memoirs, *Vietnam, the Movie* is mainly populated by Americans at war with an unseen enemy. The country is an unchanging jungle stage set, a faraway place where bad things happened to Americans who regrettably did bad things in turn.

So fixed is war-torn Vietnam in American memory that it often takes American tourists by surprise to find the country at peace. My students, like many, perhaps even most, Americans, remember the Vietnam War as something that happened among Americans. Indeed, the film that many American Vietnam veterans say is closest to their remembered combat experiences of patrol and ambush—*Platoon*—makes the Americanization of the war explicit: "We didn't fight the enemy in Vietnam," the hero declares at the movie's end, "we fought ourselves." The Vietnam War, in short, was a civil war, but—and this may puzzle the Vietnamese—it was an *American* civil war.

There is a sense in which this reading of the war is quite accurate. More divisive than any conflict Americans have engaged in since the Civil War, the Vietnam War raised questions about the nation's very identity. These questions

248

have not been settled. The battle over interpreting the Vietnam War is a battle over interpreting America and it continues to the present day. George Orwell summarized the significance of such struggles in his novel *1984*: "Who controls the past controls the future: who controls the present controls the past."

The Persian Gulf War has been a classic illustration of Orwell's dictum. The enemy in the Gulf was only in part Iraq. Equally, the Bush administration sought to defeat an older enemy, the memory of defeat in Indochina twenty years ago. Beyond this, the warmakers have hoped to convert victory over Saddam Hussein into monopoly control over how the Vietnam War is understood and remembered. It is for this reason that the presentation of the war in the Gulf was so closely monitored by the Bush administration. The press operated under censorship more rigorous than in any war the United States has ever fought, including World War II. President Bush and the military said that what they had learned from Vietnam was how to fight a war: fast, hard, massive.

But in fact the major lessons were not so much how to fight as how to market a war. As a product, the Vietnam War had been a distinct disappointment, and so the new sales force shaped their marketing strategy in the light of the old sales statistics. For example, early in the war, General Norman Schwarzkopf pointed out that inflated "body count" figures had led many Americans to distrust military press briefings. Therefore, there would be no body counts in this war. Through more than a month of bombing and a week of ground fighting, no estimates of Iraqi losses were ever offered, nor did the press demand them. The result was a televised war relatively innocent of dead bodies; a war that, except for the bombing of the Baghdad shelter and the desperate oil-soaked cormorants, would not spoil one's dinner. By the end, it had become possible to believe that the enemy were not people at all, but machines; that the tanks, buses, and cars that jammed the highway out of Kuwait City had fled on their own, that their charred hulks contained no human remains. There was thus a purity to the U.S. victory that successfully masked its savagery. "It's Vietnam revisited as it should have been," the historian Robert Dallek told a reporter, "Vietnam: The Movie, Part II, and this time it comes out right."[1] The war that was represented as a video game, the Nintendo War, has already appeared as a videocassette entitled "Schwarzkopf: How the War Was Won."[2]

Victory in the Gulf was intended to restore to Americans a vision of their country they had lost over the course of the Vietnam War, a vision featuring the belief that Americans could not commit atrocities, that wars undertaken by the United States were always just wars, that no foreign will could prevail over that of the United States, that Americans could not lose wars. From the point of view of the government, the widespread public realization that none of these propositions was any longer true constituted a real and present danger, an intolerable constraint on the making of foreign policy. For the journalists, historians, writers, whose task it is to interpret America to itself, the collapse of familiar paradigms has often been equally intolerable. One solution has been to separate out the origins of the war from its conduct. An April 1975 *Washington Post* editorial put the issue very clearly: " . . . if much of the actual conduct of the Vietnam policy over the years was wrong and misguided—even tragic—it cannot be denied that some part of the purpose of that policy was right and defensible." And wherein lay that right and defensibility? In the "hope that the people of South Vietnam would be able to decide on their own form of government and social order."[3]

The editorial writer was not being cynical. Of course he or she had available many reams of documents which made it explicit that the only criteria for a government in the South were its anti-communism and its readiness to take U.S. military direction. But the dedication of the United States to the rights of all people to self-determination had always been a fundamental element in America's national identity. This dedication was not contingent but axiomatic. And without the conviction that whatever the United States did expressed a commitment to universal self-determination, U.S. intervention was in danger of looking like an invasion of a foreign country; this was simply not acceptable, not even thinkable. The editorial writer concluded on a high note: "The American public is entitled, indeed obligated to explore how good impulses came to be transmuted into bad policy, but we cannot afford to cast out all remembrance of that earlier impulse."[4] It is important to pause here and note the contorted urgency of the editorial writer's injunction: the country *cannot afford not to remember* its benevolent intentions. Thus, to remember, in this instance, *requires* forgetting.

Most efforts to contain the wasting effects of the war on America's self-vision have preserved the myth of the benevolent origin of the war by focusing criticism on its tactics. A lengthy bibliography in that mode has been produced by civilians like Norman Podhoretz and military men like Harry Summers. Some of these analysts argue that the war in the South was largely irrelevant; the United States should have concentrated its efforts against the North. Massive bombing of Hanoi combined with mining Haiphong Harbor are frequently cited as likely to have won the war for the United States had they occurred early enough. Other writers insist that counterinsurgency was never really given a chance. The war in the South was a revolutionary war which could only have been countered by tactics that combined politics and force, as did those of the National Liberation Front (NLF) itself. Both approaches acknowledge that the tactics employed caused terrible destruction, but that way they also protect the reader from having to confront more fundamental issues: condemning the tactics leaves the basic policy intact, uncriticized.

To my knowledge, only one book has gone all the way and sought to alleviate the pain of war memories by exculpating the tactics as well. In the first book-length account of the war published after 1975, *The United States and Vietnam*, Guenter Lewy, like many critics of the way the war was fought, argued that "big unit" war as General Westmoreland pursued it had been counterproductive. The United States should have concentrated its efforts on pacification and counterinsurgency. But the trauma of Vietnam, Lewy believed, lay elsewhere. Young people in America lacked national pride and self-confidence because they were under the mistaken impression that "illegal and grossly immoral conduct" on the Vietnam battlefield had been "officially condoned." Lewy does not deny that such conduct occurred, only that it was policy. "Examined dispassionately," he wrote, "American actions in Vietnam lend no support to the accusations of criminality or of gross immorality with which America's conduct of the war is charged."[5]

None of the weapons the United States used, Lewy pointed out, violated international conventions. Napalm was just a technologically more advanced form of that ancient weapon of war, fire. He found no evidence that herbicides directly endangered people's health; cluster bombs had not been banned internationally, nor, for that matter, had white phosphorous. There was no "firm" evidence that the shackling of political prisoners caused organic paralysis; the deliberate creation of refugees was permissible under extant international rules of war and in any case, refugee camps, however unpleasant, were "not out of line with the local standard of living." It was urgent that this be understood, Lewy goes on, for "the simple reason that Vietnam continues to haunt our minds and continues to exert a powerful influence on our conception of ourselves as a nation and of our role in the world."[6] Note that Lewy's book was published in 1978, only three years after the war had ended. Given the usual lead time for books to appear in print, it is likely that he began writing it in 1976 or even earlier. Yet he seems surprised that Vietnam should continue to bother people.

Lewy's argument, like the reassurances offered by the *Washington Post* editorial affirming the benevolence of American intentions, rested solidly on the premise that the United States had a legal and moral right to be fighting in Vietnam in the first place. Without this first premise, the tactics employed, legal or illegal, officially condoned or condemned, are irrelevant to Lewy's enterprise. For it is impossible to fight a criminal war with justice.

One way or another, every presidential reference to the war, every book, every movie, every TV serial on the war has dealt with the same question: who were we, as a nation, that we fought that war? Who can we be now, having fought such a war? In the main, most have denied any exploration of the possibility that the war was, in origin and prosecution, criminal. Instead, the ongoing effort has been to restore belief, to recuperate an unblighted national identity. There are similarities here to the way American historians have long found it difficult to confront the origins of the nation in genocide, or its long history as a slave power, preferring always a discussion of tactical choices rather than fundamental structures.

On the other hand, the issues of national identity evoked by the Vietnam War are so fundamental they are also foundational. Some of the Vietnam literature seeks explanations and, if possible, exculpation in the nation's originating history. While Guenter Lewy can represent the historians who try to cleanse the Vietnam War so that it can be remembered in an untroubled fashion, Loren

Baritz's *Backfire: A History of How American Culture Led Us into Vietnam and Made Us Fight the Way We Did* is a more complicated effort to find a way to understand Vietnam, to make sense of its apparent madness by placing it in the coherent context of the nation's entire history.

Baritz's history begins and ends with the nation's dominant creation myth, which casts America as the Christian city on a hill, the country with a message for all mankind, the nation that will set the example for all nations and usher in the millenium. He is certainly correct in identifying the popular vision of national identity, a belief in the unique moral stature of the United States, a conviction that has enabled policymakers to pursue self-interest in the name of global benevolence. Baritz is illuminating in drawing out the connection between this belief and the missionary rhetoric of the Vietnam War. But then, oddly, he himself grows reluctant to let go of the myth. "An important reason we marched into Vietnam," he writes, "was liberalism's irrepressible need to be helpful to those less fortunate. But the decency of the impulse . . . cannot hide the bloody eagerness to kill in the name of virtue."[7]

He does not write: liberalism's irrepressible need *to represent itself* as helpful to the less fortunate. And by not writing this, he leaves unscathed what is precisely the essence of the myth: that liberalism *does* have "a need to be helpful to those less fortunate." In thus losing or refusing the opportunity to deconstruct a national myth he himself holds responsible for the war, Baritz's book typifies a particular kind of liberal scholarship that rejects the war and the *warmakers'* interpretation of the liberal nation without abandoning the myth of the liberal nation itself. Such scholarship seeks to wipe the shame of Vietnam from the national escutcheon without leaving a stain.

America, Baritz concludes his book, "must be for freedom, for dignity, for genuine democracy, or it is not America. *It was not America in Vietnam"*[8] (emphasis added). Then who was it? The idea that the United States is something apart from its history, or from parts of its history, casts this country in the religious mode, one that has throughout world history served to justify more killing and destruction than any other. Arguing that America was not "itself" in Vietnam, Baritz, who has identified the Puritan myth of the city on a hill as a rationale for the war, marches right back up the hill.

Baritz's book is the text for most of the Vietnam movies. In an essay entitled "War Stories: Movies, Memory, and the Vietnam War,"[9] William Adams observes that the movies incorporate Vietnam into an American symbolic universe: "the wilderness, scene of violence and desire, trial and temptation, ordeal and rebirth." In that familiar setting, the hero (or antihero; it comes to the same thing) of *Platoon, Full Metal Jacket, Off Limits,* or any of a dozen other Vietnam movies, provides the audience with "a subtle form of compensation." In the midst of the most terrible suffering, violence, and horror, familiar cultural tropes are reproduced: the rough equality of combat, a distrust for authority "cushioned by a vague and sentimental patriotism," pluralism. "The compensatory aspect of these works," Adams writes, "is precisely the notion that the American character endures, in spite of this painful episode, in the darkly charismatic, antiheroic and concrete characters who suffered and ultimately survived it." Films about Vietnam, moving between narrative poles of innocence lost and virtue sustained, are the "inevitable and inevitably awkward consequence of the attempt to retell an event that threatens the very framework of collective comprehension."

On the other hand, all these movies and books form only a part of the national memory. It is quite unclear what Americans at large actually remember about the Vietnam War. This is a problem that concerns those in charge very deeply. Successive presidents have issued public rules for remembering. President Carter, while accurately reflecting how damaged postwar America felt, refused to face the asymmetries of the damage, insisting instead that the United States owed Vietnam nothing because "the destruction was mutual." No public figure or news analyst questioned his accounting. President Reagan went one step further and suggested that the war should be enshrined in public memory as a noble crusade.

All the postwar administrations have been troubled by what they see as a disease the country caught in Southeast Asia, a kind of spiritual flu: the "Vietnam Syndrome." Officials defined the syndrome as a regrettable aversion to sending American troops overseas to kill other people for reasons that seemed less than compelling to the citizenry. Although Reagan in Grenada and Libya and Bush in Panama sought homeopathic cures for the syndrome, the public resistance to military adventures they knew about in advance held firm, as all newspaper polls on the Persian Gulf crisis prior to January 16, 1991 demonstrated. Here we can see what might be called the active memory of Vietnam at work, which was given voice when reporters asked people's opinion about the possibility of war in the Middle East. In one poll, only 1 out of 10 people questioned supported an immediate military move in the Gulf; 7 out of 10 said war should not even be considered until the economic blockade had been given a chance to work; and 2 out of 10 said they would oppose war in the Gulf under any circumstances.

Clearly recalling the Gulf of Tonkin, 47 percent of those questioned told a reporter that if Bush charged Saddam Hussein with having "provoked" a war *they would not believe him*. Remembering the same event, Congress kept shaking a warning finger at Bush—don't you dare make war behind our backs. "If there is a provocation," Representative Dante Fascell declared, "it's got to be a real one . . . it can't be two whales passing in the night. It has to be something that can stand the scrutiny of the media, and of the public, and of history."[10] Needing a war but lacking a provocation, and with Vietnam constantly in mind, the Bush administration chose to gamble on a debate on the issue of war in Congress. It won the gamble, but the result is not unambiguous: it will be more difficult for future presidents to commit the country to war without the full participation of the U.S. Congress.

Before the Gulf War, public distaste for new military engagements derived, with different degrees of awareness, from another way in which Vietnam was remembered. Apart from the ways in which young people identified with veterans, or their parents argued the merits or demerits of the Vietnam War, there remained a residue of feeling, too deep for easy articulation, from which no American who lived through the war is free. It consists of iconic images of the war: the Saigon officer, in his American flak jacket, shooting a bound, unarmed guerrilla in the head; a child running from a cloud of napalm, her hands upraised, her body burning; the women and children massacred at My Lai; the terrified ARVN soldiers pulling helicopters out of the sky in their desperate effort to escape from the failed invasion of Laos; the dead students at Kent State; the GIs throwing their medals back at the government; the faces of women imprisoned in the tiger cages.

One index of the power of such images is reflected in the extent to which viewers this time around did not seem to want to know more about the war than the military would tell them. Reporters complained, but many Americans insisted they were satisfied to know less about the Gulf than they had been forced to know about Vietnam.[11] It was clear from the repeated images of targets being blown up in both Iraq and Kuwait that the Coalition fighter bombers were well equipped with cameras. Yet the slaughter of the retreating Iraqi army was never televised. "I got a little bit sick when I saw this," an American soldier said of the heaps of bodies by the side of the road—but to my knowledge there have been no pictures of what was disturbing him.[12] The meaning of the Gulf War and its relation to Vietnam was succinctly summarized by a pair of pictures which ran in many newspapers in early March 1991: one shows U.S. Marines clamboring out of a helicopter that has landed on the roof of the U.S. embassy in Kuwait City. The other, of course, is the classic picture of the helicopter on the roof of the U.S. embassy in Saigon, loading fleeing Americans.

In every respect, Vietnam was the negative template for the Gulf War. Discomforting moments in the Gulf were read back to the past and reversed. One curious example was an account General Norman Schwarzkopf gave of the second biggest weekend in the general's life (the first, obviously being the launching of the ground war). In August 1965, the general told R.W. Apple, Jr., he had been pinned down at a Special Forces camp in the Vietnamese highlands near Pleiku. "Then a major assigned as an adviser to South Vietnamese forces [Schwarzkopf], found himself surrounded by thousands of Vietcong and North Vietnamese troops advised by Chinese Communist officers." Despite "constant pounding of enemy mortar and heavy machine-gun fire" Schwarzkopf and his men held out, albeit reduced to eating rice and fish sauce.[13] In this story, the American is besieged, but he holds out. Indeed it takes "thousands" of the enemy to pin him down. His presence is explained by the assertion of a matching "alien" force—the Chinese Communists. It does not matter that no history of the war, however pro-American, has ever alleged that in 1965 the NLF and the North Vietnamese had Chinese advisers in the field.

For the past twenty years many of us have been struggling against one or another revisionist version of the Vietnam War. This was an important thing to do not only because we cared about objective history but because we knew that the Reagan and Bush administrations were making an enormous effort to overcome the reluctance of the American public to use military force as an instrument of policy. Policymakers believed they could cure the Vietnam Syndrome by small, concentrated doses of military action—Libya, Grenada, more daringly, Panama. This, finally, is what the Gulf War has been about. As President Bush put it in a "spontaneous burst of pride" on the day after the cease-fire in the Gulf, "By God, we've kicked the Vietnam Syndrome once and for all." For much of Congress and the press, the lessons of Vietnam were that the American public would not for any length of time tolerate an undeclared unilateral U.S. war with high American casualties. The administration ticked off this list of requirements and met them all: Bush secured U.N. support through a combination of bribe and threat, parlayed success in the U.N. into success in Congress, ignored opinion polls that up to and including the January 15 deadline favored economic sanctions, and launched an air war of unparalleled force against Iraq. By ignoring Iraqi efforts to negotiate, Bush could deliver to the public a total military victory at very low cost in U.S. lives.

But for many of us the shame of Vietnam has lain in the intervention, not the defeat, and not only in the intervention but in the punishment the United States has meted out to Vietnam ever since. The very goals of the United States in Vietnam were what we opposed, not the failure to meet them. After the Russian war in Afghanistan, the Soviet foreign minister told his legislature that the government had "violated the norms of proper behavior," gone "against general human values," taken the decision for war "behind the backs of the party and the people." But no American president or secretary of state has acknowledged that the United States invaded Vietnam against our stated values and ideals, that it did so secretly and deceptively, fighting a war of immense violence in order to impose its will on another sovereign nation. Because coming to grips with this reality has never been on the checklist of prerequisites for renewed military interventions, the barrier against war provided by the Vietnam Syndrome was always partial.

Yet the fragmentation of national identity that occurred during the Vietnam War has not been, indeed cannot be, mended; the old national identity cannot be recuperated, but only reshaped, transformed. The nature of that transformation is what the struggle over how Vietnam should be remembered is all about. There is no automatic, necessary connection between the way a war is fought, nor even what it is fought for, and its impact on national self-consciousness. The Korean War, in terms of the weapons used, the casualties inflicted and suffered, and the widespread popular doubt about American war aims, resembled Vietnam in many ways. During the first three months of the Korean War, 7.8 million gallons of napalm had been dropped, and by November 1950, Bomber Command was grounded because, as its commander testified in Congress, "there were no more targets in Korea." Senator Stennis applauded this news, assuring Major-General O'Donnell that he had "demonstrated soldierly qualities that endeared [him] to the American public." Despite the apparent lack of targets, the bombing of whatever was left of North Korea resumed in the summer of 1952 with a ferocity matched only by the Christmas bombing of North Vietnam twenty years later. In July and August 1952, 697 tons of bombs and 10,000 liters of napalm were dropped on Pyongyang, killing 6,000 civilians. In May 1953 North Korean dikes and dams were heavily bombed, destroying the rice crop. There was no public outrage nor any questioning of the national character.[14]

In the wake of the Korean War, there was a brief period of national soul-searching but its focus was the alleged cowardice of American prisoners of war. This became the grounds for a kind of domestic psychological and ideological warfare campaign stressing the need for continued mobilization against communism and stricter Army discipline. What was wrong with Americans in Korea, according to one Army spokesman, was a "new failure in the childhood and adolescent training of our young men—a new softness."[15] The war itself disappeared almost without a trace.

Until the Gulf War, there was reason to feel confident that the same could not happen to Vietnam. Then, in the immediate aftermath of that war, there was reason to fear that any accurate remembering of its history would be buried in an avalanche of confetti, yellow ribbons, and flags. But the Gulf War proved to be the nation's first fully disposable war: use it once and throw it away. It may not serve to deter future "clean" wars, but it has also left Bush's confident prediction as to the fate of the Vietnam Syndrome open to serious doubt.

The Vietnam War marked not the loss of national innocence but the loss of belief in it. Rid of such illusions, Americans may begin to define the national identity as a product of the history of the United States rather than of its myths. Remembering Vietnam is central to this possibility.

"We won the [Vietnam] war after we left," General Westmoreland boasted recently "Today, Vietnam is a basket case. . . ."[16] But as Tom Wicker has pointed out, "The U.S. is not really Number One in anything but military might, which is not always usable or effective. . . ."[17] Westmoreland's dictum may this time be reversed: we shall lose the war after we have won it.

Notes

1. Peter Applebome, "Sense of Pride Outweighs Fears of War," *New York Times*, February 24, 1991, section 4, 3

2. Randall Rothenberg, "If You Liked Him in the War, You'll Love Him in the Video," *New York Times*, March 15, 1991.

3. *Washington Post*, April 30, 1975, quoted in Noam Chomsky and Edward Herman, *After the Cataclysm: Postwar Indochina and the Reconstruction of Imperial Ideology* (Boston: South End Press, 1979), 8–9.

4. Ibid.

5. Guenter Lewy, *The United States in Vietnam* (New York: Oxford University Press, 1978), vii; and Lewy "Vietnam: New Light on the Question of American Guilt," *Commentary* 65, 2 (February 1978): 49.

6. Lewy, "New Light," 49.

7. Loren Baritz, *Backfire: A History of How American Culture Led Us Into Vietnam and Made Us Fight the Way We Did* (New York: William Morrow, 1985), 42.

8. Ibid., 341.

9. William Adams, "War Stories: Movies, Memory, and the Vietnam Era," *Comparative Social Research* 11:1989.

10. For prewar poll data, see Michael Oreskes, "Poll Finds Strong Support for Bush's Goals, but Reluctance to Start a War," *New York Times*, October 11, 1990. See also, "Poll Finds Americans Divided on Sanctions or Force in the Gulf," *New York Times*, December 14, 1990.

11. William Boot, "The Press Stands Alone," *CJR*, March/April 1991.

12. Quoted in Christopher Hitchens, "Minority Report," *Nation*, March 25, 1991, 366.

13. R.W. Apple, Jr., "The General Tries Not to Seem Confident," *New York Times*, February 29, 1991.

14. Gavan McCormack, Jr., *Cold War, Hot War: An Australian Perspective on the Korean War* (Sydney: Hale and Iremonger, 1983), 126, 124.

15. Quoted in Eugene Kinkead, *In Every War but One* (New York: W.W. Norton, 1959), 156.

16. Fox Butterfield, "Voices From the Past Sound Out Again," *New York Times*, January 25, 1991.

17. Tom Wicker, *New York Times*, February 27, 1991.

18

The Antiwar Movement
after the War

David Hunt

A Second Homeland

The Paris antiwar meeting was coming to a close when they passed the microphone to Jean-Paul Sartre. "*Ils se battent pour nous,*" he began. "They fight for us." Trying not to be conspicuous, the well-meaning, but befuddled graduate student I was then (December 1966) rose along with everyone else to hail this declaration of solidarity with the Vietnamese Revolution. The evening had already shocked me more than once, as Trotskyites and Maoists rocked the hall with their chants, and, in response to documentary footage of Robert McNamara alighting from a helicopter, the crowd hurled imprecations against U.S. imperialism. Chain-smoking and scowling at the audience, Sartre posed an even more disturbing challenge: "They fight for us." But who were "they"? And how could they be fighting for people in France, let alone in the United States?

As it wrestled with such questions, one segment of the antiwar movement stopped couching its opposition to U.S. intervention on grounds that it was damaging American interests and sensibilities and began to argue that victory for the National Liberation Front (NLF) would best serve the Vietnamese people as well as the people of the United States. This shift was the product of a fundamental turn in understanding, feeling, commitment. It was a collective discovery of the world and a self-discovery, operating at many levels, down to the texts we helped each other find and interpret. Scanning my bookshelves and thinking back, I pick at random: Wilfred Burchett, *Vietnam: Inside Story of the Guerilla War* (the Communists were fighting for social justice, we were the enemy); Tom

258

Hayden, *The Love of Possession is a Disease with Them* (the NLF's liberated territory was "Indian country," racist violence was rooted in U.S. history); Alfred McCoy, *The Politics of Heroin in Southeast Asia* (the CIA trafficked in heroin, the rulers were criminals). Vietnam helped us see the world in a different way.[1]

Participation in the antiwar movement eventually led me to study the Vietnamese Revolution in the Mekong Delta province of My Tho. The Rand Corporation interviews with NLF defectors and prisoners of war that I explored brought to life the inferno created by U.S. intervention, as bombing and shelling, troop sweeps, and the destruction of crops spread terror and heartbreak throughout the province. Interviewees recalled sleepless nights hiding in canals and bunkers, napalm burning rice fields just before the harvest, traumatized children starving to death.[2]

During this ordeal, many Vietnamese lifted themselves to a very high level of devotion. When interrogators asked about the core of militants who remained in the villages, defectors usually spoke with respect of the people, mostly poor peasants, they had left behind. I couldn't take it anymore, they would say, but the cadres deep in the liberated zone, in Cai Be and Cai Lai districts, they'll never give up.

The interviews revealed that NLF activists were no cartoon characters seated around campfires singing Vietnamese folk songs. Some quarreled over promotions, slept with each other's spouses, or stole from the village treasury. Hardbitten, ruthless fighters, they were inured to suffering and prepared to kill those who stood in their way. But hatred alone did not explain the behavior of men and women who again and again were identified by their former comrades as revolutionaries. They were struggling to create a world in which Vietnam would be independent, peasants would be "masters of the countryside," and everyone would be "free to work and free to enjoy." Even defectors could not hide their lingering fondness for these watchwords or their hope that others would not desert a cause they no longer had the strength to sustain. NLF militants clung to each other with a love that all the fury of U.S. escalation could not undo, and in the process they achieved a mastery over circumstances that would have broken the will of a lesser movement.

The people we became and the lives we have lived because of the war were shaped by the Vietnamese. Ramifications of the guerrilla struggle are woven into the fabric of U.S. society and politics, in the awareness and experience of every person in this country, and not least for those on the left who came to think of Vietnam as a second homeland. As the Vietnamese would say, the war changed the balance of forces that we face. What interventions would Washington have launched if the guerrillas had not resisted and then found a way to defeat the United States? And who would we be, how would we understand the world and ourselves, if they had not stepped forward to teach us?

They did fight for us, and we came to love them for it.

End of a Romance

Soon after 1975, my attention turned from Vietnam. The liberation of Saigon occurred at a painful moment in my life, and today I recall the mid-seventies as a personal watershed. Besides, I was a historian of France, not of Vietnam, and could not even read Vietnamese. To leave a mark as a scholar—and as I approached forty, this ambition became more urgent—it seemed that my focus should be on French history.

I continued to teach about the war, but not about Vietnam after 1975, and, without an analysis of current events, I found myself evading student questions concerning the postwar situation. When Joan Baez and others criticized "reeducation camps" in Vietnam, they did not spell out the moral and political principles for treating former enemies that the Vietnamese were being castigated for violating. But still I was disturbed by these precipitous defections from the antiwar coalition. Soon younger vets claiming that there were U.S. prisoners in Indochina and Vietnamese students with harrowing personal testimonies began to appear at University of Massachusetts/Boston. Assuming that the Rambo phenomenon was crazy and that boat people could not tell the whole story, I found myself unable to deal with the passion of their anti-communism, which depended on an interpretation of the Vietnamese Revolution after its victory. The Kampuchea/Vietnam/China War that began in 1978 deepened this perplexity. Increasingly, I lacked the means to counter images of a Vietnamese gulag, of U.S. prisoners in cages, of Hanoi imperialism spreading across Indochina.

Recalling this failure aroused my curiosity about the Left in general since 1975.[3] A quick review suggested that many progressive publications ignored Vietnam after the liberation of Saigon, while others offered an analysis that sooner or later reached an impasse. *Socialist Review* has printed no articles on Vietnamese politics and society since 1975. Paul Lyons's excellent "Teaching the Sixties," published in 1985, is about debates in the United States. It offers welcome references to veterans, including women veterans, and notes that in this country the Vietnamese version of events is usually ignored. But Lyons himself says little about Vietnam.[4]

In 1979, *Socialist Review* published an editorial on the Kampuchea/Vietnam/China War that dealt with the Sino-Soviet split rather than with internal dynamics in Indochina. Its main point was that "the American left's indepen-dence from uncritical identification with existing socialist countries will be of mounting importance for its ability to act politically in this country." The reaction was understandable, given that the Vietnamese had first refrained from public criticism of the Khmer Rouge, then, in conjunction with their invasion, switched to a lurid and nonanalytic denunciation of democratic Kampuchea. In *Brother Enemy*, Nayan Chanda demonstrates that Hanoi feared that public criticism of Pol Pot would widen the gulf between Vietnam and China and preclude a peaceful resolution of the crisis.[5]

This less than candid posture embarrassed U.S. sympathizers who continued to insist on the veracity of Vietnamese leaders, but it is not the central issue raised by the conflict. The geopolitical, state-centered editorial in *Socialist Review* is not so much wrong as incomplete. It does not weigh our obligations to the peoples of Indochina.

Coverage elsewhere has also been meager. George Black's "Republican Overtures to Hanoi" in the *Nation* is a fascinating discussion of right-wing support for normalization of relations with the former enemy, but I have not retained any articles from the *Nation* on Vietnamese internal affairs. *Radical America* and *In These Times* have neglected the postwar history of Vietnam, though the latter should be credited with publishing Paul Joseph's strong "Vietnamese Trying to Find a Way Out" and other pieces on the war in Kampuchea.[6]

In the years after 1975, *Monthly Review*'s extensive coverage posited a happy ending after the war. "The socialist reconstruction of Vietnam should inspire an even stronger and more resilient international solidarity," Tran Van Dinh declared in 1976. His "Why and How the Vietnamese Won the Vietnam War," published in 1978, is a celebratory treatment. In a similar register, Kathleen Gough evoked the "dedication," "sense of purpose," "superb organization," "deep love of country," "zest for life," and "sense of fun" of the Vietnamese, who were making "amazing progress" toward a better life. Her "Green Revolution in South India and North Vietnam" praises the Vietnamese model, cited for its egalitarianism, full employment, and abolition of exploitation, its rational planning and superior productivity.[7]

These optimistic statements make painful reading today. In 1979, Vietnam again plunged into war, international solidarity gave way, and the Vietnamese found themselves almost completely isolated. Favorable comparisons with other nations had to be abandoned as mounting evidence demonstrated that Vietnam was one of the poorest countries in the world. Along with others on the Left, *Monthly Review* in the 1980s stopped talking about a Vietnamese reality that mocked the analysis we had inherited from the antiwar movement.

Aside from useful specialized publications such as *Indochina Newsletter* and *Indochina Issues*,[8] the *Guardian* is the only journal in the United States that has continued in recent years to write about Vietnam. After the war, it offered extensive treatments, for example, in articles by Wilfred Burchett in 1977 and Richard Ward in 1978. Their reports stressed the gravity of the situation, but the overall impression conveyed is of a well-organized, mass-based state moving forward. More cautious than Tran Van Dinh and Kathleen Gough, they share with the *Monthly Review* correspondents a fundamental optimism. Progress was slow, but the Vietnamese knew what they were doing and were on the right track.

The tone of *Guardian* coverage changed in the early 1980s. In "Vietnam Combating Capitalism's Comeback," published in 1983, Waldo Bello begins with a warning: "Socialist construction in Vietnam is headed for deep trouble unless decisive steps are taken to rein in the free market." The drift "to the right," a "retreat" comparable to the New Economic Policy in the Soviet Union, had begun in 1979. It consisted of encouraging "small-scale private production in both countryside and city while radically slowing down collectivization; and creating a system of differential material incentives to bring about local initiative and efficiency." In the process, reformers were handing over power to a new bourgeoisie, which was gaining control of strategic and other commodities and of the agrarian economy.[9]

In the same vein, Abe Weisburd criticized the reforms of July 1979,

> which gave free rein to the private sector in the circulation of goods, causing astronomical increases in prices, unconscionable profits, widespread corruption, usurious interest rates, and increased speculation and smuggling. Massive theft by government workers and cadre of state-supplied raw materials and equipment for use in the legal private enterprises also resulted, causing severe drains in the economy.

Fortunately, Weisburd declared, "tough laws have been recently enacted to rein in an expanding capitalist sector, which now controls 70% of all goods in circulation."[10]

By 1985, a more positive emphasis was found in such articles as Karen Gellen's "Vietnam's New 'War.'" The reforms that had been regarded with suspicion by Bello and Weisburd two years earlier were now described as "strikingly new methods of stimulating production and rationalizing an inefficient wage, price and distribution system." Whereas the earlier pieces appeared to sympathize with opponents of reform (Bello identified them as "the socialist vanguard that holds state power and controls the 'commanding heights' of the economy"), Gellen attributed resistance to "recalcitrant bureaucrats."[11]

In Weisburd's "Vietnam Purging Itself of 'Poison,'" "widespread official corruption" was identified as the toxin signaled in the title and "such capitalist principles as the law of supply and demand and how to balance books to show a profit" as the remedy. The purge of party ranks was characterized as "a kind of revolution," introducing an emphasis that is "more expert and less red." In a later piece, he portrayed capitalist-style reforms "on a scale unknown in the socialist world since the Soviet New Economic Policy of the 1920s." This approach, which the author compared to "Gorbachev's perestroika policies," faces opposition from "the entrenched bureaucracy."[12]

The articles end in theoretical confusion. One set of concepts (red vs. expert, egalitarianism vs. material incentives, social control over production vs. the free market) would have led new leftists of the sixties to criticize the reformers while another (openness vs. bureaucracy) prompts a more favorable assessment of their endeavor. The stress on a nonanalytic category such as "corruption" betrays an inability to determine what is wrong and how to regain the initiative. Reformers say that more restructuring is necessary and that the foot-dragging of venal, unimaginative officials is to blame for the crisis. Their opponents say that market forces are encouraging speculation and inequality and that more state control over the economy is required. During the war, the revolutionary route seemed clear enough, but today no one knows what socialism means in a country as desperately poor as Vietnam.

There has been little discussion on the Left of this question, as a generation of new leftists tacitly abandoned Maoist politics and then, in spite of flirtations with *glasnost*, did not succeed in finding an alternative.[13] A rough consensus dating from the 1960s in praise of socialism in Vietnam and China and disdainful of the Soviet Union did not serve well when discussion turned to the Kampuchea/ Vietnam/China War or to the disintegration of the Vietnamese economy.

This analytic failure opened the way for *mea culpas*, as in Todd Gitlin's *The Sixties*, with its recollection of the antiwar movement sliding "into romance with the other side," of Marxist-Leninists in Hanoi "snookering" emissaries from the U.S. with lies about their commitment to grass-roots democracy. Seeming to relish an image of new leftists as "innocents abroad," Gitlin regrets the way "we turned where romantics have traditionally turned: to the hot-blooded peoples of the subtropics and the mysterious East." Having lost confidence in our own country, we threw ourselves into an infatuation with "the vast poor and dark-skinned world." Twenty years later, seemingly on the basis of a more balanced assessment, he notes "the Vietnamese reign of terror in 'reeducation camps,' " and "the killing of thousands of peasants, kulak-style, in North Vietnam, and the imprisonment of thousands of others in forced labor camps, in 1955–56 (a 'mistake' Hanoi had owned up to, after the fact)."[14]

Gitlin's determination to pull back from the "mysterious" and "dark-skinned" Vietnamese can be characterized in various ways, but not as "innocent." Like the 1970s critics, he offers no analysis of the reeducation camps, and his tone in discussing land reform recalls Washington front man Hoang Van Chi whose fabricated portrait of a Communist "bloodbath" in North Vietnam was used to justify U.S. intervention. The sarcastic parenthetical aside and the reference to "kulaks" are gratuitous. There is no credible evidence that the 1956 "Rectification of Errors" campaign was a bad-faith exercise on the part of ,Hanoi leaders. In conception, Vietnamese land reform (confiscation from the rich, distribution to the poor) was akin to the peasant revolution of 1917 in Russia and fundamentally unlike Stalin's collectivization (confiscation from small holders, state ownership of the land). A different impression of land reform's human costs (and benefits) emerges from the work of reputable researchers such as Gareth Porter, Christine White, Edwin Moise, and Gabriel Kolko.[15]

Perhaps these remarks from a sophisticated scholar with clear ties to the Left should not surprise. Gitlin was not alone in distancing himself from the romanticism of the antiwar movement. For various reasons after 1975, many former activists stopped identifying with the Vietnamese.

Going Back to Vietnam

In 1985, I received an invitation to visit Vietnam as part of an educators' delegation organized by the U.S./Indochina Reconciliation Project.[16] My friends were excited, and I professed to be excited, too, but in the privacy of my own thoughts, I sought some pretext to avoid a trip that did not coincide with my personal, scholarly, or political concerns. In the end, I departed with a sense of the voyage as a pilgrimage to acknowledge an earlier, completed, phase of my life.

After our arrival, I and others in the group were embarrassed to realize how little we understood of current debates and choices within Vietnam. This sense of disorientation began in Bangkok when a well-informed observer remarked to us that Vietnam's situation was bleak, but that at least the Vietnamese were no longer "blaming the war" for their problems. So, it seemed, there was a considerable amount of "blame" to distribute, and the problem did not lie where I would have assumed, with the destructive U.S. intervention. But if Washington was not to blame, then who was?

Questions multiplied after our arrival in Hanoi. I knew about land reform in the 1960s, but not about the contract system in the 1980s. I resuscitated old arguments about U.S. intervention, but was unaware of negotiating positions adopted by the Reagan administration and the Socialist Republic of Vietnam. The polemical categories I mobilized from other contexts, such as the debate over individual and collective incentives in Cuba, were inadequate to conditions of material deprivation and government impotence in Vietnam.

Most of all, I was both touched and discomfited by the warm reception accorded to us by Vietnamese at all levels, from government officials to people in the street. As a social historian, I knew that collective action always involves a moral dimension, a confidence that one is redressing wrongs. But my memories of the antiwar movement centered more on the limits of our influence than on the meaning of our choices. When Norman Morrison immolated himself in protest against the war in 1965, we hung back from his seemingly ineffectual gesture. Struggling to go beyond moral witness, most antiwar activists continued to doubt that their efforts were shaping events.

But, our visit suggested, the Vietnamese attitude is determined more by a sense of justice than by votes or firepower, and many still speak of Morrison with a deep respect. I also could not help noticing that religious groups and especially the Mennonites and the Quakers, who are carrying on multifaceted assistance programs in Indochina, have demonstrated more staying power there than the "revolutionary" sectors of the antiwar movement. For the Vietnamese, the fundamental point is not that we succeeded in stopping U.S. intervention, but that in a moment of peril we expressed our belief in the righteousness of their cause. My experience of working against the war, one that combined pride in a commitment properly chosen and mortification that we were not more effective, remained incomplete until I received a recognition that only the Vietnamese could provide.

The warmth of our hosts, their certainty that our two countries would always be bound by a common experience, also made me uneasy. Surely they would be wounded by the indifference to Vietnam among both friends and adversaries in the United States. Without anticipating exactly how to achieve this objective, I returned to the U.S. with hopes of drawing attention to Vietnam's current situation and needs.

A few months later, I became co-director of the William Joiner Center for the Study of War and Social Consequences at the University of Massachusetts/Boston. The center is mandated to serve and advocate for veterans and to encourage scholarship on the causes, events, and results of the Vietnam War and other wars. Here, I thought, was an opportunity to build on my recent trip.

I began this job with confidence in my understanding of veterans and their issues. The first demonstration I ever attended, in 1965, featured a speech about the elitist bias, the self-described "channeling" function of the selective service system, a topic with its attendant class analysis that remained a prominent theme of the antiwar movement as I remember it. I'll never forget student–veterans who flocked to University of Massachusetts/Boston, where I began to teach in 1969, bringing insight and a tremendous surge of energy into the classroom. By 1971, veterans were the moral leaders of the struggle against U.S. intervention.

But after 1975, it is a different story. Turning away from Vietnam, the left also forgot about the soldiers who served there. The anti–draft-registration campaign of the late seventies was concerned with a new generation of soldiers rather than with the GIs who had fought in Indochina. Leftist coverage of the veterans' movement has been even more sketchy than of Vietnam. Reporting by Jack Calhoun and Tod Ensign has given veterans a fitful presence in the *Guardian*, and *In These Times* has featured notes on Agent Orange and atomic veterans, as well as occasional strong pieces such as Darcy DeMarco, "The Missing Image of Black Vets in Nam." There is even less to extract from the *Nation* and no sign at all in *Socialist Review* of interest in veterans. In 1976 and 1977, *Radical America* printed articles on the GI movement and women in the military, but the magazine has published nothing since on the topic. The Rainbow Coalition, which enlarged the audience for many progressive constituencies, thereby serving as a kind of barometer for the Left, did not address veterans' concerns.[17]

Before 1986, I knew that many veterans were strung out, but I would not have been able to define post-traumatic stress disorder (PTSD) or to explain how combat stress is similar to other trauma, as in rape and child abuse. I knew that vets had been badly treated, but had only casually followed and did not understand the Agent Orange court case and its connection to other instances where corporations have contaminated the environment. I remembered our 1960s analysis of racism in the military, but was oblivious to the ways black soldiers and veterans are being misrepresented or ignored in histories of the war, in films like *Platoon* and *Full Metal Jacket*, and even in the programs of black progressive politicians. I had never thought about the fact that there are women veterans and was surprised to discover that women vets have their own organizations and demands. I did not know that a substantial minority of the homeless are veterans; that AIDS is more common among veterans than in the general population; or that veterans did not have the right to sue Veterans Administration doctors for malpractice.

The evolution of the veterans' movement as it gravitated from antiwar work to these issues was difficult and circuitous, which in part explains the flagging support of the non-veteran Left. It nonetheless remains true that the resulting separation left unfinished the work we undertook during the war. Campaigns such as the Winter Soldier Investigation were political initiatives and also individual efforts to gain closure on events that had to be faced before the participants could go forward. Government repression expressed the fear of authorities who knew that people would listen to those who had been in the front lines in Vietnam. It also blocked the effort at recovery that veterans had initiated. In this way, their activism brought together with great emphasis the political and the personal. For others, who could not find a way to recovery when there was an oppositional culture to aid their efforts, the clock is now ticking. It is not too late for them to finish with the war, but only the support of a larger movement can promote this outcome.

In 1987, the Joiner Center helped fund a conference on Vietnam, sponsored by people with impressive and deserved left credentials, and with the center's help a veterans' presence was ensured at the proceedings. This coming together of seemingly disparate groups was not free of tension, and on several occasions in hallways and cafeterias, leftists were heard to inform veterans that their views were racist or sexist or both. I was not ready to say that these charges were false, but it was also clear that the critics had no understanding of veterans' concerns and needs, that they could imagine allying with veterans only after a process of rethinking focused on the deficiencies of the other side.

At veterans' gatherings, the reception I received as co-director of the Joiner Center and a former antiwar activist was more generous. Early in my tenure, a vociferously conservative vet approached me at a convention. He described his continuing nightmares about Vietnam and declared that soldiers had risked their lives so people like me would retain the right to protest. Wary, I rehearsed a rebuttal to this explanation for U.S. policy, but then realized that he was explaining why *he* (and not LBJ or Nixon) had fought. He went on to acknowledge that the antiwar movement had protested in order to end the war and to bring him and other soldiers home before they got killed. Then he abruptly shook my hand and walked away.

Reconnecting the Past with the Present

For this veteran and others I have met, the Vietnam War is history in the true sense, quite different from the debased notion that makes its way into the mainstream of our culture. They don't see Vietnam as a dead, past phenomenon, a bundle of "lessons" to be brandished in current quarrels. Mere remembering is not enough when people seek to pursue the mission that history imposed on them in the 1960s, first of all in the United States, but also in Vietnam. In the words of Kevin Bowen, the other co-director of the Joiner Center, going back to Vietnam "stirs the mind, rekindles the imagination, and reopens the heart to hope. It cannot change the past, but it can reconnect the past with the present."[18]

In this spirit, I have traveled several times to Vietnam with Joiner Center delegations to set up veteran-to-veteran programs, to provide medical assistance to the Vietnamese, to arrange translation of Vietnamese veteran writings into English and U.S. veteran writings into Vietnamese, and to organize an exhibit of paintings by veteran artists from Vietnam and the United States, to be toured in both countries.

Joiner trips to Vietnam have been both exhilarating and disturbing. Our delegations have toured veteran production units where most of the antiquated machinery does not work, where shortages in foreign currency prevent acquisition of raw materials, where work spaces are crowded, filthy, and poorly ventilated. We visited disabled veterans' residential centers where everyone is an amputee or blind or paralyzed, and the director worries that there will not be enough food for the residents. I have seen hospital facilities where children suffer from polio, dysentery, and hepatitis, where jars of deformed fetuses gather dust because the staff has no money to complete its research on Agent Orange, where there are no medicines and no equipment and beds are covered only with straw mats.

These scenes gave me a new understanding of the victory won by the Vietnamese in 1975. No people select the context in which they act, but history has imposed on Vietnam in this century more than its share of catastrophes. Faced with multiple obstacles, some Vietnamese drew the conclusion that a peripheral role, a footnote to the French or the United States, was the best that could be hoped for. Others yearned for a patriotic outcome, but shrank from the sacrifices necessary to give it life. Only the revolutionaries aspired to make history, and in the end their hubris was decisive. For good or ill, Vietnam would chart an original course, outside the U.S. orbit.

Having fought for their independence, the Vietnamese are now compelled to live with the consequences. Victory brought not freedom, but a new set of constraints, even more unyielding than those before 1975. In Bangkok, the visitor sees plenty of begging, homelessness, and prostitution, but there can be no doubt that foreign investment has injected a certain vitality into the city's economy. It is unquestionably more prosperous than Hanoi, where children appear undernourished and even some government officials, painfully thin and fatigued, convey an air of debility.

When the history of international politics in the twentieth century is written, the Thais, whose destiny is being determined by others, will not command a prominent place. Proudly independent, Vietnam lives in misery. During my visits, I have been startled by the readiness of leftist traveling companions to conclude that the Vietnamese like us better than the Russians and that the Soviet bloc hurt rather than helped the Vietnamese. The socialist countries could not replace what capitalism once promised Vietnam. The country's desire for better relations with the United States may be a testimonial to us as a people, but it also reflects a material reality in which capitalism still dominates the globe. Not as much blood is being shed, but, through its trade embargo and its support for China, Thailand, and the Khmer Rouge, the United States continues to do great harm to the peoples of Indochina.

Dismayed to find the Vietnamese in such straits after all they have been through, I returned home from my first Joiner Center trip determined to help them. But images from Vietnam intruded on my work, of children with infected eyes and bad teeth in the streets of Hanoi, of young women in a Ho Chi Minh City cancer ward tearfully pointing to the dioxin-induced stomach tumors that are killing them. Walking in the neighborhood around my house, I saw Vietnamese children play in a park while a man sipping from a bottle in a paper bag eyed them with hatred. I expected jet-lag sleeplessness after arriving in Boston, but not the tears that came in the middle of the night as I sat in bed, feeling out of place in my own home and ashamed of having abandoned the Vietnamese.

Frightened to find myself so unhinged by the trip, I half jokingly remarked to veteran friends that I was suffering from "antiwar activists' PTSD," then, embarrassed, tried to take back the remark, adding that of course it wasn't real PTSD, as veterans experience it. My friends were not so ready to dismiss the notion. That we participated in the war, but did not risk our lives in it, is an invitation neither to discount our distress nor to equate it with the anguish of the Vietnamese or the U.S. veteran. Our sense of helplessness, of being far from the suffering and unable to arrest its course, did create a "stress disorder." There was a time when this powerlessness threatened to drive us crazy. What a relief it was in 1975 to abandon a terrain where we had always played a marginal role.

This turn reflects a long-standing weakness of the U.S. Left, which tends to accept an agenda determined by government policy and by media-defined crises, but it also should be understood as a failure of nerve. Our celebration after the liberation of Saigon hid a determination to flee from the torment of others. And getting involved again with the Vietnamese, who face many difficulties and who need more assistance than we will ever be able to provide, is bound to reopen old wounds.

I hope that the Left will face this pain and reaffirm its intimate ties to Vietnam. Taking that route will bring us closer to others in the United States—veterans, refugees—who need us and who have something to teach us. Fighting the battles that arise as others reinterpret the war is a necessary, but also a self-serving tack that finds us defending our own credibility and past activism. Our critique of social amnesia has been accompanied by an equally problematic refusal to take notice of the present. I do not agree that the Left identified too closely with third world liberation struggles. It should be a matter of pride to have forged a bond with people we had never seen, halfway around the world, to the point where an injury to them felt like an injury to ourselves. Our romance with Vietnam helped us grasp political realities and explain them to other people. The real failure came after 1975, when events demonstrated the limits of our analysis, and, instead of persisting with efforts to understand and to help the Vietnamese, we stopped thinking about them. Our silence on a front where the Left once held forth with a brash self-confidence amounts to an abdication. We cannot turn away from people who are a part of us. To be true to ourselves, we must go back to Vietnam.

Notes

An earlier version of this essay appeared under the title "Coming to Terms with Post-War Vietnam," in *Socialist Review* 19, 2 (1989): 113–27. Among the many friends who helped me think through the issues discussed here, I would especially like to thank Kevin Bowen.

1. Wilfred Burchett, *Vietnam: Inside Story of the Guerilla War* (New York: 1965); Tom Hayden, *The Love of Possession is a Disease with Them* (Chicago: 1972); Alfred McCoy, *The Politics of Heroin in Southeast Asia* (New York: 1973). For more on Burchett, see David Marr, "Burchett on Vietnam," in Ben Kiernan, ed., *Burchett Reporting the Other Side of the World, 1939–1983* (New York: 1986), 219–39. Hayden's later thoughts on his involvement in the antiwar movement are found in Tom Hayden, *Reunion: A Memoir* (New York: 1988). An enlarged, updated version of McCoy's study is now available: Alfred McCoy, *The Politics of Heroin: CIA Complicity in the Global Drug Trade* (New York: 1991).

2. For more on the revolutionary movement in My Tho and on the Rand investigation, see David Hunt, "Villagers at War: The National Liberation Front in My Tho Province, 1965–67," *Radical America* 8, 1–2 (January–April 1974): 3–184; and "Village Culture and the Vietnamese Revolution," *Past & Present* 94 (1982): 131–57.

3. The following "literature review," conducted in 1989, is by no means systematic, and it would be a pleasure to learn that publications others than the ones I habitually read did a better job of staying in touch with the Vietnamese reality. It should also be noted that, in response to a rapidly evolving situation in Cambodia, China, and the former Soviet bloc, both the Left and the mainstream press have in the last two or three years been somewhat more attentive to Vietnam.

4. Paul Lyons, "Teaching the Sixties," *Socialist Review* 15, 1 (1985): 71–91.

5. *Socialist Review* 9, 2 (1979): 10; Nayan Chanda, *Brother Enemy: The War after the War. A History of Indochina since the Fall of Saigon* (New York: 1986).

6. George Black, "Republican Overtures to Hanoi," *Nation*, June 4, 1988; Paul Joseph, "Vietnamese Trying to Find a Way Out," *In These Times*, February 26–March 11, 1986.

7. Tran Van Dinh, "Vietnam in the Year of the Dragon," *Monthly Review* 28, 1 (1976): 19–33; and "Why and How the Vietnamese Won the War," *Monthly Review* 30, 6 (1978): 28–40. Kathleen Gough, "A Hanoi Interview," *Monthly Review* 29, 1 (1977): 20–31; and "Green Revolution in South India and North Vietnam," *Monthly Review* 29, 8 (1978): 10–21. See also Kathleen Gough, *Ten Times More Beautiful: The Rebuilding of Vietnam* (New York: 1978).

8. *Indochina Newsletter*, 2161 Massachusetts Avenue, Cambridge, MA 02140; *Indochina Issues*, Indochina Project, 2001 S Street, N.W., Suite 740, Washington, D.C. 20009.

9. Waldo Bello, "Vietnam Combating Capitalism's Comeback," *Guardian*, February 3, 1983.

10. Abe Weisburd, "Crackdown on Capitalists," *Guardian*, September 7, 1983.

11. Karen Gellen, "Vietnam's New 'War,' " *Guardian*, September 18, 1985.

12. Abe Weisburd, "Vietnam Purging Itself of 'Poison,' " *Guardian*, September 18, 1985; and "Vietnam Opens Doors Wide," *Guardian*, January 20, 1988.

13. Gabriel Kolko attempts to launch such a discussion in "The Structural Consequences of the Vietnam War and Socialist Economic Transformation," *Journal of Contemporary Asia* 18 (1988): 473–82.

14. Todd Gitlin, *The Sixties: Years of Hope, Days of Rage* (New York: 1987), 269.

15. Hoang Van Chi, *From Colonialism to Communism* (New York: 1964); Gareth Porter, *The Myth of the Bloodbath: North Vietnam's Land Reform Reconsidered* (Ithaca: 1972); Christine White, "Agrarian Reform and National Liberation in the Vietnam Revolution, 1950–57," Ph.D. dissertation, Cornell University, 1981; Edwin Moise, *Land Reform in China and Vietnam* (Chapel Hill: 1983); Gabriel Kolko, *Anatomy of a War: Vietnam, the United States, and the Modern Historical Experience* (New York: 1985).

16. U.S./Indochina Reconciliation Project, 220 West 42nd Street, Suite 1801, New York, NY 10036.

17. Darcy DeMarco, "The Missing Image of Black Vets in Nam," *In These Times*, September 30–October 6, 1987; Linda Alband, et al., "The GI Movement Today: The Volunteer Armed Forces and Movement in the Ranks," *Radical America*, 10, 3 (1976): 27–45; and "Women and the Volunteer Armed Forces: First Report on a Rocky Romance," *Radical America* 11, 1 (1977): 19–31.

18. Kevin Bowen, "Seeking Reconciliation in Vietnam," *Christian Science Monitor*, November 10, 1988. See also Kevin Bowen, "U.S. Veterans: The War and the Long Road Home," in Douglas Allen and Ngo Vinh Long, *Coming to Terms: Indochina, The United States, and the War* (Boulder: 1991), 250–64.

19

China and Vietnam:
Looking for a New Version
of an Old Relationship

Keith W. Taylor

Sino-Vietnamese relations have been evolving for more than 2,000 years within the context of a strategic dilemma. This dilemma arose from the fact that the Vietnamese territories lay within the reach of Chinese armies but beyond the reach of the sinicizing process. For several centuries, Vietnam was a restive frontier jurisdiction of the Chinese empire. Then, for several centuries, it was an independent kingdom posing as a tributary of the Chinese empire. For 2,000 years, the culture, the political ideals, and the military power of imperial China were the dominant factors shaping the outlook of ruling-class Vietnamese. Offering formal deference to Chinese imperial claims was the only alternative to warfare for Vietnamese; acknowledging Chinese cultural norms became a habit of ruling-class Vietnamese. However, in the twentieth century, a historic reorientation of Vietnamese thought and culture away from China occurred as a result of two developments.

First, French efforts to stop the use of Chinese and Vietnamese characters among literate Vietnamese led to the adoption of a twenty-nine-letter alphabet for writing the Vietnamese language, which by the 1920s and 1930s resulted in a cultural revolution that became the basis for the modern nationalist awakening. Modern Vietnamese nationalism looked to Europe rather than China for intellectual inspiration. The centuries-long cultural link with China, whereby all educated Vietnamese mastered the Chinese language and the cultural values embedded in it, was irrevocably broken. A sense of cultural affinity, of shared "Asian" values, remains, but the mechanism of a shared language and literature is gone.

An important implication of this is that Vietnamese leaders today are less susceptible to Chinese claims of cultural and moral precedence than they were in the past. Furthermore, Vietnamese leaders are today, in an unprecedented way, restricted in their relations with China by the cultural edifice that has in this century been erected upon a new conception of an indigenous Vietnamese tradition. This tradition, though not entirely invented, is in large part an aspect of modern Vietnamese nationalism, and has produced the "democratic" constraints of popular opinion; having indoctrinated millions of Vietnamese about what it means to be citizens of a modern nation, Vietnamese leaders are now in large measure prisoners of the expectations they have taught to their people. What this means is that Vietnamese leaders today no longer monopolize public discussion but must react to new voices in their society that use their slogans against them. This point will be developed in greater detail below. Here I wish to note that the matter of going to China to "kowtow," after the vast uproars of the twentieth century, can no longer be kept as a simple matter between governments, or communist parties.

Second, the emergence of an independent, united Vietnam took place in a world where China was no longer the only great power. In the mid-twentieth century, Vietnamese nationalists labored to establish a modern state in a polycentric world. France, the Soviet Union, Japan, and the United States all offered options to a Sinocentric world. This was a temporary phenomenon, but it has nevertheless been an important factor in twentieth-century Vietnamese political behavior. The process of adjusting to a shrinking world, where all roads again lead to Peking, will be resisted by Vietnamese leaders; all other options will be fully explored.

What has not been generally recognized is that the role of the United States in Vietnamese affairs has always been and continues to be congruent with, if not in overt support of, long-term Chinese interests in Vietnam. The United States, in the actual effect of its successive policies more than with any clearly articulated intention, has systematically endeavored to remove every obstacle to the realization of Chinese ambitions in Indochina: the defeat of Japan, the removal of France, even U.S. withdrawal itself, and, of course, opposition to Soviet influence in Indochina. The historic effect of American intervention in Vietnam has been to thwart the efforts of Vietnamese to establish themselves in a polycentric world and to force Vietnam back into the Chinese fold.

This appears puzzling when we recall that U.S. intervention in Vietnam was initially rationalized as an effort to contain, if not to prevent, the spread of Chinese influence into Vietnam. Despite this, beneath the blithe certitudes of Cold War rhetoric, one of the truly great unrecognized ironies of the Cold War was that, since the Geneva Conference of 1954, the U.S. and People's Republic of China (PRC) governments have perceived their respective interests in Vietnam in ways that were in fact complementary. China's patronage of the Democratic Republic of Vietnam (DRV) was conditioned by its interest in an international security system on its southern border that would stabilize South-east Asia and answer the American fears embodied in the "domino theory." The Americans were incapable of understanding this.

On June 23, 1954, four days after forming his government, Pierre Mendes-France, prime minister of France, met with Chou En-lai. In the report on this meeting forwarded to the French Ministry of Foreign Affairs by Jacques Roux, the ministry's director for Asia and the Pacific,[1] Chou En-lai makes several interesting points. First, in Vietnam, the military and political settlements must be separated, and the military settlement is first priority. Second, the three In-dochinese countries can remain in the French Union; this will, in the words attributed to Chou En-lai, "contribute to the establishment of friendly and peace-ful relations between France and China." Third, all Vietnamese military forces must withdraw from Cambodia and Laos. These three points were all, more or less, at variance with DRV priorities. The DRV believed that any military settle-ment should facilitate a political settlement, and, although the DRV was not categorically opposed to membership in the French Union, its idea of what this should mean differed from French expectations;[2] as late as June 12, DRV mili-tary negotiators had informed their French counterparts that Vietnamese rela-tions with Laos and Cambodia were not open for discussion.[3] China was clearly endeavoring to find common ground with France, and its motive was to work for a Sino-French relationship that would oversee Indochinese affairs.

A fourth point made by Chou En-lai was that there were to be no U.S. bases in Laos and Cambodia. This needs some elaboration. Mendes-France responded by referring to this as "a very important point" and he affirmed that he was in absolute agreement that there should be no U.S. bases established in "Laos and Cambodia."[4] The unstated assumption being made by both Chou En-lai and Mendes-France was that some kind of French presence would continue, at least for a time, in part of Vietnam, which would seem to make unnecessary any mention of U.S. bases in Vietnam itself; French forces were to be withdrawn from the newly independent Laos and Cambodia, and both China and France were in agreement that U.S. forces should not replace them. Chou En-lai's reply to Mendes-France's assurances on the question of U.S. bases went on to raise a fifth point having to do with there being two Vietnamese governments:

> I want to thank Mr. Mendes-France for what he has just said, especially for the response, the good response, that he has made on the last point. The peoples of the three Indochinese countries, of China, of France, and of all Southeast Asia are happy that France is not disposed to permit the establishment of American military bases. This will be a basis for our future conversations. I am in agreement on the necessity for international control for solving the military problem in Laos and Cambodia. In Vietnam, the situation is a bit different, and more difficult; there it is a matter of an agreement in principle to act upon (intervienne sur) the political and military aspects of the problem. In practice, this comes down to regroupment zones and a cease-fire. Study of political

questions will come later. Therefore, we are in agreement on the necessity to distinguish two stages, the length of which will depend upon the efforts made by the two [Vietnamese] sides. There are, of course, two governments in Vietnam, but France must contribute to bringing them together, not in putting them in opposition. One obstacle to the armistice is that [the two Vietnamese governments] are not talking with each other. I believe that you already know that the Chinese delegation is pushing the DRV delegation to approach not only the French delegation but also the delegation of Bao Dai's Vietnam. But this [DRV–Bao Dai talks] seems more difficult [than DRV–French talks]. Where does this difficulty come from? I believe that you can imagine. . . .[5]

Mendes-France replied by citing all the difficulties in the way of an agreement between the two Vietnamese governments; he had apparently misunderstood Chou En-lai, for Chou replied:

In reference to what has just been said, it is necessary to avoid any misunderstanding: it is obviously not yet a question of *rapprochement* or of cooperation between the two parties in Vietnam. For the moment, it is nothing more than a matter of contacts. But I want to say that France must use its influence to encourage these contacts so that [the two Vietnamese parties] not be influenced by exterior forces.[6]

Obviously, Chou En-lai had the United States in mind when he talked about "exterior forces" here. He was willing to forsee an indefinite French presence in southern Vietnam as a guarantee against American intervention. What the Americans could not understand was that this was also in their best interests, and may have relieved them of the heavy price in blood and treasure that their eagerness to replace the French in Vietnam eventually cost.

One of the most controversial parts of the Geneva settlement in succeeding years has been the temporary partition of Vietnam into two military regroupment zones, each containing a rival Vietnamese government, with elections to produce a unified Vietnamese government after two years. The comment of Chou En-lai about French responsibility to foster contact between the two Vietnamese governments, cited in the previous paragraph, was in the context of concern about American interference in the future political settlement in Vietnam. The Bao Dai government, led by Ngo Dinh Diem since June 16, 1954, claimed to represent all of Vietnam and was adamantly opposed to any form of partition; the U.S. government publicly supported this position. Thus, there were already signs that the United States was positioning itself as a spoiler of any agreement that conferred legitimacy upon the DRV. China was hoping that continued French influence over the Saigon government would not only preclude American intervention, but would also result in a Vietnamese government in the South that would enter into dialogue with the DRV. It was in light of American intentions that the question of partition was understood by the people endeavoring to reach a settlement at Geneva.

It is clear that the DRV rather quickly came to accept a temporary partition that would allow consolidation of a viable state territory under the protection of an international agreement. The idea of partition had been in the minds of British and Soviet diplomats as early as February and March 1954; the British Foreign Ministry produced a paper, approved by Foreign Minister Anthony Eden on April 1, that mentioned "a solution based on the partition of Vietnam" as, among other things, something that "might be best as a *pis-aller* [last resort]."[7] Partition was being informally discussed by journalists and commentators when the Geneva Conference took up the Indochina question.[8] As early as May 11, the Bao Dai government publicly rejected the idea of partition.[9] Two weeks later, on May 25, Pham Van Dong tabled a proposal for "temporary *de facto* partition."[10] This was the first official proposal to the conference that envisaged partition. This was followed up in meetings between French and DRV military negotiators on June 10, 12, and 13, when Ta Quang Buu, DRV delegate, vigorously pushed for a temporary partition to be followed by a political process to result in a unified Vietnamese government.[11] By the time Pierre Mendes-France and Chou En-lai had their first meeting on June 23, the idea of partition was recognized by all interested parties, except for the Bao Dai government and the United States, as an essential part of any agreement.

If a temporary partition were to be a successful step toward a peaceful settlement of Vietnamese political problems, then parties that threatened to undermine this process, namely the Saigon government and the United States, would have to either be brought under control or excluded. This is apparently what Chou En-lai had in mind when he urged Mendes-France to bring the South Vietnamese government into fruitful contact with the DRV and prevent U.S. intervention. Chou En-lai clearly favored a continuing French presence in Vietnam as a stabilizing factor, not only in avoiding future hostilities between the two Vietnamese governments but also in excluding the destabilizing influence of an American government preoccupied with an anti-Communist crusade.

The question of whether or not and under what conditions Vietnam would eventually be united was not urgent. This does not necessarily mean that China preferred to keep Vietnam divided; but it simply means that Vietnamese unification was not a critical priority for China in the light of China's desire to stabilize the situation beyond its southern border. It is a reasonable conjecture that, for China, peaceful settlement of the Vietnamese political problem and exclusion of U.S. intervention, two inseparable priorities, did not necessarily preclude the existence of two Vietnamese governments, each ensconced in its own territory, for the foreseeable future. The DRV certainly had a more definite expectation of a speedy settlement of the political problem through peaceful means; this, according to Robert F. Randle in his study of the Geneva conference, is the only reasonable explanation for their willingness to submit to a "temporary *de facto* partition."[12] That Chinese priorities were not identical to Vietnamese priorities should be no cause for surprise or blame.

There is no clear evidence that the DRV accepted the idea of partition only after heavy pressure from the Soviet Union and/or China. There were naturally misgivings and even outrage about the idea of partition, even temporary, among Vietnamese of all political persuasions. But, after initial hesitation following the euphoria of Dien Bien Phu, the DRV leadership seems to have read the threat of future U.S. intervention and concluded that partition was the best option. On the other hand, it is obvious that Chinese persuasion and Soviet diktat were critical in determining the actual manner in which the partition was made.

Up until July 13, the DRV held fast to their proposal for a partition at the 13th parallel, in contrast to the French proposal for the 18th parallel. On July 13, Pierre Mendes-France met for the second time with Chou En-lai. Chou En-lai had just returned from a visit to India, Burma, and an interview with Ho Chi Minh on the Sino-Vietnamese border. According to the report of this meeting on file in the Quai d'Orsay archives,[13] Mendes-France immediately raised the question of where the partition line should be drawn and argued at length for the 18th parallel. He admitted that this line would lie north of large areas inhabited by people loyal to the DRV, but he claimed this would be more than offset by the loss to France of " . . . northern Vietnam, the part of the country that is richest, most populated, and has the capital as well as the most important economic enterprises."[14]

Chou En-lai replied by disagreeing that French loss of northern Vietnam was a greater sacrifice than DRV loss of areas in the south inhabited by people with whom it had established close ties of loyalty; "[the DRV] will deeply resent the loss, even temporarily, of these territories."[15] But he went on to take a fresh tack:

> It is the armistice that we now find at the center of our attention. As for the political declaration that must conclude our work, we will naturally take into account the interests of the Vietnamese people. We also hope that Vietnam will establish, in terms of equality, friendly relations with France. . . . It is regrettable that the question of the demarcation line is at an impasse. The two sides must be prepared to make concessions, though one may make more important concessions than the other. I do not see how else this question can be resolved. And bear in mind that we are being watched by those who want war. France has control of certain regions in the north as the DRV has control of certain regions in the south. There will be a fixed time limit for the evacuation of these regions. The DRV will be able to take into consideration the difficulties that France will experience in this regard. I hope that M. Mendes-France will wish to reflect seriously on this. I believe that if you make a first step, the other side will go to meet you and, in doing so, will move further than you.[16]

Mendes-France restated his position that France was giving up more than the DRV was giving up in the south and that the 18th parallel was the only reasonable line of partition. Chou En-lai said: "I must make my idea more precise: I did not propose that it be a matter of the two sides making equivalent concessions. I simply wanted to say that if France concedes a little, the DRV will concede much; and I repeat, I believe that Mr. Pham [Van Dong] wishes to see you before your departure for Paris."[17]

In his final comments Mendes-France said:

> You know that I must go to Paris this evening to meet Mr. Dulles, along with Mr. Eden. I do not yet know the ultimate intentions of the American government on the subject of their representation at Geneva. But it seems to me that in the interest of peace it will be good if the accord on which we are working receives the approval of all the participants of the conference. Yesterday, I said to Mr. Pham Van Dong, in a light-hearted manner, that if I were in his place, I would prefer to take less with the approval of the Americans than to take more without their approval.[18]

The meeting ended with Chou En-lai complaining about American efforts to "sabotage" the conference and Mendes-France affirming that such an attitude could not help because any successful agreement had to have the assent of the Americans.[19] This meeting clearly suggests that expectations of future American policy were critical factors in shaping the French, Chinese, and Vietnamese negotiating positions.

Within a few hours of this meeting, before his departure for Paris, Mendes-France met again with Pham Van Dong, who offered to draw the line of partition at the 16th parallel.[20] This Vietnamese concession looks like a response to Chinese pressure, which is how François Joyaux, in his study of the Chinese role in the conference, understands it.[21] On the other hand, it may have come simply as part of a coordinated Sino-Vietnamese negotiating strategy, considering that the DRV had been pushing hard for a temporary partition into two relatively equal parts since late May.

It is tempting to see the PRC coercing the DRV into making concessions; but in the absence of evidence it may be more flattering to the DRV leaders to assume that they understood and accepted, with whatever misgivings, what was necessary to gain international recognition of Vietnamese "sovereignty, independence, unity, and territorial integrity"[22] and to secure at once a viable state territory without further war or threat of war. Certainly, among DRV leaders there was resentment that the PRC and the USSR were unwilling to tempt American ire on their behalf. But the Vietnamese were not unfamiliar with the facts of life for smaller countries.

The final act was orchestrated by Molotov, who, on July 20, with Mendes-France's time limit for an agreement nearly up, proposed the 17th parallel for the demarcation line, and a two-year waiting period before elections to unify Vietnam.[23] According to François Joyaux, the Chinese delegation had by this time already communicated these concessions to the French.[24] The DRV had wanted to wait only six months before elections; the French publicly preferred no specified date for elections, while confidentially estimating that a minimum of eigh-

278   KEITH W. TAYLOR

teen months would be necessary to prepare for elections. Why did Molotov, presumably in consultation with the Chinese, make it two years, longer than the previously stated Soviet position of sixteen months?[25] Was he trying to put the Vietnam conundrum into the closet with the idea that with enough time the situation would resolve itself quietly? Robert F. Randle surmised that the Soviets, British, Americans, and "perhaps the Chinese" actually favored a permanent rather than a temporary partition to avoid the seemingly inevitable uproar that any effort to unify the country would provoke.[26] In the eyes of the Soviets and the Chinese, any such uproar would almost certainly involve the Americans, and that was to be avoided if at all possible. Point four of the Anglo-American seven-point position paper of June 29, 1954, which France accepted, implied permanent partition, for it affirmed support of an agreement that "does not contain political provisions which would risk loss of the retained area to Communist control."[27] The two-year waiting period was an unmistakable signal that the proposed political process for bringing an end to the "temporary" partition of Vietnam was not a priority for the major powers at the conference. If the Americans were satisfied with half of Vietnam for the "free world," then perhaps the Indochina situation could calm down.

What I hope to have gained by this brief excursion into the Geneva Conference of 1954 is an appreciation of the degree to which the agreement was influenced by perceptions of American intentions, and, at least in the case of China, by a desire to retain a French presence in Vietnam as a means of moderating American actions in the region. A quiet and stable Indochina would not attract unwanted American attention.

The success of Ngo Dinh Diem, well-known for his anti-French attitude, in gaining control of the situation in Saigon and the speed with which the United States elbowed aside the French and established a dominant position in southern Vietnam were not foreseen when the delegates to the Geneva Conference completed their work on Indochina. The Americans, full of disdain for the French and sure of their own destiny, were incapable of understanding that a continued French presence in southern Vietnam would not only relieve them of a great deal of trouble but would also contribute to a stable free-world position on China's southern border; judging from the encounters between Chou En-lai and Pierre Mendes-France, the Chinese and French were capable of working together on the Vietnamese problem. It is doubtful that the Vietnamese would have acquiesced indefinitely to Sino-French tutelage, but the scourge of American intervention may have been avoided.

The Geneva settlement was built around a Sino-French understanding of joint responsibility for the security of Indochina, which included the recognition of two Vietnamese governments coexisting under the watchful eyes of their patrons. China expected a continued French presence in southern Vietnam to moderate the Bao Dai government and to contain, if not exclude, U.S. Cold War enthusiasm. The reluctance of the DRV in moving from political to military

struggle after 1956, implies acceptance of this scenario. The initiative to destabi-
lize this Geneva scenario came from Ngo Dinh Diem and the United States, not
through failure to hold elections in 1956 but in ousting the French, thereby
nullifying the Sino-French understanding. This in itself need not have been fatal
to a peaceful resolution, except that Diem's alienation of the southerners and
American readiness to wage war provoked a return to violence. The joint messages from the U.K. and the USSR, co-chairmen of the Geneva Conference, to
the French government, the two Vietnamese governments, and the International
Supervisory Commission (ISC) in May 1956 cited the "dissolution of the French
Union High Command" in Vietnam as the cause for increased "difficulties" of
the ISC in "carrying out the functions specified in the Geneva Agreements."[28]
The dissolution of the French command was hastened by Diem and the United
States.

One of the curiosities of U.S. intervention in Vietnam is that its effect was
exactly counter to its stated aim. The most effective barrier to the expansion of
Chinese influence in Southeast Asia has historically been a strong and united
Vietnam. By trying to enforce a permanent partition of Vietnam, the United
States was in fact endeavoring to establish a situation that would serve Chinese
interests in the long run. One of the effects of U.S. intervention in Vietnam, as
well as U.S. post-intervention policy toward Vietnam, has been to facilitate the
development of China's role as the regional power in Southeast Asia. If this
development represents U.S. interests as presently understood, then the "lesson"
of the so-called "Vietnam War" has more to do with U.S. perceptions of China
than with U.S. perceptions of Vietnam.

Of course, the shift in U.S. perception of China was a large factor in facilitat-
ing U.S. abandonment of its policy of intervention in Vietnam. But U.S. failure
in Vietnam was also a setback for Chinese interests. A united Vietnam that was
not tethered to a "special relationship" was immediately perceived by China as a
problem. In pre-French times, this "special relationship" was anchored in Chinese and Vietnamese ruling classes which shared a common language, classical
Chinese, for education, government, scholarship, and literature.

During the century since China passed its claim of suzerainty over Vietnam to
France, both the Chinese and the Vietnamese have experienced deep changes
that have affected the way they are able to deal with each other. The advent of
modern nationalism has enmeshed the Chinese and Vietnamese in more particu-
larist forms of cultural and ideological commitment, which have erected unprecedented barriers to re-establishing a "special relationship."

The Chinese may be ready to play the overlord again, but the Vietnamese are
not as ready to play the vassal. As long as the Soviet Union provided the
Vietnamese an alternative to accepting Chinese terms for a "special relationship," the Vietnamese could postpone the day of reckoning with China. With the
disintegration of the Soviet bloc, and until the United States is willing to offer
Vietnam the option of developing a relationship with Japan and the West that

would constitute a genuine alternative, Vietnam has no place to turn except China. Geographical proximity will eventually require the Vietnamese to establish some kind of special relationship with China.

The chief beneficiary of this turn of events, as in previous centuries, will be the ruling elite, in this case the Vietnamese Communist Party. While the Chinese Communist Party can expect deference from the rest of the world, the Vietnamese Communist Party, in its present embattled condition, has no viable option other than to appeal to China's paternalistic instincts. If the Chinese and Vietnamese Communist Parties can work out a satisfactory arrangement, it is unlikely that political reform in Vietnam will be able to evolve very far beyond the political framework that exists in China at any given time.

Is it in the American interest to deny to the Vietnamese the luxury of a non-Chinese option, to force Vietnam to make their kowtow to China? This is probably a question that American policymakers do not even consider worth asking. Being kind to Chinese Communists in hopes that they will thereby be inspired to improve themselves while at the same time being unkind to Vietnamese Communists in hopes that they will thereby be inspired to improve themselves is, at least superficially, a double standard of current U.S. policy. But this so-called double standard is irrelevant if the U.S. government has decided, as all indications suggest it has, that it intends to support the extension of Chinese influence in Southeast Asia as a "stabilizing" factor in international affairs.

Such an abdication of genuine American interest in Vietnam, not only economic and diplomatic, but also cultural and psychological given the legacy of U.S. intervention, would be consistent with the level of rationality that has always been displayed in U.S. policy toward Vietnam. After years of war, the United States has finally come to understand regional security in Southeast Asia along the lines that governed Chou En-lai's negotiating priorities in 1954. Only now there is no countervailing non-Chinese power in the region capable of moderating Chinese ambitions.

Even with the fundamental reorientation of Vietnamese cultural and political life away from China in the twentieth century, Chinese influence in Vietnam will never be unimportant. The French came and went. The Japanese came and went. The Americans came and went. The Soviets came and went. But China has always been there and it will never go away.

The relationship between the Communist parties of China and Vietnam has been close, and at times vital, since the 1920s. More recently, they have shared the fear of being overcome by the peaceful penetration of capitalism into their countries. Elements in both parties have begun to look to one another for reassurance and moral support. But this cannot be an equal relationship. The Chinese will insist upon defining the terms of accommodation. The Vietnamese will, as always, be the little brother.

The effect of Chinese influence upon Vietnamese government, now as in centuries past, is to reinforce the mechanisms of state authority. In previous periods of strong Chinese influence upon Vietnamese leadership, 1950–58 and 1963–66, there were relatively large numbers of Vietnamese party cadres who had been trained in China and who tended to understand political problems from a Chinese point of view. However, in the present moment of ascending Chinese influence upon Vietnamese affairs, since 1989, there is no similar constituency within the Vietnamese Communist Party for a pro-Chinese line; today, there is a new generation of Vietnamese officials and intellectuals trained in Eastern Europe. Furthermore, the Chinese and Vietnamese have just experienced a decade of warfare and confrontation, the causes of which have not yet been settled. In the present situation, a Vietnamese turning toward China will be the result of hard calculation with little or no sentimental or psychological bondage, which figured prominently in earlier eras of Sino-Vietnamese rapprochement. Despite this, the Vietnamese are heirs to a political wisdom that requires some formal acknowledgment of Chinese ascendance.

But a Vietnamese kowtow to China today will not be the same as it was in the past. Modern nationalism with mass literacy in an easy-to-learn alphabet has made Vietnamese leaders more vulnerable to popular sentiment and more confined by their own rhetoric. The degree to which Vietnamese leaders can move beyond the anti-Chinese rhetoric of recent years will be a test of their control over public attitudes. Vietnamese understand that a deal with China will entrench the most conservative members of the government and shrink the opportunities for rapid reform. Public opinion may be a new factor in Sino-Vietnamese relations. The current lack of consensus in the Vietnamese government on how to respond to the critical novels and short stories of a new generation of writers suggests that the Communist Party no longer enjoys absolute control over public opinion.

The Vietnamese Writers Association has managed to compromise Communist Party discipline. When the weekly magazine of the Association, *Van Nghe*, published three controversial short stories by Nguyen Huy Thiep in 1988, its editor, Nguyen Ngoc, was removed.[29] Within a year, however, Nguyen Ngoc was elected to the executive committee of the Writers Association and, in an interview published in May 1990, he saw his election as vindication of his editorial work with *Van Nghe*.[30] In this interview, he said that "writers go further and deeper than a purely political viewpoint. The party and the nation, if they know how to listen to the voice of literature, will be able to avoid politics that is temporary [i.e., suitable for one era but unable to adjust to a new era]."[31] These words imply that Vietnam is changing and that literature can serve to alert political leaders to the dangers of resisting change.

Nguyen Huy Thiep has become a favorite target of party critics, who now participate in rather than dominate literary debate in Vietnam. His stories that provoked the uproar over the editorship of *Van Nghe* in 1988 were especially resented by conservative party members because they challenged the notion of heroism that has been at the heart of the historical image nurtured by the party.

In 1989, these stories, along with several others of his, were published in a book, but half of the book was taken up by essays written by his critics. The editor's "Preface" said of Nguyen Huy Thiep, "There are those who sing his praises until they run out of words; there are those who disparage and denounce him; and there are even those who call for him to be brought to court and imprisoned."[32]

The lack of consensus in Vietnam about writers like Nguyen Huy Thiep reveals that party conservatives must now jostle with a new generation of writers. In 1990, Nguyen Huy Thiep accepted an invitation to be a member of the Writers Association.[33] The frustration of party critics is revealed in their continuing strident but ineffectual, even pathetic, attacks upon what threatens to become the literary mainstream. In September 1990, the party newspaper, *Nhan Dan*, published two Sunday articles by critics who, in responding to essays published elsewhere that praised the work of Nguyen Huy Thiep, argued that Nguyen Huy Thiep had betrayed the Vietnamese Revolution by toppling sacred heroes in Vietnamese history, had not distinguished properly between Mencius and Aristotle, had been discredited by association with the racist theories of Nietsche and the fascism of Hitler, had gotten lost in the existentialism of Camus and Sartre, and had been deceived by the chimera of pre-1975 Saigon.[34]

These critics also try to resurrect the *Nhan van-Giai pham* affair of the late 1950s when a post–Dien Bien Phu generation of young writers tried to espouse a literature without politics, "art for art's sake."[35] At that time, "socialist realism" was reaffirmed and the deviant authors were disciplined. Party critics appear to hope that there will be a similar solution to their current exasperation. But the situation is much different now than it was on the eve of the American War. The new writers today are not interested in "art for art's sake"; they fully accept that their writing has social relevance. In fact, it is precisely over the terrain of "realism" that the new writers are contesting their legitimacy; they claim to be the true realists because they are describing what they see with their own eyes. In their view, their critics have their heads stuffed with theory and are oblivious to what is going on in the society around them. And, in fact, it is apparent that their critics dare not criticize them for saying what is obvious to any Vietnamese. Rather, as in the case of Nguyen Huy Thiep, attacks are launched in the fields of history and philosophy, the final refuge of dogmatism.

The Vietnamese Communist Party has so far refrained from calling in the army to discipline the intellectuals, as the Chinese did in June 1989. If the Vietnamese manage in the years ahead to avoid a dramatic suppression of opinion, it will be because recent literary and intellectual developments in Vietnam have been occurring before an alert and appreciative audience, a relatively large reading and thinking public, in which the party is itself embedded. The intellectual turmoil in Vietnam today will not easily be directed by command. Public opinion is an increasingly significant factor in the resolution of Vietnam's political and foreign policy dilemmas. Any new relationship with China will have to be understood and accepted by Vietnamese public opinion.

In the past, Vietnamese intellectuals could be ignored, bought, or disciplined by governments who took only the peasantry seriously. But today, the peasantry and intellectuals are no longer so far apart. Modern education has raised the level of intellectual awareness among Vietnamese peasants and workers; the new generation of bureaucrats, teachers, professors, and researchers in Vietnamese government organs, schools, universities, and institutes come largely from the peasantry and working class, thanks to an educational system that encourages students with proletarian and peasant backgrounds. The reading public is not a small entrenched group of literati families as had been the case during centuries past. Today, the reading public encompasses a large majority of the total population. Furthermore, tens of thousands of peasant and working-class people have had experience working overseas in Soviet bloc, Middle Eastern, and African countries. They have learned foreign languages. They have attended foreign universities and worked in foreign industries. They see their country in an international context. For these reasons, the Vietnamese government understands that disciplining a small group of intellectuals can never be a solution as it was for China, for Vietnam is relatively exposed to the outside world and enjoys a relatively unified and widespread literary scene.

The traditional Sino-Vietnamese relationship is sometimes stereotyped as uniformly adversarial, as if for 2,000 years there has been nothing but tension and warfare. This is, of course, not true. There have been long eras of peaceful contact, and there is no reason why these eras should not be equally as prominent as the eras of confrontation in exposing the possibilities for a future relationship. However, one unprecedented element in the present effort to establish a new Sino-Vietnamese relationship is the popular attitudes that have been fostered in each country toward the other through the use of twentieth-century methods of propaganda. Literacy and nationalism make these attitudes difficult to manipulate, especially if, as in Vietnam, public opinion has begun to take on a momentum of its own. Reforms embraced by the Communist Party in recent years have to a significant degree been driven by public opinion.

The possibility of Vietnam establishing counterbalancing relationships with the rest of the world remains. However, it is unlikely that this option will materialize sufficiently to provide an alternative without active U.S. support. Without U.S. leadership, no other country is likely to cross Chinese interests in Vietnam. This may mean that those who would like to see Vietnam break out of China's shadow into the world of nations may yet find virtue in the old Cold War argument about containing China. But it should be remembered that the Vietnamese were in the business of containing China long before the Americans stumbled onto the scene. Ultimately, as the Vietnamese know from long experience, they will have to deal with China alone. For them, it has always come back to this.

In the early 1990s, there appear to be three trends in the Vietnamese leadership. One is to diversify foreign relations and to promote cooperation with all countries in an effort to balance Vietnamese interests amidst many global forces; this trend is not realistic so long as the United States maintains the embargo and non-recognition policy. Another is to diversify relations but with greater emphasis upon the Association of Southeast Asian Nations (ASEAN) countries and the West; this is an effort to shift away from Chinese cultural, political, and ideological influence and to absorb Western influence as beneficial to Vietnamese development. This is also unrealistic so long as the United States maintains the embargo and non-recognition policy. Third, and increasingly prominent, is to diversify relations but with greater emphasis upon relations with China in order to defend the structure of socialism, meaning the party's control of the government.

The only way to exclude or contain Chinese influence is by modernization and the establishment of a Vietnamese industrial structure; this will not happen so long as the United States maintains the embargo and non-recognition policy. U.S. policy is apparently driven by a "sore loser" psychosis that blinds American policymakers to the possibility of a constructive relationship with Vietnam. Vietnam and the United States have no fundamental conflict of interest. On the other hand, there is long-term potential for conflict of interest between China and the United States in the South China Sea and Southeast Asia. But, for the moment, the United States appears to acknowledge a kind of overlord status to China in Southeast Asia that it reserves for itself in Central America and other parts of the world.

Notes

1. Pierre Mendes-France, *Ouvres Completes*, vol. 3 (Paris: Gallimard, 1986), 71–77.

2. Robert F. Randle, *Geneva 1954* (Princeton, NJ: Princeton University Press, 1969), 190, 191.

3. Ibid., 277–78.

4. Mendes-France, *Ouvres Completes*, 75.

5. Ibid., 75.

6. Ibid., 76.

7. James Cable, *The Geneva Conference of 1954 on Indochina* (New York: St. Martin's, 1986), 44–45, 82.

8. Randle, *Geneva 1954*, 200.

9. Ibid., 211.

10. Ibid., 232. Francois Joyaux, *La Chine et le reglement du premier conflit d'Indochine (Geneve 1954)* (Paris: Sorbonne, 1979), 187.

11. Joyaux, *La Chine et le reglement*, 274, 277–78; Cable, *The Geneva Conference*, 94.

12. Cable, *The Geneva Conference*, 34–36.

13. Mendes-France, *Ouvres Completes*, 115–19.

14. Ibid., 116.

15. Ibid., 117.

16. Ibid., 117–18.

17. Ibid., 118.

18. Ibid., 118.

19. Ibid., 118–19.

20. Randle, *Geneva 1954*, 319.

21. Joyaux, *La Chine et le reglement*, 277.

22. From the Final Declaration; see Cable, *The Geneva Conference*, 148.

23. Ibid., 339–40.

24. Joyaux, *La Chine et le reglement*, 281–85.

25. Ibid., 334.

26. Ibid., 202.

27. Ibid., 297, 334.

28. *Vietnam and the Geneva Agreements*, Vietnam no. 2, 1956 (London: Her Majesty's Stationery Office, reprinted 1965), 10–12.

29. Murray Hiebert, "One Step Backward," *Far Eastern Economic Review*, May 4, 1989, 15.

30. "Gap va phong van Nguyen Ngoc" [Meeting and Interviewing Nguyen Ngoc], *Doan Ket*, May 1990, 24.

31. Ibid.

32. Nguyen Huy Thiep, *Tac pham va du luan* [Works and Opinions] (Nha Xuat Ban Tre, 1989), 5.

33. Barry Wain, " 'Pitiful' Writer Jolts Vietnamese Minds," *The Asian Wall Street Journal Weekly*, August 13, 1990, 13.

34. Phan Cu De, " 'Dinh huong rong' va tu do sang tac," ["The Vast Orient" and the Freedom to Create], *Bao Nhan Dan (Chu nhat)* 38 (September 16, 1990); and Hoang Nhan, "Khoang trong trong tu tuong mot nha van," [The Empty Space in the Thought of a Writer], *Bao Nhan Dan (Chu nhat)* 39 (September 23, 1990).

35. See Georges Boudarel, "The Nhan-van Giai-Pham Affair," *Vietnam Forum* 13 (1990): 154–74.

Index

A

Abrams, Creighton, 51, 161, 194, 195–96
AC–130 gunship, 135
Acheson, Dean, 146
Adams, William, 252–53
Adas, Michael, 22n
Advance Research Projects Agency on Marine Operations, 154
Agent Orange, 265, 267
Aircraft losses, 136
Air strikes. *See* Bombing
Air-to-air war, 136
Allman, T.D., 221
American International Engineering Group, 6
Americans Talk Security Foundation, 180
Anatomy of a War (Kolko), 59, 152–53, 205
An Giang, 46
Angkor Borei, 222
An Hao, 161
Antiwar movement, xxi-xxii, 39, 199, 200- 201, 203, 264
  advocacy of NLF victory, 258–59
  ambiguous results in, 182n
  anger as motive in, 106
  in armed forces, 177
  characterized, 166–67
  cultural change and, 172–73
  defections from, 260, 263
  effectiveness of, 167–81
  elite opinion and, 170–71
  goals of, 165
  latent power of, 177, 179–80
  media coverage and, 171–72

Antiwar movement *(continued)*
  national security experts and, 171
  policy impact of, xxi-xxii, 165–66, 168- 69
  and post-1975 Vietnam, 264–69
  public attitudes and, 169–70
  social context for, 175–77
  social movements and, 172
  Vietnamese view of, 166, 245
  and Vietnam veterans, 266
Ap Bac, battle of, 31, 37, 76, 77, 78
Apple, R.W., Jr., 254
Armed forces, U.S.
  in air-to-air war, 136
  antiwar movement in, 177
  assessment of performance, 122–24, 152–55
  attitude toward Vietnamese, 158–59
  in Cambodia, 181n, 218
  morale of GIs, xxi, 157–61
  principles of war, 115
  reserves, 176
  search and destroy operations, 38, 51, 52, 63n, 169, 239
  Special Forces, xxiv, 129n, 181n, 192, 193–94, 218, 221, 254
  sweep and hold strategy of, 239
  in Tet offensive, 47, 49, 50, 51, 53, 56- 57, 62, 73
  See also Bombing
Armed forces, U.S., units of
  1st Cavalry Division (Airmobile), 141
  9th Division, 49
  1st Infantry Division, 50
  25th Infantry Division, 50
  26th Marines, 161